Frommer's®

Atlanta

12th Edition

by K. K. Snyder

WILEY

Wiley Publishing, Inc

Published by:

WILEY PUBLISHING, INC.

111 River St.

Hoboken, NJ 07030-5774

ISBN 978-0-470-88869-8 (paper); ISBN 978-1-118-06403-0 (ebk); ISBN 978-1-118-06404-7 (ebk); ISBN 978-1-118-06405-4 (ebk)

Editor: Anuja Madar
Production Editor: Heather Wilcox
Cartographer: Andrew Dolan
Photo Editor: Richard Fox
Production by Wiley Indianapolis Composition Services
Front Cover Photo: High Museum of Art Atlanta Georgia ©Mark & Audrey Gibson/PhotoLibrary
Back Cover Photo: Sculpture, Exterior of Turner Field ©IndexStock/SuperStock, Inc.

For information on our other products and services or to obtain technical support, please contact our Customer Care Department within the U.S. at 877/762-2974, outside the U.S. at 317/572-3993 or fax 317/572-4002.

Wiley also publishes its books in a variety of electronic formats. Some content that appears in print may not be available in electronic formats.

Manufactured in the United States of America

5 4 3 2 1

CONTENTS

LIST OF MAPS

ABOUT THE AUTHOR

K. K. Snyder admits that, while she wasn't born in the south, she got there as quickly as she could and has loved the region and its people for nearly 30 years. A freelance writer who lives to travel and travels to live, she edits and writes for a number of publications.

ACKNOWLEDGMENTS

Once again, the fine people of the melting pot that is Atlanta went above and beyond to assist me in finding those cultural, culinary and classic experiences that can only be had in this incredible city. Atlanta continues to live up to the gracious Southern hospitality expectations of those who visit here.

For Jacob Elijah Snyder, whose recent arrival into this sometimes harsh, sometimes wonderful world has melted hearts, opened minds, and improved dated attitudes—forever.

HOW TO CONTACT US

In researching this book, we discovered many wonderful places—hotels, restaurants, shops, and more. We're sure you'll find others. Please tell us about them, so we can share the information with your fellow travelers in upcoming editions. If you were disappointed with a recommendation, we'd love to know that, too. Please write to:

Frommer's Atlanta, 12th Edition
Wiley Publishing, Inc. • 111 River St. • Hoboken, NJ 07030-5774
frommersfeedback@wiley.com

AN ADDITIONAL NOTE

Please be advised that travel information is subject to change at any time—and this is especially true of prices. We therefore suggest that you write or call ahead for confirmation when making your travel plans. The authors, editors, and publisher cannot be held responsible for the experiences of readers while traveling. Your safety is important to us, however, so we encourage you to stay alert and be aware of your surroundings. Keep a close eye on cameras, purses, and wallets, all favorite targets of thieves and pickpockets.

FROMMER'S STAR RATINGS, ICONS & ABBREVIATIONS

Every hotel, restaurant, and attraction listing in this guide has been ranked for quality, value, service, amenities, and special features using a **star-rating system.** In country, state, and regional guides, we also rate towns and regions to help you narrow down your choices and budget your time accordingly. Hotels and restaurants are rated on a scale of zero (recommended) to three stars (exceptional). Attractions, shopping, nightlife, towns, and regions are rated according to the following scale: zero stars (recommended), one star (highly recommended), two stars (very highly recommended), and three stars (must-see).

In addition to the star-rating system, we also use **seven feature icons** that point you to the great deals, in-the-know advice, and unique experiences that separate travelers from tourists. Throughout the book, look for:

Special finds—those places only insiders know about

Fun facts—details that make travelers more informed and their trips more fun

Best bets for kids and advice for the whole family

Special moments—those experiences that memories are made of

Places or experiences not worth your time or money

Insider tips—great ways to save time and money

Great values—where to get the best deals

The following **abbreviations** are used for credit cards:

AE	American Express	**DISC**	Discover	**V**	Visa
DC	Diners Club	**MC**	MasterCard		

TRAVEL RESOURCES AT FROMMERS.COM

Frommer's travel resources don't end with this guide. Frommer's website, **www.frommers. com**, has travel information on more than 4,000 destinations. We update features regularly, giving you access to the most current trip-planning information and the best airfare, lodging, and car-rental bargains. You can also listen to podcasts, connect with other Frommers. com members through our active-reader forums, share your travel photos, read blogs from guidebook editors and fellow travelers, and much more.

THE BEST OF ATLANTA

"How do I get to Tara?"

"Where are Scarlett and Rhett buried?"

"Why do you put sugar in iced tea but not on grits?"

"Just what is a grit anyway?"

Some visitors come to Atlanta looking for Old South stereotypes—white-columned mansions surrounded by magnolias, owned by slow-moving folks with accents as thick as molasses. Instead, they discover a region that's more cosmopolitan and a heck of a lot more interesting than what they'd expected.

When General William Sherman burned Atlanta to the ground in 1864, the city rose from those smoldering bitter ashes and hasn't looked back since. Instead, it has spent the last 145 years building what's been described as the Capital of the New South and the Next Great International City. Atlanta's heritage may be southern, but the current dynamic is brashly Sunbelt, and straight-up economic vitality now drives this city's engines.

Atlanta is and always has been a city on the move. Longtime mayor William B. Hartsfield called it the city "too busy to hate," and the spirit of Atlanta is one of working together to get the job done. The dramatic downtown skyline, with its gleaming skyscrapers, is testimony to Atlanta's inability to sit still—even for a minute. And its role as host for the Centennial Olympic Games in 1996 finally convinced the rest of the world that Atlanta is a force to be reckoned with—and a great place to visit. Recent projects have only reinforced that notion. These ventures include the World of Coca-Cola; the addition of the Atlanta Dream, the city's first venture into women's professional basketball; and the onslaught of new hotels and restaurants that call Atlanta home.

Consistently ranked as one of the best cities in the world in which to do business, Atlanta is headquarters for hundreds of corporations, including Coca-Cola, Delta Air Lines, UPS, Holiday Inn, Georgia-Pacific, Home Depot, BellSouth, and Cox Enterprises, and it has become a magnet for many Internet-related companies. A major convention city and a crossroads where three interstate highways converge, Atlanta is home to the country's busiest airport. And all those conventiongoers certainly find many places to spend money—Atlanta is considered the shopping capital of the Southeast. Although the city limits are only 131 square miles, the metro area is vast and sprawling. With a population nearing 5.5 million (and still counting), Atlanta was recently named the ninth-largest metropolitan area.

But commerce and development are not the only things that characterize this bustling metropolis. Its success is due in no small part to its quality of life, which is hard to beat. Atlanta is often called the City of Trees, and the streets are indeed filled with dogwoods and azaleas. The city has a small-town quality to it, with dozens of neighborhoods and parks. A temperate climate makes Atlanta a magnet for anyone who enjoys the outdoors, and the city's southern roots ensure graciousness and hospitality. As Atlanta has grown in stature, it has attracted residents from across the continent and around the world, further enriching the city's social fabric. You'll still hear gentle southern accents here, but at least half of Atlanta's citizens were born outside the South. Interestingly, many of these transplants find themselves bending to the local customs, saying "please" and "ma'am" and holding doors open for one another.

When H. L. Mencken came south earlier in the century, he branded Atlanta a cultural wasteland. He should visit now. Media mogul Ted Turner inaugurated CNN here in 1980, and subsequently launched Superstation TBS, Headline News, and TNT. Also in 1980, the revitalized black neighborhood of Sweet Auburn became a national historic district, with 10 blocks of notable sites including Martin Luther King, Jr.'s, boyhood home, his crypt, the church where he preached, a museum, and the Martin Luther King, Jr., Center for Nonviolent Social Change. It is probably *the* major black historical attraction in the country, and in the last several years it has undergone a major revitalization and restoration.

Atlanta is home to major art, science, nature, and archaeology museums; a vibrant theater community; an outstanding symphony orchestra; a well-regarded ballet company; opera, blues, and jazz performances; Broadway musicals; a presidential library; Confederate and African-American heritage sites; and dozens of art galleries. To those leisure options, add such attractions as Stone Mountain Park, a regional theme park, a botanical garden, and professional sports teams, and you have the makings of a lively and sophisticated city. The culinary spectrum here ranges from grits and biscuits to caviar and sushi. Sure, you can still feast on fried chicken and barbecued beef, but Atlanta also serves up cuisine from across the globe.

Of great significance is the ongoing development downtown. For years, city leaders have tried to encourage central city living, and it's finally taken hold as developers renovate old buildings into attractive apartments and lofts. The mark of a great city is an appealing and vital downtown area where people live as well as work, and Atlanta finally appears to be living the dream.

Atlanta recently said goodbye to Shirley Franklin, the first African-American female elected as mayor of this busy city, and welcomed the newly elected Kasim Reed, who shares much of Franklin's expansive vision for this heart of the New South. So if you've set your heart on hoop skirts and plantations, go on down to your local bookstore and pick up a copy of *Gone With the Wind*. But if you want to visit a vibrant, energetic city that's rich in heritage, culture, fine cuisine, entertainment, and commerce, Atlanta runs right up there with the big dogs.

FROMMER'S favorite
ATLANTA EXPERIENCES

- **Stepping Back in Time at the Atlanta History Center:** A re-created farm (with original buildings from the 1840s) shows how rural southern folks really lived before the Civil War. The beautifully restored 1928 Swan House, an estate on the property, gives a fascinating glimpse into the lifestyle enjoyed by upper-crust Atlantans in the early 20th century. Kids will love the hands-on discovery areas at the history museum. Explore the walking trails after you take in the exhibits. It all adds up to a great look at the rich tapestry of Atlanta's past and present. See p. 115.

- **Frolicking in the Fountain:** The biggest attraction at Centennial Olympic Park is the Fountain of Rings, where young and old can get delightfully soaked on warm days. The fountain is a simple but ingenious design on the plaza floor, consisting of 251 water jets in the shape of the five Olympic rings. Take a deep breath and zip in and around the 12-foot water bursts, or just sit and watch the timed light-and-sound-effects show, when the water bursts 35 feet into the air. See p. 117.

o **Touring the CNN Studios:** The network that started round-the-clock television news lets you take a peek behind the scenes to see how it's all done. You can even have a videotape made of yourself reading the day's top stories from behind a CNN anchor desk. See p. 118.

o **Time-Traveling at Fernbank Museum of Natural History:** Check out the 45-foot-long model of a *Giganotosaurus,* then travel back 15 billion years and experience the Big Bang that jump-started the formation of the universe. The museum's stunning architecture is notable. IMAX films are shown here, too. See p. 120.

o **Discovering the Fox Theatre:** This Moorish-Egyptian palace exemplifies the glamorous movie-theater architecture of the 1920s, complete with onion domes, minarets, and a twinkling starlit sky over the auditorium. See p. 121.

o **Marveling at the Creatures in the Georgia Aquarium:** Even if you have only a day or two to spend in the city, this is a must-see. The Georgia Aquarium, the largest in the world, continues to draw mind-boggling numbers of visitors every day. The highlights include giant whale sharks and unforgettable exhibits in five major categories, from river life to sea life in foreign waters around the planet. A 4-D movie, numerous opportunities for dining and shopping, and amazing play spaces for the little ones provide a full day of fun. Plan to order advance tickets online, as huge crowds usually converge on this attraction. See p. 122.

o **Exploring the King Center:** It's an inspiring experience to visit this living memorial to a true American hero. You'll see lots of memorabilia for Dr. Martin Luther King, Jr., and a film on his life and works. Especially moving is Freedom Plaza, where he's buried. The tomb is inscribed with his words: "Free at Last. Free at Last. Thank God Almighty I'm Free at Last." See p. 127.

o **Strolling Around Oakland Cemetery:** This 88-acre cemetery is a peaceful place, and its Victorian graves are of aesthetic, historic, and symbolic interest. The guided tour is recommended. Bring a picnic lunch; even your dog is welcome to hang out here (on a leash). See p. 131.

o **Relaxing in Stone Mountain Park:** Hike to the top of the big granite rock or spend a leisurely day taking in the diverse attractions, from a paddlewheel cruise to a living museum of southern history. You can also choose from an array of activities—golf, tennis, swimming, hiking, boating, and more. See p. 132.

o **Touring the World of Coca-Cola:** Atlanta is Coke's hometown, so it's only fitting that there's a museum dedicated to the world's most renowned beverage. Come see the gigantic collection of memorabilia, explore the interactive exhibits, and sample Coke products from around the world. See p. 135.

o **Hanging Out at the Zoo:** Ever since the giant pandas Yang Yang and Lun Lun arrived at Zoo Atlanta and welcomed baby pandas—Mei Lan in 2006 and Xi Lan in 2008—this has been one of the hottest tickets in town. It's been even more popular since the arrival of the zoo's first baby giraffe, Zuri, last summer. You don't have to be a kid to be fascinated by these adorable creatures. See p. 150.

o **Getting a Breath of Fresh Air in Piedmont Park:** Atlanta's favorite public park is fun, funky, and a terrific place to watch the world go by. Take your in-line skates, or pack a lunch and find a shady spot for a picnic. See p. 154.

o **Spending a Day at the Ballpark:** Pack up the kids and take them out to the old ballgame. Even if there isn't an Atlanta Braves game scheduled, you can take a tour

APPLAUSE FOR THE REVITALIZED
downtown

Downtown revitalization was at the top of the list for Atlanta leaders and developers when the city won the bid for the 1996 Olympics. Since then, the downtown area has continued to improve and today is the biggest draw in the city for visitors, especially visiting families. The World of Coca-Cola opened in its new home a few years ago right next to the well-attended Georgia Aquarium, touted as the world's largest. Both offer experiences that are both interactive and engaging.

These two jewels in Atlanta's crown, along with the expansive Centennial Park, Imagine It! Children's Museum, the CNN Center, and Philips Arena—have proved to be a much-needed shot in the arm for the downtown residential and commercial markets. New hotels in the area, including Hilton Garden Inn and Twelve Centennial Park, make staying right in the middle of the action an easy task. And the area offers enough variety of restaurants that visitors don't have to venture far for a great meal. These developments no doubt make the downtown area *the* place to be in this city for visitors, residents, and conventiongoers alike.

of Turner Field, play in Tooner Field playground, and visit the museum. The ballpark served as the Olympic Stadium for the 1996 Olympic Games. See p. 161.

o **Trekking Through Virginia-Highland:** Atlanta's version of New York's Greenwich Village or London's Soho, this trendy neighborhood is full of coffee bars, galleries, cafes, and funky little boutiques. It all makes for a pleasant stroll on a sunny afternoon. For some of the shopping highlights, see p. 174.

o **Shopping at Lenox Square:** One of the most popular malls in the Southeast, Lenox Square is a mecca for affluent shoppers. It's hard to visit every store, even if you spend the whole day, but many visitors think it's a worthy goal. You'll enjoy good restaurants and great people-watching, too. See p. 177.

o **Spending the Morning at the Market:** Atlanta is home to two gigantic indoor farmers' markets, both jammed with locals who are shopping in earnest and visitors who have a hard time keeping their eyes from bugging out. Choose from the DeKalb Farmers' Market, which has an international flavor, and Harry's, which is a little more upscale. Each has loads of gourmet goodies you can take home or consume on the spot. See p. 181.

o **Taking in a Chastain Park Amphitheatre Concert:** Big-name entertainers perform under the stars, and everyone brings elaborate picnic fare (some people even bring tablecloths and candelabra for the picnic table). Even the entertainers seem dazzled by the setting. See p. 187.

best HOTEL BETS

o **Best for Business Travelers:** All the major downtown megahotels—which cater largely to a business and convention clientele—are fully equipped to meet your business needs. The finest is the **Ritz-Carlton Atlanta,** 181 Peachtree St. NE (© **800/241-3333**), which combines a full business center and a can-do concierge with superb service. See p. 50.

o **Best for Families:** The **Residence Inn by Marriott Atlanta Buckhead,** 2960 Piedmont Rd. NE (✆ **800/331-3131**), offers accommodations large enough to ensure privacy for all, plus fully equipped kitchens, washers and dryers, indoor and outdoor swimming pools, barbecue grills, and basketball, volleyball, and paddle tennis courts. Many rooms even have fireplaces. See p. 66.

o **Best for a Romantic Getaway:** You'll fall for each other all over again at the luxurious **Four Seasons Hotel,** 75 14th St. (✆ **800/819-5053**), an elegant choice with lavish guest rooms, luxurious marble tubs, and impeccable service. See p. 55.

o **Best Moderately Priced Hotel:** It's hard to beat the **Residence Inn by Marriott Downtown,** 134 Peachtree St. NW (✆ **800/331-3131**). It offers a convenient location, large rooms, and a bundle of amenities for a very reasonable price. See p. 53.

o **Best Inexpensive Accommodations:** It's nothing fancy, but the convenient Buckhead location of the **Country Inns & Suites,** 800 Sidney Marcus Blvd. (✆ **800/596-2375**), makes this a good deal. See p. 67.

o **Best Location:** Buckhead is one of the loveliest—and busiest—parts of town, offering exceptional nightlife, dining, and shopping. There are two MARTA stations (Buckhead and Lenox) where you can connect to other parts of the city, and any hotel within walking distance of either of those stations is a sure bet. A good example is the **JW Marriott Hotel Buckhead,** 3300 Lenox Rd. NE (✆ **800/613-2051**), adjacent to the upscale Lenox Square mall. See p. 62.

o **Best Service:** The **Mansion on Peachtree,** 3376 Peachtree Rd. NE (✆ **888/767-3966**), takes the cake when it comes to guest service, employing three staff members to every overnight guest. Where else does a private butler come with every hotel room? The **Ritz-Carlton Atlanta,** 181 Peachtree St. NE (✆ **800/241-3333**), and the **Ritz-Carlton Buckhead,** 3434 Peachtree Rd. NE (✆ **800/241-3333**), are tied for a close second. See p. 62, 50, and 62 for each hotel, respectively.

o **Best Architectural Digest Interior:** The towering **Grand Hyatt Atlanta,** 3300 Peachtree Rd. (✆ **800/233-1234**), offers a stunning combination of 18th-century American architecture and Japanese attention to aesthetic detail. A 9,000-square-foot garden features waterfalls viewable from the lobby overlook. See p. 61.

o **Best Trendy Hotel:** Atlanta's four W Hotels (more than any other city outside New York) are trendy, but the **W Atlanta Midtown,** 188 14th St. (✆ **877/822-0000**), with its popular lobby bar, is definitely the trendiest. The **Westin Buckhead Atlanta,** 3391 Peachtree Rd. NE (✆ **404/365-0065**), with its clean Euro-modern style, is a favorite among visiting celebrities. See p. 56 and p. 64.

o **Best for Travelers with Disabilities:** The **Embassy Suites Atlanta Buckhead,** 3285 Peachtree Rd. NW (✆ **800/362-2779**), is fully accessible, with 10 suites completely equipped for visitors with disabilities (some with roll-in showers, too). The hotel is just a block away from the Buckhead MARTA station. See p. 65.

o **Best for Pets:** Some hotels get downright snooty if you try to check in with your pooch, but not the trendy **Hotel Indigo,** 683 Peachtree St. (✆ **404/874-9200**). All pets are welcome—no fees, no weight limit. If you're in town on Tuesdays, don't miss Canine Cocktail Hour in the bar. See p. 58.

best DINING BETS

o **Best Spot for a Business Lunch:** Power brokers head for steaks at **Bone's,** 3130 Piedmont Rd. NE (© **404/237-2663**), in Buckhead, where the food is serious and the service is impeccable and unobtrusive. See p. 88.

o **Best Spot for a Romantic Dinner:** There's no better spot than the tree-shaded terrace at **Horseradish Grill,** 4320 Powers Ferry Rd. (© **404/255-7277**). See p. 93.

o **Best Spot for a Celebration:** Why not pick one of the most sought-after tables in town? That would be at **Bacchanalia,** 1198 Howell Mill Rd. (© **404/365-0410**). See p. 79.

o **Best Newcomer: Antico Pizza Napoletana,** 1093 Hemphill Ave. (© **404/724-2333**), is pizza the way it was supposed to be made and eaten. Other pizza will never measure up after you experience these recipes perfected over generations and prepared the old-fashioned way. See p. 85.

o **Best View: Canoe,** 4199 Paces Ferry Rd. NW, in Vinings (© **770/432-2663**), is perched on the north side of the Chattahoochee River. Ask for a table on the large, canopied patio, surrounded by landscaped gardens, and watch the river go by. See p. 106.

o **Best Wine List: Craft** at the Mansion on Peachtree, 3376 Peachtree Rd. (© **404/995-7580**), is Tom Colicchio's first Atlanta venture. His regional cuisine is complemented by a vast and eclectic wine list. See p. 90.

o **Best Italian Cuisine:** It's noisy as the devil, but **Sotto Sotto,** 313 N. Highland Ave. (© **404/523-6678**), gets my vote for its inspired northern Italian cuisine. See p. 104.

o **Best Italian on a Budget: Pasta Da Pulcinella,** 1123 Peachtree Walk (© **404/876-1114**), serves gourmet pasta for next to nothing. See p. 84.

o **Best Seafood:** The **Atlanta Fish Market,** 265 Pharr Rd. (© **404/262-3165**), is the ticket, with an enormous selection of fresh seafood dishes that are done to perfection. See p. 92.

o **Best New Southern Cuisine:** The competition is stiff, but the **Horseradish Grill** (see "Best Spot for a Romantic Dinner," above) wins by a hair. See p. 93.

o **Best Traditional Southern Cuisine:** It's a tie between **Colonnade,** 1879 Cheshire Bridge Rd. NE (© **404/874-5642**), keeper of the best heirloom recipes; and **Mary Mac's Tea Room,** 224 Ponce de Leon Ave. NE (© **404/876-1800**), a legend in this city for more than 60 years. See p. 96 and 84, respectively.

o **Best Southwestern Cuisine: Nava,** 3060 Peachtree Rd. (© **404/240-1984**), is a stunning restaurant with food to match. See p. 94.

o **Best Steakhouse:** There's quite a turf war going on, but **Bone's** (see "Best Spot for a Business Lunch," above), that powerhouse for powerbrokers, gets my vote. See p. 88.

o **Best Fried Chicken:** There are lots of New Southern restaurants trying to invent newfangled ways to cook fried chicken. Well, they should just cut it out. You should head to the **Colonnade** (see "Best Traditional Southern Cuisine," above) for some of the best fried chicken you've ever tasted. This establishment has been turning it out for years, and they know what they're doing. See p. 96.

💬 SAY cheese

P.C. is a big priority in Atlanta. No, no—not *P.C.*, as in political correctness. P.C., as in pimento cheese. And let's get the pronunciation down right off the bat. It's puh-*men*-uh cheese, an utterly simple but delightful mixture, usually consisting of just three main ingredients—canned pimentos, cheese, and some sort of binder, probably mayonnaise—slapped between two pieces of white bread. Southern cooks have hot debates over the fine points. Cheddar or Monterey Jack? Sharp or extra-sharp? Duke's mayonnaise or Hellmann's? Is onion okay? How about red-pepper flakes?

Regardless of the mixture, a pimento-cheese sandwich is right up there with grits as one of the ultimate southern comfort foods. It's usually a homemade concoction, not found on many restaurant menus. But Watershed (p. 108) in Decatur has seen fit to include it among lunch *and* dinner offerings, as there is such a demand for it from patrons. Here is Watershed's take on the venerable southern classic.

WATERSHED'S PIMENTO CHEESE

2½ cups (10 oz.) extra-sharp cheddar cheese, grated

⅛ teaspoon cayenne pepper, or to taste

salt to taste, if needed

5 or 6 grinds of black pepper

¾ cup homemade mayonnaise

3 tablespoons finely chopped pimento

In a mixing bowl, stir together all of the ingredients until well mixed and creamy. Taste carefully for seasoning and adjust as needed. Cover and keep refrigerated until ready to use. Makes about 2 cups.

---

o **Best Brunch:** The winner of this category can be none other than **Murphy's,** 997 Virginia Ave. NE (✆ **404/872-0904**), where the serving of American and Continental cuisine has transitioned right along with this funky neighborhood. See p. 102.

o **Best Breakfast:** The fun and funky **Flying Biscuit Cafe,** 1655 McLendon Ave. (✆ **404/687-8888**), fulfills all the usual breakfast expectations, and also has a great selection of offbeat specialties. See p. 105.

o **Best Afternoon Tea:** Fresh-baked scones with Devonshire cream, finger sandwiches, pastries, and tea are served every afternoon in the posh lobby lounge of the **Ritz-Carlton Buckhead,** 3434 Peachtree Rd. NE (✆ **800/241-3333**). See p. 62.

o **Best Desserts: Bacchanalia** (see "Best Spot for a Celebration," above) takes this category with its warm Valrhona chocolate cake with vanilla-bean ice cream—a flourless confection with a sinful, gooey center. They tried to take it off the menu once, but the public outcry was too great. See p. 79.

o **Best Late-Night Dining:** Head to the 24/7 **R. Thomas Deluxe Grill,** 1812 Peachtree St. NW (✆ **404/872-2942**), where you can eat some of the healthiest fare in town at any hour of the day. See p. 98.

o **Best Decor: Bluepointe,** 3455 Peachtree Rd. NE (✆ **404/237-9070**), is an energy-filled multilevel restaurant in a soaring contemporary space. Its dramatic decor feels very of-the-moment and classy. See p. 87.

- **Best People-Watching:** Famous beefeaters flock to **Bone's** (see "Best Spot for a Business Lunch," above), which has welcomed the likes of Bob Hope, George Bush, and the Atlanta Braves. See p. 88.
- **Best Pre- & Post-Theater Dining:** If you're attending a show at the Woodruff Arts Center—Atlanta's major performance facility—dine at **Veni Vidi Vici,** 41 14th St. (☎ **404/875-8424**), which opens early enough to have a relaxing meal. For post-theater noshing, try **South City Kitchen,** 1144 Crescent Ave. (☎ **404/873-7358**). See p. 85 and 80, respectively.

ATLANTA IN DEPTH

Atlanta is a bright light on the southern horizon and has certainly come a long way since it burned to the ground during General William Tecumseh Sherman's "March to the Sea" in 1864. This is the city from which Martin Luther King, Jr., launched his social revolution, and the city where Ted Turner launched his media empire. It is home to many of America's largest corporations and is one of the top convention destinations in the country.

Atlanta may be best known, however, for hosting the 1996 Summer Olympics. The city went all out in its preparations for the 1996 Games, with new parks, hotels, and sports venues. In the center of downtown is Woodruff Park, which was spruced up to the tune of $5 million. The Olympic Village, erected just north of the central business district, now provides housing for Georgia State University students. South of Olympic Village, and stretching to the CNN Center, is the 21-acre Centennial Olympic Park—a major gathering place during the Olympics, with lawns, gardens, and the dramatic (and hot-weather fun) Fountain of Rings. The park regularly hosts concerts, street festivals, and other cultural events, and anchors the city's efforts to revitalize commercial and residential development in this once-neglected corner of downtown. The Olympic Stadium, site of the opening and closing ceremonies, as well as track and field events, has been reincarnated as Turner Field, home of the Atlanta Braves baseball team.

Since the Olympics, Atlantans have had some time to think about their future and how to shape it. They've always been an optimistic bunch, but the breakneck development that began with the Olympics and still continues has many local citizens wondering if they have too much of a good thing. Atlanta has had big-city problems such as crime, urban blight, and clogged freeways for some time now, but the overall quality of life remains high. Currently, the spotlight is not on growth and how to encourage it, but on growth and how to manage it. Of great concern is traffic—horrendous by any standards—and the accompanying decline in air quality. Everyone is rethinking the role that the automobile plays—even more so now that gas prices have seen record highs—and there's a lot of discussion about how to improve public transportation and make the metro area more pedestrian friendly. Of great significance is the recent development downtown. For years, city leaders have tried to encourage "in-town" living, but it's quickly taken hold as developers remake old buildings into attractive apartments and lofts, and home buyers are breathing new life into the city's old neighborhoods. The mark of a great city is an attractive and vital downtown area where people live as well as work, and Atlanta continues to head quickly in that direction, with in-town addresses among the most desirable of residences.

ATLANTA TODAY

For Atlanta, a new century has meant a new effort to spruce up its image, especially that of the downtown area, which for years was a seedy section of town where not even the locals ventured after dark. Today, attractions such as the Georgia Aquarium, Centennial Olympic Park, the CNN Studio, and the World of Coca-Cola are drawing scores of residents and visitors to a shiny new downtown area that sprouts new offerings with great frequency—and much success. In 2004, Atlanta was named the number-one city for African Americans by *Black Enterprise* magazine. Former Mayor Shirley Franklin—an African-American female—was highly active in the quest to pitch Atlanta as a tourist destination: In 2006, the city branded itself with a spirally red "ATL" logo and the slogan "Every day is opening day." Atlanta's current mayor, Kasim Reed, follows in those footsteps to maintain Atlanta's favorable reviews. The number of visitors to this heart of the South continues to increase, averaging 36 million a year, nearly double what it was just 10 years ago. National recognition of Atlanta also continues to improve, including being named "Best City for Singles" by *Forbes* magazine in 2008, citing a hopping nightlife, high number of singles, and sizzling job growth among its many assets.

LOOKING BACK AT ATLANTA

It is most fitting that Atlanta in the 21st century is an international gateway and transportation hub. The city was conceived as a rail crossroads for travel north, south, east, and west, and its role as a strategic junction has always figured largely in its destiny. It all began with a peach tree.

In 1826, surveyors first suggested this area of Georgia as a practical spot for a railroad connecting the state with northern markets. This was not yet the heyday of railroads, and the report was more or less ignored for a decade. But in 1837, the state legislature approved an act establishing the Western & Atlantic Railroad here. Look for the marker known as Zero Milepost when you visit Underground Atlanta; this marks the W & A Railroad site around which the city grew. The new town was

---

The Standing Peachtree

Today, just about everything in Atlanta is called "Peachtree" something, but the first Peachtree reference dates from 1782, when explorers discovered a Cherokee village on the Chattahoochee River called Standing Peachtree. Since peach trees are not native to the region, some historians maintain the village was actually named for a towering "pitch" tree (a resinous pine). Nevertheless, the Indian village became the location of Fort Peachtree, a tiny frontier outpost, during the War of 1812; a Peachtree Road connecting Fort Peachtree to Fort Daniel (in Gwinnett County) was completed by 1813.

unimaginatively dubbed "Terminus," but future governor Alexander H. Stephens, visiting what was still dense forest in 1839, predicted that "a magnificent inland city will at no distant date be built here."

The Trail of Tears

One aspect of the city's inception, however, was far from magnificent. In the early 1800s, most of Georgia was still Native American territory. White settlers coveted the Cherokee and Creek lands because they wanted to expedite the building of the railroad and further expand their settlements. Throughout the 1820s, in order to keep the peace, Native American leaders signed numerous treaties ceding millions of acres. They adopted a democratic form of government similar to the white man's, complete with a constitution and Supreme Court; erected schools and shops; built farms; and accepted Christianity. But the white frontiers-people cared little whether the Native Americans adapted—they wanted them to leave.

With President Andrew Jackson's support, Congress passed a bill in 1830 forcing all southern tribes to move to lands hundreds of miles away on the other side of the Mississippi River. When the U.S. Supreme Court ruled against the order, Jackson ignored the ruling and backed the Georgia settlers. In 1832, the state gave away Cherokee farms in a land lottery, and the white settlers used guns to force the Cherokee off their land. In 1837, 17,000 Native Americans were rounded up by federal soldiers, herded into camps, and forced on a cruel westward march called the "Trail of Tears." Some 4,000 died on the 800-mile journey to Oklahoma, and those who survived suffered bitterly from cold, hunger, and disease. Terminus and its surroundings were now firmly in the hands of the white settlers.

A City Grows

Terminus soon began its evolution from a sleepy rural hamlet to a thriving city, a meeting point of major rail lines. In 1843, the town was renamed Marthasville, for ex-governor Wilson Lumpkin's daughter Martha. No one in Marthasville took note in 1844 when a 23-year-old army lieutenant, William Tecumseh Sherman, was

DATELINE

1782 Explorers discover Cherokee village of Standing Peachtree.

1820s Cherokee and Creek leaders cede millions of acres to white settlers in hopes of keeping peace.

1837 The town, newly named Terminus, is selected as the site of a railroad terminus connecting Georgia with the Tennessee River. The same year, 17,000 Native Americans are forced to march westward on a "Trail of Tears."

1843 Terminus is renamed Marthasville.

1845 The first locomotive chugs into town. The city is renamed Atlanta.

1851 Georgia secedes from the Union, the Civil War begins, and Atlanta becomes a major Confederate supply depot and medical center.

1864 Union forces under General Sherman burn Atlanta.

1865 Civil War ends.

1877 Atlanta becomes the capital of Georgia.

stationed for 2 months in their area, but the knowledge he gained of local geography would vitally affect the city's history 2 decades later. The first locomotive, the *Kentucky*, chugged into town in 1845, and shortly thereafter, the name Marthasville was deemed too provincial for a burgeoning metropolis. J. Edgar Thomson, the railroad's chief engineer, suggested Atlanta (a feminized form of Atlantic).

In 1848, the newly incorporated city held its first mayoral election, an event marked by dozens of street brawls. Moses W. Formwalt, a maker of stills and member of the Free and Rowdy Party, was elected over temperance candidate John Norcross. But if Atlanta was a bit of a wild frontier town, it also had civic pride. An 1849 newspaper overstated things poetically:

> *Atlanta, the greatest spot in all the nation, The greatest place for legislation, Or any other occupation, The very center of creation.*

Storm Clouds Gather: Antebellum Atlanta

By the middle of the 19th century, the 31-state nation was in the throes of a westward expansion, and the institution of slavery was the major issue of the day. In his 1858 debate with Stephen Douglas, Abraham Lincoln declared, "This government cannot endure permanently half slave and half free." A year later it was obvious that only a war would resolve the issue. In 1861 (a year that began dramatically in Atlanta—with an earthquake), Georgia legislators voted for secession and joined the Confederacy.

In peacetime, the railroads had fashioned Atlanta into a center of commerce. In wartime, this transportation hub would emerge as a major Confederate military post and supply center—the vital link between Confederate forces in Tennessee and Virginia. Atlanta made the following ridiculous bid to become the capital of the Confederacy: "The city has good railroad connections, is free from yellow fever, and can supply the most wholesome foods and, as for 'goobers,' an indispensable article for a Southern legislator, we have them all the time." The lure of plentiful peanuts notwithstanding, the Confederacy chose Richmond, Virginia, as its capital. However, from early on, federal forces saw Atlanta's destruction as essential to Northern victory.

1886 Newspaper editor Henry Grady inspires readers with vision of a "New South." John S. Pemberton introduces Coca-Cola.

1900 Atlanta University professor W. E. B. Du Bois founds the NAACP.

1904 Piedmont Park designed.

1917 Fire destroys 73 square blocks of the city.

1929 Atlanta's first airport opens; Delta Air Lines takes to the skies and becomes Atlanta's home carrier.

1936 Margaret Mitchell's blockbuster novel, *Gone With the Wind*, is published.

1939 The movie version of *Gone With the Wind* premières in Atlanta.

1952 The city of Atlanta incorporates surrounding areas, increasing its population by 100,000 and its size from 37 to 118 square miles.

1960 Sit-ins and boycotts protesting segregation begin. The million-square-foot Merchandise Mart is erected.

continues

A City Burns

Atlanta served as not only a major Southern supply depot, but also the medical center of the Confederacy. Throughout the city, buildings were hastily converted into make-shift hospitals and clinics, and trains pulled into town daily to disgorge sick and wounded soldiers. By 1862, close to 4,000 soldiers were convalescing here, and the medical crisis was further aggravated by a smallpox epidemic.

That same year, Union spy James J. Andrews and a group of Northern soldiers disguised as civilians seized a locomotive called the *General*, with the aim of blocking supply lines by destroying tracks and bridges behind them. A wild train chase ensued, and the raiders were caught and punished (most, including Andrews, were executed). The episode came to be known as the "Great Locomotive Chase," one of the stirring stories of the Civil War and the subject of two subsequent movies. Today, you can see the *General* on display at the Southern Museum of Civil War and Locomotive History (p. 143).

The locomotive chase was an Atlanta victory, but the Northern desire to destroy the Confederacy's supply link remained intact. In 1864, General Ulysses S. Grant ordered Major General William T. Sherman to "move against Johnston's army to break it up, and get into the interior of the enemy's country as far as you can, inflicting all the damage you can against their resources." Georgians had great faith that the able and experienced General Joseph E. Johnston, whom they called "Old Joe," would repel the Yankees. As Sherman's Georgia campaign got underway, an overly optimistic editorial in the *Intelligencer* scoffed at the notion of federal conquest, claiming "we have no fear of the results, for General Johnston and his great and invincible satellites are working out the problem of battle and victory at the great chess board at the front." Johnston himself was not as sanguine. Sherman had 100,000 men to Johnston's 60,000, and the Union troops were better armed.

By July, Sherman was forcing the Confederate troops back, and Atlanta's fall seemed a foregone conclusion; Johnston informed Confederate President Jefferson Davis that he was outnumbered almost two to one and was in a defensive position.

1961 Ivan Allen, Jr., defeats segregationist Lester Maddox in mayoral election. Atlanta's public schools and the Georgia Institute of Technology are peacefully desegregated.

1964 Atlanta native Martin Luther King, Jr., wins Nobel Peace Prize.

1965 A plane crash at Orly Airport in Paris kills 106 of Atlanta's civic and cultural leaders. Atlanta Fulton County Stadium is built.

1966 Baseball's Braves move from Milwaukee and the Falcons become a new NFL expansion team. The Beatles perform in Atlanta.

1968 Martin Luther King, Jr., is assassinated in Memphis.

1974 Atlanta's first black mayor, Maynard Jackson, is inaugurated. Atlanta Braves' Hank Aaron hits his record-breaking 715th home run.

1976 Georgian Jimmy Carter elected president. Georgia World Congress Center, the nation's largest single-floor exhibit space, is completed.

Impressions

I want to say to General Sherman, who is an able man . . . though some people think he is kind of careless about fire, that from the ashes he left us in 1864, we have raised a brave and beautiful city; that we have caught the sunshine in our homes and built therein not one ignoble prejudice or memory.
—Henry Grady, *Atlanta Constitution* editor, 1886

His candid assessment was not appreciated, and Davis removed him from command, replacing him with the pugnacious 32-year-old General John Bell Hood. The change of leadership only further demoralized the ranks, and Sherman openly rejoiced when he heard the news.

Some disgruntled Confederate soldiers deserted. Hood abandoned the defensive tactics of Johnston, aggressively assaulting his opponent. His policy cost thousands of troops and gained nothing. In the Battle of Peachtree Creek on July 20, 1864, Union casualties totaled 1,710; Confederate, 4,796. Throughout the summer, the city suffered a full-scale artillery assault. More than 8,000 Confederates perished in the Battle of Atlanta on July 22, while Union deaths totaled just 3,722. The Confederates lost another 5,000 men during hours of fierce fighting on July 28, while the Yankees lost just 600. The Yankees further paralyzed the city by ripping up train rails, heating them over huge bonfires, and twisting them around trees into useless spirals of mangled iron that came to be known as "Sherman's neckties." The most devastating bombardment came on August 9—"that red day . . . when all the fires of hell, and all the thunders of the universe, seemed to be blazing and roaring over Atlanta."

By September 1, when Hood's troops pulled out of the area, first setting fire to vast stores of ammunition (and anything else that might benefit the Yankees), the town was in turmoil. Its roads were crowded with evacuees, and its hospitals, hotels, and private residences were flooded with wounded men. Crime and looting were rife, and

1979 MARTA rapid-transit train system opens.

1980 New Hartsfield International Airport dedicated.

1983 Martin Luther King, Jr.'s, birthday becomes national holiday.

1988 Atlanta hosts Democratic National Convention.

1989 Underground Atlanta reopens with great fanfare.

1992 Atlanta completes the new 70,500-seat Georgia Dome.

1994 Atlanta hosts Super Bowl XXVIII at the Georgia Dome.

1995 On their third try, the Atlanta Braves win the World Series.

1996 Atlanta completes the 85,000-seat Olympic Stadium and hosts the Centennial Olympic Games.

1997 Atlanta reopens Olympic Stadium as the new Turner Field, home of the Atlanta Braves baseball team.

1998 A renovated Centennial Olympic Park opens as a major city gathering spot and a lasting legacy of the Centennial Olympic Games.

continues

food was almost unavailable; the price of a ham-and-eggs breakfast with coffee soared to $25. Rooftops were ripped off houses and buildings, there were huge craters in the streets, and many civilians were dead. The railroads were in Sherman's hands.

On September 2, Mayor James M. Calhoun, carrying a white flag to the nearest federal unit, officially surrendered the city. The U.S. Army entered and occupied Atlanta, raising the Stars and Stripes at city hall for the first time in 4 years. Claiming he needed the city for military purposes, Sherman ordered all residents to evacuate. Atlantans piled their household goods on wagons, abandoned their homes and businesses, and became refugees. Before departing Atlanta in November, Union troops leveled railroad facilities and burned the city, leaving it a wasteland—defunct as a military center and practically uninhabitable. The Yankees marched out of the city to the strains of "The Battle Hymn of the Republic."

As of January 1865, there was $1.64 in the treasury, the railroad system was destroyed, and most of the city was burned to the ground.

> **Impressions**
>
> *No one goes anywhere without passing through Atlanta.*
> —Francis C. Lawley, *London Times* reporter, 1861

A City Rebuilds

Slowly, exiled citizens began to trickle back into Atlanta. Confederate money had become worthless. At the inauguration of his second term in 1865, Lincoln pledged "malice toward none, charity for all"—but after his assassination later that year, this policy was replaced with one of harsh Republican vengeance. It wasn't until 1876 that federal troops were withdrawn and Atlanta was freed from military occupation.

Still, the city was making a remarkable recovery. Like the ever-resilient Scarlett O'Hara ("It takes more than Yankees or a burning to keep me down"), Atlanta rolled up its sleeves and began rebuilding. A Northern newspaper reported, "From all this

1999 Atlanta completes the Philips Arena, home to the Atlanta Hawks basketball team and the Atlanta Thrashers hockey team.

2000 The city hosts Super Bowl XXXIV.

2003 The $95-million Georgia International Convention Center—featuring a 40,000-square-foot ballroom—opens for business.

2005 The 5-million-gallon Georgia Aquarium opens in the middle of revitalized downtown Atlanta.

2007 The all-new, bigger and better World of Coca-Cola opens downtown next to the Georgia Aquarium.

2009 Atlanta's population continues to climb, having recently bypassed the five million milestone.

2011 The Georgia Aquarium pumps $110 million into a new dolphin exhibit, making the world's largest aquarium an even bigger draw.

ruin and devastation a new city is springing up . . . the streets are alive from morning till night with drays and carts and hand-barrows and wagons . . . with loads of lumber and loads of brick."

In the years after the war, Atlanta was filled with carpetbaggers (Northern adventurers and politicians who went south to take advantage of the unsettled postwar conditions) and other adventurers hoping to turn a quick buck, and with them came gambling houses, brothels, and saloons. But the city also boasted hundreds of new stores and businesses, churches, schools, banks, hotels, theaters, and a new newspaper, the *Atlanta Constitution*. The railroads began operating again. In 1867, African Americans chartered Atlanta University, today the world's largest predominantly black institution of higher learning. Newspaper editor Henry Grady, Atlanta's biggest civic booster, inspired readers with his vision of an industrialized and culturally advanced "New South." A new constitution in 1877 made Atlanta the permanent capital of the state of Georgia. Two years later, General Sherman visited the city he had destroyed and was welcomed with a ball and, lest he get any funny ideas, a grand military review.

In 1886, a new headache cure was introduced to the city—a syrup made from the coca leaf and the kola nut, which would eventually become the world's most renowned beverage, Coca-Cola. Atlanta adopted the symbol of a phoenix rising from the ashes for its official seal in 1888 and, the following year, dedicated the gold-domed state capitol and opened a zoo in Grant Park. Piedmont Park was built in 1904 as the site of the Cotton States and International Exposition—a $2.5-million world's fair–like extravaganza with entertainment ranging from Buffalo Bill and His Wild West Show to reconstructed "international villages." Former slave Booker T. Washington gave a landmark address, and John Philip Sousa composed the "King Cotton March" to mark the event.

The 20th Century

At the turn of the 20th century, Atlanta's population was 90,000, a figure that more than doubled 2 decades later. Though a massive fire destroyed almost 2,000 buildings in 1917, the city was on a course of rapid growth. In 1929, Atlanta opened its first airport on the site of today's Hartsfield International, presaging the growth of a major air-travel industry. The same year, Delta Air Lines took to the skies and became Atlanta's home carrier.

Margaret Mitchell's blockbuster Civil War epic, *Gone With the Wind,* which went on to become the world's second-best-selling book (after the Bible) and the basis for domestically the biggest-grossing picture of all time (when adjusted for inflation), was published in 1936. Louis B. Mayer turned down a chance to make the film version for MGM, because "no Civil War picture ever made a nickel."

A grimmer legacy of the Civil War and the institution of slavery was racial strife, and the early years of the 20th century were marked by violent race riots. Atlanta University professor W. E. B. Du Bois founded the National Association for the Advancement of Colored People, or NAACP, in 1900. In 1939, black cast members were unable to attend the glamorous première of *Gone With the Wind* because the theater was segregated. And as late as 1960, segregation in Atlanta (as everywhere in the South) was still firmly entrenched and backed by state law. Unlike much of the South, though, the city adopted a progressive attitude regarding race relations. Even before the civil rights movement, there were hints of tolerance—the hiring of black police officers, the election of a black professional to the Atlanta Board of Education, the desegregation of a public golf course in 1955, and, in 1959, the desegregation of public transit. Mayor Bill Hartsfield (who held office for almost 3 decades) called Atlanta "a city too busy to hate." And his successor, Mayor Ivan Allen, Jr., called on Atlantans to face race problems "and seek the answers in an atmosphere of decency and dignity."

Atlanta peacefully desegregated its public schools and the Georgia Institute of Technology in 1961. Atlanta native Dr. Martin Luther King, Jr., headquartered his Southern Christian Leadership Conference here and made Ebenezer Baptist Church, where he was a copastor with his father, a hub of the civil rights movement. In 1974, Atlanta inaugurated its first black mayor, Maynard Jackson, and, following a term by another black mayor, Andrew Young, Jackson was reelected.

In 1966, Atlanta went big league when the Braves and the Falcons came to town. And Atlantans went wild in 1974, when Hank Aaron broke Babe Ruth's home-run record here.

All About Atlanta

There's so much to learn about this gateway city and so many ways to do it. For an overview, start with the **Atlanta History Center,** which includes the Atlanta History Museum and a wing dedicated to the 1996 Olympic Games.

Or schedule a tour of the **Georgia State Capitol,** which was modeled after the nation's Capitol, another neoclassical edifice atop a "crowning hill." Its 75-foot dome, covered in gold leaf and topped by a Statue of Freedom, is a major Atlanta landmark. The building is fronted by a massive four-story portico with a pediment supported by six Corinthian columns set on large stone piers. In the rotunda, with its soaring 237-foot ceiling, are busts of famous Georgians, including signers of the Declaration of Independence and the Constitution. The governor's office is off the main hall. The capitol building's public spaces have been restored to their 1889 grandeur. The fourth floor houses legislative galleries and the Georgia Capitol Museum, with exhibits on cotton, peach, and peanut growing; cases of mounted birds, fish, deer, insects, and other species native to Georgia; rocks and minerals; American Indian artifacts; and more. Note, too, the museum displays on the first floor.

You'd be surprised by how many folks come to Atlanta expecting to tour the *Gone With the Wind* mansion or see where Scarlett and Rhett are buried—no joke. But the story is so much a part of the fiber of Atlanta that you really should plan to visit the **Margaret Mitchell House & Museum,** "the dump" she lived in while crafting the famous tale of the South. The museum contains movie memorabilia and chronicles the making of the movie, its première in Atlanta, and the impact of the book and movie on society. The tour concludes in the museum shop, which features a variety of *GWTW* collectibles. If you finish your tour around mealtime and you're ready for a real change of pace, walk a few blocks south on Peachtree to the Vortex, a rowdy burger joint and bar that serves some of the best burgers in town.

The **Atlanta Preservation Society** offers a number of guided historic walking tours throughout the city, including the fabulous Fox Theatre, Piedmont Park, down-town Atlanta, Grant Hill, Inman Park, and the Sweet Auburn/Martin Luther King, Jr., historic district. All of these tours provide insight to the history of Atlanta and the people and places that make this city what it is today.

Civil War Trail

Atlanta was obviously in the midst of the action throughout the Civil War, and many opportunities exist to learn about what many here still refer to—with tongue in cheek—as "the war of Northern aggression." Begin with a visit to the **Atlanta Cyclorama & Civil War Museum,** in Grant Park. The building that houses the Cyclorama also contains a museum of related artifacts, the most important being the steam locomotive *Texas* from the 1862 Great Locomotive Chase. Other exhibits include displays of Civil War arms and artillery, Civil War–themed paintings, portraits of Confederate and Union leaders, "life in camp" artifacts and photographs, and uniforms.

Next, venture northwest to the **Kennesaw Mountain/National Battlefield Park,** a 2,884-acre park established in 1917 on the site of a crucial Civil War battle in the Atlanta campaign of 1864. Some two million visitors come annually to explore the Confederate entrenchments and earthworks, some of them featuring Civil War artillery. Located in the same vicinity is the **Southern Museum of Civil War and Locomotive History,** operated in association with the Smithsonian Institute, which means that Civil War and transportation objects from the Smithsonian are incorporated into the exhibits here. It was here that the wild adventure known as the Great Locomotive Chase began. The museum, occupying a building that was once the Frey cotton gin, houses the *General* locomotive; a walk-through caboose; exhibits of Civil War artifacts, memorabilia, and photographs (including those relating to the chase and its participants); and exhibits on railroads. You can view a 20-minute narrated video about the chase, but if you really want the full story, pick up the Disney movie *The Great Locomotive Chase,* starring Fess Parker, available in the museum gift shop.

Even **Oakland Cemetery** is ripe with Civil War history, as Confederate and Union soldiers, including five Southern generals, are among the more than 48,000 people buried here. Listed on the National Register of Historic Places, this outstanding 88-acre Victorian cemetery was founded in 1850. Two monuments honor the Confederate war dead. Standing at the marker that commemorates the Great Locomotive Chase, you can see the trees from which the Yankee raiders were hanged; the Confederate train conductor Capt. William Fuller is buried nearby.

African-American History

Atlanta is ripe with ties to the rich history of African Americans and the civil rights movement. After all, this is the birthplace of Martin Luther King, Jr. And all of the sites are full of learning opportunities, so bring the whole family along this sightseeing trail, beginning with the **APEX (African-American Panoramic Experience) Museum** in the Sweet Auburn district. Featuring exhibits on the history of Sweet Auburn and the African-American experience, the museum includes a children's gallery with interactive displays.

Leaving the APEX, follow the walking tour for **Sweet Auburn** (p. 163), which includes the **King Center,** Dr. King's final resting place; his late wife Coretta Scott King is buried next to him. Next, the **Birth Home of Martin Luther King, Jr.,** is open for half-hour guided tours. Though the tour is free, you must get tickets at the National Park Service Visitor Center on Auburn Avenue. Don't miss **Ebenezer Baptist Church** or the **Herndon Building,** named for an ex-slave who went on to found the Atlanta Life Insurance Company, the second-largest black insurance company in the country. Built in the early 1900s, the **Butler Street YMCA** was a popular meeting place for civil rights leaders. And the **Sweet Auburn Curb Market** offers fare not often enjoyed outside of the South.

For answers about African-American history, visit the **Auburn Avenue Research Library on African-American Culture and History.** Several churches along the avenue, such as **Big Bethel AME** and **First Congregational,** helped build and maintain the heritage of the street. The **Royal Peacock Club** provided an elegant setting where many African Americans could perform and bring the changing styles of black popular music to Atlanta.

Famous Atlantans

HENRY LOUIS "HANK" AARON (b. 1934) An outfielder with the Milwaukee (later Atlanta) Braves, Aaron broke Babe Ruth's record in 1974 with his 715th home run, in Atlanta–Fulton County Stadium. He remained cool and dignified in the face of the media frenzy surrounding his pursuit of the record, despite receiving countless death threats and bags of hate mail from bigots who felt that Ruth's achievement should never be surpassed by a black man. He retired in 1976 with 755 homers.

HENRY W. GRADY (1850–89) Managing editor of the *Atlanta Constitution,* Grady preached post–Civil War reconciliation and worked passionately to draw northern capital and diversified industry to the agrarian South. His name is synonymous with the phrase "The New South."

JOEL CHANDLER HARRIS (1848–1908) Called "Georgia's Aesop," he created Uncle Remus, the wise black raconteur of children's fables. His tales of Br'er Rabbit and Br'er Fox were the basis for Disney's delightful animated feature *Song of the South.* See chapter 10 for more on Harris.

ROBERT TYRE "BOBBY" JONES (1902–71) The founder of the Masters tournament, Jones won golf's Grand Slam at age 28 and has been called the world's greatest golfer. He also held academic degrees in engineering, law, and English literature.

MARTIN LUTHER KING, JR. (1929–68) Civil rights leader, minister, orator, and winner of the Nobel Peace Prize, King preached Gandhi's doctrine of passive resistance.

MARGARET MITCHELL (1900–49) Originally a journalist, Mitchell was the author of the definitive southern blockbuster novel, *Gone With the Wind.* She began writing "the book" in 1926 when a severe ankle injury forced her to give up reporting. *GWTW* is still one of the world's best-selling books.

JOHN C. PORTMAN (b. 1924) An architect/developer who revolutionized hotel design in the United States with his lofty atrium-lobby concept, Portman almost single-handedly designed Atlanta's skyline in the 1960s. He has been called "Atlanta's one-man urban-renewal program."

ROBERT EDWARD "TED" TURNER III (b. 1938) Dubbed "the mouth of the South," America's most dynamic media mogul, Ted Turner, created 24-hour cable news networks CNN and Headline News, along with entertainment networks Superstation TBS and TNT. Turner is vice chairman of Time Warner, Inc., and owns a portion of MGM, the Atlanta Braves, and the Atlanta Hawks.

ALFRED UHRY (b. 1936) One of the most winning present-day playwrights (an Oscar, a Tony, and a Pulitzer Prize), Uhry, who was born and reared in Atlanta and spent much of his adult life here, has since moved away from the city. But he still has

It stinks, I don't know why I bother with it, but I've got to have something to do with my time.
—Margaret Mitchell, author of *Gone With the Wind*

Gone With the Wind *is very possibly the greatest American novel.*
—Publishers Weekly

2

ATLANTA IN DEPTH | Atlanta in Pop Culture

Atlanta on his mind: Many of his plays, the most notable of which are *Driving Miss Daisy* and *The Last Night of Ballyhoo,* take place in this city. Uhry's early scripts were produced when he was a student at Druid Hills High School in the mid-1950s, including one about rural life that was upstaged by a boisterous live chicken.

ROBERT W. WOODRUFF (1889–1985)   Woodruff was the Coca-Cola Company president, a philanthropist, and a leading Atlanta citizen for more than half a century. He put Coca-Cola on the map worldwide; promoted civil rights; and gave more than $400 million to educational, artistic, civil, and medical projects in Atlanta, such as Emory University, the Woodruff Arts Center, and the High Museum.

ATLANTA IN POP CULTURE

BOOKS   Many books have been written—both fiction and nonfiction—about this beloved city. And while most nonfiction can be taken for fact, many natives will tell you that a lot of the fiction holds nearly as many truths (and some not-so-secret skeletons) about Atlanta and the folks who've lived here through the decades.

Archival Atlanta: Forgotten Facts and Well-Kept Secrets from Our City's Past, by Perry Buffington and Kim Underwood, is a light read, packed with fascinating historical tidbits—some of which are sure to surprise even the most knowledgeable Atlanta history buff. The book includes its share of humorous anecdotes.

For those more interested in looking at pictures than reading, Andy Ambrose, deputy director of the Atlanta History Center, compiled *Atlanta: An Illustrated History,* filled with images from Atlanta's archives. From the days of saloons and brothels in the early 1800s to the city's renaissance beginning in the 1960s, this account explores everything from Atlanta's troubling racial past to the celebrated, historically rich neighborhoods of Ansley Park and Buckhead.

Michael Rose's *Atlanta Then and Now* delivers an illustrated juxtaposition of Atlanta's past and present. The photos allow first-time visitors as well as old friends to see just how far this southern city has come in the past century.

For an account of some of the down-and-dirty backroom dealings that brought Atlanta to the forefront as an international city, many readers swear by Frederick Allen's *Atlanta Rising: The Invention of an International City 1946–1996.* This mostly objective account of Atlanta's dealings over the past 50 years describes the relationships among the city's decision makers as various events unfold.

Of course, Margaret Mitchell's novel *Gone With the Wind* is a given for those who wish to take in a Civil War–era depiction of this area.

Author Fred Willard has a big following, which began with his Atlanta-based satirical mystery, *Down on Ponce,* and continued with *Princess Naughty and the Voodoo Cadillac.* Those folks who know the area intimately will swear to the authenticity of the Deep South social outcasts who inhabit a side of Atlanta that most residents would rather keep quiet.

Anne Rivers Siddons was reared just 20 miles from the big city, and **Hills Town, King's Oak,** and **Homeplace** are all set in Georgia. Her **Peachtree Road** is a dark, hypnotic tale of Buckhead high society in the mid–20th century, when money and civil rights were the fuel on which the city ran. Her **Downtown** depicts Atlanta's last years of innocence: "Atlanta in the autumn of 1966 was a city being born, and the energy and promise of that lying-in sent out subterranean vibrations all over the just-stirring South, like underground shock waves—a call to those who could hear it best, the young. And they came, they came in droves, from small, sleeping towns and large, drowsing universities, from farms and industrial suburbs and backwaters so still that even the building firestorm of the civil rights movement had not yet rippled the surface."

And while he doesn't live in Atlanta, Tom Wolfe ruffled more than a few feathers with his 1998 tome **A Man in Full.** As Wolfe states in the book, Atlanta is a place "where your 'honor' is the thing you possess." More critics than not thought his depiction of the slums and socialites of Atlanta might do more harm than good in boosting the tourism economy here.

FILM Atlanta's biggest connection to film is, of course, **Gone With the Wind,** taken from the Pulitzer Prize–winning novel of the same name written in 1936 by Margaret Mitchell of Atlanta. The 1939 Academy Award–winning film depicted Atlanta and the Old South during the Civil War as seen from the viewpoint of a rebellious southern belle, Scarlett O'Hara, whose home, a plantation called Tara, is taken over by the Northern opposition. The movie première was held in the ballroom of Atlanta's Georgian Terrace, still a grand working hotel today, on Peachtree Street, across from the Fox Theatre. In attendance were actors from the film, including Vivien Leigh (Scarlett) and Clark Gable (Rhett Butler).

Atlanta playwright Alfred Uhry penned a play from which the movie **Driving Miss Daisy** was adapted. The plot follows a 72-year-old Atlanta widow, Miss Daisy Werthan, in 1948 as she deals with issues of aging, race relations (she is white and Jewish; her son hires an African-American chauffeur after she has a fender bender), religion, fear, and relationships. Miss Daisy was played by Jessica Tandy and Morgan Freeman starred as Hoke Colburn, the chauffeur. She's initially embarrassed—because of age or her fear of appearing too rich—to be driven around and even walks to the grocery store in defiance. Once she accepts the fact that she is unable to drive herself, she and Colburn warm up to one another and she teaches him to read. On a trip out of town for a family occasion, Miss Daisy is awakened to the prejudicial treatment her new friend encounters. When her synagogue is bombed, she realizes that she, too, is subjected to racism as a Jew. The elderly lady eventually goes into a retirement home, to be visited frequently by Colburn, the two having become best friends. The film took four awards from nine nominations at the 62nd Academy Awards in 1989. It is the only film based on an off-Broadway production ever to win an Academy Award for Best Picture. At age 80, Tandy was the oldest winner in the Best Actress category.

Also an Atlanta-related film is Disney's **The Great Locomotive Chase,** starring Fess Parker as the dashing Union spy James J. Andrews. The movie tells how the story of the wild adventure known as the "Great Locomotive Chase" began. The Civil War had been underway for a year on April 12, 1862, when Andrews and a group of 21 Northern soldiers disguised as civilians boarded a locomotive called the *General* in Marietta, buying tickets for diverse destinations to avert suspicion. When the train made a breakfast stop at the Lacy Hotel in Big Shanty, they seized the locomotive and several boxcars and fled northward to Chattanooga. The goal of these daring raiders was to destroy tracks, telegraph wires, and bridges behind them, thus cutting off the Confederate supply route between Virginia and Mississippi.

Conductor William A. Fuller, his breakfast interrupted by the sound of the *General* chugging out of the station, gave chase on foot, then grabbed a platform car and poled along the tracks. With him were a railroad superintendent and the *General*'s engineer. At the Etowah River, Fuller and crew commandeered a small locomotive called the *Yonah* and made better progress. Meanwhile, the raiders tore up track behind them, and when the pursuers got close, the raiders slowed them down by throwing ties and firewood onto the tracks. Andrews, a very smooth talker, managed to convince station attendants en route that he was on an emergency mission running ammunition to Confederate General Beauregard in Mississippi.

Fuller's chances of catching the *General* improved when he seized the southbound *Texas* and began running it backward toward the raiders, picking up reinforcements along the way and eventually managing to get a telegraph message through to General Danville Leadbetter, commander at Chattanooga. The chase went on, with Andrews sending uncoupled boxcars careening back toward Fuller as obstructions. Fuller, who was running in reverse, merely attached the rolling boxcars to his engine and kept on. At the covered Oostanaula Bridge, the raiders detached a boxcar and set it on fire in hopes of finally creating an impassable obstacle—a burning bridge behind them. But the *Texas* was able to push the flaming car off the bridge. It soon burned out, and Fuller tossed it off the track and continued.

By this time the *General* was running low on fuel and water, the *Texas* was hot on its heels, and the raiders realized that all was lost. Andrews gave his final command: "Jump off and scatter! Every man for himself!" All were captured and imprisoned within a few days. Some escaped, others were exchanged for Confederate prisoners of war, and the rest were hanged in Atlanta, most of them at a site near Oakland Cemetery. Though the mission failed, the raiders, some of them posthumously, received the newly created Medal of Honor for their valor.

Today, Atlanta is a hopping scene in the film industry, with such homegrown film products as **The Lady from Sockholm, Last Goodbye, Freez'er, The Adventures of Ociee Nash,** and **No Witness.** Of greatest note is **Last Goodbye,** starring David Carradine and Faye Dunaway among others. The movie brings six very different individuals together on a hot summer day in Atlanta. Carradine, as a whacked-out Bible salesman, and Dunaway, as a film director, play the role of saviors to some needy younger people.

In addition, Tyler Perry, whose numerous stage plays continue to be reborn as movies, also lives in Atlanta, where his talent as a playwright first wowed audiences. In 2005, Perry opened at the top of the box office with his instant hit **Diary of a Mad Black Woman,** which he wrote, produced, and starred in. That success was followed by additional movies adapted from his plays, including **Meet the Browns, Why Did I Get Married, Daddy's Little Girls, Madea's Family Reunion, The Family That Preys,** and **Madea Goes to Jail.** Perry's latest blockbuster, **For Colored Girls,** opened late 2010. His Tyler Perry Studios, the first independent studio of its size to open in Georgia, is located in Atlanta.

MUSIC Atlanta seems to be a magnet for talented musicians, and a long list of singers, musicians, and entire bands hail from the city. Among the most popular are Atlanta Rhythm Section, Mother's Finest, Indigo Girls, Black Crowes, Georgia Satellites, SOS Band, Heart to Heart, and Mose Davis.

ATLANTA GETS crunk

East Coast, West Coast, or Dirty South, the multibillion-dollar hip-hop music scene is as strong as ever, and Atlanta is respectfully recognized as a major player in this genre.

Home to high-profile record labels such as So So Def Records, established by producer Jermaine Dupri in 1992, Atlanta, called "Motown of the South," is a huge draw for hip-hop and rap artists. Twenty years ago, Dupri signed Kris Kross as his first act and soon established himself as a key player in the industry, putting Atlanta on the hip-hop map. Other acts followed Dupri's first success, including Bow Wow, Dem Franchise Boyz, and J-Kwon.

Through the years, Dupri's label has been affiliated with multiple larger record labels through the years, as Dupri has aligned himself and then parted ways with labels including Columbia, Arista (where he was named president of Black Music), Sony, BMG, and Virgin. Yet another label, Grand Hustle Records, is owned by Atlanta native rapper T.I. and is a subsidiary of Warner Music Group and distributed by Atlantic Records.

Atlanta producers and artists even coined a signature style called Dirty South hip-hop, made popular by Outkast, Goodie Mob, and others. A rapper and producer in his own right, Lil Jon is the force behind a party-style hip-hop variety known as "crunk," which fuses hip-hop music with the Memphis-born electro genre. Crunk has also come to be used as an all-inclusive term for southern hip-hop music. Lil Jon and the East Side Boyz, with the Ying Yang Twins, brought the national spotlight to crunk music with their song "Get Low."

Whether they were born and raised in "Hotlanta" or came here to be part of a growing hip-hop scene, many multiplatinum rappers call this city home. Among them are Ludacris, Young Jeezy, B.o.B., Lloyd, Gorilla Zoe, Big Boi, Andre 3000, Young Dr., Pastor Troy, Crime Mob, Lil Scrappy, Ying Yang Twins, D4L, Yung Joc, Usher, Ciara, and Cee-lo Green.

Hip-hop celebrity sightings are frequent in Atlanta, whether it's Andre 3000 enjoying a Braves baseball game (we sat next to him a couple of years ago and he graciously signed autographs with one hand while eating with the other) or any number of other hip-hop icons shopping at high-end malls at Lenox Square and Phipps Plaza.

You can even spot a famous face or two—especially on Sunday nights—at 300 Atlanta, an upscale bowling alley featuring lounge-style lane-side seating in a classy bar-type atmosphere. The Castelberry Hill district is a celebrity draw, as is Eight, Young Jeezy's clothing store on the historic Auburn Avenue.

Atlanta venues hosting hip-hop artists and related events include Bankhead area's Club Crucial, owned by rapper T.I.; Magic City, a popular strip club where Snoop Dogg held his latest CD release party; Straits, a Midtown restaurant owned by Ludacris; and the Velvet Room, previously Vision nightclub, where celebrities go to party en masse.

Because of its high-profile standing in the music industry, Atlanta is also home to the annual BET Hip-Hop Awards show each October and hosted by such big names as comedian Katt Williams, rapper T-Pain, and the multi-talented performer Mike Epps. Like peers in other hip-hop music scene cities, Atlanta's hip-hop industry has expanded into other ventures, including branded fragrance and clothing lines.

Today, Atlanta is a mecca for rap and hip-hop artists, with major recording studios based here, such as Jermaine Dupri's So So Def. Among the artists hailing from Atlanta or now calling the city home are Lil Jon, Usher, Outkast, Ludacris, T.I., Ying Yang Twins, Young Jeezy, and Jermaine Dupri.

The country music scene is also well tied to Atlanta, including Trisha Yearwood, who frequents the city but wasn't born here, and Sugarland, the darling duo of Jennifer Nettles and Kristian Bush, both of whom now call the city home. In 2008, they recorded their number-one album, *Love on the Inside,* here at Southern Tracks, a studio with a long Atlanta history and an even longer client list of all the top musicians, from the '50s through today. Musicians of all genres have recorded here at one time or another, including Pearl Jam, Aerosmith, Creed, Third Day, Newsong, Gladys Knight, Collective Soul, Keith Sweat, and Bruce Springsteen. The original studio was founded by music producer Bill Lowery in the mid-1950s. He's best known for producing such jewels as "Be Bop a Lula," "I Never Promised You a Rose Garden," and "Games People Play."

EATING & DRINKING

Atlanta runs right up there with the big dogs when it comes to fine dining. With cuisine from nearly every ethnic group in the universe, the city isn't just about sweet tea and fried chicken—though you can certainly get your fill of authentic southern cooking here as well. But when you've tired of turnip greens, fried okra, and cheese grits (p. 82 for the scoop on this southern staple), prepare to dazzle your taste buds with fare ranging from Russian and Indian to Moroccan and Greek. Whatever you choose to dine on, you can always wash it down with one of many local brews, including the most popular, Sweetwater 420 Extra Pale Ale. A number of brewpubs in Atlanta serve their own house brews, so take a taste drive at 55 Seasons, Park Tavern Brewery, or Max Lager's American Grill & Brewery.

In addition, some of the country's top chefs operate successful restaurants here, including Richard Blais (a former competitor on *Iron Chef America*), who always has a new venture in the works (his latest is FLIP Burger Boutique, a modern hamburger joint concept for which Blais serves as creative director). The legendary Anne Quatrano and Clifford Harrison—the wife/husband team and owners of Bacchanalia, Quinones, Floataway Café, and Star Provisions—were recently jointly named the James Beard Foundation's "Best Chef in the Southeast."

DINING LIKE A TRUE SOUTHERNER   In the South, we call our first meal of the day breakfast, like the rest of the country, but the water gets murky after that. What most of the country calls "lunch," southerners often refer to as "dinner." And to differentiate between it and the evening meal, we typically refer to "dinner" as "supper." But don't worry, even Atlanta's Southern cuisine eateries use the standard breakfast, lunch, and dinner references.

It's no surprise that many folks visiting Atlanta and/or the South for the first time have some curiosity about southern or "country" cooking, and visitors here won't be disappointed. While many establishments serve what they consider southern dishes, many of them miss the mark. But that reliable handful of seasoned cooks (and some are true chefs) serving authentic, "down home" cooking do us all proud. One anomaly for many unfamiliar with southern fare is **grits.** There's really no mystery here, folks; grits are ground corn, similar to what our northern counterparts do with wheat and call "cream of wheat." Now, what you do with grits is a whole 'nother story. While the traditional style is hot grits topped with butter, salt, and pepper, cheese grits is another tasty option, especially popular as a side to fried fish. However, even cheese grits have taken on a new spin, with chefs constantly trying to find some fancy cheese to mix in rather than sticking to the Velveeta upon which most southern cooks rely for flavoring. Today's cooks are liable to do all manner of dishes with grits, including the popular **shrimp and grits,** quail and grits, and even baked garlic cheese grits. Many chefs use grits much like others would use polenta, and the taste isn't terribly different. Transplants to the South have been known to eat their grits with sugar, much to the dismay of natives, of course. But even locals add a twist to their grits on occasion, such as cream cheese, ham, or **red eye gravy,** not really a gravy at all, but rather a thin sauce made from the drippings of country ham and coffee (it tastes much better than it sounds—trust me).

While among us dwells a small percentage of vegetarians, most southerners do like their meat, especially if it's fried, such as fried chicken, fried pork chops, and country fried steak. Wild game is typically easy to come by and includes venison, wild hog, quail, turkey, dove, and even alligator and rattlesnake for the most daring amongst us. Barbecued meat of all types is another southern favorite, and if you're going to eat it, you've got to have **Brunswick Stew,** for which the most traditional recipe calls for cooking down a hog's head (or even squirrel). Whatever meat is used—pork, chicken, beef—is combined with corn, tomatoes, potatoes, and a wide variety of ingredients, depending on who's cooking. We're also fond of fried seafood, especially catfish and **mullet** (it's got to be fresh to be good).

Another large sector of southern food is fresh vegetables, including black-eyed peas; **collard, turnip, or mustard greens;** okra (fried or stewed with tomatoes are favored among southerners); fried green tomatoes; and squash, most tasty when baked into a casserole with cheese and cracker crumbs. Other southern sides include pear salad (a canned pear half topped with a dollop of mayonnaise and sprinkled with shredded cheddar cheese) and sweet-potato soufflé, both of which are almost des-sertlike. Speaking of desserts, southerners will charm you with pecan pie, **red velvet cake** (the cake really is red, thanks to food coloring, and then topped with rich cream-cheese frosting), banana pudding, peanut butter pie, and 12-layer caramel cake.

Between meals, you might try some southern snacks, such as fried pork skins in any variety of flavors, **boiled peanuts** (a truly acquired taste—I think it's the texture that throws first-timers), or **cheese straws,** a cheesy crumbly cracker and a staple at any respectable shower, tea, reception, or other such event that calls for southern hospitality.

Bread is on the table for all southern meals, from morning to night. But what we consider "bread" in the South takes on a wide definition, including your standard grocery store loaf of white bread, or **"light bread"** as we are known to call it. It also includes such high-carb treats as buttermilk biscuits, thick slabs of cornbread, and **lace hoecake cornbread**—a thin, lacy bread fried in a cast-iron skillet. There's nothing better with any southern meal than a good ol' **cat head biscuit,** so called because they are as big as a cat's head. And don't be surprised if you see one of us dipping (or sopping, as it's known here) our biscuit in the gravy or drowning it in cane syrup, blackstrap molasses, Tupelo honey, Mayhaw jelly, or any number of sweet concoctions.

Wash it all down with a tall glass of **sweet tea** (iced tea with sugar and usually a slice of lemon), that southern nectar that leaves northerners scratching their heads when we try to order it in a restaurant north of the Mason-Dixon line (Mary Macs, a southern dining tradition in Atlanta, refers to sweet tea as "the table wine of the South"). RC (Royal Crown) Cola and, of course, **Coca-Cola** (pronounced "co-cola" by southerners) are other staples. And many old-timers still belly up to the bar for a nice cold glass of fresh buttermilk.

If you're looking for something a little stronger in the drink category, Atlanta is home to many brewpubs, bubbling up their own beers, among the most popular of which is Sweetwater 420. Of course, some folks do still drink their **mint juleps,** but not with the frequency that outsiders might think. This stereotypical libation is a strong combination of whiskey, sugar, mint, and crushed ice, and it'll knock your socks off.

WHEN TO GO

Although there is no high season for tourism here, Atlanta is a major convention and trade-show destination. Before choosing travel dates, it's wise to ask the Atlanta Convention & Visitors Bureau (ACVB; p. 145) or your travel agent what major events will be taking place in Atlanta when you plan to visit. Large conventions can mean an increase in hotel prices and longer waits at popular restaurants. Among the largest conventions that occupy a high percentage of Atlanta hotels each year are the twice-a-year Atlanta International Gift and Home Furnishings Markets, with 93,000 attendees in early to mid-January and 72,000 attendees in mid-July, as well as the Cheer Sport gathering of about 70,000 attendees in the third week of February. With more than 93,000 hotel rooms, Atlanta can accommodate both conventiongoers and tourists, the first of which tend to rely on the MARTA public transportation system rather than clogging up already congested roadways.

Spring and autumn are long seasons, and in terms of natural beauty and moderate temperatures, they're ideal times to visit. April, when the dogwoods and azaleas put on a brilliant, colorful display, is especially lovely, but May and October are excellent months here, too.

If you come during July and August, when Atlanta gets a little steamy, you may find some hotels offering summer discounts. Almost all accommodations offer reduced rates during the Christmas holiday season.

The Weather

Atlanta's climate is mostly temperate year-round. The city enjoys four distinct seasons, but the variations are less extreme than in other parts of the United States.

It does get cold here in winter. The mercury dips below freezing—usually at night—an average of 50 days a year, and at least once a year there's a snowfall or an ice storm. (Northern transplants think it's pretty hilarious the way an inch or two of snow can paralyze the city.) But for the most part, winter days are mild, and it's often possible to enjoy the parks and even the outdoor restaurants in the middle of January or February.

Don't let the low average daytime temperatures for July, August, and early September fool you. Summers can be hot and humid, with daytime highs reaching into the 90s, although the really stifling spells usually last just a few days at a time. Annual rainfall is about 48 inches, and the wettest months are December through April, plus July.

Atlanta's Average Daytime Temperature & Rainfall

	JAN	FEB	MAR	APR	MAY	JUNE	JULY	AUG	SEPT	OCT	NOV	DEC
TEMP. °F/°C	52/11	57/14	65/18	73/23	80/27	87/31	89/32	88/31	82/28	73/23	63/17	55/13
RAINFALL (IN.)	5.0	4.7	5.4	3.6	4.0	3.6	5.1	3.7	4.0	3.1	4.1	3.8

HOLIDAYS

Banks, government offices, post offices, and many stores, restaurants, and museums are closed on the following legal national holidays: January 1 (New Year's Day), the third Monday in January (Martin Luther King, Jr., Day), the third Monday in February (Presidents' Day), the last Monday in May (Memorial Day), July 4 (Independence Day), the first Monday in September (Labor Day), the second Monday in October (Columbus Day), November 11 (Veterans Day/Armistice Day), the fourth Thursday in November (Thanksgiving Day), and December 25 (Christmas). The Tuesday after the first Monday in November is Election Day, a federal government holiday in presidential-election years (held every 4 years, and next in 2012).

Atlanta Calendar of Events

Note: Some events, such as the Georgia Renaissance Festival and the Georgia Shakespeare Festival, begin in one month and continue for several months thereafter. These are listed under the month in which they start, so do look back and ahead a few months for information on ongoing events. The ACVB's website (www.atlanta.net) also has a terrific calendar of events.

For an exhaustive list of events beyond those listed here, check http://events.frommers.com, where you'll find a searchable, up-to-the-minute roster of what's happening in cities all over the world.

JANUARY

Martin Luther King, Jr., Weekend. This major event begins with an interfaith service and includes musical tributes, seminars, awards dinners, and speeches by notables. There are also concerts by major performers (in past years, Stevie Wonder and the Neville Brothers, among others, have performed). For details, contact the **King Center** (☎ **404/526-8900;** www.thekingcenter.org). Second weekend of January.

Cathedral Antiques Show. For 4 days, 30 to 35 high-quality antiques dealers display their wares at the Cathedral of St. Philip, 2744 Peachtree Rd. (at W. Wesley Rd.). The merchandise ranges from 18th- and 19th-century furnishings to vintage jewelry and Oriental rugs. Admission is $15 per day. On the first day of the show, a tour of homes and mansions in Buckhead is offered for an additional $25. For details, call ☎ **404/365-1000.** Last week in January.

FEBRUARY

Southeastern Flower Show. One of the South's premier gardening events, the flower show takes place for 5 days toward the beginning of the month at Cobb Galleria Centre, 2 Galleria Pkwy. You'll find nearly 4 acres of stunning landscapes and gardens displaying both flowers and plants. Garden-related products are sold at the 90-vendor marketplace; there are also events for children and demonstrations of gardening techniques. Admission is $12 in advance, $16 at the door, with discounts for seniors and children. For information, directions, and tickets, call ℂ **404/351-1074,** or visit www.flowershow.org. Five days in late January/early February.

MARCH

Lasershow Spectacular. This 45-minute extravaganza of laser lights and fireworks, held for the past 25 years at Stone Mountain Park, is choreographed to popular, patriotic, country, and classical music. Admission is free, but you must pay $8 for a parking permit to the park. For details, call ℂ **770/498-5690,** or visit www.stonemountainpark.com. Beginning in March, the show is held on Saturdays at 8:30pm. From Memorial Day weekend through Labor Day, the show takes place nightly at 9:30pm. After Labor Day, it resumes its Saturday 8:30pm schedule through October.

International Auto Show. Held at the Georgia World Congress Center, this annual showcase features more than 500 current-year import and domestic cars, light trucks, vans, and SUVs. Special attractions include concept cars, exotics, and next year's intros. Tickets are $8 for adults and $5 for children. For details, call ℂ **770/916-1741,** or visit www.ajcautoshow.com. Mid-March.

APRIL

Easter Sunrise Services. This service is held at the top and the base of Stone Mountain at 30 minutes before sunrise. Park gates open at 4am, and the sky lift begins operating at 5am. For details, call ℂ **770/498-5690,** or visit www.stonemountainpark.com. Easter Sunday.

Atlanta Dogwood Festival. Held in Piedmont Park, this huge festival features concerts, food booths, kite-flying contests, children's activities, a juried arts-and-crafts show, the National Disc-Dog Championship (a canine Frisbee tournament), and an exciting display of hot-air balloons. For details, call ℂ **404/329-0501,** or visit www.dogwood.org. Three days in mid-April.

Atlanta Film Festival. The IMAGE (Independent Media Artists of Georgia Etc.) Film & Video Center, 535 Means St., features hundreds of films by some of the country's most important independent media artists. Admission averages $10 per movie, and films are shown at several venues around the city, including some newly added outdoor ones. For details, call ℂ **404/352-4225,** or visit www.atlantafilmfestival.com. Ten days in mid-April.

Georgia Renaissance Festival. This re-creation of a 16th-century English county fair (held in Fairburn—8 miles south of the airport on I-85, exit 61) boasts a 30-acre "village," a juried crafts show and marketplace with more than 100 craftspeople (many of them demonstrating 16th-c. skills), continuous entertainment on 12 stages (there are more than 100 shows each day), period foods, a birds-of-prey show, and a cast of costumed characters including jousting knights, jugglers, storytellers, giant stilt-walkers, minstrels, magicians, and choral groups. King Henry VIII and one of his wives oversee the festivities. Admission is $20 for adults, $18 for seniors, $9 for kids 6 to 12. For details, call ℂ **770/964-8575,** or visit www.garenfest.com. Saturdays and Sundays, mid-April to early June (plus Memorial Day).

Inman Park Spring Festival. This Atlanta suburb (the city's oldest) is noted for its gorgeous turn-of-the-20th-century Victorian mansions and Craftsman-style cottages. Activities include a tour of homes, live entertainment (theater, jazz bands, cloggers, Irish music, country music, and more), an arts-and-crafts festival/flea market, a parade, and food vendors. Tickets to the tour of homes are $10 in advance, $12 on the day of the tour. All other events are free. For more information, call ℂ **770/635-3711,** or visit www.inmanparkfestival.org. Last weekend in April.

MAY

Gardens for Connoisseurs Tour. Gardening buffs will enjoy this excellent tour, which allows a peek into several outstanding private gardens. Tickets, which benefit the Atlanta Botanical Garden, are $20 for all the gardens or $10 for an individual garden. For details, call ℂ **404/876-5859,** or visit www.atlantabotanicalgarden.org. Mother's Day weekend.

Decatur Arts Festival and Garden Tour. This 3-day event features an art show on the south lawn of the Old Courthouse in Decatur, various juried shows nearby, garden tours, mimes, jugglers, puppet shows, clowns, children's art activities, great food, and performances by music, dance, and theater groups. The literary arts are celebrated with storytelling, readings, and book signings. Events are free. For details, call 🕐 **404/371-8386.** Memorial Day weekend, but most events take place on Saturday and Sunday.

Atlanta Jazz Festival. This is a week of jazz in different venues around the city, beginning the week before Memorial Day and continuing through the holiday weekend. Past concerts have included such major stars as Wynton Marsalis, Nancy Wilson, Shirley Horn, Cyrus Chestnut, Max Roach, and Sonny Rollins. Admission is charged to most events, but concerts in Piedmont Park on Memorial Day weekend are free. The celebration in the park also includes artists' booths and food vendors. For details, call 🕐 **404/853-4234,** or visit www.atlanta festivals.com. Week before Memorial Day through Memorial Day.

JUNE

Virginia-Highland Summerfest. This weekend neighborhood arts and music festival takes place along Virginia Avenue near the intersection of North Highland Avenue. There's a juried arts-and-crafts show, an artists' market, food booths, and plenty of free entertainment in John Howell Park. Afterward, take a stroll through Virginia-Highland, which has lots of galleries and shops. All events are free. For more information, call 🕐 **404/898-8986,** or visit www.vahi.org. Weekend in early June.

Georgia Shakespeare Festival. Five productions are presented from mid-June through November on the campus of Oglethorpe University, 4484 Peachtree Rd., in the intimate 510-seat Conant Performing Arts Center. Before the summer performances, audiences enjoy farcical vignettes on the lawn. Everyone brings a preperformance picnic or arranges in advance to purchase it on the premises. The company, made up of Actors Equity pros for the most part, offers both traditional and innovative Shakespearean productions as well as other classics. Picnic grounds open 1½ hours before summer performances, and the preshow begins 1 hour before curtain time. There are both matinees and evening performances. Admission is $15 to $40 for adults. Call for tickets as far in advance as possible, especially for weekend performances. For information about tickets or picnic lunches, call 🕐 **404/264-0020,** or visit www.gashakespeare.org. Mid-June through November.

Stone Mountain Village Annual Arts & Crafts Festival. This family-oriented festival has something for everyone. More than 125 southeastern craftspeople display their wares in a juried show, and entertainment (cloggers, clowns, country music, and more) is offered continually in the Village. There are food booths and lots of activities for kids, too. Admission is free. For details, call 🕐 **770/879-4971.** Father's Day weekend.

JULY

Independence Day. If you're willing to get up early on July 4th, you can start the day's celebrations by watching 55,000 runners pound the pavement in the **Peachtree Road Race,** a 10K run down Peachtree Road from Lenox Square to Piedmont Park. For details, call 🕐 **404/231-9064.**

Later in the afternoon, take in Atlanta's star-spangled **Salute 2 America Parade.** The floats, marching bands, and giant helium-filled balloons start their marching, rolling, and floating at Peachtree and Ralph McGill at 1pm, winding up at Centennial Olympic Park. For information, call 🕐 **404/ 897-7855.** Afterward, there's more free entertainment and music in Centennial Olympic Park; the best part is the stunning fireworks display at night. For information, call 🕐 **404/222-7275.**

An old-fashioned **Fourth of July Parade,** complete with floats, bands, baton twirlers,

We're going to ride these buses deseg-regated in Atlanta, Georgia, or we're going to ride a chariot in heaven or push a wheelbarrow in hell.
—Rev. William Holmes Borders, civil rights leader, 1957

Atlanta is like Los Angeles was before it went bad.
—Jane Fonda, activist, 1996

cloggers, and more, takes place in **Stone Mountain Village,** traveling from Mountain Street at the foot of the west gate of Stone Mountain Park along Main Street through the Village shopping area. The stores are open, and when the parade's over, there's free watermelon for everyone at the visitor center. The parade begins at 10am, pre-ceded by a 5K run at 7am. For details, call ✆ **770/879-4971.** The biggest attraction at Stone Mountain Park's **Fantastic Fourth Celebration** is the extravagant fireworks display after the star-spangled laser show. Many people make a day of it, coming early for the race and parade, picnicking in the park, and staying through the grand finale of the fireworks. For details, call ✆ **770/ 498-5690,** or visit www.stonemountainpark. com.

National Black Arts Festival. More than 150 events (most of them free) take place throughout the city during this festival. Billed as "a celebration of the sights, sounds, and expressions of the African Diaspora," it features concerts (including such big names as Gladys Knight and Wyn-ton Marsalis), theater, film, dance, storytell-ing, poetry readings, performance art, art and folk-art exhibitions, children's activi-ties, workshops, African puppet shows, and more. For details, call ✆ **404/730-7315,** or visit www.nbaf.org. A 10-day affair in mid-July.

Asian Cultural Experience. The Gwinnet Center, 6400 Sugarloaf Pkwy., Duluth, cel-ebrates Asian culture with demonstrations of crafts, musical performances, children's activities, an art show, and dancing, among other offerings. Admission is $10 for adults, $8 for seniors, and $5 for students. For details, call ✆ **770/998-8375,** or visit www.asianculturalexperienceinga.com. Weekend in late July.

AUGUST

Decatur Book Festival. Held in and around the downtown Decatur Square, the Decatur Book Festival brings more than 200 authors to town for readings, talks, and panel discussions. Authors include Pulitzer Prize winners and bestsellers of fiction in many genres and nonfiction on diverse topics. The event also includes writing workshops, a street fair with many vendor booths, arts performances, cooking dem-onstrations, activities for children, and opportunities to meet the writers. Events are free. For details, call ✆ **404/370-4100,** or visit www.decaturbookfestival. com. Three days at the end of August.

SEPTEMBER

Art in the Park. This Labor Day weekend art show, on the historic square in Marietta (just northwest of Atlanta), offers fine art by more than 120 artists, plus food and antiques. Admission is free. Call ✆ **770/429-1115** for details. Labor Day weekend.

Yellow Daisy Festival. Stone Mountain Park hosts a vast outdoor arts-and-crafts show (more than 400 exhibitors) with musical entertainment, a flower show, great food, clogging, and storytellers. About 200,000 people attend each year. For details, call ✆ **770/498-5690,** or visit www.stone mountainpark.com. Weekend after Labor Day.

OCTOBER

Annual Scottish Festival and Highland Games. This gathering of the clans at Stone

Mountain comprises 2 days of Highland dancing, pipe and drum concerts, Scottish harping and fiddling, sword dancing, reel dancing, lilting, and athletic events such as the hammer throw and caber toss. Fee is $15 for adults and $4 for children. For details, call ✆ **770/498-5690,** or visit www.stonemountainpark.com. Mid-October.

Sunday in the Park at Oakland Cemetery. On an October Sunday every year, this graveyard party is attended by several thousand visitors and features storytellers, historians, guided tours, a hat and costume contest, turn-of-the-20th-century music, and Victorian boutiques. Admission is free. For a small charge, you can reserve a picnic lunch. Call ✆ **404/688-2107,** or visit www.oaklandcemetery.com for details. One Sunday in October.

NOVEMBER

Veterans Day Parade. Atlanta mounts an impressive version of this parade each year, with floats, drill teams, marching bands, clowns, color guards, and more. The parade begins at 11am at West Peachtree Street and proceeds to Centennial Olympic Park. Visit www.gavetsdayparade.org for details. Veterans Day.

An Olde-Fashioned Christmas. The holiday season kicks off with an array of events at Stone Mountain Park from mid-November to December 30 (daily 6–10pm, except for Dec 24–25). Tour the authentically decorated Antebellum Plantation, where you'll find a five-story poinsettia Christmas tree, crafters, carolers, storytellers, and a live nativity scene. The open-air Scenic Railroad is decorated to the hilt, too, and travels through a spectacular array of Christmas-light displays as it makes its way around the base of Stone Mountain. Santa Claus is here, and there's also a Polar Express 4-D attraction. Crossroads features more than two million lights and "snow" is abundant. Admission is $20 for adults and $17 for children 3 to 11, in addition to the $8 parking charge. For details, call ✆ **770/498-5690,** or visit www.stonemountainpark.org. Mid-November through December 30.

Stone Mountain Village Candlelight Shopping. This charming village lures holiday shoppers with candlelight and the aroma of mulled cider. A jolly St. Nick, strolling carolers, gaily lighted trees, and carriage rides are part of the fun. Admission is free. The Village also hosts the **Sugar Plum Festival,** a breakfast with Santa Claus from 7 to 11am on the first Saturday of December. The $5 admission includes breakfast and a photograph with Santa. Call ✆ **770/879-4971,** or visit www.stonemountainvillage.com for details. Every Thursday and Friday night, beginning the Thursday before Thanksgiving and continuing until Christmas.

Ride the Pink Pig. From its 1953 debut as a children's ride at the downtown Richs department store to a brief stint at the Festival of Trees, the Pink Pig has found a new holiday home at Macy's in Lenox Square on Peachtree Road NE. Four generations have heralded in the holiday season with a ride on the pig. Fee is $3 per child with proceeds benefiting Children's Healthcare of Atlanta. Ride open daily from late November through New Year's Day. For information, call ✆ **404/231-2800.**

Holidays in the Garden. The Atlanta Botanical Garden is beautifully decorated, and highlights of the month-long list of events include a dog parade, a holiday train, photos with St. Nick, puppet shows, a moonlight event, high tea, and holiday greenery displays. For details, call ✆ **404/876-5859,** or visit www.atlantabotanicalgarden.org. Events run from late November through early January.

DECEMBER

Children's Healthcare of Atlanta Christmas Parade and Festival of Trees. The parade is a major to-do, with award-winning bands, lavish holiday-themed floats, helium-balloon cartoon characters, and, of course, Santa Claus. It kicks off the 9-day Festival of Trees at the Georgia World Congress Center, for which Atlanta artists and designers lavishly decorate more than 200 trees, wreaths, and other holiday ornaments, which are exhibited and auctioned off to benefit Children's Healthcare of Atlanta. The festival also features live entertainment, cooking demonstrations, an antique carousel, a roller coaster, a giant slide, a balloon ride, international holiday displays, and more. Admission to the festival is $8 for adults, $5 for seniors and children 2 to 12. The parade begins at 10:30am, and the festival follows. For information, call ✆ **404/325-NOEL** (6635), or visit www.choa.org/festival. First Saturday in December.

Peach Bowl Game. This exciting football game is held annually at the Georgia Dome. Tickets are hard to come by; reserve well in advance. Call ✆ **404/586-8496,** or visit www.peachbowl.com for information.

Sometime between Christmas and New Year's Eve (occasionally in early Jan).

New Year's Eve. The Big Peach that rings in Atlanta's New Year is dropped at the stroke of midnight from the 138-foot light tower at Underground Atlanta. Festivities begin earlier (about noon) with children's activities, followed later by live music for dancing in the streets, a pyrotechnic display and laser show, balloons, and usually a marching band. Call ✆ **404/523-2311,** or visit www. peachdrop.com for details.

RESPONSIBLE TRAVEL

Atlanta is a bit slow on the draw when it comes to taking the initiative on responsible travel, but there is some definite movement in that direction. In late 2010, the city received $47.6 million in federal funding to build a 2.6-mile streetcar line. The project will not only be a huge nod from the city to the importance of sustainability, but (hopefully) will also ease some of the gridlock that gives Atlanta traffic such a bad name. In addition, the streetcar line will connect with MARTA, the city's rapid-transit system. Officials project the four-car line will have the capacity to shuttle 4.7 million tourists and residents annually. Offering this option for environmentally sustainable transportation will certainly be a feather in the city's cap. The project is slated for completion in 2013.

In the meantime, a couple of Atlanta's top tourist attractions have acknowledged the impact their facilities can have on the environment and have implemented policies to oversee their sustainability measures. As the largest aquarium in the world, the **Georgia Aquarium** (p. 122) obviously recognizes the value of water and other resources. The aquarium has already cut water usage by 10% with a plan to cut an additional 10% once all sustainability projects are complete. Initiatives include waterless urinals that save 1 million gallons per year (who knew?) and not watering the landscape. Additionally, the aquarium strives to educate visitors about the importance of water conservation by posting tips throughout the facility.

Just up the street, the **World of Coca-Cola** (p. 135) has an environmental commitment that includes a "Gold" rating from the U.S. Green Building Council, earned through their emphasis on energy and water efficiency, recycling, reuse of resources, and waste reduction. It's one of just a handful of buildings in the entire state with Leadership in Energy and Environmental Design (LEED) designation. One cool feature is the cups in the popular Taste It! Lounge; they're produced from 100% compostable cornstarch.

While a handful of hotels have actively sought "green" certification of one type or another, the city continues business as usual, despite the ongoing water wars between neighboring states. Some hotels have taken the lead in adopting ecofriendly practices, including the **Ellis** (p. 51), **Emory Inn** (p. 72), **Hotel Palomar** (p. 55), and the **Westin Peachtree Plaza** (p. 50), all recipients of the National Green Seal Lodging approval. In addition, Hilton, Hyatt, Sheraton, Omni, and Marriott properties in the city have all implemented their company's sustainable practices. **Doubletree Hotel Atlanta Buckhead** (p. 68) was the first Buckhead hotel to practice green and sustainable initiatives. Elsewhere in the city, **Stonehurst Place** (p. 56) is likely the most ecofriendly lodging option, emphasizing recycling, rainwater reclamation, air purification, and solar energy, and serving strictly organic meals and snacks.

Speaking of organic, scores of Atlanta eateries have jumped on the farm-to-table bandwagon, creating menus to promote local sustainable and/or organic ingredients. Among those sustainable-supporting restaurants are **Bacchanalia** (p. 79), **Restaurant Eugene** (p. 95), **Woodfire Grill** (p. 95), **Leon's Full Service** (p. 107), **Pura Vida** (p. 104), and **Craft** (p. 90).

Outside the city, **Serenbe Southern Country Inn** (p. 74) is located in the Serenbe Community, a neighborhood built entirely on sustainability practices, including the lodging, dining, shopping, and residential offerings.

See Frommers.com/planning for more tips on responsible travel.

SUGGESTED ATLANTA ITINERARIES

W hether it's your first visit or your 10th, a trip to Atlanta is always a new experience, as the city keeps evolving and providing visitors with more to see each year. This chapter will provide you with essential information, helpful tips, and advice for creating the perfect itinerary for your upcoming trip to "the ATL."

Neighborhoods in Brief

You can't really get the feel of a city until you understand the characteristics of its neighborhoods. Here's a brief rundown of Atlanta's diverse districts.

DOWNTOWN

Unlike some big cities, Atlanta has been slower to draw a large residential population to its downtown area, though that has changed drastically in the past few years. In-town living is gradually becoming quite popular. Currently, downtown consists primarily of businesses, hotels, restaurants, and sports venues, and is slowly gaining that round-the-clock big-city excitement found in places such as New York.

Atlanta's financial and business hub, this area of sleek skyscrapers includes the Peachtree Center hotel/convention center/trade mart/office-tower complex. Here, too: Underground Atlanta, a mix of shops, restaurants, and nightclubs fronted by a 138-foot light tower; the mammoth Georgia World Congress Center, one of the largest meeting and exhibition halls in the nation; the 71,500-seat Georgia Dome, home of the Atlanta Falcons and site of Super Bowl XXXIV; Philips Arena, home of the Atlanta Hawks and Atlanta Thrashers; CNN Center; Georgia State University; the golden-domed, century-old State Capitol, a major landmark; the 21-acre Centennial Olympic Park, the city's best gathering place; and Woodruff Park.

Just south of downtown is Turner Field, home of the Atlanta Braves. Also in the general area are Oakland Cemetery (it's mentioned in *Gone With the Wind*, and Margaret Mitchell is one of the many notables buried here), Grant Park, Zoo Atlanta, and Cyclorama.

People are beginning to move into newly renovated lofts and other buildings downtown, but there's still not a lot of activity after business hours. For that reason, visitors should stick to the hotel district and the sports venues in the evening.

SWEET AUBURN

This traditionally African-American neighborhood, also called the **Martin Luther King, Jr., Historic District,** is just below downtown's central area. In 1980, under the auspices of the National Park Service, the neighborhood was designated a park to honor King, whose boyhood home, crypt, and church are located here. In spite of the yoke of segregation, affluent black businesspeople and professionals flourished here from the early part of the 20th century through the 1950s. Recently revitalized, Sweet Auburn is one of Atlanta's major sightseeing draws.

MIDTOWN

Though its boundaries have never been definitively decided, Midtown basically encompasses the area north of downtown from about Ponce de Leon Avenue to I-85. It includes Piedmont Park, the central city's major recreation area; the Woodruff Arts Center, home of the Atlanta Symphony Orchestra, the Alliance Theatre, and the High Museum of Art; the famed Fox Theatre, a 1920s Moorish-motif movie palace; the Atlanta Botanical Garden; Ansley Park, a 230-acre residential greenbelt area, designed at the turn of the 20th century by Frederick Law Olmsted (of New York's Central Park fame); and Colony Square, an office/hotel/retail complex. AT&T, IBM, Bank of America, and BellSouth maintain corporate offices in Midtown.

BUCKHEAD

Named for an 1838 tavern called the Buck's Head, this is Atlanta's silk-stocking district—one of America's most beautiful and affluent communities. It begins about 6 miles north of downtown, just above I-85. You'll find tree-shaded residential areas filled with magnificent mansions that are surrounded by verdant acreage, as well as many smaller middle-class homes. Shops and boutiques (Lenox Square and Phipps Plaza, two exclusive shopping malls, are here), superb restaurants, and first-class hotels abound. On weekends, the bars and clubs in the center of Buckhead attract crowds of revelers.

Buckhead is also a burgeoning business area, with high-rise office buildings concentrated near Peachtree and Lenox roads. The area's major sightseeing attraction is the Atlanta History Center, surrounded by 32 woodland acres, with a Palladian villa designed by noted architect Phillip Schutze. The Greek Revival Governor's Mansion is also in Buckhead.

VIRGINIA-HIGHLAND

Every major American city has a district that claims kinship (however slight) with New York's Greenwich Village. In Atlanta, it's the Virginia-Highland section (so named for its central avenues), located northeast of downtown. Here you'll find ethnic restaurants, antiques shops, bookstores, sidewalk cafes, art galleries, lively bars and bistros, and shops selling everything from gourmet gadgets and woodworking tools to ecofriendly clothing. The surrounding area is full of tree-lined streets with charming little cottages, many of them recently renovated.

LITTLE FIVE POINTS

Just below Virginia-Highland—and a funkier offshoot of it—Little Five Points offers an offbeat ambience, attracting young and old members of the tie-dyed and pierced set. The neighborhood is home to the Jimmy Carter Library/Carter Presidential Center, which opened in 1986 to house the correspondence and memorabilia of this Georgia-born president. The area's many Victorian homes make for an architecturally interesting stroll. The neighborhood is centered at the junction of Euclid and Moreland avenues. Don't confuse this area with **Five Points,** which is a major downtown intersection.

WEST END & CASCADE ROAD

Southwest of town lies a booming area populated by well-to-do African-American singles and families. The historic West End, Atlanta's oldest neighborhood, is full of lovely Victorian homes and is the gateway to the Cascade Road area. This is where you'll find the Wren's Nest, the former home of writer Joel Chandler Harris.

DECATUR

Founded in 1823 by Commodore Stephen Decatur, a dashing naval hero of the War of 1812 who died in a duel, this charming suburb centers on an old courthouse square and has become a new favorite destination for residents and visitors alike. About a 15-minute drive east of downtown, Decatur is the scene of numerous annual events, festivals, and concerts, and houses the sprawling DeKalb Farmers' Market, an international food market that must be seen to be believed. Like Virginia-Highland and Little Five Points, Decatur weaves a splash of funky color and texture into Atlanta's tapestry of neighborhoods.

DULUTH

Duluth, located in Gwinnett County just north of the city, is a bustling town with shopping, dining, and entertainment. Major roadways here include Buford Highway and its impressive list of ethnic restaurants; Pleasant Hill Road, home of many retail opportunities; and Peachtree Industrial Boulevard, which offers a little of everything for visitors—dining, lodging, theater, shopping, and more. Every summer, the town hosts the "Flicks on the Bricks" outdoor family film festival and the Summer-Stage concert series, enjoyed by residents and visitors alike.

THE BEST OF ATLANTA IN 1 DAY

If your travels to Atlanta allow you just 1 day to take in the sights, you might feel overwhelmed trying to decide how to make the most of your time. However, you certainly don't want to miss a handful of special attractions among the many worthwhile ones in this city. Plan your day accordingly and, by the end of it, you'll have a strong feel for what this city is all about. Build your schedule around enjoying lunch at the Atlanta History Center's Swan House before leaving the premises. Not only will you dine in a historic setting, but you'll also save valuable travel time by not having to find a restaurant. Whether you choose to drive yourself or use public transportation to navigate the city, a full day of touring can be satisfying; it also might encourage you to return to see what you couldn't squeeze in during a 1-day visit. **Start:** *Atlanta History Center (drive or MARTA to Lenox station).*

If driving, take I-75 N. to exit 252A Northside Dr. and turn right; right on Arden Rd.; and right on W Paces Ferry Rd. NW. Or, take MARTA to the Lenox Station; bus 23 to Peachtree St. and W. Paces Ferry Rd.; then walk 3 blocks west on the latter.

1 Atlanta History Center ★★★

Grab your coffee and head up to Buckhead to tour the Atlanta History Center for a good overview of the city's history—it will make the rest of your visit a richer experience. The 20,000-square-foot Centennial Olympic Games Museum addition houses a permanent exhibition about the 1996 Olympic Games hosted by the city of Atlanta. Another highlight of the center is the beautifully restored Swan House. House-tour tickets are limited and can be purchased only on the day of your visit, so arrive early to avoid disappointment. Enjoy lunch at the on-site restaurant, the Swan Coach House, where lunch is served from 11am to 2:30pm, Monday through Saturday. Get in on the early seating so you won't be pressed for time at your next stop. Consider choosing the signature chicken salad, served in delicate timbales. No reservations are required for dining. See p. 115.

It's about a 15-min. drive back downtown via I-75 S. to the Williams St. exit; right on Baker St., right on Luckie St.; and park in the Pemberton Place deck on the right. Or, take MARTA from the Lindbergh station to either Peachtree Center or Omni/Dome/ GWCC station and walk a couple of blocks to Baker St.

2 Georgia Aquarium ★★★

While the main attraction in Atlanta these days is the Georgia Aquarium, the world's largest indoor aquarium, it takes about 3 hours to see and enjoy it all, so head here quickly after an early lunch at the Swan House. Order tickets online first, and you'll be able to choose an entrance window that helps cut down on bottlenecking at the front gate. Of course, weekends are extremely busy, and you may find yourself shoulder to shoulder trying to nudge your way up close to see the fantastic exhibits. There's also a 4-D movie that shows every half-hour. When you enter the aquarium, decide what time to check out the show, and then work in your exhibits before and after. There are areas designed specifically for the little kids, too, so if they get antsy, they can run around and let off steam. See p. 122.

From the aquarium exit, walk west on Baker St. and turn left on Marietta St. NW. Continue walking until you reach:

3 CNN Studio Tour ★★★

Spend the next hour enjoying a CNN Studio Tour, the last one scheduled for 5pm daily. To save precious time, you can purchase advance tickets online, securing your spot when you arrive for the 55-minute guided walking tour that takes you behind the scenes of this international newsroom. Don't miss the gift shop, where visitors can don news-announcer garb and record themselves "reporting" the news. Buy your recording and take it home to share with friends and family. See p. 118.

From the main entrance to the CNN Center, walk across the street to:

4 Centennial Olympic Park ★★★

This park was the main gathering place during the 1996 Olympic Games. Kids love to splash in the Fountain of Rings here, especially during a hot Georgia afternoon. The park often plays host to live entertainment, activities for children, art festivals, and other fun events, so check the online calendar to see what's going on during your visit. See p. 117.

From the parking deck, drive east on Baker St.; right on Centennial Olympic Park Dr.; left on Harris St. NW; left on Piedmont Rd. NE; right on Ponce de Leon Ave. NE; and left on Monroe to reach the Virginia-Highland neighborhood. Or, take MARTA from Peachtree Center or Omni/Dome/GWCC station to North Avenue station.

5 Virginia-Highland

Early in the evening, visit the shops and galleries in the very popular Virginia-Highland neighborhood. You've had a full day and have probably worked up a voracious appetite, so treat yourself to a great dinner at one of the many restaurants. Later, enjoy a nightcap or coffee and dessert in a bar or cafe along North Highland Avenue, where the nightlife is always jumping. See the Virginia-Highland sections of the dining and shopping chapters of this guide.

THE BEST OF ATLANTA IN 1 DAY
1 Atlanta History Center
2 Georgia Aquarium
3 CNN Studio Tour
4 Centennial Olympic Park
5 Virginia-Highland

THE BEST OF ATLANTA IN 2 DAYS
1 Martin Luther King Jr. National Historic Site
2 World of Coca-Cola
3 Atlanta Cyclorama
4 Zoo Atlanta
5 Atlantic Station

THE BEST OF ATLANTA IN 2 DAYS

Follow the suggestions above for your first day in town. On your second day, get up early, go over to Auburn Avenue (p. 163 for the walking tour), and visit the many sites operated by the National Parks Service, a touching tribute to Martin Luther King, Jr., and Atlanta's rich African-American history. Depending on how much energy you're willing to put into day 2, you may decide to skip a site or two, opting to stay longer at one or more of the others. You could while away many hours at most of these sightseeing options. *Start: Martin Luther King, Jr., National Historic Site (drive or MARTA to Five Points station).*

If driving, take I-75/85 north- or southbound, then exit 248C Freedom Pkwy.; right on Boulevard NE; right at next light on John Wesley Dobbs Ave.; parking on left. Or, take MARTA bus 3 to Five Points station to:

1 Martin Luther King, Jr., National Historic Site

Start your morning in the Auburn district early, as the entire neighborhood is packed full of historic treasures, starting with the Martin Luther King, Jr., National Historic Site. Designated a national historic site, these blocks include the Birth Home of Martin Luther King, Jr., and the Ebenezer Baptist Church, where King's father and grandfather were ministers and King served as a copastor. In the area, you'll also find the King Center, where King is buried, and the APEX Museum. See p. 130.

Drive west on Auburn Ave. NE; right at Fort St. NE; take ramp to I-75/85 N. for exit 249D Spring St.; right on Spring St. NW; left at Centennial Olympic Park Dr., and right at Baker St. NW. Park in Pemberton Place deck. Or, from Five Points station, take MARTA to Peachtree Center or Omni/Dome/GWCC station to:

2 World of Coca-Cola ★★

At the World of Coca-Cola, you can meet the Coke polar bear, mingle in the Pop Culture Gallery, and drink free carbonated beverages from around the world until your head spins from the sugar and caffeine buzz. Memorabilia galore awaits those interested in the history of this popular beverage invented right here in Atlanta. A short film in the Happiness Factory Theater allows visitors a behind-the-scenes look at the bottling process, which they later see at the actual in-house bottling line. See p. 135.

Drive east on Baker St. and turn right on Centennial Olympic Park Dr.; left on Marietta St. NW; continue on Decatur St. SE; right on Hill St. SE; left at Memorial Dr. SE; and right onto Cherokee Ave. Take MARTA bus 97 to Cherokee Ave.

3 Atlanta Cyclorama ★★

Located in Grant Park next to Zoo Atlanta, the Atlanta Cyclorama features a 42-foot-high rotating cylindrical oil painting, depicting the events of the Battle of Atlanta on July 22, 1864, in meticulous detail. The total program here lasts just 35 minutes but packs a historic wallop. See p. 114.

Exit the Cyclorama and turn left to find the Zoo Atlanta ticket booths just yards away.

4 Zoo Atlanta ★★

Among the highlights in this world-class zoo are the giant pandas. The happy couple welcomed their second baby in 2008, named Xi Lan, after the traditional 100-day waiting period for naming baby pandas. Cute as she is, though, Xi Lan isn't the only draw; Zuri, the baby giraffe, arrived last summer to a hail of cheers. The 40-acre Zoo Atlanta features some 200 species of animals from around the world. See p. 150.

From I-75/85 N., take exit 250 10th/14th sts.; merge onto Williams St.; right on 10th St. NW; left on W. Peachtree St. NW; left on 17th St. NW. Or, take MARTA to Arts Center station and hop the free shuttle to:

5 Atlantic Station

You might be too tired for shopping at this point, but you've got to eat, right? Atlantic Station, a mixed-use development packed with your favorite stores, from Ann Taylor LOFT to IKEA, also has a wide variety of dining options. And who knows, once you refuel, you just might be ready to hit the shops before calling it a day. See p. 169.

THE BEST OF ATLANTA IN 3 DAYS

On your first 2 days, see as many of the sights described above as a comfortable pace allows. While many of your sightseeing decisions may be based on the weather—Atlanta summers can be scorching, making indoor attractions more appealing—you certainly won't want to miss Stone Mountain Park on day 3. You can, however, pass an entire day here, taking in all the activities and dining on-site. *Start: Stone Mountain Park (drive).*

Take I-85 N. to I-285 E.; then exit 39B for U.S. Hwy. 78 E.; and exit 8 for Stone Mountain Park. There is no public transportation from the city to Stone Mountain Park.

1 Stone Mountain Park ★

Georgia's number-one tourist attraction, Stone Mountain Park has lots of things to do, including visiting Crossroads, a re-created 1870s southern town with costumed characters, craft demonstrations, and diversions for kids, including the Treehouse Challenge and the Great Barn. The park's Sky Hike attraction is a family-friendly adventure course that allows visitors to "walk" through the treetops. There are also an Antique Car and Treasure Museum and cruises on the *Scarlett O'Hara* paddlewheel riverboat. In summer, be sure to stay late and see the laser show—it's truly one of a kind. See p. 132.

From the park, take U.S. Hwy. 78 W. for 15 miles; left at Boulevard NE; left on Freedom Pkwy. Using MARTA from downtown, take train to Five Points station and a Noble bus 16 to:

2 Jimmy Carter Library & Museum

If you opt out on a morning in the park, or even if you don't, plan to tour the Jimmy Carter Library & Museum. Here you'll find an impressive collection of some 27 million pages of documents, memoranda, and correspondence, as well as 1.5 million photographs from Carter's White House years. See p. 126.

Head north on Freedom Pkwy.; left on Ponce de Leon Ave.; right on Peachtree St. Or, take MARTA to the Midtown station and walk 1 block east to:

3 Margaret Mitchell House & Museum ★

Affectionately referred to as "the dump" by *Gone With the Wind* author Margaret Mitchell, her former residence and adjoining museum give great insight into this intriguing author who met with an early demise. Guided tours of 60 and 90 minutes are scheduled throughout the day. See p. 128.

Head north on Peachtree St. and take a left on Spring St. NW to:

4 Center for Puppetry Arts ★

If you're traveling with kids, you may choose to forgo the Carter Library and Mitchell House Museum and instead spend the afternoon at the Center for Puppetry Arts. In addition to its permanent exhibits and regular performances, this attraction now displays a number of Jim Henson's Muppets, part of the collection of more than 500 Henson puppets and scenes from *The Muppet Show* and *Sesame Street*. See p. 146.

Head south on Spring St. NW; turn left on 17th St. NW; turn right on Peachtree St. NE; turn left on Ponce de Leon Ave. NE; left on Clifton Rd. On MARTA, take the train to the North Avenue station, then board bus 2 for Ponce de Leon Ave. Ask the driver to drop you at the corner of Clifton Rd. Walk down Clifton Rd. to:

5 Fernbank Museum of Natural History ★★

Adults don't have to have a kid in tow to enjoy all the Fernbank Museum of Natural History has to offer, including an IMAX theater and a complete mounted skeleton of the largest dinosaur ever found, the *Argentinosaurus*. A number of permanent exhibits include one highlighting Georgia's landscape, from the Piedmont Plateau to the Okefenokee Swamp. See p. 120.

THE BEST OF ATLANTA IN 4 DAYS

You're in the home stretch now, so take it easy. Over the busy first 3 days, juggle the above suggestions as you see fit. Enjoy your fourth and final day in the city by taking in the home of the Atlanta Braves baseball team, some Civil War history, and the beautiful collections of the Atlanta Botanical Garden and the High Museum of Art. **Start:** *Turner Field (drive or MARTA to Georgia State University station).*

Take I-75/85 to exit 246 Fulton St./Turner Field; left on Fulton St.; right on Capitol Ave./Hank Aaron Dr. Using MARTA, take train to Georgia State University station and less than a mile on Capitol Ave. to:

1 Turner Field ★★

Even if it isn't game day in Atlanta, Turner Field has a lot to offer visitors year-round, including stadium tours, a Braves Museum and Hall of Fame, and Cartoon Network's Tooner Field playground for kids. See p. 161.

Take I-75/85 N. to exit 250 10th/14th sts.; merge onto Williams St. NW and turn right on 10th St. NW; left on Charles Allen Dr. NE; slight left at Park Dr. NE and gardens are on the right. For MARTA, take train to Arts Center station and bus 36 (bus 27 from Monroe or Lindbergh stations on Sun) to:

2 Atlanta Botanical Garden

Occupying 30 acres in the heart of the city, Atlanta Botanical Garden is home to the 25,000-square-foot Fuqua Orchid Center, a must-see at this attraction. Other highlights include the misty Tropical Rotunda with its exhibit of Central and South American poison dart frogs in colors and patterns you'd never imagine on such a creature. An English herb knot garden and the children's garden are also big draws. See p. 113.

It's a good 45-min. drive to the next stop, depending on traffic. Take I-75 N. to exit 273 for Wade Green Rd.; left on Wade Green Rd., and continue on Cherokee St. NW to destination. There is no public transportation from Atlanta to:

3 Southern Museum of Civil War and Locomotive History

Operated in association with the Smithsonian Institute, the museum marks the site where the wild adventure known as the Great Locomotive Chase began during the Civil War. The museum is located in a former cotton gin and houses the *General,* the locomotive from the aforementioned chase, as well as Civil War artifacts, memorabilia, and photographs. See p. 143.

Head west on Cherokee St. NW; left on S. Main St./Old Hwy. 41, and continue to intersection with Stilesboro Rd. NW. Follow entrance signs to park. No public transportation available to:

4 Kennesaw Mountain/National Battlefield Park

Established in 1917 on the site of a crucial Civil War battle in the Atlanta campaign of 1864, Kennesaw Mountain covers nearly 3,000 acres, including a visitor center, which is where your visit should begin. Start with the 20-minute film about the battle and view Civil War artifact exhibits before hiking the trails to see actual Confederate entrenchments and earthworks. See p. 141.

Take I-75 S. toward Atlanta; exit 250 16th St.; right at 16th St.; right at Market St. NW; right at 17th St. NW; and right on Peachtree St. NE. Or, take MARTA to the Arts Center station and a covered walkway to:

5 High Museum of Art ★★★

Atlanta's finest art museum, the High is home to extensive permanent exhibits featuring 19th- and 20th-century American paintings, a collection of American decorative arts, and Italian paintings and sculpture from the 14th through the 18th centuries. The High is also host to major traveling exhibitions each year, such as a recent exhibit on loan from the Louvre, a Dalí exhibit, and one of work by iconic 20th-century photographer Henri Cartier-Bresson. See p. 123.

Take I-75/85 S. to exit 248A MLK Dr.; keep right and merge onto Butler St.; right on Decatur St. SE; right at Grant St. SE; left at Biggers St. SE, which veers right and turns into Oakland Ave. SE. Or, take MARTA to the King Memorial station near:

6 Oakland Cemetery ★

Oakland Cemetery can be visited any time of day, but it's especially intriguing in the evening light. If you're visiting during the long light hours of summer, consider picking up a meal from the nearby aptly named Six Feet Under restaurant or other eateries in the vicinity. It might seem weird, but folks frequently enjoy picnics on the grounds, surrounded by both the dead and the exquisite monuments to life in this Victorian cemetery on the National Register of Historic Places. See p. 131.

ITINERARIES BY INTEREST

Beat the Heat

The Georgia heat can be relentless, but not to worry: If you can't take the heat, the city has options for fun days in air-conditioned facilities, with everything from museums and shopping to sea life and live entertainment. For a couple of days out of the elements, start with a trip to the world's largest aquarium, the **Georgia Aquarium,** with 100,000 animals from more than 500 species in 80 million gallons of fresh and marine water. You'll be amazed at the massive whale sharks that swim overhead in the glass tunnel as you walk through or glide along on the moving sidewalk. These gentle beasts can grow to be as large as a school bus. Beluga whales, jellyfish, penguins—they're all here in amazing habitats.

Next, make a visit to the **World of Coca-Cola** to browse the world's largest collection of memorabilia celebrating this popular beverage, created right here in Atlanta in 1886. While Coca-Cola was first served at a small pharmacy soda fountain near Underground Atlanta, it is now served more than one billion times a day and is enjoyed in more than 200 countries across the globe. Come discover the history of this global brand and sample Coca-Cola products from around the world. Some will leave you longing for another sip, while others are worse than castor oil. For big fans of Coke, the Everything Coca-Cola gift shop is an outstanding outlet for memorabilia and literally can't be missed, as you have to pass through it to exit the facility. The museum is open from 9am to 5pm most days, though it may open later or close earlier on certain Sundays.

Plan ahead and schedule a **CNN Studio Tour,** just across the street from the World of Coca-Cola and the Georgia Aquarium. The 55-minute guided walking tour allows a look at one of the world's most trusted names in news, as well as the inventor of 24-hour news. You'll get to journey into the heart of CNN Worldwide and enjoy an up-close, in-depth look at global news in the making. There are a number of behind-the-scenes demonstrations: In the special-effects room, you'll learn just how they make images—such as weather maps—appear behind the anchors and correspondents. At the interactive-exhibit area, you can view video clips of the top 100 news stories that CNN has covered during the past 20 years, test your knowledge with the journalism ethics display, and trace the growth of CNN as it parallels world events. The gift shop features a faux newsroom setup where visitors can deliver the news from behind the anchor's desk, then purchase the DVD for themselves.

If you like to spend money while staying cool, Atlanta has no shortage of retail opportunities. **Lenox Square** and **Phipps Plaza** are two of the poshest, most exclusive malls in the city, and Atlanta's popular shopping destination, **Atlantic Station,** is a mixed-use community being recognized as a national model for smart growth and sustainable development. Tenants here include the Southeast's first IKEA, a full-day adventure in itself; its restaurant is the company's first to serve grits and sweet tea. Or, dine outside at one of the dozens of eateries in the complex. You'll also find a movie theater here if the weather warrants an afternoon in the dark watching one of the latest flicks. Shopping options include American Eagle Outfitters, Ann Taylor and Ann Taylor LOFT, City Sports, Express, the Gap, Nine West, Old Navy, West Elm, and Z Gallerie.

The Great Outdoors

One of the best things about visiting the South is that much of the year can be enjoyed outdoors. Start with a day at **Stone Mountain Park.** A monolithic gray-granite outcropping (the world's largest) carved with a massive monument to the Confederacy, Stone Mountain is a distinctive landmark on Atlanta's horizon and the focal point of its major recreation area, which includes 3,200 acres of lakes and beautiful wooded parkland. It's Georgia's number-one tourist attraction, and one of the 10 most-visited paid attractions in the United States. Although the best view of the mountain is from below, the vistas from the top are spectacular. Visitors with lots of energy and lung capacity can take the walking trail up and down the moss-covered slopes, especially lovely in spring when they're blanketed in wildflowers. The trail is 1.3 miles each way. Or you can ride the Skyride cable car to the top, where you'll have an incredible view of the city and the Appalachian Mountains. The best approach is to take the cable car up and then walk back down.

For a different perspective, check out the park from onboard a World War II amphibious vehicle—the park's new Ride the Ducks Tour is a 40-minute adventure that moves from the land into the waters of Stone Mountain Lake. End your day at the park with Stone Mountain's Lasershow Spectacular, an astonishing display of laser lights and fireworks with animation and music. The brilliant laser beams are projected on the mountain's north face, a natural 1-million-square-foot screen. Bring a picnic supper and arrive early to get a good spot on the lawn at the base of the mountain. Shows are free with park admission.

Zoo Atlanta is another popular outdoor venue, with all the excitement these days surrounding the newest addition: a baby giraffe, Zuri, born last summer to proud parents, Glenda and Abu. In addition, giant pandas Lun Lun and Yang Yang and their two offspring are always a hit, and a third panda baby was expected as this guidebook went into production. Although the pandas' rowdiest period is in the afternoon, the family puts on quite a show most of the day: munching bamboo, tussling with each other, playing on their log swing, or climbing on the swinging ladder. When Lun Lun has had enough of Yang Yang's roughhousing, she heads for the water. In the summer, the two can be especially entertaining; if it's really sweltering, zoo officials give each of them a huge block of ice to help them cool off. Of course, there's much more to see at the zoo—you can easily spend a full day here.

Baseball fan? The spectacular 50,000-seat Atlanta Braves stadium at **Turner Field** is a popular spot. The ballpark started life as an 80,000-seat stadium built to host the Centennial Olympic Games in 1996. Don't miss the Braves Museum and Hall of Fame, featuring memorabilia commemorating legendary stars and key moments in Braves history (take a gander at the bat Hank Aaron used to hit his 715th home run). Scouts Alley is designed to teach fans about the fine art of scouting. Fans can test their hitting and throwing skills, call up scouting reports on former and current Braves, play a trivia game, call a play-by-play inning of a game, learn about Hank Aaron's "hot" spot, and much more. Add to that a number of restaurants, the Cartoon Network's Tooner Field playground for kids, and lots of souvenir shopping opportunities, and you'll see that the stadium has something for every member of the family—not to mention a great game of baseball. Stay for the fireworks displays that follow every Friday-night home game.

The delightful **Atlanta Botanical Garden,** occupying 30 acres in Piedmont Park, includes the 25,000-square-foot Fuqua Orchid Center, a children's garden, an education center, and the Dorothy Chapman Fuqua Conservatory. In the Fuqua Orchid Center, a collection of rare high-elevation orchids, which flourish on cool, wet mountains in South America, are being grown in the warm Southeast. Typically, one would have to go to San Francisco or Seattle to see such plants. An "Olympic" olive tree presented by Greece in honor of the 1996 Centennial Olympic Games in Atlanta resides in the botanical garden as well. There are flower shows throughout the year, along with lectures and other activities. Call or check the website to find out what's scheduled during your stay (www.atlantabotanicalgarden.org).

If you want to add thrills and excitement to your trip, Atlanta has a number of amusement parks, including **Six Flags Over Georgia,** the **White Water** water park, and **American Adventures,** a theme park that caters to younger children and families.

WHERE TO STAY

With the variety of lodging options available in Atlanta, choosing where to lay your head at night can be an overwhelming decision. But rest assured that no matter which area of the city you choose to make your headquarters, there is certainly something to suit your needs.

As a major convention city, metro Atlanta is capable of accommodating hordes of visitors. It has more than 94,000 rooms at 783 properties, including budget digs, bed-and-breakfast lodgings, and bastions of penultimate luxury. The choices listed below—offering good value in several different price brackets—are in parts of the city that travelers frequent most often. If you have trouble finding a vacancy at the places listed here, look to the suburbs, where nearly every chain is represented. If you have a car and you're near one of the major interstates, getting into the city from the suburbs should be relatively simple, especially if you avoid rush hours, which last from around 6:30 to 9:30am and 4 to 7:30pm.

Although 100% occupancy is a rarity in Atlanta, this is a major convention city; booking well in advance assures you of a room in the hotel of your choice. Many accommodations, especially those downtown hotels that cater to business travelers, are at full capacity during the standard Monday-through-Friday business week, with more open beds and reduced rates offered over the weekend.

RATES The hotels reviewed below are classified first by area, then by price, using the following categories: **Very Expensive:** more than $200 per night; **Expensive:** $150 to $200; **Moderate:** $100 to $150; **Inexpensive:** less than $100. All rates are for double occupancy (two people in one room) and are subject to change.

The prices listed in this book are "rack rates"—the highest that the hotel will charge. If you ask about discounts and packages, or if you book through a travel agent, you can often do better than these posted rates. Reduced-price packages may include extras such as meals, parking, theater tickets, and golf fees, and lower rates are often available for seniors, families, and active-duty military personnel. Preferential rates are also often available when you reserve via toll-free reservation numbers or the Internet. Websites and toll-free telephone information are supplied in all applicable listings below.

Any extras included in the rates (for example, breakfast or other meals) are listed for each property. A 15% tax will be added onto your hotel or motel bill within the city of Atlanta and Fulton County (8% sales tax plus 7% room tax); the rates listed below do not include that tax. If you have a car, be sure to consider the price of parking in the hotel garage at an average of $25 per overnight. Finally, remember that hotel rates often increase during special events.

BED & BREAKFASTS Bed & Breakfast Atlanta (ⓒ 800/967-3224 or 404/875-0525; www.bedandbreakfastatlanta.com) is a free reservations service that has been carefully screening facilities in the Atlanta area since 1979. Its list comprises more than 100 homes and inns; all accommodations have private bathrooms. Among the offerings are a turreted Queen Anne–style Victorian home with nine fireplaces, located near the Carter Library; a delightful honeymoon cottage with a Jacuzzi in Druid Hills; and an elegant 1920s Tudor-style home in Buckhead. The company even has kosher homes on its roster. All rates include continental breakfast, in many cases with more than the usual pastry and coffee. To make sure that you get a room in your top B&B choice, make sure you reserve as early as possible. Call during office hours, which are Monday through Friday from 9am to 5pm.

B&B rates run the gamut from $90 to $399 (the latter for the überluxurious owner's suite in a Midtown EarthCraft property). Rates during special events may be higher. Weekly and monthly rates are available (in guesthouses and apartments) for long-term visitors. American Express, Diners Club, MasterCard, and Visa are accepted.

DOWNTOWN

Downtown hotels no longer cater primarily to the business/convention traveler because the area now offers so much for the leisure traveler, too, including the Georgia Aquarium, the World of Coca-Cola, the CNN Center, Centennial Olympic Park, Imagine It! Children's Museum of Atlanta, and the Georgia Dome.

Very Expensive

Glenn Hotel ★★ The Atlanta lodging scene has never seen anything like this before. The seductive Glenn Hotel, with its wispy-sheer drapery, wraparound lounging sofas, and erotic art, is all about pleasure and was downtown Atlanta's first boutique hotel. Guests can shower in small bathrooms with all-glass stalls that open onto the bedroom, or enjoy a soaking tub for two in one of the 13 roomy and stylish suites. Need a bedtime story? You'll find a pop-up book version of the *Kama Sutra* on the coffee table. This is luxury boutique lodging at its finest.

110 Marietta St. NW, Atlanta, GA 30303. ⓒ **404/521-2250.** www.glennhotel.com. 109 units. $209–$269 double; $349 suite. AE, DC, MC, V. Valet parking $25. MARTA: Dome/GWCC/Philips Arena/CNN Center. **Amenities:** Restaurant; bar; concierge; room service. *In room:* TV, CD player, hair dryer, minibar, Wi-Fi.

Marriott Downtown ★ This small, upscale property with warmth and charm boasts a central downtown location. The hotel is close to Peachtree Center and a short walk from the Georgia Aquarium, Centennial Olympic Park, the new World of Coca-Cola, Philips Arena, the CNN Center, and the Georgia World Congress Center. The rooms, decorated with traditional quiet prints, dark woods, and overstuffed chairs, are not huge, but they're nicely appointed. Marble floors and counters in the bathrooms lend a handsome touch. The oversize tubs are nice, though not whirlpool tubs. Some units have views of Centennial Olympic Park, and 12 are accessible to travelers with disabilities.

Where to Stay Downtown

Days Inn Atlanta Downtown **11**	Hyatt Regency Atlanta **14**
The Ellis **6**	Marriott Downtown **9**
Embassy Suites at Centennial Olympic Park **2**	Marriott Marquis **15**
Glenn Hotel **4**	Omni Hotel at CNN Center **3**
Hilton Atlanta **16**	Residence Inn by Marriott Downtown **5**
Hilton Garden Inn **1**	Ritz-Carlton Atlanta **7**
Holiday Inn Atlanta Downtown **10**	W Atlanta Downtown **12**
Hyatt Place Downtown **13**	Westin Peachtree Plaza **8**

160 Spring St. (at International Blvd.), Atlanta, GA 30303. ☎ **866/316-5959** or 404/688-8600. www.marriott.com. 312 units. $179–$220 double; $290 suite. Children 17 and under stay free in parent's room. Weekend rates often available; higher rates during special events. AE, DC, DISC, MC, V. Valet parking $28. MARTA: Peachtree Center. **Amenities:** Restaurant; bar; babysitting; concierge; health club; large outdoor heated pool; room service. *In room:* TV, hair dryer, Wi-Fi.

Marriott Marquis ★★   A dramatic downtown landmark, the Marriott Marquis is a first-class megahotel that recently underwent a renovation that has put this hotel at the top of the list for downtown lodging, with an ultra-contemporary lobby bar as the main attraction. However, the lobby level is so open and attractive that event receptions are often held here and, while they are typically held early in the evening, the noise from a large gathering funnels straight up the atrium and into the rooms. The rooms are attractively decorated in a contemporary style. Guest rooms and bathrooms are of average size. Forty-two rooms are wheelchair accessible. The Marriott is connected by a covered walkway to shops in the Peachtree Center mall.

265 Peachtree Center Ave. (btw. Baker and Harris sts.), Atlanta, GA 30303. ☎ **888/855-5701** or 404/521-0000. Fax 404/586-6299. www.marriott.com. 1,675 units. $189–$289 double; $389 suite. Children 11 and under stay free in parent's room. Packages available. AE, DC, DISC, MC, V. Valet parking $28. MARTA: Peachtree Center. **Amenities:** 2 restaurants; 2 bars; free airport shuttle; concierge; fitness center; room service. *In room:* TV, fridge, hair dryer, Wi-Fi.

Ritz-Carlton Atlanta ★★★   A 2008 renovation glamorized the lounge, guest rooms, and suites, and revamped the technology. The impeccable service you'd expect from a Ritz property harkens back to another, more gracious era; you'll be pampered (for instance, housekeeping stops by twice daily). Elegant, spacious rooms, many with bay windows, are furnished with dark hickory bachelor's chests and ostrich-patterned leather headboards. Ample marble and granite bathrooms have rain shower heads. Four rooms are accessible to travelers with disabilities.

Overlooking all the action along Peachtree Street, Atlanta Grill features steaks, chops, and seafood as well as southern favorites. Diners can count on a warm, club-like atmosphere, accompanied by the soothing sounds of live jazz every night. The Atlanta Grill is a popular Atlanta dining choice with both guests and nonguests.

181 Peachtree St. NE (main entrance on Ellis St.), Atlanta, GA 30303. ✆ **800/241-3333** or 404/659-0400. Fax 404/688-0400. www.ritzcarlton.com. 444 units. $269 double; $319–$679 suite. AE, DC, DISC, MC, V. Valet parking $30. MARTA: Peachtree Center. **Amenities:** Restaurant; babysitting; concierge; executive-level rooms; fitness center; room service. *In room:* TV/DVD, fax, hair dryer, minibar, MP3 docking station, Wi-Fi.

W Atlanta Downtown ★   This location brings the total of W Hotels in Atlanta to four, but it's the first to be built from the ground up; all other locations were other hotels in previous lives. With its very chic interior, W Atlanta Downtown is right in the heart of things regarding attractions and restaurants. Rooms are ultramodern in design and color scheme. Ask for a large corner room with two walls of windows overlooking the city. W's signature bedding is notable, as is the full service Bliss spa. This W prides itself on being hip, so make time to experience the handcrafted cocktails at DRINKSHOP, one of two bars on-site. Their Whatever/Whenever service philosophy means what it says: Ask and you shall receive (as long as it's legal). They've acquired lots of attention for their creativity and offer five types of special ice, each designed to melt at just the right pace for the drink in which it's served. Service here is impeccable. If you choose to skip dining at **BLT Steak** (p. 77) on-site (though I can't imagine why you would), walk up the street to **FAB** (French American Brasserie; p. 78), which is excellent.

45 Ivan Allen Jr. Blvd., Atlanta, GA 30308. ✆ **877/946-8357** or 404/582-5800. Fax 404/582-5805. www.watlantadowntown.com. 237 units. $219–$265 double; $339–$599 suite. AE, DC, DISC, MC, V. Valet parking $30. MARTA: Civic Center. **Amenities:** Restaurant; 2 bars; concierge; fitness center; pool; room service; spa. *In room:* TV, hair dryer, MP3 docking station, Wi-Fi.

Westin Peachtree Plaza ★★   You wouldn't expect a 73-story, 1,000-room hotel to be described as cozy, but that fits here. The 300-square-foot rooms are both elegant and intimate, and floor-to-ceiling windows provide dramatic views of the city. The Westin's "Heavenly Beds"—boasting a custom-designed pillow-top mattress set, a down blanket, three luxury-brand sheets, a comforter, a duvet, and five of the softest pillows ever—guarantee you a good night's sleep. Bathrooms are of average size. The revolving Sun Dial Restaurant, on the 71st floor, serves sophisticated American fare and has an impressive 360-degree view of the city skyline. The revolving Sun Dial bar, on the 72nd floor, is a good spot for cocktails and light fare. Twenty-eight rooms are accessible to travelers with disabilities.

210 Peachtree St. NW (at International Blvd.), Atlanta, GA 30303. ✆ **800/228-3000** or 404/659-1400. Fax 404/589-7424. www.westin.com. 1,068 units. $190–$270 double; $335–$1,450 suite. Extra person $20. Children 17 and under stay free in parent's room. Package rates available. AE, DC, DISC, MC, V. Valet parking $23; self-parking $19. MARTA: Peachtree Center. **Amenities:** 2 restaurants; 2 bars; concierge; fitness center; large indoor/outdoor pool; room service. *In room:* TV, hair dryer, Internet.

> ## Rooms & a View
>
> For a bird's-eye view of the city, take a trip up to the top of the **Westin Peachtree Plaza.** You'll ride up 72 stories in a glass elevator to a viewing area with telescopes where you can get a 360-degree look at Atlanta and the surrounding area. On a clear day, you can see the foothills of the Appalachian Mountains. Open from 10am to 11pm daily; the cost is $5 for adults, $3 for children. Call ✆ **404/659-1400** for details.

Expensive

The Ellis ★   The Ellis on Peachtree is downtown Atlanta's most historic boutique hotel. Formerly the Winecoff Hotel, destroyed by fire in 1946, the Ellis is the result of a $28-million investment and a vision for returning this grand old landmark to the bustling hotel of former years. The rooms are quite small, but nicely appointed, as are the bathrooms. Unusual is the ecofriendly hotel's "female only" floor, with keyed entry, a throwback to earlier times, but comforting for women traveling alone who like the added privacy and security. The Ellis is a good location for those looking to explore downtown, as many places, including the Georgia Aquarium and World of Coca-Cola, can be reached on foot. Entrance is on a steep side street and parking can be an issue. Valet parking from an outside vendor is available, and self-parking is offered at a couple of nearby parking garages. The Ellis is one of only four hotels in the city to receive the National Green Seal for their sustainability practices.

176 Peachtree St. NW, Atlanta, GA 30303. ✆ **404/523-5155.** www.ellishotel.com. 127 units. $125–$188 double; $139–$202 suite. AE, DC, MC, V. Valet parking $23. MARTA: Peachtree Center. **Amenities:** Restaurant; lounge; concierge; room service. *In room:* TV, CD player, hair dryer, minibar, free Wi-Fi.

Embassy Suites at Centennial Olympic Park ★ ☺   This Centennial Olympic Park location is a good bet for tourists, conventioneers, and sports fans, since the hotel is just across the street from the Georgia Aquarium, the World of Coca-Cola, and the Georgia World Congress Center, and within walking distance of MARTA, the CNN Center, Philips Arena, and the Georgia Dome. Kids will immediately spot the fountains at Centennial Park, designed to allow visitors to run through them and get soaked from head to foot.

Each two-room standard suite is decorated with contemporary furniture and includes a pullout sofa in the living room. Ask for a park-side room, which has a nice view of the park and the city skyline; there's no extra charge. Complimentary cooked-to-order breakfasts and an evening reception will keep a few bucks in your pocket. Seventeen suites are accessible to travelers with disabilities.

267 Marietta St., Atlanta, GA 30313. ✆ **404/223-2300.** Fax 404/223-0925. www.embassysuites1.hilton. com. 321 units. $209–$279 suite. Children 17 and under stay free in parent's room. Rates include full breakfast. Packages and weekend rates available; higher rates during special events. AE, DC, DISC, MC, V. Valet parking $24. MARTA: Omni/Dome/GWCC. **Amenities:** Restaurant; free airport shuttle; concierge; health club; large outdoor pool; room service; sauna. *In room:* TV, fridge, hair dryer, Internet, kitchen.

Hilton Atlanta ★★   If you want to stay in one of the downtown megahotels, this is a good choice. One of Atlanta's top convention hotels—with 104,000 square feet of meeting and exhibit space—the Hilton is surprisingly upscale for a chain lodging.

4

WHERE TO STAY

Downtown

Renovations to the executive level lounge, the entrance, and lobby took place within the last few years. Rooms have high ceilings and large windows (ask for one with views of downtown). Suites will make you feel as if you're sitting at home in your own living room; some have Murphy beds for extra guests.

The Hilton's premier restaurant is **Nikolai's Roof,** a 30th-floor dining room with spectacular skyline vistas. Multicourse prix-fixe French and Russian dinners are the specialty, as are the flavored vodkas steeped in-house. Adjacent to Nikolai's Roof is A Point of View bar. Trader Vic's, a Polynesian restaurant found at numerous Hiltons, provides its signature setting of palm trees and tiki torches, plus potent rum drinks.

255 Courtland St. (btw. Baker and Harris sts.), Atlanta, GA 30303. ✆ **800/HILTONS** (445-8667) or 404/659-2000. Fax 404/524-0111. www.hilton.com. 1,224 units. $152–$229 double. Children stay free in parent's room. AE, DC, DISC, MC, V. Valet parking $24; self-parking $17. MARTA: Peachtree Center. **Amenities:** 4 restaurants; 2 bars; airport shuttle; concierge; 2 basketball courts; fitness center w/jogging track; Jacuzzi; outdoor pool; room service; sauna; 4 outdoor tennis courts. *In room:* A/C, TV, hair dryer, minibar.

Hilton Garden Inn ★ ☺   One of downtown's newest hotels, the Hilton Garden Inn provides one more option for staying near the mix of attractions in downtown Atlanta. Within walking distance to Centennial Olympic Park, the Georgia Aquarium, the World of Coca-Cola, and Imagine It! Children's Museum, this is a great place for families to use as headquarters during a trip to the city. The hotel has a video arcade and playground, as well as special activities to keep the little ones busy. Rooms are welcoming but pretty basic and of average size, as are the bathrooms; ask for one with a city view for a more interesting stay. Suites have a separate living room so parents can relax after putting the kids to bed. Rooms include a refrigerator and microwave.

275 Baker St., Atlanta, GA 30303. ✆ **800/HILTONS** (445-8667) or 404/577-2001. Fax 404/577-2002. www.hilton.com. 273 units. $135–$179 double; $494 suite. Children stay free in parent's room. AE, DC, DISC, MC, V. Valet parking $24; self-parking $18. MARTA: Peachtree Center. **Amenities:** Restaurant; bar; airport shuttle; concierge; fitness center; pool; room service. *In room:* A/C, TV, fridge, Internet access, microwave.

Hyatt Place Downtown ★   Formerly AmeriSuites, this place got a fresh start under new ownership and now features the double-plus Hyatt Grand Beds and 42-inch flat-panel HD televisions. Still ideal for the business traveler as it's just a few blocks from downtown, Hyatt Place offers a lot, including free Wi-Fi. Leave your car in the parking lot and don't even worry about fighting the Atlanta rush-hour traffic— the hotel offers a free shuttle to and from local offices. Rooms are large and nicely furnished, making them particularly appealing for business travelers on extended stays. Bathrooms are of standard size. Five units are accessible to travelers with disabilities. A complimentary deluxe continental breakfast buffet is served each morning. Don't miss the guest reception every Tuesday evening.

330 Peachtree St. NE (btw. Baker St. and Ralph McGill Blvd.), Atlanta, GA 30308. ✆ **888/492-8847** or 404/577-1980. Fax 404/688-3706. www.hyatt.com. 94 units. $169–$299 double. Children 16 and under stay free in parent's room. Packages available. AE, DC, DISC, MC, V. Self-parking $22. MARTA: Peachtree Center or Civic Center. **Amenities:** Restaurant; fitness center. *In room:* A/C, TV, minibar, fridge, hair dryer, microwave.

Hyatt Regency Atlanta ★★   One of the city's major convention hotels, this Hyatt was designed in 1967 by famed Atlanta architect John Portman and recently underwent a major renovation. Rooms have a contemporary flavor and feature the Hyatt's "premium bedding" concept—beds are graced with pillow-top mattresses, high-thread-count sheets, and feather blankets. Rooms and bathrooms are of average size. The main building's 22nd floor houses the Regency Club accommodations, featuring a private concierge, lounge, continental breakfast, evening hors d'oeuvres, and plush robes. Business Plan rooms are on the 21st floor. The hotel is connected to the Peachtree Center mall by a covered walkway.

Accommodations, rates, and service at the Hyatt are comparable to those at the Hilton, thus any preference is usually based on habit. The Hilton is, however, the more suitable property for large conventions.

265 Peachtree St. NE (btw. Baker and Harris sts.), Atlanta, GA 30303. © **800/233-1234** or 404/577-1234. Fax 404/588-4137. www.hyatt.com. 1,260 units. $229–$254 double. Extra person $25. Children 17 and under stay free in parent's room. Packages and promotional rates available. AE, DC, DISC, MC, V. Valet parking $24. MARTA: Peachtree Center. **Amenities:** 3 restaurants; bar; concierge; fitness center; large outdoor pool; room service. *In room:* A/C, TV/VCR, hair dryer, high-speed Internet access, minibar.

Omni Hotel at CNN Center ★★ ☺ The Omni has an excellent location, especially if you're attending a sporting event. It adjoins the Georgia World Congress Center, Philips Arena, the Georgia Dome, and the CNN Center, and is across from the Georgia Aquarium, the World of Coca-Cola, Centennial Olympic Park, and Imagine It! Children's Museum of Atlanta. Be sure to request a room with a view of Centennial Olympic Park or the downtown skyline. On-site, the Natural Body Spa can be a treat at the end of a busy day.

Standard rooms and bathrooms are of average size, but the suites here include huge living/dining areas with wet bars. If you don't have a problem dropping a few grand a night, ask for the two-level Omni Suite extraordinaire. Eleven rooms have been modified for visitors with disabilities. Digs are comparable to the Embassy Suites across the street, but the service here is better. If you're traveling with kids, ask about the Omni Kids program.

100 CNN Center (at Marietta St. and International Blvd.), Atlanta, GA 30335. © **800/THE-OMNI** (843-6664) or 404/659-0000. Fax 404/525-5050. www.omnihotels.com. 1,067 units. $199–$209 double; $999 suite. Children 17 and under stay free in parent's room. Weekend packages sometimes available; higher rates during special events. AE, DISC, MC, V. Valet parking $30. MARTA: Omni/Dome/GWCC. **Amenities:** Restaurant; concierge; health club; room service. *In room:* A/C, TV, minibar, hair dryer, high-speed Internet access.

Residence Inn by Marriott Downtown ★★ 🔥 This is the best deal downtown: It's close to all the action; the accommodations are quiet, nicely appointed studios or suites; and it's incredibly well priced—especially for an extended stay. The building itself was constructed in 1928 and is listed on the National Register of Historic Places. The ceiling in the marble lobby was painted by European artists when the building was new, and it has been restored to its original splendor. The most recent renovations were completed in late 2008. The rooms, which are like small apartments, have queen-size beds and kitchens outfitted with all the necessary equipment. Bathrooms are of standard size. High ceilings lend a feeling of spaciousness. For a nice view of downtown, ask for one of the suites on the higher floors. In addition to a complimentary breakfast, the hotel provides a light supper with beer and wine from Monday through Thursday.

134 Peachtree St. NW (1 block north of Woodruff Park), Atlanta, GA 30303. © **800/331-3131** or 404/522-0950. Fax 404/577-3235. www.residenceinnatlanta.com. 160 units. $169–$189 suite. Higher rates during special events. Children 17 and under stay free in parent's room. AE, DC, DISC, MC, V. Valet parking $23; offsite parking $23. MARTA: Peachtree Center. **Amenities:** Fitness center; room service. *In room:* A/C, TV, hair dryer, kitchen/kitchenette.

4

WHERE TO STAY | Downtown

family-friendly HOTELS

Embassy Suites at Centennial Olympic Park (p. 51) Kids will love this location, just yards away from Centennial Park, which is home to festivals, art markets, and concerts—plus fountains that invite playing and splashing.

Four Seasons Hotel (p. 55) A special kids program here includes cookies and milk upon check-in, a toiletries box with baby shampoo and a rubber duck, chocolates at nightly turndown, board games, and children's movies and video games.

Holiday Inn Express Hotel & Suites (p. 68) All-suite hotels are almost always the most economical way to travel as a family, and this one has an excellent location to boot. Rates include deluxe continental breakfast, and each suite has a fully equipped kitchen and a DVD player. On-site are a lovely pool and a patio with barbecue grill. You'll find a city park with a playground down the street.

Marriott Evergreen Conference Resort (p. 70) Kids will love this "castle" nestled in a pine forest. The location is excellent for families that want to take advantage of all of Stone Mountain Park's activities.

Omni Hotel at CNN Center (p. 53) The Omni's fabulous central location

puts the family-friendly attractions of the city at your fingertips. Kids receive a welcome gift here, too.

Residence Inn by Marriott Atlanta Buckhead (p. 66) This place not only has a swimming pool but boasts fully equipped kitchens—a potential money-saver for families. Rates here include breakfast, and there are barbecue grills and picnic tables on the premises. It's like having your own Atlanta apartment, with parking at your door. The property also offers basketball, volleyball, and paddle-tennis courts, and guests can rent movies at the front desk.

Serenbe Southern Country Inn (p. 74) Kids will love the open spaces and farm animals here, not to mention activities that range from playing in a treehouse to roasting marshmallows around a bonfire.

Stone Mountain Inn (p. 71) Located in Stone Mountain Park, this lovely inn is the perfect spot for families that want to take full advantage of the park's recreational opportunities. Fishing, boating, miniature golfing, bicycling, hiking, and more are at your doorstep, and the inn features an outdoor pool as well.

Moderate

Days Inn Atlanta Downtown   In a great central location, this Days Inn has balcony rooms on floors 3 to 10, with views toward Midtown. Although you don't get all the luxury-hotel frills here, the accommodations are just fine. Guest rooms are large and comfortable. All units boast flatscreen televisions. Bathrooms, with tub/shower combinations, are separate from the vanity area, a plus for those traveling in packs and trying to get ready for dinner all at the same time. Six rooms are wheelchair accessible.

The athletic center and large outdoor pool are other highlights. In-house conference rooms and a location in the heart of the business district make this hotel a great choice for folks in town on business; the rooms and facilities are quite suitable for families as well. This place is also conveniently located for those who want to enjoy all those downtown attractions or take in a game at the Dome.

300 Spring St. (at Baker St.), Atlanta, GA 30308. © **800/DAYS-INN** (329-7466) or 404/523-1144. Fax 404/577-8495. www.daysinn.com. 263 units. $77–$135 double. Extra person $10. Special weekend rates available. Children 17 and under stay free in parent's room. AE, DC, DISC, MC, V. Self-parking $15. MARTA: Peachtree Center. **Amenities:** Exercise room; large outdoor pool. *In room:* A/C, TV, fridge, hair dryer, microwave.

Holiday Inn Atlanta Downtown ★ This property offers appealing rooms and one of the better locations for business accommodations, including full conference facilities and services, at a rate that won't break you or your expense account. They've just freshened the place up with a multimillion-dollar renovation, too. The hotel is adjacent to the Gift, Apparel, and Merchandise Marts, the Georgia Aquarium, the World of Coca-Cola, and Centennial Olympic Park, and it's 2 blocks from the CNN Center, Philips Arena, and the Georgia World Congress Center. Guest rooms are of average size, as are the bathrooms. Sixteen rooms are accessible to travelers with disabilities, eight of them with roll-in shower stalls.

101 International Blvd. (at Williams St.), Atlanta, GA 30303. © **800/972-2404** or 404/524-5555. Fax 404/221-0702. www.hidowntownatlanta.com. 260 units. $102–$149 double. Rates can go up to $250 a night during major conventions. Children 18 and under stay free in parent's room; children 12 and under eat free. AE, DISC, MC, V. Valet parking $20. MARTA: Peachtree Center. **Amenities:** Restaurant; bar; concierge; fitness center; Jacuzzi; pool; room service. *In room:* TV, hair dryer, free Wi-Fi.

MIDTOWN

Travelers interested in the cultural highlights of Atlanta will appreciate the hotel choices in Midtown, an area that's home to the Woodruff Arts Center, the High Museum of Art, the Fox Theatre, and the Margaret Mitchell House. Joggers and other outdoor enthusiasts will enjoy the proximity to Piedmont Park and the Atlanta Botanical Garden.

Very Expensive

Four Seasons Hotel ★★★ ☺ This elegant hotel is the one to choose if you're looking for luxurious surroundings and impeccable service in the heart of Atlanta's cultural area. Accommodations are lavish and sophisticated, with large windows. The gorgeous, large marble bathrooms have huge tubs perfect for soaking, and some have separate showers as well. Thirteen of the rooms have been modified to accommodate travelers with disabilities.

The Spa at Four Seasons offers a wide variety of treatments, many available in-room. The hotel provides several amenities for children, including a gift upon arrival, board and video games, movies, and books. For older kids, trips can be arranged to nearby kid-friendly attractions.

The **Park 75** restaurant, open all day, has redefined southern steakhouse cuisine and features the freshest goods from local markets (and their own rooftop gardens) combined in extremely creative contemporary dishes by Chef Robert Gerstenecker.

75 14th St. (btw. Peachtree and West Peachtree sts.), Atlanta, GA 30309. © **800/819-5053** or 404/881-9898. Fax 404/873-4692. www.fourseasons.com. 244 units. From $400 double; from $650 suite. Children 17 and under stay free in parent's room. Weekend cultural packages available. AE, DC, DISC, MC, V. Valet parking $30. MARTA: Arts Center. Pets under 15 lb. accepted. **Amenities:** Restaurant; bar; concierge; health club; Jacuzzi; pool; room service; sauna; spa. *In room:* TV/DVD, hair dryer, minibar, Wi-Fi.

Hotel Palomar Atlanta-Midtown ★★ The first Atlanta venture by San Francisco–based Kimpton Hotels, Palomar is in the heart of the action in Midtown and within walking distance to many popular attractions and eateries. However, you won't want to go any farther than the hotel's **Pacci Ristorante** (p. 82), an Italian steak-house heaven. Guests enjoy the wine reception and hors d'oeuvres in the lobby lounge from 5 to 6pm each evening. Rooms are contemporary and comfortable, with a sofa for lounging around. The hotel is both kid and pet friendly, so inquire about the perks when you make reservations. Pets of any size are welcome for free.

866 W. Peachtree St. NW, Atlanta, GA 30308. ✆ **866/945-6285** or 678/412-2400. Fax 678/412-2401. www.HotelPalomar-AtlantaMidtown.com. 304 units. $250–$280 double; from $300 executive level; $500 suite. AE, DC, DISC, MC, V. Valet parking $30. MARTA: Midtown. Pets accepted free. **Amenities:** Restaurant; 2 bars; babysitting; children's program; concierge; health club; room service. *In room:* TV/DVD, fridge, hair dryer, Internet, minibar.

Loews Atlanta Hotel ★★ Atlanta's latest luxury offering, Loews opened in spring 2010 to high acclaim. The hotel offers bird's-eye views of Piedmont Park and is within walking distance of the park, the High Museum of Art, Fox Theatre, and other attractions, so leave your car in the garage and save the hassle of navigating traffic and finding a parking space. Accommodations are modern and feature floor-to-ceiling windows in every room. Techies will love the televisions that "appear" from behind the bathroom mirrors, making it easy to catch up with the morning news while getting ready for the day.

Loews is making use of the "mixology" method of handcrafted cocktails at Bar eleven, featuring the Lavender Drop Martini made with real lavender grown on the roof garden. The bar's LIVE at Loews program highlights local music talent, including some big names you just might recognize, such as Ed Roland from a little Georgia band known as Collective Soul. The hotel is both kid and pet friendly, offering special incentives and room service menus for both.

1065 Peachtree St., Atlanta, GA 30309. ✆ **800/235-6397** or 404/745-5000. Fax 404/745-5001. www. loewshotels.com/atlanta. 414 units. $204–$309 double; $389–$539 suite. AE, DC, DISC, MC, V. Valet parking $30; self-parking $15. MARTA: Arts Center. Pets accepted with fee. **Amenities:** Restaurant; bar; children's programs; concierge; health club; room service; spa. *In room:* TV/DVD, fridge, hair dryer, minibar, Wi-Fi.

Stonehurst Place ★★★ A one-of-a-kind EarthCraft House, built in 1896 and on the National Register of Historic Places, Stonehurst was extensively refurbished in 2008. Its two guest rooms and three suites are all finely appointed. A true "green lodg-ing," Stonehurst emphasizes recycling, rainwater reclamation, air purification, and solar energy. Lovely gardens and porches are great for unwinding at the end of a busy day. It's a convenient walk to Midtown restaurants and MARTA. Beds boast 1,000-thread-count Egyptian cotton bedding. Multiple shower heads and heated Car-rara marble floors are available in some bathrooms. Splurge for the luxurious master suite when available. Four units have working fireplaces. A full organic gourmet break-fast is served, along with complimentary (and delicious) home-baked goods and a variety of beverages available throughout the day. Dog friendly, Stonehurst welcomes well-behaved dogs of up to 75 pounds. The pet fee varies, depending on the size of the dog, and includes treats. A dog walking service is available for an additional fee.

923 Piedmont Ave. NE, Atlanta, GA 30309. ✆ **404/881-0722.** www.stonehurstplace.com. 5 units. $159–$249 double; $199–$399 suite. AE, MC, V. Free off-street parking. MARTA: Midtown. Pets accepted. **Amenities:** Computers. *In room:* TV/DVD, CD player, hair dryer, MP3 docking, Wi-Fi.

W Atlanta Midtown ★ This former Sheraton underwent a major transformation, and the sleek W Atlanta Midtown now rivals the Glenn boutique hotel as Hotlanta's sexiest hotel. From the thumping dance music that (very loudly) greets you in the

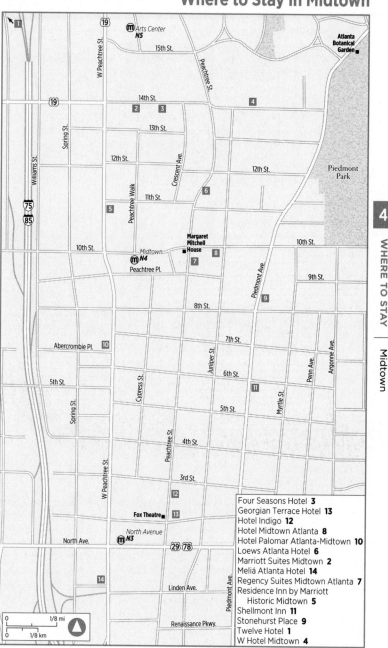

Four Seasons Hotel **3**
Georgian Terrace Hotel **13**
Hotel Indigo **12**
Hotel Midtown Atlanta **8**
Hotel Palomar Atlanta-Midtown **10**
Loews Atlanta Hotel **6**
Marriott Suites Midtown **2**
Meliá Atlanta Hotel **14**
Regency Suites Midtown Atlanta **7**
Residence Inn by Marriott
  Historic Midtown **5**
Shellmont Inn **11**
Stonehurst Place **9**
Twelve Hotel **1**
W Hotel Midtown **4**

4

WHERE TO STAY | Midtown

lobby and the Whiskey Park bar to the ultramodern, slightly above-average-size rooms appointed in black and silver and oh-so-hip decor, W has put this address back on the Midtown map. Bathrooms are attractive and of average size. At the W, where staff promises to meet requests with its signature "Whatever/Whenever" service, the attention to detail is hard to beat. Whether it's the miniature martini shaker with all the makings available in-room or the "Intimacy Kit" in the hanging minibar, there isn't much you'd want for in this hot spot.

What's more, the W is home to Bliss, the hotel's signature spa, featuring hot R&B music (instead of nature tunes) and a brownie buffet (who said you had to be on a diet to enjoy pampering?). Atlanta is now home to four W hotels, so take your pick.

188 14th St. NE (at Peachtree St.), Atlanta, GA 30361. © **877/822-0000** or 404/892-6000. Fax 404/872-9192. www.watlantamidtown.com. 467 units. $249–$279 double; $575 suite. AE, DC, DISC, MC, V. Valet parking $28; self-parking $16. MARTA: Arts Center. **Amenities:** Restaurant; 2 bars; concierge; fitness center; pool; room service; spa; free Wi-Fi in lobby. *In room:* TV/DVD, CD player, hair dryer, Internet, minibar, MP3 docking station.

Expensive

Georgian Terrace Hotel ★★ 🛄 Listed on the National Register of Historic Places, the Georgian Terrace opened in 1911 as a luxury hotel. Clark Gable and Vivien Leigh stayed here in 1939 and attended the première party of *Gone With the Wind*. The marble floors, soaring columns, and dramatic French windows hark back to the opulence and grandeur of a bygone era, though the rooms are thoroughly modern. The whole place just underwent a multimillion-dollar freshening, and it shows. The hotel has studios and one-, two-, and three-bedroom suites, with large bathrooms, and is convenient to all that Midtown has to offer. The Fox Theatre is right across the street. If you'd like a view of Stone Mountain, ask for a suite on the east side of the hotel. Breakfast is offered in the original hotel lobby, while cocktails are served in the parlor.

Note: Although the suites have full-size kitchens, they lack pots and pans and have only enough dinnerware for two people. Call the front desk for additional accouterments.

659 Peachtree St. (just north of Ponce de Leon Ave.), Atlanta, GA 30308. © **800/651-2316** or 404/897-1991. Fax 404/724-9116. www.thegeorgianterrace.com. 317 units. $169–$189 double; $209 1-bedroom suite; $239–$289 2-bedroom suite. Weekend packages available; reduced rates for stays of more than 30 days. AE, DC, DISC, MC, V. Valet parking $25; self-parking $22. MARTA: North Ave. **Amenities:** Restaurant; bar; concierge; fitness center; heated junior Olympic swimming pool; room service. *In room:* TV, hair dryer, kitchen.

Hotel Indigo ★ 🛄 This fun boutique hotel boasts a welcoming foyer, hardwood floors, and beds with oversize pillows in funky color combinations. Also oversize are the Adirondack lobby chairs in each unit. The spa-style showers are the perfect treat after a long day of sightseeing, though the bathrooms themselves are very tiny (and only two have tubs). Dog owners, take note: This is Atlanta's number-one pet-friendly hotel, with no weight limit and no fee. During Tuesday night's Canine Cocktail Hour, guests and locals bring their dogs to the lobby and bar, where the dogs are served special treats and water from a silver pitcher, while their owners socialize. The hotel is right across the street from the Fox Theatre, so you can just roll into bed after attending a performance.

683 Peachtree St. (btw. Third St. and Ponce de Leon Ave.), Atlanta, GA 30308. © **404/874-9200.** www.hotelindigo.com. 139 units. $119–$179 double. Rates may be higher during conventions and special

events. AE, DC, DISC, MC, V. Self-parking $18. MARTA: North Ave. Pets accepted. **Amenities:** Restau-
rant. *In room:* A/C, TV, hair dryer, high-speed Internet access.

Hotel Melia Atlanta   Straddling Midtown and downtown, Melia puts you in a
good position for exploring the city. Rooms facing up Peachtree offer a magnificent
view of the city, the Georgia Aquarium, and the World of Coca-Cola. Just across I-75
from Georgia Tech, Melia is a good base if you're in town to see the Yellow Jackets
play. You can also amble across the street and belly up to the "whaddya have?" counter at the Varsity for a world-famous chili dog. Melia is the first U.S. venture for
Spanish-based Sol Melia, and there are big plans in store for the property, including
a renovation scheduled for completion in late 2012. In the meantime, you can enjoy
a great drink in the lobby bar and get a good night's sleep in one of the comfortable
guest rooms. If you want to go all out, ask for one of four suites with private pools on
the balcony.

590 W. Peachtree St. NW, Atlanta, GA 30308. ✆ **888/95-MELIA** (63542) or 404/877-9000. Fax
404/588-4137. www.melia-hotels.com. 502 units. From $149 double; $269–$329 suite. AE, DC, DISC,
MC, V. Valet parking $28; self-parking $15. MARTA: Peachtree Center. **Amenities:** 2 restaurants; bar;
concierge; fitness center; outdoor pool; room service. *In room:* TV, CD player, fridge, hair dryer, Internet.

Hotel Midtown Atlanta ★   This 11-story red-brick hotel is close to many Midtown cultural attractions, including Piedmont Park and the Margaret Mitchell House
and Museum. It's also convenient to Georgia Tech, making it a favorite among visitors
to the campus and on game weekends. The nicely appointed rooms include a comfy
armchair for enjoying a relaxing read. Pillow-top mattresses and custom bedding
ensure a good night's sleep. Suites feature separate sitting areas with sofas, extra TVs
and phones, and refrigerators. Eight rooms are accessible to travelers with disabilities.

125 10th St. NE (just east of Peachtree St.), Atlanta, GA 30309. ✆ **877/999-3223** or 404/873-4800.
Fax 404/870-1530. www.hotelmidtownatlanta.com. 191 units. $155–$175 double. AE, DC, DISC, MC, V.
Valet parking $20; self-parking $15. MARTA: Midtown. **Amenities:** Restaurant; state-of-the-art fitness
center; Jacuzzi; large heated indoor pool; room service. *In room:* TV, hair dryer, Internet.

Marriott Suites Midtown ★   Located in the heart of Midtown, this all-suite hotel
is a perfect choice for culture buffs, and its proximity to MARTA makes it easy to get
to the rest of the city's attractions, too. Each spacious suite, attractively decorated in
a warm, homey style, offers a king-size bed and a full living room with a convertible
sofa. Bedrooms are set off from living-room areas by lace-curtained French doors.
Large marble bathrooms have a separate shower. Twelve units are accessible to travelers with disabilities.

35 14th St. NE (btw. Peachtree and W. Peachtree sts.), Atlanta, GA 30309. ✆ **888/855-5701** or
404/876-8888. Fax 404/876-7727. www.marriott.com. 254 units. From $199 1-bedroom suite; from $219
executive suite. AE, DC, DISC, MC, V. Valet parking $24; self-parking $18. MARTA: Arts Center. **Amenities:** Restaurant; bar; concierge; fitness center; Jacuzzi; indoor/outdoor swimming pools; room service.
In room: TV, fridge, hair dryer, Internet.

4

WHERE TO STAY

Midtown

Regency Suites Midtown Atlanta ★ This all-suite property is ideally located right in the midst of Midtown activity. The latest renovation enhanced guest suites with new granite counters, marble flooring, and pillow-top mattresses. Regency Suites is ideal for business travelers, who are drawn to the complimentary expanded continental breakfast and the full dinner for two served on Monday through Thursday nights when booked direct. Suites and bathrooms are of average size. If you choose to venture out for meals, numerous restaurants are within walking distance—as is the Fox Theatre, if you're in town to catch a performance. Accommodations include fully equipped kitchenettes with standard appliances and table service for four. Additionally, all units have noise-reduction windows in case the Midtown partying scene goes on too late for your comfort.

975 W. Peachtree St. NE, Atlanta, GA 30309. ✆ **404/876-5003.** Fax 404/817-7511. www.regencysuites. com. 96 units. $129–$209 suite. AE, MC, V. Parking $15. MARTA: Midtown. **Amenities:** Fitness center. *In room:* TV, hair dryer, kitchenette, free Wi-Fi.

Residence Inn by Marriott Historic Midtown ★ The complimentary evening reception, offered Monday through Thursday, and a full hot breakfast sets this property apart from others in the area. If the free food doesn't tempt your taste buds, you can opt for the complimentary grocery-shopping service from Monday through Friday. The studios and spacious suites here boast handsome oak or mahogany furnishings— mostly antique reproductions, including Chippendale-style beds. Most rooms have balconies with French doors. Ten rooms are accessible to travelers with disabilities. There aren't many attractions within walking distance, but you're not far from the Midtown MARTA station. The inn provides hot tea and coffee all day in the lobby.

1041 W. Peachtree St. (at 11th St.), Atlanta, GA 30309. ✆ **404/872-8885.** Fax 404/724-9218. www. marriott.com. 78 units. From $159 studio; from $189 1-bedroom suite; from $299 2-bedroom suite. AE, DC, DISC, MC, V. Parking $19. MARTA: Midtown. Pets accepted with $100 nonrefundable fee. **Amenities:** Restaurant; exercise room; Jacuzzi; Wi-Fi. *In room:* TV, kitchen, hair dryer, free Internet.

Shellmont Inn ★ This charming two-story Victorian mansion looks like a fairy-tale house, its exterior embellished with ribbons, bows, garlands, and shells. The building, which dates from 1891, is on the National Register of Historic Places and is a city landmark. Innkeepers Ed and Debbie McCord have done a superb job of restoring the place, meticulously researching original paint colors, stencil designs, woodwork, and period furnishings, and reproducing them with 100% accuracy. Upstairs are the four guest rooms, which can be reserved individually or in pairs (as two-room units). On your way up, be sure to stop on the landing to check out the five-paneled stained-glass window, believed to be an authentic Tiffany. Rooms have elegant queen-size beds, leaded-glass or bay windows, and Oriental rugs on pine floors. Three rooms have whirlpool baths. The carriage house has a luxurious master bedroom, a modern bathroom with steam shower, a fully equipped kitchen, a living room, and a dressing area.

821 Piedmont Ave. NE (at Sixth St.), Atlanta, GA 30308. ✆ **404/872-9290.** Fax 404/872-5379. www. shellmont.com. 4 units, plus carriage house. $185–$225 double; $225–$260 whirlpool suite; $245–$350 carriage house. Rates include full breakfast. Children 12 and under allowed in carriage house only. AE, DC, DISC, MC, V. Free parking. MARTA: Midtown. **Amenities:** Innkeepers/concierge services. *In room:* TV/DVD, Wi-Fi.

Twelve Hotel ★★ This posh, all-suite boutique hotel in Atlantic Station, the Southeast's largest live/work/play community, will leave guests wishing they could move in for good. While the use of high ceilings and concrete in the large rooms lends an industrial feel, the creature comforts—including track lighting, in-room computers, and beautiful marble counters—will make you feel right at home. The property's high-tech system, known as GHOST (Guest Hotel Operating System Terminal), allows guests to order room service, make specific housekeeping requests, contact the concierge, request their car from valet, and more, all from the hotel computer in your room. Suites include full kitchens and large bathrooms.

Don't miss the opportunity to dine at the on-site restaurant, **Lobby at Twelve** (☎ **404/961-7370**), where diners can choose from an extensive wine list, including some rare vintages. Even breakfast is a treat—try the ricotta, fried egg, and arugula wrap cooked in the wood oven. See p. 83 for more details.

361 17th St., Atlanta, GA 30363. ☎ **404/961-1212.** Fax 404/961-1221. www.twelvehotels.com. 102 units. $209–$229 1-bedroom suite; from $329 2-bedroom suite. AE, MC, V. Valet parking $24. MARTA: Arts Station, then free shuttle to Atlantic Station. **Amenities:** Restaurant; bar; concierge; fitness center; outdoor pool; room service. *In room:* TV, hair dryer, kitchen, computer w/high-speed Internet access.

BUCKHEAD

There's something for everyone in Buckhead—shoppers, foodies, history buffs, business travelers, and night owls will all find their niche. The neighborhood's offerings and the ease of getting around (a free community shuttle allows access to popular Buckhead hotels, shopping malls, and restaurants) make Buckhead the ideal place to stay. A word about dining: There are so many fine restaurants and nightspots in Buckhead that it's foolish to limit yourself to hotel fare. There are three notable exceptions, however—the Westin Buckhead Atlanta, the Mansion on Peachtree, and InterContinental Buckhead all have outstanding restaurants. You'll find these establishments reviewed in chapter 5.

Very Expensive

Grand Hyatt Atlanta ★   The towering Grand Hyatt Atlanta offers a winning combination of 18th-century American architecture and Japanese flavor. The lobby overlooks a 9,000-square-foot garden with traditional Japanese plantings, rock formations, and splashing waterfalls created by noted Kyoto landscape architects. A collection of museum-quality Japanese art, spanning 4 centuries, is displayed throughout the hotel. The Grand Hyatt is just one of many hotels at this price and level of service in the area. You'll be in the heart of Buckhead—the "Beverly Hills of the South," with a world of options when it comes to fine dining, high-end shopping, and a jumping nightlife scene. Ask for a room with a view of Stone Mountain. Every luxury imaginable is provided at this plush establishment—you'll even find an umbrella in your closet.

3300 Peachtree Rd. (just east of Piedmont Rd.), Atlanta, GA 30305. ☎ **800/233-1234** or 404/365-8100. Fax 404/233-5686. www.grandatlanta.hyatt.com. 438 units. $329–$354 double; $379 Regency Club floor; $429 executive suite. AE, DC, DISC, MC, V. Valet parking $30; self-parking $20. MARTA: Buckhead. Pets under 25 lb. accepted with $100 nonrefundable fee. **Amenities:** Restaurant; bar; airport shuttle; free shuttle (2-mile radius); babysitting; children's programs; concierge; executive rooms; fitness center; seasonal outdoor heated pool; room service; sauna. *In room:* TV, fax, fridge, hair dryer, MP3 docking station, Wi-Fi.

InterContinental Buckhead ★★   An elegant luxury hotel, InterContinental is designed to cater to the most discriminating guests. This property is an especially great choice if you're in town to take advantage of the city's high-end shopping at Phipps Plaza and Lenox Mall, both just a couple of blocks away. Rooms are spacious and quiet, with ultra-comfortable bedding for a sweet night's sleep. Suites and executive-level rooms include daily cocktail hour. The InterContinental is also home to the fabulous 24-hour **Au Pied de Cochon** European brasserie (p. 93), with an extensive raw seafood bar and sinful desserts. The adjoining XO bar specializes in cognac and has live jazz Tuesday through Saturday evenings. The bar crowd can get rather rowdy late in the evening, as Buckhead is a hot spot for partygoers, so dine early if you're not up for the action, as the noise from the bar can get pretty intense.

3315 Peachtree Rd., Atlanta, GA 30326. ✆ **404/946-9000.** Fax 404/946-9001. www.intercontinental. com. 422 units. $252–$279 double; $319 club level; $540 suite. AE, DC, MC, V. Valet parking $30; self-parking $20. MARTA: Buckhead. Pets under 25 lb. accepted with $100 nonrefundable fee **Amenities:** Restaurant; bar; concierge; executive-level rooms; health club; Jacuzzi; outdoor pool; room service; spa. *In room:* TV, fax, hair dryer, minibar, Wi-Fi.

JW Marriott Hotel Buckhead ★   This luxurious Marriott property has an excellent location. Connected to the Lenox Square mall, it's across the street from MARTA and within walking distance of the posh Phipps Plaza mall and many good restaurants. It's popular with business travelers and die-hard shoppers alike. Rooms are charmingly furnished with Chippendale-style mahogany pieces; the picture windows afford great views of Buckhead or the downtown skyline. Well-appointed rooms reek of luxury and pampering. Ask for a room with a view of downtown Buckhead to see all the action for yourself. Corner rooms are superior and spacious. Nineteen units have been modified for travelers with disabilities.

3300 Lenox Rd. NE (a few blocks east of Peachtree Rd. at E. Paces Ferry Rd.), Atlanta, GA 30326. ✆ **800/613-2051** or 404/262-3344. Fax 404/262-8689. www.marriott.com. 371 units. From $260–$299 double; from $329 concierge level. AE, DC, DISC, MC, V. Valet parking $30; self-parking $20. MARTA: Lenox. **Amenities:** Restaurant; airport shuttle; concierge; executive rooms; health club; Jacuzzi; large indoor pool; room service; sauna. *In room:* TV/DVD, minibar, fridge, hair dryer, Internet.

The Mansion on Peachtree ★★★   Long awaited, the Mansion opened in 2008, offering travelers a whole new level of luxury and service (you even get your own butler). Coffee and tea are delivered to your room upon request each morning. Rooms have 9½-foot ceilings and are lush, with neutral velvets and satins. An LCD television is hidden behind a framed piece of art that retracts at the touch of a button. All 31 suites have balconies; rooms with balconies and double balconies are available. Luxury extends to the spacious bathrooms, where you can soak in a deep tub or enjoy a marble steam shower.

The hotel has two excellent restaurants, Tom Colicchio's **Craft** (p. 90) and **NEO,** with a contemporary Italian-inspired menu (don't miss the foie gras). On-site **29 Spa** by Lydia Mondavi offers exclusive treatments with grape-seed antioxidant products.

When it comes to luxury, the recently opened St. Regis is giving the Mansion a run for its money, though both are bastions of grandeur.

3376 Peachtree Rd., Atlanta, GA 30326. ✆ **888/767-3966** or 404/995-7500. Fax 404/995-7501. www. rwmansiononpeachtree.com. 127 units. $389 double; $569 suite. AE, DC, DISC, MC, V. Valet parking $28. MARTA: Lenox. **Amenities:** 2 restaurants; bar; limousine and shuttle service; concierge; executive-level rooms; health club; large indoor pool; room service; spa. *In room:* TV/DVD, CD player, hair dryer, minibar, Wi-Fi.

Ritz-Carlton Buckhead ★★★   The Ritz-Carlton Buckhead is the Rolls-Royce of Atlanta hotels. Every inch of this hotel oozes luxury, from the lobby to the public areas, now saturated in a color palette representative of a southern garden. A renovation, completed in late 2008, brought the hotel to the next level, as well as doubled the number of suites. The rooms, all with large bay windows, are exquisitely decorated with

Where to Stay in Buckhead

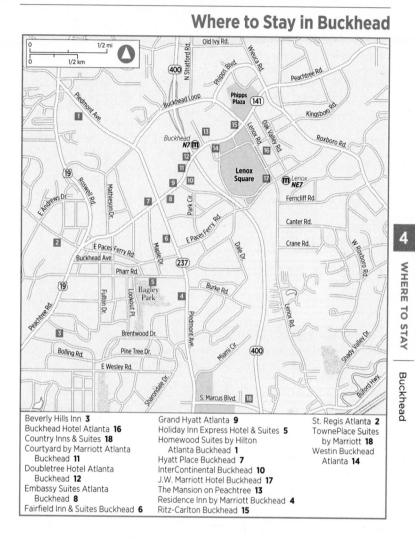

Beverly Hills Inn **3**	Grand Hyatt Atlanta **9**	St. Regis Atlanta **2**
Buckhead Hotel Atlanta **16**	Holiday Inn Express Hotel & Suites **5**	TownePlace Suites
Country Inns & Suites **18**	Homewood Suites by Hilton	by Marriott **18**
Courtyard by Marriott Atlanta	Atlanta Buckhead **1**	Westin Buckhead
Buckhead **11**	Hyatt Place Buckhead **7**	Atlanta **14**
Doubletree Hotel Atlanta	InterContinental Buckhead **10**	
Buckhead **12**	J.W. Marriott Hotel Buckhead **17**	
Embassy Suites Atlanta	The Mansion on Peachtree **13**	
Buckhead **8**	Residence Inn by Marriott Buckhead **4**	
Fairfield Inn & Suites Buckhead **6**	Ritz-Carlton Buckhead **15**	

armoires, luxuriously upholstered sofas or armchairs, and marble-topped desks. Twelve units are accessible to travelers with disabilities. Executive-level guests can enjoy the comfortable Club Lounge, which serves complimentary meals, snacks, and cocktails.

The Café is a hot spot for Sunday brunch, and nonguests pour in for the dining event. The Lobby Lounge is the setting for afternoon English-style teas and features live jazz in the evenings.

3434 Peachtree Rd. NE (at Lenox Rd.), Atlanta, GA 30326. (C) **800/241-3333** or 404/237-2700. Fax 404/239-0078. www.ritzcarlton.com. 517 units. $359 double; $434–$599 suite. AE, MC, V. Valet parking $32. Pets under 30 lb. accepted with $250 nonrefundable deposit. MARTA: Buckhead or Lenox. **Amenities:** Restaurant; bar; airport shuttle; mall shuttle; babysitting; concierge; executive rooms; fitness center; Jacuzzi; indoor pool; room service; sauna; spa. *In room:* TV/DVD, minibar, high-speed Internet access, Wi-Fi.

4

WHERE TO STAY | Buckhead

The St. Regis Atlanta ★★★ This property is nothing less than the lap of luxury, and few hotels can even call themselves peers in comparison. Like the Mansion, St. Regis provides a butler service with each room, someone to arrange coffee in your room each morning or to ensure your ironing makes it back in time for the afternoon meeting. Just ask and it shall be yours. You can also ask the butler to reserve a space for you at the elegant afternoon tea served daily in the Long Gallery.

The 40,000-square-foot pool piazza is an oasis in the middle of a bustling city, and guests spend hours there sunning, reading, or enjoying a cold drink from the poolside bar. It includes a billiards room, fireplace, and Jacuzzi. When you're ready to wind down for the evening, enjoy dinner at the property's **Paces 88** restaurant (p. 94).

88 W. Paces Ferry Rd., Atlanta, GA 30305. ✆ **866/716-8116** or 404/563-7900. Fax 404/563-7905. www.StRegis.com/Atlanta. 150 units. $335–$400 double; $455–$480 1-bedroom suite; $535–$560 deluxe suite. AE, DC, DISC, MC, V. Valet parking $32. MARTA: Buckhead. **Amenities:** Restaurant; bar; free shuttle (2-mile radius); concierge; fitness center; Jacuzzi; large outdoor pool; room service; spa. *In room:* TV, hair dryer, MP3 docking station, Wi-Fi.

Westin Buckhead Atlanta ★★ If the Ritz-Carlton is the Rolls-Royce of Atlanta hotels, the Westin is the Ferrari. Its fresh Euro-modern design makes it a favorite among trendsetters visiting the city. In the heart of Buckhead between Lenox Square and the Atlanta Financial Center, it's a top choice among business travelers and serious shoppers.

The Westin Buckhead boasts postmodern European architecture, including a pristine white-tile exterior with a graceful curve. Interior spaces employ minimalist Bauhaus design elements and feature original works by renowned contemporary artists, including Warhol, Rauschenberg, Chagall, Schnabel, and Stella. Rooms are sleekly furnished with Beidermeier-style maple pieces. The Westin's signature "Heavenly Beds" are so cushy, you might sleep right through breakfast. Corner king rooms are especially luxurious.

The superb **Palm** restaurant serves one of the best lobster dinners in town (p. 91).

3391 Peachtree Rd. NE (btw. Lenox and Piedmont roads), Atlanta, GA 30326. ✆ **404/365-0065.** Fax 404/365-8787. www.westin.com. 365 units. From $292–$329 double; $379–$459 executive level. AE, DC, MC, V. Valet parking $30; self-parking $20. MARTA: Buckhead. **Amenities:** Restaurant; shuttle service (2-mile radius); concierge; health center; large indoor pool; room service; sauna; spa. *In room:* TV/DVD, CD player, fridge, hair dryer, minibar, Wi-Fi.

Expensive

Buckhead Hotel Atlanta ★ This Marriott property has abundant services and facilities, plus a great location that's close to MARTA, Lenox Square, Phipps Plaza, and many restaurants. A recent renovation updated an aging interior, and for the price it's an excellent location in the heart of this business and shopping district. Like most Buckhead hotels, this one is conveniently located so you can set out on foot to try one of numerous top-notch eateries. Take advantage of the shuttle service and hit one of two nearby high-end malls and shop till you drop. Several units have balconies, and those with king-size beds have plush armchairs with ottomans as well. Eleven rooms are accessible to travelers with disabilities.

3405 Lenox Rd. NE (btw. Peachtree and E. Paces Ferry roads), Atlanta, GA 30326. ✆ **800/241-8260** or 404/261-9250. Fax 404/848-7391. www.buckheadhotelatlanta.com. 369 units. $167 double. Extra person $20. Children 16 and under stay free in parent's room. AE, DC, DISC, MC, V. Self-parking $12. MARTA: Lenox. **Amenities:** Restaurant; bar; shuttle service (3-mile radius); health club; outdoor swimming pool; room service. *In room:* TV, hair dryer, Internet.

THE vine THAT ATE THE SOUTH

If you're visiting Georgia in the summer and traveling its interstate highways or country lanes, it's impossible to ignore the wild-looking vines growing along the roadside. That's kudzu, a frighteningly robust plant that upholsters billboards and fences, swallows up whole trees, and creeps eerily toward asphalt lanes, threatening everything in its path. It would surely blanket the pasturing cows if they were to stand still for a couple of days.

A native of the Far East, kudzu was introduced to the United States in the late 1800s and became treasured as a porch vine whose prolific tendrils would shoot straight up at the rate of a foot a day, quickly covering a roof or trellis, providing welcome shade from the midday sun. It was touted as an excellent forage crop (a crop used for grazing and for hay), and because it would grow almost anywhere, it was promoted as a means to control erosion.

By the turn of the 20th century, some horticulturists were having their doubts about kudzu, pointing out (to no avail) that the seemingly virtuous vine had the really bad habit of growing *everywhere* at an alarming rate. However, their warnings went unheeded, and the federal government continued to urge farmers to plant kudzu on worn-out farmland to keep it from washing away. It wasn't until the 1960s that the Soil Conservation Service stopped recommending its use. By then, the dense tangles had a lock on the landscape, not to mention barns and telephone poles.

Nobody's found a practical way to eradicate the stuff yet. Burning it won't work. Chemicals are impotent, unless each root and crown is hunted down relentlessly and sprayed and sprayed for years. And there are no natural predators, unless you count goats or other grazing animals—and there just aren't enough goats to go around. For now, the only thing to do is continue to hack away at the formidable vine—and remember to close our windows at night.

Embassy Suites Atlanta Buckhead ★★ This all-suite hotel stacks up well against the more expensive hotels in the same area. A favorite with business travelers, the suite arrangement is also ideal for families, and the location can't be beat, with Lenox Square, Phipps Plaza, and many fine restaurants within walking distance. The Buckhead MARTA station is less than a block away.

Each elegantly appointed, 800-square-foot, two-room suite has a bed and a pullout queen-size sofa. Although the entire hotel is accessible to travelers with disabilities—most of the participants in the wheelchair division of the Peachtree Road Race stay here—10 of the suites are completely equipped for those with disabilities, and two have roll-in showers.

Two popular bonuses: the complimentary cooked-to-order breakfast, served in the 16-story atrium lobby (check out the waterfall), and complimentary afternoon cocktails.

3285 Peachtree Rd. NW (1 block north of Piedmont Rd.), Atlanta, GA 30326. ℂ **800/362-2779** or 404/261-7733. Fax 404/261-6857. www.embassysuites1.hilton.com. 317 units. $209 suite. AE, DC, DISC, MC, V. Valet parking $19; self-parking $16. MARTA: Buckhead. **Amenities:** Restaurant; shuttle service (1-mile radius); concierge; exercise room; Jacuzzi; large outdoor pool/small indoor pool; sauna. *In room:* TV, fridge, hair dryer, free Wi-Fi.

Homewood Suites by Hilton Atlanta Buckhead ★ ✔ This well-run all-suite hotel is an excellent value, perfect for an extended business stay or a long weekend. Although you won't be within walking distance of most of the Buckhead attractions or the MARTA station, there is a courtesy van that will take you anywhere within a 3-mile radius. The spacious and homey apartment-style suites have pullout sofas and large kitchen areas with full-size appliances, dishwashers, and toasters. Some of the two-bedroom suites can easily sleep eight people—a great option for large families. Four suites are accessible to travelers with disabilities. The hotel is set back from a busy street, so all units are quiet; ask for one overlooking the pool and patio.

In addition to a complimentary hot breakfast buffet, there is an evening social from Monday through Thursday with free beer, wine, and light snacks or meals.

3566 Piedmont Rd. (btw. Peachtree and Roswell roads), Atlanta, GA 30305. © **800/225-5466** or 404/365-0001. Fax 404/365-9888. www.homewoodsuites1.hilton.com. 92 units. $169 1-bedroom suite; $219 2-bedroom suite. AE, DC, DISC, MC, V. Free parking. MARTA: Buckhead; bus 59 stops in front of hotel. Pets accepted with $100 nonrefundable deposit. **Amenities:** Shuttle service (3-mile radius); concierge; exercise room; small heated outdoor pool. *In room:* TV, fridge, free Internet, kitchen, MP3 docking station.

Residence Inn by Marriott Atlanta Buckhead ★★ ☺ This home away from home was designed to meet the needs of travelers making extended visits, but it's great even if you're spending a single night. Staying here is like having your own apartment, with a private entrance and a large, fully equipped kitchen. Spacious accommodations include comfortable living-room areas; about half the suites have working fireplaces (during the winter, logs are available through the front desk). The most luxurious units are the duplex penthouses with vaulted ceilings, full dining-room/office areas, two standard-size bathrooms, and living-room fireplaces. Two rooms have been modified for travelers with disabilities. The hotel offers a free hot breakfast buffet daily and cocktail-hour parties Monday through Thursday. The location is good, near several excellent restaurants and not far from shopping and nightlife. There's a free shuttle service within a 3-mile radius.

2960 Piedmont Rd. NE (just south of Pharr Rd.), Atlanta, GA 30305. © **800/331-3131** or 404/239-0677. Fax 404/262-9638. www.marriott.com. 136 units. $159 studio suite; $169 1-bedroom suite; $219 2-bedroom suite. Discount for extended stay. AE, DC, DISC, MC, V. Free parking. MARTA: Bus 5 from Lindbergh station stops at Pharr and Piedmont roads, about half a block away. Pets accepted with $100 nonrefundable deposit. **Amenities:** Shuttle service (3-mile radius); fitness center; Jacuzzi; outdoor pool. *In room:* TV, fridge, hair dryer, Internet, kitchen.

TownePlace Suites by Marriott Atlanta Buckhead ★ This good-value choice caters to both business and leisure travelers, with its extended-stay, all-suite layout. Attractively furnished, large suites include full kitchens with all the appliances you need for cooking and eating. Though you are in the heart of busy Buckhead and won't need for a thing, this property is still only 4 miles from downtown Atlanta and all the attractions offered there. If you don't feel like navigating yourself, hop the hotel's free shuttle to the MARTA station and don't worry about traffic. Five rooms are accessible to travelers with disabilities. There isn't a restaurant on the property, but rates include a deluxe continental breakfast. Shuttle van service is within a 3-mile radius of the hotel.

820 Sidney Marcus Blvd. (btw. Lenox and Piedmont roads), Atlanta, GA 30324. © **404/949-4000.** Fax 404/949-4810. www.marriott.com. 142 units. $119–$174 suite. AE, DC, DISC, MC, V. Free parking. MARTA: Lindbergh; bus 39 stops in front of hotel. Pets accepted with $75 nonrefundable deposit. **Amenities:** Shuttle service (3-mile radius); small fitness center; large outdoor pool. *In room:* TV, fridge, hair dryer, kitchen, free Wi-Fi.

Moderate

Beverly Hills Inn ★★   British owner/host Mit Amin offers warm hospitality in this charming B&B, housed in a former women's apartment building from the 1920s. Located on a tree-lined residential street, this is a good spot for an extended stay, especially for families that prefer a B&B atmosphere. On the first floor is a parlor/library where a decanter of port is available all day. Another library is downstairs in the garden room, which has a sky-lit conservatory area filled with plants.

Spacious bedrooms are cheerful and attractive, decorated in a mix of antiques and collectibles. All are equipped with kitchenettes, and there's a private balcony through the French doors. A supermarket is within easy walking distance, should you want to cook in your room, though you may be tempted by the several good restaurants close by. Rates include a deluxe continental breakfast, and you'll also find a half-bottle of burgundy in your room upon arrival. Within walking distance to the Governor's Mansion, the Atlanta History Center, and the Swan House.

65 Sheridan Dr. NE (just off Peachtree Rd.), Atlanta, GA 30305. ℂ **800/331-8520** or 404/233-8520. Fax 404/233-8659. www.beverlyhillsinn.com. 18 units. $129 double; $149 balcony suite; $169 2-bedroom suite; $169 whirlpool suite. AE, DC, DISC, MC, V. Free parking. MARTA: Bus 23 stops at the corner of Peachtree St. and Sheridan Dr. Pets accepted with $125 nonrefundable deposit. **Amenities:** Access to nearby health club; fax/computer. *In room:* TV, kitchenette.

Country Inns & Suites   This hotel caters to business and leisure travelers who need a suite and are more interested in spending their money on a fabulous dinner in one of Buckhead's many restaurants than on lodging. Each unit has a bed, a pullout sofa, and a kitchen with full-size appliances. Studios have one TV; suites have two. Outdoor grills are available. A nice touch is the guest supply closet from which visitors can get replacement toiletries and towels whenever they want. Five rooms are accessible to travelers with disabilities. Free coffee and cookies are available 24 hours a day. Rates include breakfast. There's complimentary van service between the hotel and the MARTA Lindbergh station.

800 Sidney Marcus Blvd. (btw. Lenox and Piedmont roads), Atlanta, GA 30324. ℂ 800/596-2375 or 404/949-4000. Fax 404/949-4010. www.countryinns.com/hotels/gabuckhd. 80 units. $119–$139 double; $169–$189 suite. Rates include continental breakfast. Lower rates for extended stays. AE, DC, DISC, MC, V. Free parking. MARTA: Lindbergh; bus 39 stops in front of hotel. **Amenities:** Shuttle service; concierge; fitness center; outdoor pool. *In room:* TV, fridge, hair dryer, free Wi-Fi.

Courtyard by Marriott Atlanta Buckhead ★ 🦺   This provides a lot of bang for the buck. It's a favorite among business travelers, but anyone will enjoy it. The Courtyard has a terrific location, near everything that Buckhead has to offer, and within 2 blocks of the Atlanta Financial Center, the Lenox Square and Phipps Plaza shopping malls, and a MARTA station.

The rooms are large and bright, and the suites—perfect for families in town for a few days—come with a full-size pullout couch. Some units are equipped with whirlpool tubs that surprisingly are located in the bedroom rather than in the bathroom. Ask for one of the end rooms, which are a little larger than the others. Eight units are equipped for travelers with disabilities.

3332 Peachtree Rd. NE (btw. Lenox and Piedmont roads), Atlanta, GA 30326. ℂ **404/869-0818.** Fax 404/869-0939. www.marriott.com. 181 units. From $109 double; from $119 suite. AE, DC, DISC, MC, V. Valet parking $21; self-parking $18. MARTA: Buckhead. **Amenities:** Restaurant; bar; shuttle service (1-mile radius); exercise room; small heated indoor pool; room service. *In room:* TV, hair dryer, minibar, MP3 docking station, Wi-Fi.

Doubletree Hotel Atlanta Buckhead ★ Located within the Tower Place complex and designed with the business traveler in mind, this is also a good choice for leisure travelers, as it's so convenient to both Lenox Mall and Phipps Plaza. It's the first Buckhead hotel to practice green and sustainable initiatives. You'll be welcomed with Doubletree's signature freshly baked chocolate-chip cookies before you go up to your comfortable guest room, outfitted with an ergonomic work area and a large desk. All standard rooms come with a rich marble bathroom and an armchair with ottoman—perfect for putting your feet up after you've shopped, explored, or worked all day. The large units with king-size beds are especially desirable; other units are of average size. Suites offer parlor rooms with spacious sitting areas, leather couches, and a full dining-room ensemble for eight.

3342 Peachtree Rd. NE (btw. Lenox and Piedmont roads), Atlanta, GA 30326. ℂ **800/833-TREE** (8733) or 404/231-1234. Fax 404/231-5236. www.doubletree1.hilton.com. 230 units. $139–$209 double. AE, DC, DISC, MC, V. Valet parking $25; self-parking $20. MARTA: Buckhead. **Amenities:** Restaurant; bar; airport shuttle; free shuttle service (3-mile radius); fitness center; room service. *In room:* TV, hair dryer, Wi-Fi.

Fairfield Inn & Suites Buckhead A stone's throw from several excellent restaurants and close to everything else in upscale Buckhead, this is an economical choice for business and leisure visitors who are more interested in location than in luxury. There's nothing fancy about the Fairfield Inn except for the surrounding neighborhood. The large rooms are well maintained and pleasant, with high ceilings. If you're in town for an extended stay, try to book one of the suites, which have fridges, microwaves, 32-inch TVs, DVD players, and CD players, along with king-size beds and sofa beds. *Tip:* Rooms near the elevators and ice machines can be a little noisy, so ask for one away from those locations for a better night's sleep.

3092 Piedmont Rd. NE (btw. Peachtree and E. Paces Ferry roads), Atlanta, GA 30326. ℂ **404/846-0900.** Fax 404/467-9878. www.marriott.com. 103 units. $109 double; $139 suite. AE, DC, DISC, MC, V. Free parking. MARTA: Bus 5 from Lindbergh station. **Amenities:** Fitness center; Jacuzzi; small indoor pool; free Wi-Fi. *In room:* TV, hair dryer, free Internet.

Holiday Inn Express Hotel & Suites ★ ☺ ✦ This is a good choice if you're looking for a great Buckhead location at less than the usual Buckhead price. It's within walking distance of several fine restaurants (Pricci is across the street; the Atlanta Fish Market is a few blocks away) and close to Buckhead nightlife. There's also good shopping in the area, as well as a park nearby for the kids. Accommodations include spacious one- and two-bedroom suites with a separate living room, queen-size beds, and a vanity/dressing area with sink. Six suites are equipped for travelers with disabilities. The complimentary hot breakfast buffet is served in a bright room next to the lobby. Evening guest receptions are held Tuesday through Thursday. Complimentary shuttle service is within a 3-mile radius and to Lindbergh MARTA station.

505 Pharr Rd. (about a block off Piedmont Rd.), Atlanta, GA 30305. ℂ **800/972-2404** or 404/262-7880. Fax 404/262-3734. www.ichotelsgroup.com. 87 units. $119–$127 double; $136–$157 suite. AE, DISC, MC, V. Free parking. MARTA: Bus 5 from Lindbergh station stops at Pharr and Piedmont roads, about a block away. Pets accepted. **Amenities:** Shuttle service (3-mile radius); exercise room; Jacuzzi; heated outdoor pool. *In room:* TV, fridge, hair dryer, Internet, kitchen.

Hyatt Place Buckhead ★ ✦ This rather plain-Jane all-suite hotel is the best bargain buy in the heart of Buckhead, and rates include a continental breakfast buffet. The 24/7 Guest Kitchen offers made-to-order snacks and entrees. Accommodations here are more like a studio or efficiency than a typical suite, with the "bedroom" separated from the rest of the unit by a low wall. A pullout couch offers some extra sleeping space. A complimentary shuttle runs within a 3-mile radius of the hotel.

3242 Peachtree Rd. NE (at Piedmont Rd.), Atlanta, GA 30305. (Ⓒ) **877/774-6467** or 404/869-6161. Fax 404/869-6093. www.amerisuites.com. 172 units. $124–$189 suite. AE, DC, DISC, MC, V. Free parking. MARTA: Buckhead. **Amenities:** Shuttle service (3-mile radius); exercise room; small heated outdoor pool. *In room:* TV/VCR in most units, fridge, hair dryer, minibar, MP3 docking station, free Wi-Fi.

VIRGINIA-HIGHLAND & INMAN PARK

Virginia-Highland is a marvelous choice for visitors, as it's within easy walking distance of shops, galleries, and restaurants. The only problem is that there are few accommodations available because this is a mostly residential area. Nearby Inman Park, though not as convenient to attractions, is equally charming. You'll find the following properties on the "Where to Stay in Midtown" map (p. 57).

Moderate

King-Keith House Bed & Breakfast   The lovely 1890 King-Keith home, built by hardware magnate George King, is in Inman Park, a neighborhood of Victorian homes that is on the National Register of Historic Places. Built in the Queen Anne style, the B&B boasts 12-foot ceilings and carved fireplaces, plus a huge wraparound porch. Beds range from double to king-size, and each room has a private bathroom. The large downstairs suite has a private entrance and sitting room with an extra twin bed. The one-room cottage, which is very spacious, has a king-size bed, sitting area, two-person Jacuzzi, and fireplace. There is a 2-night minimum for reservations.

Coffee is delivered to your room every morning, and the complete breakfast might include French toast, homemade pancakes, or eggs cooked to order. The property is not far from the funky Little Five Points commercial district, the Martin Luther King, Jr., National Historic Site, the Jimmy Carter Presidential Library and Museum, and several restaurants.

889 Edgewood Ave. NE (at Waverly Way), Atlanta, GA 30307. (Ⓒ) **800/728-3879** or 404/688-7330. Fax 404/584-8408. www.kingkeith.com. 5 units, 1 cottage. $120–$175 double; $185 suite; $225 cottage. $20 per additional adult and child over 10. No charge for up to 2 infants or toddlers. Rates include full breakfast. AE, DISC, MC, V. Free parking. MARTA: 2 blocks from Inman Park station. *In room:* TV, free Internet.

DECATUR/LAKE CLAIRE

Originally a streetcar suburb of Atlanta, the quaint and quiet Lake Claire neighborhood is becoming a popular residential area. Don't waste your time looking for the namesake lake—it doesn't exist.

Moderate

Laurel Hill Bed & Breakfast   This B&B is actually two individual houses and named for the laurel that grows wild on the property. The venture is the result of a lot of hard work by innkeeper Dave Hinman, who lived in one of the homes for about 15 years. When the house next door—a mirror image of his own—became available, he purchased it and renovated both English Tudors to create this comfortably furnished bed-and-breakfast. Winding paths lead up through the property to secluded and tranquil seating areas—perfect places for reflecting quietly and enjoying a relaxing moment.

Individually prepared full American breakfasts are served each morning in intimate dining rooms on an open schedule, beginning with the first request and ending with a relaxed last call at 11am. Baked goods, spring water, coffee, and tea are available throughout the day. The dining environment is laid-back, enjoyable, and a good opportunity to interact with other guests, but you can also request to have a special private dinner. (See p. 57 for the "Where to Stay in Midtown" map.)

1992 McClendon Ave., Atlanta, GA 30307. © **404/377-3217.** Fax 404/262-7618. www.laurelhillbandb. com. 5 units. $109–$179 double. Rates include hot breakfast. AE, DISC, MC, V. Free parking. MARTA: Eastlake Rail station is half a mile away. *In room:* A/C, TV, hair dryer.

Inexpensive

Garden House Bed & Breakfast   Decatur is one of the fastest-growing areas in Atlanta, but it's still severely lacking in places to stay. This bed-and-breakfast, while offering only one suite (there's another bedroom available in a pinch), is a delightful, homey lodging owned by Decatur natives Rhoda and Doug Joyner, who have enjoyed more than 66 years in this city. The suite features a sitting room with a desk and workspace, perfect for getting some work done, reading, or watching TV. A pullout couch accommodates parents traveling with children, and a crib is available. The suite also includes a large private bath.

Guests are invited to relax on the spacious screened porch overlooking gardens and a pond with a waterfall. Refreshments, a stocked library, a smoke-free environment, and fresh flowers all add to the experience. The hosts will cook basically whatever their guests prefer, from a full southern breakfast—with eggs, grits, sausage, and biscuits—to a more gourmet selection of blintzes, quiche, and home-baked walnut wheat bread. They're also able to accommodate special health requirements, such as low-fat or low-sodium diets.

135 Garden Lane, Decatur, GA 30030. © **404/377-3057.** www.gardenhousebedandbreakfastdecatur. com. 1 unit. $100 double; $89 double for 2 or more nights. Rates include full breakfast. MC, V. Free parking. MARTA: Decatur. *In room:* TV, free Wi-Fi.

STONE MOUNTAIN PARK

Stone Mountain Park, just 16 miles east of downtown Atlanta, is a recreation area with 3,200 acres of lakes and wooded parkland. It's a major tourist destination, visited by more than four million people annually. *Note:* There's a $10 parking fee upon entering the park.

Expensive

Marriott Evergreen Conference Resort ★ ☺   Geared primarily to business groups, Evergreen is also a good choice for vacationing families that want to take advantage of the activities in Stone Mountain Park. A turreted stucco lakefront "castle," Evergreen is nestled in a fragrant pine forest. Each of the large, luxuriously appointed rooms has a private balcony or veranda, and lake-view rooms are available. The suites boast a lovely, spacious bedroom; however, those who wind up on the uncomfortable pullout couch in the living room may be in for a resless night.

4021 Lakeview Dr., Stone Mountain Park, Stone Mountain, GA 30086. © **770/879-9900.** Fax 770/465-3264. www.evergreenresort.com. 336 units. From $179 double; $349 suite. AE, DC, DISC, MC, V. Free valet parking. **Amenities:** Restaurant; bar; airport shuttle; concierge; fitness center; Jacuzzi; 3 pools (indoor/outdoor/kiddie); room service; 2 18-hole golf courses; 16 tennis courts. *In room:* TV, fridge, hair dryer, Wi-Fi.

Stone Mountain Inn ★ ☺ ✐   This charming inn, across the street from the tennis venue built for the 1996 Olympics, is managed by Marriott and housed in a two-story, white-colonnade brick building that wraps around a central courtyard. Rooms are lovely, featuring Chippendale-reproduction furnishings; most have large vanity/dressing areas and spacious parlors. Honeymoon suites have king-size, four-poster beds. Almost all of the units have courtyard-facing balconies or patios with rocking chairs. Five rooms are accessible to travelers with disabilities. Tickets for all park attractions are sold at the inn.

1058 Robert E. Lee Dr., Stone Mountain Park, Stone Mountain, GA 30086. ✆ **770/469-3311.** Fax 770/876-5009. www.marriott.com. 92 units. $119–$139 double (rates vary seasonally). AE, DC, MC, V. Free parking. **Amenities:** Restaurant; shuttle service; outdoor pool. *In room:* TV, fridge, hair dryer, Wi-Fi.

A Campground

Stone Mountain Family Campground   Nestled in the woods, this large campground with sections for pop-ups, RVs (hookups available), and tents is a great place to stay. The area has many sites overlooking the lake, especially in the tent section. All sites have barbecue grills, and picnic tables are scattered throughout the area. Public facilities include a dining pavilion, playgrounds, laundries, and showers. The park's beach is close by, and the swimming pool is new. Pets are permitted if kept on a leash. This is a popular place, so be sure to call ahead. You may reserve a spot up to 90 days before you stay; all reservations must be made at least 1 week in advance.

Stone Mountain Park, P.O. Box 778, Stone Mountain, GA 30086. ✆ **800/385-9807** or 770/498-5710. Fax 770/413-5082. www.stonemountainpark.com. $25–$65 per night, depending on type of site and time of year. Rates cover 2 adults and 4 children; additional guests $2 per night. Children 11 and under stay free. AE, DISC, MC, V. Pets accepted. **Amenities:** Outdoor pool; barbecue grills; showers.

DRUID HILLS/EMORY UNIVERSITY

Though it's not a happening section of town in terms of restaurants or attractions, this area, east of Midtown and Buckhead, offers good value for your hotel dollar. And if you have a car, the lodgings listed below are only about a 10-minute drive from the center of things.

Moderate

Courtyard by Marriott Atlanta Executive Park/Emory   This limited-service, moderately priced lodging is slightly outside the usual tourist areas, but it's close to town and convenient to I-85—making it popular with business travelers. Don't expect a spartan, no-frills atmosphere; accommodations feature large desks and sizable dressing-room areas. Suites have full-size pullout sofas, extra phones, and TVs. Eight rooms are accessible to guests with disabilities. There's also airport shuttle service.

1236 Executive Park Dr. (off N. Druid Hills Rd.), Atlanta, GA 30329. ✆ **404/728-0708.** Fax 404/636-4019. www.marriott.com. 145 units. $139 double; $169 suite. AE, DC, DISC, MC, V. Free parking. MARTA: 3 miles from Lindbergh station. **Amenities:** Restaurant; bar; airport shuttle; exercise room; Jacuzzi; outdoor pool; room service. *In room:* TV, hair dryer, free Internet.

Emory Inn   Inspired by the architectural design of Frank Lloyd Wright, this delightful hotel, owned by Emory University, is an approved Atlanta "green" hotel and popular with visitors to Emory and the nearby Centers for Disease Control and Prevention. Rooms, furnished with Early American–style knotty-pine pieces, are attractively decorated. Nine units are accessible to travelers with disabilities. Guests enjoy free use of a vast fitness complex on the university campus, with a heated indoor pool, 12 tennis courts lit for night play, basketball courts, indoor track, racquetball, and a full complement of Nautilus equipment. There's also complimentary shuttle service to the campus and hospital, and an airport shuttle on request.

1641 Clifton Rd. NE (btw. Briarcliff and N. Decatur roads), Atlanta, GA 30329. © **800/933-6679** or 404/712-6700. Fax 404/712-6701. www.emoryconferencecenter.com. 107 units. From $149 double. AE, DC, DISC, MC, V. Free parking. MARTA: Bus 6 Emory stops in front of the hotel. **Amenities:** Restaurant; airport/campus/hospital shuttle; access to campus fitness complex w/heated indoor pool; Jacuzzi; outdoor pool; room service. *In room:* TV, hair dryer, Internet.

DULUTH

Located in Gwinnett County, one of the fastest-growing counties in the country, Duluth manages to retain its small-town charm just minutes from the hustle and bustle of the big city. You'll find lots of shopping here, including the Mall of Georgia and Gwinnett Place Mall. Duluth's Buford Highway is also home to an incredible variety of ethnic restaurants, which draw diners from Atlanta looking for everything from Korean to Vietnamese to Caribbean cuisine.

Moderate

Courtyard by Marriott Atlanta Gwinnett Mall   Rooms here are nicely appointed with cherry furnishings, including a dining table and workspace. Both rooms and bathrooms are of average size. Some units have a patio overlooking the pool area. The Courtyard Cafe, an on-site restaurant, serves an affordable breakfast buffet each morning. For snacks or beverages, the Market is always open. The property is in close proximity to the Mall of Georgia on I-85.

3550 Venture Pkwy., Duluth, GA 30096. © **770/476-4666.** Fax 770/623-0198. www.marriott.com. 146 units. From $94 double; from $124 suite. AE, MC, V. Free parking. **Amenities:** Restaurant; fitness center; Jacuzzi; outdoor pool. *In room:* TV, fridge, hair dryer, Internet.

Inexpensive

Candlewood Suites   Perfect for families or business travelers on the go, Candlewood Suites boasts spacious rooms. An oversize workspace doubles as the kitchen table, dividing the full-size kitchen from the living room. Kick back in a comfy recliner and watch a DVD—which you can borrow free of charge from the front desk—while you munch on popcorn purchased from the on-site convenience store (which is open 24 hr. a day and operates on the honor system). Even the bathrooms are big here. If the weather is nice, you can cook dinner outside, on the grill under the gazebo, for a change of pace.

3665 Shackleford Rd., Duluth, GA 30096. © **678/380-0414.** Fax 678/380-0413. www.ichotelsgroup. com. 122 units. $60–$93 suite. AE, MC, V. Free parking. Pets accepted with $75 nonrefundable fee for stays of 14 days or less. **Amenities:** Fitness center. *In room:* TV/DVD, fridge, hair dryer, Internet, kitchen.

AIRPORT

There are more than three dozen hotels near the airport, most of them well-known chains. If you're flying out very early or in very late, a room in this area can be quite convenient. Although most airport-hotel guests are business travelers, it's not out of the question for leisure travelers to choose accommodations here. Weekend rates are often very low, and many of the hotels offer free shuttles to the Airport MARTA station, making it easy to reach other parts of the city. Buckhead, for instance, is about 35 minutes away by MARTA rail. The hotels listed below are three of the finest, but there are numerous other chains in the area.

Expensive

Hilton Atlanta Airport ★   Mercifully, this airport hotel is not under the normal flight pattern. That, and its triple-paned windows, makes it quieter than many hotels, especially the less expensive ones. (For the *most* quiet location, ask for a room with a city view.) The rooms are a good size, with tasteful contemporary decor and one king-size or two double beds. The bathrooms have generous vanities, though the sound of the toilet flush will make you think you're already on the plane. For an excellent value, ask for one of the Executive Corner rooms, which are only $20 more than the standard units. They're twice as big, though, and are spacious enough to accommodate a sofa and two easy chairs in the sitting area. Suites are quite large and luxurious. Twenty-five of the standard rooms have been modified for guests with disabilities. There's a complimentary airport shuttle.

1031 Virginia Ave. (at I-85, exit 73A), Atlanta, GA 30354. ✆ **800/HILTONS** (445-8667) or 404/767-9000. Fax 404/768-0185. www.hilton.com. 503 units. $159–$189 double. Rates may be lower during summer, higher during special events. Weekend packages available. AE, DC, DISC, MC, V. Valet parking $15; self-parking $10. **Amenities:** 2 restaurants; sports bar; free airport shuttle; state-of-the-art fitness center; Jacuzzi; outdoor pool; small indoor heated pool; room service; lit tennis court. *In room:* TV, hair dryer, minibar, Internet.

Renaissance Concourse Hotel ★   If you're an airplane buff or you just travel with one, this is the ticket. Built on the site of an old airport terminal in 1992, the Renaissance is literally on the edge of the runway. Each of the renovated guest rooms opens onto the beautiful 11-story interior atrium. Half the rooms also open to the runway, so you can step out on your balcony and watch the planes take off and land; on the other side, rooms have views of the downtown skyline. It sounds noisy, but the soundproofing is more than adequate, and back in your room, you'll hardly know you're at the airport. The rooms themselves are luxuriously decorated, light, open, and quite large. Twenty rooms have been specially modified for travelers with disabilities; 19 have roll-in showers. Guests use the complimentary airport shuttle.

1 Hartsfield Center Pkwy., Atlanta, GA 30354. ✆ **404/209-9999.** Fax 404/305-2343. www.marriott.com. 387 units. From $149 double; from $189 executive level. AE, DC, DISC, MC, V. Valet parking $19; self-parking $11. **Amenities:** Restaurant; free airport shuttle; concierge; fitness center; Jacuzzi; medium outdoor pool; large indoor heated pool; room service; sauna. *In room:* TV, minibar, hair dryer, Internet.

Sheraton Gateway Hotel Atlanta Airport ★   If you're looking for convenience when flying in or out of Atlanta, this is a great location from which to base yourself. Half a mile from the airport—and just 10 minutes from downtown—Sheraton Gateway is fresh from a multimillion-dollar renovation and very comfy Sheraton Sweet

Sleeper beds. The double rooms and bathrooms are of average size. Grab a meal at the 1900 Grill or the 1900 Bar, both serving tasty American fare. Amenities here are similar to those at nearby properties, including AmeriSuites, Hampton Inn, and Holiday Inn Express. There's a complimentary airport shuttle.

1900 Sullivan Rd., Atlanta, GA 30337. © **770/997-1100.** Fax 770/991-5906. www.starwoodhotels.com. 395 units. $134–$184 double. AE, MC, V. Free parking. **Amenities:** Restaurant; bar; fitness center; Jacuzzi; indoor/outdoor pools; room service. *In room:* TV, hair dryer, Internet.

SOUTH OF TOWN

Expensive

Serenbe Southern Country Inn ★★ ☺ 👜 This sustainable community retreat is on 284 acres of farmland, 32 miles southwest of Atlanta, amid rolling meadows, horse pastures, verdant woodlands, and fields of sage. Children play in a treehouse, pet the baby animals, or feed the chickens. Activities include croquet, occasional hayrides, marshmallow roasts around a bonfire, fishing from a well-stocked lake, hiking along trails dotted with streams and waterfalls, and moonlit canoe rides. The "town" includes residential properties and rental lodging and boasts shopping, a bakery, and a restaurant.

The 94-year-old main house includes the dining room, where you'll enjoy a hearty breakfast—perhaps cheese grits, baked ham, fresh eggs, fried green tomatoes, and biscuits. The rooms—all with private bathrooms, one with a Jacuzzi tub—are charming and unpretentious, with unique features such as knotty-pine floors strewn with rag rugs, antique furnishings, a bed piled high with decorative pillows, and lace-curtained windows. One room has been modified for guests with disabilities. The lake house has four bedrooms with private entrances and private bathrooms. There's also a communal kitchen with an unstocked fridge, along with a barbecue grill. Rates include a full farm breakfast, afternoon tea, and bedtime sweets.

The Serenbe community also offers lodging in a variety of spaces, from a single room in the inn to a one-bedroom loft apartment in the Serenbe Community to a four-bedroom lake house.

10950 Hutcheson Ferry Rd., Palmetto, GA 30268. © **770/463-2610.** Fax 770/463-4472. www.serenbe. com. 18 units. $130–$235 room at inn; $190–$360 cottage; $255–$395 community properties. Rates include full breakfast. AE, MC, V. Free parking. Call ahead for directions. **Amenities:** Babysitting; bikes; children's programs; exercise room; Jacuzzi; pool. *In room:* TV, hair dryer, Internet, kitchenette.

WHERE TO DINE

The down economy thinned Atlanta's restaurant offerings a bit, but like that famous phoenix that is the symbol of this southern city, things have risen once again. Unfortunately, some longtime favorites are among the deceased, including City Grill, the Dining Room at Ritz-Carlton, and Pano's & Paul's—all high-end eateries. But where some culinary efforts have fallen, others have moved in to offer the latest in dining crazes such as gourmet burgers, street vendor foods, and that still-strong farm-to-table movement.

Atlanta's contributions to gastronomy were once mostly limited to Coca-Cola and Varsity hot dogs. Not so today. In the last decade, the dining scene has exploded, and Atlanta has emerged as a sophisticated restaurant town, where establishments have veered away from uninventive American fare and inauthentic down-home southern cooking (happily, there are still lots of places to feast on *authentic* down-home southern cooking).

Innovative chefs, who once left Atlanta for the great food capitals, have brought their expertise and ideas back to the New South. As a result, there's now a little bit of everything available—from all around the world. You can munch on pierogi in East Atlanta, nibble fragrant Thai basil rolls in Virginia-Highland, dig into *osso buco* in Buckhead, and so on. There's French cuisine as authentic as any you'll find on the Left Bank, and Italian pasta that tastes like it came from Naples.

The Colonnade and Mary Mac's Tea Room, two bastions of tradition, still turn out some of the best southern food you'll ever put in your mouth, but the current trend in many kitchens is to take heirloom southern recipes and give them a contemporary twist. So, pork chops might be stuffed with eggplant and andouille sausage, collard greens sautéed and seasoned with balsamic vinegar, and comfy, familiar grits spiked with Stilton cheese.

The audience for all these culinary concoctions is huge. Atlantans love to eat out, spending half their annual food budget on dining away from home. The debut of a new restaurant is more eagerly awaited than the opening of a new play, and Atlantans avidly peruse the local newspapers to find out about the hottest names in the food game.

Restaurants listed below are divided first by area, then by price, using the following guide: **Very Expensive:** more than $30 per dinner main course; **Expensive:** $20 to $30 per dinner main course; **Moderate:** $10 to $20 per dinner main course; **Inexpensive:** less than $10 per dinner main course.

Valet parking is listed where applicable.

RESTAURANTS BY CUISINE

ASIAN
Bluepointe ★★★ ($$$$, p. 87)
Doc Chey's Noodle House ($, p. 105)
Spice Market ★ ($$$, p. 83)

BAKERY/CAFE
Corner Café/Buckhead Bread
Company ★ ($, p. 99)

BARBECUE
Fat Matt's Rib Shack ($$, p. 96)

BRAZILIAN
Fogo de Chão ★ ($$$$, p. 90)

CHINESE
Little Szechuan ($$, p. 110)

CONTEMPORARY SOUTHERN
Horseradish Grill ★ ($$$, p. 93)
Restaurant Eugene ★ ($$$, p. 95)
South City Kitchen ★ ($$$$, p. 80)

CONTINENTAL
Swan Coach House ($$, p. 98)

COUNTRY FRENCH
Floataway Café ★★ ($$$, p. 107)

ECLECTIC
Aria ★★ ($$$$, p. 87)
R. Thomas Deluxe Grill ★★
($$, p. 98)

EUROPEAN
Ecco ★★ ($$, p. 83)

EUROPEAN PROVINCIAL
Babette's Café ★★ ($$, p. 102)

FRENCH
Anis Café & Bistro ★ ($$$, p. 92)
Au Pied de Cochon ★★ ($$$, p. 93)
French American Brasserie ★★
($$$, p. 78)

GASTROPUB
Brick Store Pub ($, p. 109)
Leon's Full Service ★ ($$, p. 107)

GREEK
Athens Pizza House ($, p. 109)
Kyma ★★ ($$$, p. 93)

ITALIAN
Floataway Café ★★ ($$$, p. 107)
NEO ★ ($$$$, p. 91)
Pasta Da Pulcinella ★ ($$, p. 84)
Pacci Ristorante ★★★ ($$$, p. 82)
Pasta Vino ($$, p. 98)
Pricci ★ ($$, p. 98)
Sotto Sotto ★★ ($$, p. 104)
Thirsty Dog Tavern ★ ($$$, p. 95)
Veni Vidi Vici ★★ ($$, p. 85)

KOREAN
Han il Kwan ★ ($$, p. 110)
Hankook Taqueria ★ ($, p. 86)

MEDITERRANEAN
Anis Café & Bistro ★ ($$$, p. 92)

MEXICAN
Raging Burrito ($, p. 110)
Willy's Mexicana Grill ★ ($, p. 79)

NEW AMERICAN
Bacchanalia ★★★ ($$$$, p. 79)
Bluepointe ★★★ ($$$$, p. 87)
Buckhead Diner ★★ ($$, p. 96)
Canoe ★★ ($$$, p. 106)
Craft ★★ ($$$$, p. 90)
Flying Biscuit Cafe ★ ($, p. 105)
Lobby at Twelve ★★ ($$, p. 83)
ONE Midtown Kitchen ★ ($$, p. 104)
Paces 88 ($$$, p. 94)
Toulouse ★ ($$, p. 99)
TWO Urban Licks ★ ($$$, p. 100)
Warren City Club ★ ($$, p. 105)
Woodfire Grill ★★ ($$$, p. 95)

PIZZA
Antico Pizza Napoletana ★★
($, p. 85)
Athens Pizza House ($, p. 109)
Fellini's Pizza ($, p. 100)
Pasta Vino ($$, p. 98)

KEY TO ABBREVIATIONS:
$$$$** = Very Expensive   **$$$** = Expensive   **$$** = Moderate   **$ = Inexpensive

SEAFOOD

Atlanta Fish Market ★★ ($$$, p. 92)
Chops Lobster Bar ★★ ($$$$, p. 88)
New York Prime ★★ ($$$$, p. 91)
The Palm ★★ ($$$$, p. 91)
Prime ★★ ($$$, p. 95)

SOUTHERN/REGIONAL

Colonnade ★ ($$, p. 96)
Mary Mac's Tea Room ★ ($$, p. 84)
Watershed ★ ($$, p. 108)
Wisteria ($$$, p. 102)

SOUTHWESTERN

Nava ★★ ($$$, p. 94)
Taqueria del Sol ★ ($, p. 86)

SPANISH

La Fonda Latina ($, p. 100)

STEAK

BLT Steak ★★★ ($$$$, p. 77)
Bone's ★★★ ($$$$, p. 88)
Chops Lobster Bar ★★ ($$$$, p. 88)
New York Prime ★★ ($$$$, p. 91)
The Palm ★★ ($$$$, p. 91)
Prime ★★ ($$$, p. 95)

SUSHI/JAPANESE

Atlanta Fish Market ★★ ($$$, p. 92)
Magic Fingers Sushi ★★ ($$, p. 84)
Prime ★★ ($$$, p. 95)

TAPAS

Pura Vida ($$, p. 104)

THAI

Surin of Thailand ★ ($$, p. 104)
Tamarind Seed Thai Bistro ★★
  ($$, p. 85)
Thai Chili ★ ($$, p. 108)

TRADITIONAL AMERICAN

Blue Ridge Grill ★ ($$$$, p. 87)
Bone's ★★★ ($$$$, p. 88)
Buckhead Diner ★★ ($$, p. 96)
George's Restaurant and Bar ($, p. 106)
Houston's ★ ($$, p. 97)
Murphy's ★★★ ($$, p. 102)
OK Café ($$, p. 97)
Swan Coach House ($$, p. 98)
The Varsity ★ ($, p. 78)
The Vortex ($, p. 86)
Woody's Famous Philadelphia
  Cheesesteaks ($, p. 106)

DOWNTOWN

Your restaurant choices in downtown Atlanta range from the fabulous French American Brasserie to the world's largest drive-in, the Varsity.

Very Expensive

BLT Steak ★★★ STEAK   Meat eaters were excited when this posh chain made its way into Hotlanta via the W Atlanta Downtown hotel. Not your average hotel eatery, BLT Steak offers top-notch beef selected by Chef de Cuisine Jean Luc Mongodin. Cuts are naturally aged, broiled at 1,700°F, buttered, and served with a variety of sauces. But don't let the name fool you: BLT Steak stands for Bistro Laurent Tourondel, and its French bistro side shines. Black cod, roasted Maine lobster, duck, and lamb are all available, as is a generous offering of sides. Don't be concerned that trying to have something for everyone means nothing is special; it's all good. The raw bar menu is a great place to start, with the tuna tartar an excellent choice. A selection of East and West Coast oysters is also a good bet. And make sure your server brings you some of the light-as-air popovers.

45 Ivan Allen Jr. Blvd. 🕐 **404/577-7601.** www.bltsteak.com. Reservations recommended for dinner. Lunch items $14–$30; dinner items $16–$85. AE, MC, V. Daily 6:30–10pm. MARTA: Civic Center.

☺ family-friendly RESTAURANTS

Doc Chey's Noodle House (p. 105) This casual neighborhood favorite has two special children's entrees, but there are also several other rice and noodle dishes that will appeal to the younger set.

Fellini's Pizza (p. 100) The New York–style pizza served here is a treat that will please everyone, and it's available by the slice. Salads are also superb, and you can sit outside if you choose.

Houston's (p. 97) There are always lots of families in Houston's, where there's prime rib for the grown-ups, burgers for the kids, and reasonable prices that won't bust the budget. It's casual, but still a good place to take the family for a special occasion.

OK Café (p. 97) OK Café's classic comfort food and jukebox are sure to please kids of all ages.

Pasta Vino (p. 98) Do kids like this place? One 3-year-old from the neighborhood insisted on having his birthday party here so he could have his favorite food—a slice of white-cheese pizza with pesto. There's plenty for parents, too, including fresh veal, seafood, and excellent lasagna.

Thai Chili (p. 108) While there isn't a children's menu here, the restaurant is very kid friendly and makes families feel right at home, with dishes cooked to order and without any spice at all (if your kids can't take the heat).

The Varsity (p. 78) The greasy feasts at the world's largest drive-in restaurant are big kid-pleasers.

Woody's Famous Philadelphia Cheese-steaks (p. 106) A great stop with kids in tow, whether you're coming from a day at nearby Piedmont Park or headed that way with your sandwiches. The menu is simple and prices are reasonable, making selections easy. If the cheesesteak is too much for your little one to handle, they have great hot dogs as well. Kids also love the orange freezes.

Expensive

French American Brasserie ★★ FRENCH   FAB—as it's better known—has added some much-needed fine dining to the downtown area. FAB serves classic French cuisine and American chops. Take the grand spiral staircase to the canopied rooftop terrace where you can enjoy a cocktail and a great view of the city's skyline.

Executive chef Stephen Sharp learned to cook in his grandmother's kitchen, but has worked elsewhere in the city, including Four Seasons Park 75 and the Oceanaire Seafood Room. Sharp likes to prepare simple food with complex layers, remaining true to a brasserie concept. Of note is the Le Plateau for two or four people, brimming with oysters, clams, mussels, king crab, shrimp, and lobster with sauces. Colorado lamb loin chops are also a sure bet. The sausage and sauerkraut made in-house are truly "fab." The menu is vast, so take your time ordering.

30 Ivan Allen Jr. Blvd. ✆ **404/266-1440.** www.fabatlanta.com. Reservations recommended. Lunch items $14–$30; dinner items $15–$45. AE, DC, DISC, MC, V. Mon–Thurs 11:30am–10pm; Fri–Sat 11:30am–11pm. MARTA: Civic Center.

Inexpensive

The Varsity ☺ TRADITIONAL AMERICAN   Atlanta grew up around the Varsity, the world's largest drive-in restaurant, opened in 1928 by Frank Gordy (today all six locations are run by his daughter Nancy Simms). This fast-food mecca's greasy feasts are an essential element of the Atlanta experience, and the Varsity draws more celebrities than any other restaurant in town. A 150-foot stainless-steel counter is the hub of the operation, behind which red-shirted cooks and counter people rush out thousands of orders. It's a constant chorus of "What'll ya have? What'll ya have?" with customer responses translated into such esoteric orders as "walk a dog sideways, bag of rags" (a hot dog with onions on the side and potato chips). It takes 200 employees to process the ton of onions, 2,500 pounds of potatoes, 2 miles of hot dogs, 300 gallons of chili, and 5,000 fried pies consumed here by throngs of hungry customers each day.

Order up a slaw dog or a couple of chili burgers (they're only 2 oz. each), with fries, onion rings, and a frosted orange (a creamy frozen orange drink). Barbecued pork, homemade chicken salad, and deviled-egg sandwiches are other options. And since none of this is health food (though it's all fresh and made from scratch), don't resist the fried apple or peach pie a la mode for dessert. The Varsity's interior is spartan, with seating in large, windowed rooms with Formica tables. Big TVs are always on. Can't get enough of that Varsity hot dog chili? You can now buy it by the can at all Varsity locations or through their website.

61 North Ave. (at Spring St.). © **404/881-1706.** Reservations not accepted. All items under $7. MC, V. Sun-Thurs 10am-11:30pm; Fri-Sat 10am-12:30am. Closed Thanksgiving and Christmas. MARTA: North Ave.

Willy's Mexicana Grill ★ MEXICAN   Voted to have Atlanta's best burritos by *Atlanta* magazine, Willy's isn't exactly a place you'd take someone you really want to impress. However, if it's a close friend who doesn't judge you by the joints you hang out in, this is the place to go. You'll stand in line to direct the construction of your burrito, first selecting the type of tortilla to hold it all together. Protein options include green-mole chicken, grilled cilantro-garlic steak, chipotle-barbecue pork, grilled chicken, and even marinated tofu. Next, you can pile on the goodies, including rice, black beans, roasted peppers, and all your typical burrito toppings, including the freshest salsa I've ever tasted. Aside from burritos, Willy's serves nachos, quesadillas, and tacos—it has the basic menu down. It also serves a few domestic and imported beers. Once you've got the goods, choose a booth along the brightly decorated wall or go outside where it's a bit less hectic.

There are 18 locations in Atlanta, including ones at 2074 N. Decatur Rd. (© **404/321-6060**) and 4377 Roswell Rd. NE (© **404/252-2235**).

235 Peachtree St. NE. © **404/524-0821.** Reservations not accepted. Burritos $5-$8. No credit cards. Daily 11am-10pm. Located on the square in Decatur (by the courthouse).

MIDTOWN

Midtown is an increasing hot spot, with new businesses, apartments, and restaurants springing up constantly. This is the theater district, and several restaurants in this part of town are good pretheater choices.

Very Expensive

Bacchanalia ★★★ NEW AMERICAN   Bacchanalia's edgy and sophisticated space in a meatpacking plant on the outskirts of an industrial area takes first-time diners aback, but just for a second. The airy space hits just the right note—plus the food is better than ever.

Owner/chefs Anne Quatrano and Cliff Harrison, who consistently win reams of accolades, place an emphasis on using locally produced natural and organic ingredients whenever possible, from farmstead cheeses to heirloom tomatoes to Georgia blackberries, much of which is grown on their own Summerland Farm. Everything is absolutely the freshest, and perfectly prepared. The blue-crab fritter appetizer with avocado, citrus, and Thai-pepper essence is a signature dish—a plump, sweet, all-lump crab cake that is not to be missed. A longtime dessert favorite is the warm Valrhona chocolate cake, oozing a puddle of rich chocolate from its gooey middle and served with vanilla-bean ice cream. The American wine list is overflowing with excellent choices, and there's a full bar, too. Service is smooth and professional, but it's also warm, inviting, and remarkably free of attitude.

This is one of the best restaurants in town, and reservations are difficult to come by, especially on weekends. When planning a trip to Atlanta, a call to book a table here should be at the top of your list (reservations are taken up to a month in advance). On the same premises, you'll find **Quinones,** a lavish, prix-fixe, multi-course restaurant that stresses the use of southern ingredients to create a menu that changes regularly. Dinner is served only on Saturdays, beginning at 6pm. Be sure to save time to browse Star Provisions, the upscale market also on-site. Stocked with excellent meats, seafood, cheeses, wine, pastries, tableware, cookbooks, and other cooking accessories, it's worth a separate trip. Open Monday through Saturday 10am to 10pm.

1198 Howell Mill Rd. (just north of 14th St.). (📞 **404/365-0410.** www.starprovisions.com. Reservations essential. 4-course prix-fixe menu $85; higher with wine pairing. AE, DC, MC, V. Mon–Sat from 6pm. Closed Christmas Eve to New Year's Eve and 2 weeks in summer. MARTA: Midtown.

South City Kitchen ★ CONTEMPORARY SOUTHERN   South City Kitchen is set in a converted two-story house fronted by a brick patio lined with pear trees. It's a bright space with light filtering through large windows; a bustling exhibition kitchen serves as a visual focus. There's a lot of meeting and greeting here, and the place can be a little loud, but the crowds of well-dressed professionals—sometimes four and five deep at the small bar—seem to thrive on the buzz. If the weather's nice, try the patio, which is more sedate and provides a great people-watching spot.

The seasonally changing menu reflects widely varied southern influences. This is a good destination if you're not in the mood for a full meal or want to do a little post-theater noshing; there are several options for light fare, such as the she-crab soup (a perennial favorite), and side dishes can be ordered a la carte. If you've never tried grits, this is a good time to take the plunge—the cheese-laced grits are exceptional. Entrees range from smoke-braised beef brisket to Low Country shrimp and grits. A basket of freshly baked buttermilk biscuits and corn muffins accompanies all main courses. This is also a good stop for Saturday and Sunday brunch (11am–3:30pm)—you'll find everything from crab hash to a fried green tomato BLT. The wine list includes small signature acquisitions, plus about 20 wines available by the glass.

South City Kitchen has a second location in Smyrna, at 1675 Cumberland Pkwy. (📞 **770/435-0700**).

1144 Crescent Ave. (btw. 11th and 14th sts.). (📞 **404/873-7358.** www.southcitykitchen.com. Reservations recommended. Brunch and lunch items $8–$17; dinner main courses $18–$29. AE, DC, MC, V. Daily 11am–3:30pm; Mon–Thurs and Sun 5–10pm; Fri–Sat 5–10:30pm. MARTA: Arts Center.

Where to Dine in Midtown/Downtown

Antico Pizza Napoletana **2**
Bacchanalia **1**
Ecco **10**
French American Brasserie **15**
Lobby at Twelve **3**
Magic Fingers Sushi **14**
Mary Mac's Tea Room **13**
Pacci Ristorante **9**
Pasta Da Pulcinella **5**
South City Kitchen **6**
Spice Market **8**
Tamarind Seed Thai Cuisine **7**
Taqueria del Sol **1**
The Varsity **12**
Veni Vidi Vici **4**
The Vortex **11**
Willy's Mexicana Grill **16**

💬 TRUE grits

In the South, a good ol' country breakfast isn't complete unless it includes grits. It's a staple here, kind of like potatoes, rice, and pasta are in the rest of the world, and we think everybody else is downright foolish for preferring hash browns or home fries to a heaven-sent bowl of buttered grits. Celestine Sibley, the late *Atlanta Journal-Constitution* columnist, called grits "nature's finest gift to mankind." And Celestine always told it like it was.

Grits are simply crushed kernels of dried corn. A trendier cousin, polenta, is the same thing, just more finely ground and cleaned of all traces of flour. If you've had grits and thought they were bland and tasteless, you probably just didn't have them prepared right. They can be yellow or white (usually white), but the best are stone ground and are cooked for a long time (never instant), boiled with water and salt into a thick porridge and slathered with a big slab of real butter. If you want to expose yourself to ridicule—and ruin your grits—top them with sugar and milk, which is something akin to pouring gravy over a hot fudge sundae.

The beauty of grits is that they soak up flavors like a sponge, allowing them to travel easily from breakfast to dinner. Chicken broth or a little piece of country ham can transform a whole pot, and although many purists gnash their teeth at the thought, some folks cook their grits in milk or cream.

The best addition by far is a little cheese, which turns grits into the ultimate southern comfort food. Sharp cheddar has been traditional for years, especially in a cheese-grits casserole, but goat cheese added to grits transforms them into a tangy, creamy wonder—a sinful and sophisticated enough dish to serve at a fancy dinner party.

Expensive

Pacci Ristorante ★★★ ITALIAN   Johnson and Wales–trained chef Keira Moritz put this new classic steakhouse on the map quickly after its opening in 2009. Pacci, short for the signature carpaccio beef, has a warm and welcoming atmosphere, offering tables as well as oversize, romantically tucked-away booths. The menu is both rustic and modern, from *bistecca fiorentina,* T-bone Italian-style, to *burrida,* a seasonal seafood stew. Moritz's efforts to work the room have won over many a patron, and she is happy to suggest an entree for you if you are undecided (maybe even something not on the menu). Ingredients are the freshest available, and Moritz's signature is on every dish. Squeeze in some space for dessert, and try the chocolate strata or Guinness gingerbread cake with crème fraîche.

Because Pacci is located in Hotel Palomar, they serve three meals a day and a weekend brunch. While they say they are still perfecting their wine selection, you'd be hard pressed to not find something spectacular. And while the bottles can be pricey, the list will always include a $19.81 bottle, a nod to the year Kimpton Hotels was created. Don't be overwhelmed by the wine offerings, however, as the sommelier goes above and beyond to please. After dinner, head up to AltoRex Rooftop Lounge to enjoy any of a number of handcrafted specialty cocktails, including the Ruby Red made with Absolut Ruby Red, Aperol, grapefruit, and apricot jam.

866 W. Peachtree St. (in Hotel Palomar). ℂ **678/412-2402.** www.paccirestaurant.com. Reservations recommended for dinner. Breakfast items $4–$15; lunch entrees $13–$22; dinner entrees $14–$44. AE, DC, DISC, MC, V. Mon–Fri 7–10am and 11am–2pm; Sat–Sun 8am–2pm; daily 5–11pm. MARTA: Midtown.

Spice Market ★ ASIAN From restaurants of the same name in New York and Istanbul, Spice Market has made it to Atlanta, and owner and executive chef Jean-Georges Vongerichten has changed our taste buds forever. Inspired by the hustle and bustle of Southeast Asian street life, Spice Market combines exotic curries and spices in bold dishes such as pork vindaloo, red curried duck, and cod with Malaysian chili sauce and Thai basil. The setting is as warm and inviting as the menu, as long as you don't mind the thumping music coming from Whiskey Park, the hoppin' bar in the lobby of W Midtown Atlanta, where this restaurant is located. The music gets increasingly louder as the night goes on. There is also a very nice bar within the restaurant and some casual seating areas for enjoying conversation and cocktails before or after dinner.

Forgoing the old lunch offering, Spice Market now serves breakfast instead, including such early morning options as brioche French toast and homemade granola. In the evening, you can order a five-course dinner, featuring 10 flavors, for just $48 per person. However, our gracious hostess clued us in that the menu is plenty of food for two healthy eaters to share, and she was right. You'd be miserable trying to eat one by yourself. Specialty cocktails are also worth the money, including the Saketini made with ruby red grapefruit vodka and sake.

188 14th St. NE (in W Atlanta Midtown hotel). ✆ **404/549-5450.** www.spicemarketatlanta.com. Reservations recommended. Breakfast items $9–$17; dinner entrees $16–$32. AE, DC, DISC, MC, V. Breakfast Mon–Fri 6–10:30am and Sat–Sun 7–11am; dinner Mon–Wed 5:30–10pm, Thurs–Sat 5:30–11pm, and Sun 5–10pm. MARTA: Arts Center.

Moderate

Ecco ★★ EUROPEAN Don't look now, but Atlanta's reputation in the culinary world went way, way up in 2008, when Ecco was named "Best Restaurant in the U.S." by the International Restaurant and Hotel Awards. It was second in line for the award of "Best Restaurant in the World," no small feat for a restaurant that just opened in 2006. Featuring a seasonal European menu that teases first with a delicious array of meat and cheese boards, followed by house-made pastas and wood-fired pizzas, Ecco is fast becoming a favorite, especially among locals.

Executive chef Micah Willix, most recently at Seasons 52 in Fort Lauderdale, has a fairly straightforward approach to cooking, but wows patrons with such dishes as the roasted blue cod with sweet onion, saffron, and rouille, and the *conchiglie* (seashell pasta) with eggplant, San Marzano tomatoes, and garlic. The menu lists a host of small plates and appetizers.

40 7th St. NE. ✆ **404/347-9555.** www.ecco-atlanta.com. Reservations recommended. Entrees $13–$29. AE, DC, DISC, MC, V. Daily 5:30–10pm (until 11pm Fri–Sat). Bar and patio open 4pm. MARTA: Midtown.

Lobby at Twelve ★★ NEW AMERICAN Lobby at Twelve features contemporary American cuisine at its finest. Even breakfast is a treat here for guests of the boutique hotel Twelve, which houses the restaurant, or those lucky enough to duck in for a bite on their way to work. Don't miss the ricotta, fried egg, and arugula wrap prepared in the wood oven. Come dinnertime, executive chef Nick Oltarsh wows diners with dishes such as succulently grilled skirt steak or his seared flounder. But save room for dessert and try the warm brownie with ice cream and Heath bar.

361 17th St. ✆ **404/961-7370.** www.lobbyattwelve.com. Reservations recommended Fri–Sun. Breakfast items $5–$12; lunch items $12–$24; dinner entrees $12–$28. AE, DC, DISC, MC, V. Daily 6:30–10:30am and 11:30am–2:30pm; Bistro menu 2:30–10pm (Fri–Sat until 11pm). MARTA: Arts Station, then free shuttle to Atlantic Station.

Magic Fingers Sushi ★★ SUSHI/JAPANESE   Atlanta finally has a real, live, honest-to-goodness sushi bar, also known as M. F. Sushi, for "magic fingers." Chef Chris Kinjo has worked his magic fingers all around the country, and his brother Alex takes care of greeting the guests as they enter this sushi fantasy world. Whether you choose to sit at a table or the sushi bar (where you can keep a close eye on the action), you'll be privy to a menu filled with the freshest fish. It's all there—from tuna to yellowtail, mackerel to eel. Don't wait until you're starving to show up here, as you might wait awhile if it's crowded, especially on the weekends (a typical Atlanta dining problem).

265 Ponce de Leon Ave. ⓒ **404/815-8844.** www.mfsushibar.com. Reservations recommended. Sashimi $8-$15 for 3 pieces; nigiri sushi $4-$10; rolls $4-$19 for 6-8 pieces. AE, DC, MC, V. Mon-Fri 11:30am-2:30pm; Mon-Sat 5:30-10:30pm (until 11:30pm Fri-Sat); Sun 6-10pm. Valet parking. MARTA: North Ave.

Mary Mac's Tea Room ★ SOUTHERN/REGIONAL   Mary Mac's is a colorful Atlanta institution, a bastion of classic Southern cuisine that has been patronized since 1945 by everyone from truck drivers to bank presidents to Jimmy Carter, who sometimes came by for lunch when he was governor. You'll find a glass of pencils on your table; check off the menu items you desire (they change daily) and hand your selections to your server.

Among the famous lunch and dinner entrees are fried chicken dredged in buttermilk and flour, country-fried steak, and chicken pan pie topped with thick giblet gravy. Steaks, chops, and burgers all come with a choice of side dishes, including expertly prepared fresh veggies. You might also select corn bread with *pot likker,* a tasty ham broth made with turnip greens that first-timers can sample for free. The list of sides is endless, including black-eyed peas, fried green tomatoes, whipped potatoes, fried okra, macaroni and cheese, sweet-potato soufflé, and more. Fresh-from-the-oven corn and yeast rolls are served with lunch; at night, there are hot cinnamon rolls, too. Desserts include peach cobbler and banana pudding—a favorite with locals. There's a full bar, but the drink of choice is sweet tea (sweetened iced tea). Mary Mac's can seat groups of up to 150.

224 Ponce de Leon Ave. NE (at Myrtle St.). ⓒ **404/876-1800.** www.marymacs.com. Reservations accepted for groups of 10 or more. Lunch $9-$17; dinner $10-$18. AE, MC, V. Daily 11am-9pm. MARTA: North Ave.

Pasta Da Pulcinella ★ 🍴 ITALIAN   Pasta Da Pulcinella was known for years as a humble hole in the wall serving up great pasta at rock-bottom prices. Some things have changed since the restaurant moved into new digs. Now tucked away in a charming but crowded cottage, the interior is fancier, though still casual, with table service and a full bar. Prices are fancier, too, but still sensible. What has stayed the same is a commitment to excellent pastas, made from scratch and beautifully presented with a surprising and innovative combination of flavors in each concoction.

The most popular dish is *tortelli di mele*—plump round pasta filled with sweet Italian sausage, browned Granny Smith apples, and Parmesan, then topped with browned butter and sage. You'll see nightly specials each day, but your best bet is to stick with the pastas or risottos. There is a small selection of Italian wines that changes often. Pulcinella is near a number of theaters and makes an easy pretheater stop.

1123 Peachtree Walk (near 12th St.). ⓒ **404/876-1114.** www.pastadapulcinella.com. Reservations accepted weekends only for groups of 5 or more. Main courses $10-$20. AE, DC, MC, V. Mon-Fri 11:30am-2pm and 5:30-10pm (until 11pm Fri-Sat); Sun 5:30-9pm. MARTA: North Ave.

Midtown

WHERE TO DINE

Tamarind Seed Thai Bistro ★★ 📖 THAI   If you like Thai, you'll love Tamarind. And if you've never tried Thai food, this is the place to start. Tamarind is a serious, upscale restaurant, and the quality of the food is higher than you'll find in most other Thai restaurants in the city. Once inside, you'll find white tablecloths, fresh flowers, sophisticated decor, and impeccable service. It's a good choice for a romantic evening, business lunch, or pretheater dinner.

The menu includes all the usual Thai standbys—*pad Thai* (Thai-style stir-fried noodles), chicken-coconut milk soup, fresh basil rolls, curries, and so on—and even the most ordinary dishes are carefully prepared and artfully presented. You won't be disappointed with the more inventive dishes, either, such as *neua yang nam tok,* or "waterfall beef," consisting of tender strips of steak marinated in tamarind and chili peppers and cooked with shallots, sesame seeds, and mint leaves. Keep in mind that Thai cuisine is designed to stimulate five taste senses: sweet, sour, neutral, salty, and hot. And they do mean hot: Tamarind doesn't skimp on the chilies, and many of the dishes are downright fiery. Be sure to pay attention to the "hotness guide" on the menu.

1197 Peachtree St. NE. 🕐 **404/873-4888.** www.tamarindseed.com. Reservations recommended. Entrees $10–$32. AE, MC, V. Mon–Fri 11am–2:30pm; Mon–Thurs 5–10pm; Fri–Sat 5–11pm; Sun 11am–9pm. MARTA: Arts Center.

Veni Vidi Vici ★★ ITALIAN   This elegant theater-district restaurant manages to create an intimate feel in a 5,000-square-foot space. Cutting-edge design (handsome cherrywood wine cabinets, stenciled oak flooring, and sophisticated track lighting that replaces the glow of candles with a pinpoint splash of light on each table) complements the bustling exhibition kitchen.

The specialties here are *piatti piccoli* (small plates, such as skewers of shrimp or prosciutto and pear, traditionally served with cocktails), fresh handmade pastas, and meat or seafood from the wood-fired rotisserie and grill. It's easy to make a meal of the *piatti piccoli* or other appetizers, but the pastas are so lovely that it's a shame to pass them up. Especially good is the house specialty—linguine with plump littleneck clams in a white or spicy red sauce. Other excellent traditional dishes include the risotto, *osso buco,* and veal scaloppine. The well-chosen wine list is almost 100% Italian.

41 14th St. (btw. W. Peachtree and Spring sts.). 🕐 **404/875-8424.** www.buckheadrestaurants.com. Reservations recommended. *Piatti piccoli* $8; lunch items $9–$21; dinner pastas $12–$18; dinner main courses $18–$34. AE, DC, DISC, MC, V. Mon–Fri 11:30am–11pm (until 11:30pm Fri); Sat 5–11pm; Sun 5–10pm. MARTA: Arts Center.

Inexpensive

Antico Pizza Napoletana ★★ PIZZA   I challenge you to find a better pizza anywhere in this city. When Antico opened in 2010, it immediately drew a huge fan base, and return customers lined up again and again for another hit. Its no-nonsense approach to authentic Italian pizza employs artisan techniques and requires ingredients available only from Napoli and Campania in southern Italy, which they fly in weekly. (I told you this was authentic.) Hand-kneaded dough is crafted in small batches. Stone ovens slightly char the crust, to which few toppings are added. The menu is limited to pizzas, calzones, and a couple of homemade Italian desserts, so don't come looking for pastas and breadsticks. This is certainly one case in which less is more—much more. Try the margherita, the most popular pizza by far. Be sure to get here early: Once the dough runs out, they close for the day.

1093 Hemphill Ave. ℂ **404/724-2333.** www.anticopizza.it. Reservations not accepted. Pizzas and calzones $18–$22. MC, V. Mon–Sat 11:30am until out of dough.

Hankook Taqueria ★ KOREAN   Hankook is Korean all right, but make that Korean as in barbecue tacos and other delicacies. Originally birthed by Chef Thomas Lee via a Korean taco truck that kept fans racing around the city to find its location of the day, Hankook draws a crowd looking for cheap and authentic Korean barbecue. I literally ordered everything on the menu when feeding a group of friends recently. We were not disappointed. Especially tasty are the calamari taco and the *dae ji gogi,* the pulled pork taco topped with spicy Korean barbecue sauce. The pork sliders with kimchi were a hit, as was the *bibimbap,* featuring beef, veggies, and a fried egg with pepper sauce on top of rice. Don't be put off by the aging interior; the food is well worth it and the restaurant is clean. Even with a permanent spot doing great business, Lee's tacos are still available on the Yumbii food truck.

1341 Collier Rd. NW. ℂ **404/352-8881.** www.hankooktaqueria.com. Tacos $2.25–$3.50; burritos $6.25–$7.50; street snacks $2–$6. MC, V. Mon 11am–4pm; Tues–Fri 11am–9pm.

Taqueria del Sol ★ SOUTHWESTERN   This is what fast food ought to be— quick and good, not to mention affordable. Taqueria del Sol resembles an extremely well-dressed taco stand, with inventive tacos, enchiladas, side dishes, soups, and chilies. You put together your own "plate," ordering as much or as little as you'd like. Use your imagination, picking a couple of tacos (the Memphis barbecue taco with tequila barbecue sauce is a standout), an enchilada, and maybe a side of the addictive jalapeño coleslaw. There is usually one special at lunch and one or two at dinner, which might include a southwestern interpretation of a southern dish, such as boneless fried chicken with ancho mashed potatoes, Low Country gravy, serrano-chili sauce, and turnip greens. There are 25 or so different kinds of beer to choose from, plus a full bar. Don't expect table service, and do expect to wait during prime time, but the inconveniences are small, especially if you can snag a table on the covered patio.

There are two additional locations including Decatur, located at 359 W. Ponce de Leon Ave. (ℂ **404/377-7668**).

1200-B Howell Mill Rd. NW. ℂ **404/352-5811.** www.taqueriadelsol.com. Reservations not accepted. Tacos $2; sides and soups $2; enchiladas $3; lunch specials around $8; dinner specials under $11. AE, MC, V. Mon–Fri 11am–2pm; Sat noon–3pm; Tues–Sat 5:30–9pm (until 10pm Fri–Sat). From I-75, take the 14th St. exit and head west to Howell Mill Rd. Turn right on Howell Mill Rd. The restaurant is a few blocks up on the left, just before Huff Rd. MARTA: North Ave.

The Vortex TRADITIONAL AMERICAN   The laughing-skull logo should give you a clue that this is a wild little bar and grill with a big attitude. If you're easily offended, don't go. Or at least don't read the "stuff you really need to know" on the back of the menu, which, among other things, decrees the restaurant an Idiot-Free Zone and suggests you don't get a knot in your shorts if you aren't served within 5 minutes. All kinds of weird flea-market stuff covers the walls, and kids 17 and under are not allowed here.

Attitude aside, this is the place to come for a big, fat, juicy chargrilled burger, one of the best in town. If you don't want a beef burger, you can substitute a turkey burger, chicken breast, veggie burger, or bison burger for a nominal charge. There's even a $26 "super-stack heart attack burger." Noncarnivores will find plenty to choose from, including soups, generous sandwiches, and fresh salads. You can also get breakfast all day, including a build-your-own omelet menu, featuring many unusual toppings. There's a full bar, out-of-the-ordinary soft drinks, and more kinds of beer than you can imagine (imports and domestic), not to mention 72 varieties of single-malt scotch. This is a great people-watching stop, and the late hours make it a great place to eat after a night on the town.

There's another Vortex at 438 Moreland Ave., in Little Five Points (© **404/688-1828**).

878 Peachtree St. NE. © **404/875-1667.** www.thevortexbarandgrill.com. Reservations not accepted. Starters $7–$9; sandwiches $4.50–$10; burgers $7–$26. AE, MC, V. Mon–Wed 11am–2am; Thurs–Sat 11am–3am; Sun 11am–midnight. MARTA: Midtown.

BUCKHEAD

Buckhead is home to most of Atlanta's posh restaurants. Keep in mind that this is *the* area to dine, so plan in advance and make reservations as soon as you know where you want to go.

Very Expensive

Aria ★★ ECLECTIC   Since opening a dozen years ago, Aria has remained a hit among the dozens of top-quality dining choices in the busy Buckhead area. The eclectic gourmet makings of chef/owner Gerry Klaskala are consistently delightful. He seems to have hit the nail on the head with his version of "slow food"—braised, roasted, stewed, and patiently simmered savory meats paired with scrumptious, innovative sides. Here, cooking is considered an art form—and anything less than spectacular is not allowed. Seasonal ingredients are the norm, as are fresh seafood selections. The artisan cheese tasting has three offerings. Among my favorite entrees is the Niman Ranch slow-roasted pork with sautéed spinach. The extensive wine selection wins raves, and delights from pastry chef Kathryn King complete the meal.

490 E. Paces Ferry Rd. © **404/233-7673.** www.aria-atl.com. Reservations recommended. Dinner entrees $31–$50. AE, DISC, MC, V. Mon–Sat 6–10pm. MARTA: Lenox.

Bluepointe ★★★ ASIAN/NEW AMERICAN   At the corner of Peachtree and Lenox roads, in the heart of upscale Buckhead, is one of the many big stars in the constellation of fine-dining establishments that make up the locally owned and operated Buckhead Life Restaurant Group. Part of the restaurant's success comes from the setting itself: a dramatic, multilevel space with a flashy lounge and sushi bar, soaring ceilings, and a plush contemporary decor with Asian touches. There's a lot of energy and noise in the lounge/sushi bar in the "point" of the building, but it's possible to have a decent conversation in the restaurant portion of the establishment.

The specialty here is seafood, with Asian flavors that give the dishes a contemporary edge. Menus change frequently, depending on what's fresh and available, but might include such delicious options as peanut-crusted grouper in Indian curry, or perhaps scallops with sushi-rice cakes and passion-fruit butter. There are also prime steaks and a delectable coconut curry lobster. Everything is beautifully presented, and the service is impeccable.

3455 Peachtree Rd. NE (at Lenox Rd.). © **404/237-9070.** www.buckheadrestaurants.com. Reservations highly recommended. Entrees $19–$44. AE, DC, MC, V. Mon–Sat 5–10pm (until 11pm Tues and Fri–Sat); Sun 5:30–10pm. Complimentary valet parking. MARTA: Lenox or Buckhead.

Blue Ridge Grill ★ TRADITIONAL AMERICAN   The Blue Ridge Grill's Adirondacks-style interior has the woodsy warmth of a national park lodge: stone pillars, weathered logs, and a soaring pine ceiling with massive heart pine beams salvaged from an old cotton mill. But this spot is as upscale as it is rustic, with antiques, original artwork, and cozy leather booths.

Blue Ridge Grill used to specialize in contemporary Southern cuisine, but the menu now includes traditional American fare such as steaks, chops, and seafood. As in many other restaurants these days, the emphasis is on two-fisted portions: a 22-ounce rib-eye, a 14-ounce veal chop, and huge sides of spinach, mashed potatoes, asparagus, and so on. *Note:* As you drive here along West Paces Ferry Road, remember to look for Northside *Parkway,* not Northside *Drive,* which you'll pass first.

1261 W. Paces Ferry Rd. (at Northside Pkwy., in the Paces Ferry Plaza Shopping Center). ℰ **404/233-5030.** www.blueridgegrill.com. Reservations recommended. Lunch and brunch items $11–$22; dinner main courses $22–$42. AE, DC, DISC, MC, V. Sun–Fri 11:30am–2:30pm; daily 5:30–10pm. Closed major holidays. Complimentary valet parking. MARTA: Lenox.

Bone's ★★★ STEAK/TRADITIONAL AMERICAN Atlanta's best and most famous steakhouse, Bone's is a top power-lunch venue for the expense-account crowd. As many deals as steaks are cut here, and the place is rich with celebrity lore. When Bob Hope dined here, everyone respected his privacy until he rose to leave; then the entire dining room gave him a standing ovation. The setting is traditional masculine-clubby.

The star of the menu is prime-aged, corn-fed Iowa beef, hand cut on the premises and always prepared exactly as ordered. Thick, juicy lamb chops are excellent alternatives to the beef. Noted for its seafood as well as for its steaks and chops, Bone's flies Maine lobsters in daily and serves fresh Gulf Coast crab and shrimp. Lighter entrees are available at lunch, along with salads, sandwiches, and soups. The wine gallery houses more than 500 selections, international in scope, and it highlights French and California vintages. The ultrarich desserts include "Mountain-high Pie"—layers of chocolate chip, rum raisin, and vanilla ice cream.

3130 Piedmont Rd. NE (half a block below Peachtree Rd.). ℰ **404/237-2663.** www.bonesrestaurant.com. Reservations essential. Lunch items $10–$75; dinner main courses $50–$75. AE, DC, DISC, MC, V. Mon–Fri 11:30am–2:30pm; daily 5:30–10pm. Closed most major holidays. MARTA: Lindbergh.

Chops Lobster Bar ★★ SEAFOOD/STEAK Steaks are the specialty at Chops, while lobster (not surprisingly) is the main attraction at the Lobster Bar. However, seafood and lobster are available at Chops, while steaks are also served at the Lobster Bar.

The steakhouse boasts extremely elegant, clubby surroundings—definitely macho, but less so than its arch rival, Bone's (see above). Tri-level seating is in comfortable upholstered armchairs and roomy banquettes. Entrees require a hefty wallet and a hearty appetite for the likes of a 24- or 48-ounce porterhouse steak, a 20-ounce New York strip, triple-cut loin lamb chops, salt- and garlic-crusted prime rib, and so on. You won't need dessert, which is just as well since they're nothing special. A large selection of wines is available; at lunch, filling sandwiches are an option. This is power dining at its best and seats are much in demand, so reserve in advance.

The elegant Art Deco Lobster Bar is reminiscent of the Oyster Bar in New York's Grand Central Terminal. The menu lists steaks and seafood items from Chops, plus additional seafood choices. Lobster is prepared just about every way imaginable—there's lobster cocktail, baked lobster oreganato, lobster bisque, fried lobster tail, steamed lobster, and even lobster fingers. You get the picture. The star of the menu is the crab lobster entree, one or two Maine 1-pounders prepared six different ways. For the purist, there's good old live Maine lobster (3–9 lb.), steamed and cracked.

Where to Dine in Buckhead

Anis Café & Bistro **15**
Aria **17**
Atlanta Fish Market **14**
Au Pied de Cochon **23**
Bluepointe **28**
Blue Ridge Grill **9**
Bone's **22**
Buckhead Diner **19**
Chops Lobster Bar **12**
Colonnade **30**
Corner Café/Buckhead
 Bread Company **18**
Craft **25**
Fat Matt's Rib Shack **32**
Fellini's Pizza **6**
Fogo de Chão **21**
Horseradish Grill **10**
Houston's **29**
Kyma **20**
La Fonda Latina **7**
Nava **13**
NEO **25**
New York Prime **27**
OK Café **9**
Paces 88 **11**
The Palm **24**
Pasta Vino **5**
Pricci **16**
Prime **26**
R. Thomas Deluxe
 Grill **1**
Restaurant Eugene **3**
Swan Coach House **8**
Thirsty Dog Tavern **2**
Toulouse **4**
Woodfire Grill **31**

5

WHERE TO DINE | Buckhead

PICNIC FARE & picnic SPOTS

There are plenty of opportunities to picnic in Atlanta, and loads of outdoor spots to spread your picnic blanket. Good bets include Centennial Olympic Park downtown, Piedmont Park in Midtown, Stone Mountain Park, and Grant Park. Here are some places that can help you round up a great picnic lunch:

Alon's Bakery, 1394 N. Highland Ave. NE (© **404/872-6000**), has loads of delectable baked goods (some of the best pastries in town) and a variety of made-to-order sandwiches at reasonable prices. Try the garlic-roasted lamb or the Tuscany (goat cheese, arugula, roasted eggplant). There's also a selection of interesting, easily portable side dishes and salads.

The **Mercantile,** 1660 DeKalb Ave. (© **404/378-0096**), in Candler Park is a specialty food store stocked to the brim with gourmet delicacies and homemade stocks and sauces. Their signature sandwiches, named for area neighborhoods, are perfect picnic fare and include the Kirkwood with bacon, avocado, watercress, onion and mayo, and the Inman with roasted eggplant, zucchini, and goat cheese on country loaf bread. Add to your basket from a selection of soups, cheeses, and wines.

Adjacent to the Corner Café, the upscale **Buckhead Bread Company,** 3070 Piedmont Rd. (© **404/240-1978**), prepares unusual sandwiches to go, as well as authentic French pastries that taste as good as they look.

And for those who don't like lobster (what are you doing here anyway?), there's a wide variety of impeccably prepared fish, shrimp, and crab. Stone-crab claws are popular during winter months.

70 W. Paces Ferry Rd. (at Peachtree Rd.). © **404/262-2675.** www.buckheadrestaurants.com. Reservations highly recommended. Lunch entrees $15–$44; dinner main courses $18–$85; tasting menu $49; market prices for lobster. AE, DC, DISC, MC, V. Mon–Fri 11:30am–2:30pm; Mon–Thurs 5:30–11pm; Fri–Sat 5:30pm–midnight; Sun 5:30–10pm. MARTA: Lindbergh.

Craft ★★ NEW AMERICAN   Featuring the bounty of local farmers and other purveyors of regional food, Craft and its creator/chef, Tom Colicchio, have embraced Atlanta since their opening a couple of years ago at the ultraluxurious Buckhead hotel, the Mansion on Peachtree. Colicchio's menu highlights the ultrafresh ingredients and prepares them without heavy sauces that mask real flavor. Typical finds are Gulf red snapper, farm chicken, and North Carolina flounder. Pair any with roasted vegetables for a complete dinner. A short list of mushrooms and another of oysters is also the norm. The menu also includes some of the favorites from the original Craft New York location, such as the beef short ribs.

3376 Peachtree Rd. © **404/995-7580.** www.craftrestaurant.com. Reservations highly recommended. Entrees $29–$44. AE, DC, MC, V. Daily 5:30–10pm (Sat–Sun until 11pm). Complimentary valet parking. MARTA: Buckhead.

Fogo de Chão ★ BRAZILIAN   No vegetarian would be caught dead in this place, as the highlights here are meat, meat, and more meat. From top sirloin, filet mignon, and pork ribs to lamb, rump steak, and pork loin, Fogo de Chão seasons each meat selection to perfection before slow-roasting it over a flame to bring out the natural flavors. As you make your way to the 30-item salad bar—one of the best in the city, I might add—and enjoy your side dishes of black beans, fried yucca, garlic mashed potatoes, and cheese bread, the traditional "Gaucho" cooks and waiters will present the savory cuts of meat on skewers and slice them tableside. It's a one-price-fits-all menu. Fogo has become one of the city's most popular restaurants, so reserve in advance if possible.

3101 Piedmont Rd. © **404/266-9988.** www.fogodechao.com. Reservations highly recommended. Lunch $33 per person; dinner $49 per person. AE, DC, MC, V. Mon–Fri 11:30am–2pm and 5–10pm (until 10:30pm Fri); Sat 4:30–10:30pm; Sun 4:30–9:30pm. MARTA: Lindbergh.

NEO ★ ITALIAN NEO was the first restaurant to open in the opulent Mansion on Peachtree. Serving a contemporary Italian menu for breakfast, lunch, and dinner, NEO has some standout dishes, including the can't-miss foie gras appetizer at dinner, as well as a melt-in-your-mouth *beef brasato* (beef braised in Barolo wine). Nightly specials are always a good bet, but the risottos and pasta—including a squid ink pasta—are also popular. The restaurant has a great selection of wines, by the glass or by the bottle.

At the Mansion on Peachtree, 3376 Peachtree Rd. © **404/995-7500.** www.rwmansiononpeachtree. com. Reservations recommended. Breakfast items $5–$15; lunch items $14–$24; dinner main courses $27–$44. AE, DC, MC, V. Daily 6:30am–10pm (until 11pm Fri–Sat). MARTA: Lenox or Buckhead.

New York Prime ★★ SEAFOOD/STEAK Located next to the Ritz-Carlton Buckhead, this is one of Atlanta's favorite steak-and-seafood see-and-be-seen eateries. Using only USDA prime cuts that melt in your mouth, New York Prime doesn't skimp on the seafood either, offering live lobsters from 3 pounds to a whopping 13 pounds. Triple-cut lamb chops and double-rib veal chops are other popular menu items. Service here is always impeccable, and the dark-wood furnishings and wrought-iron chandeliers give the place a dressed-up, masculine look. All the desserts are homemade and memorable. Finish off your evening with live entertainment—and perhaps a choice cigar—in the Martini Bar.

3424 Peachtree Rd. © **404/846-0644.** www.newyorkprime.com. Reservations recommended. Appetizers $9.50–$18; dinner main courses $22–$45, except for the $84 40-oz. porterhouse for 2. Seafood at market prices. AE, DC, DISC, MC, V. Mon–Sat 5–11pm; Sun 5–10pm. MARTA: Lenox or Buckhead.

The Palm ★★ SEAFOOD/STEAK New York's legendary purveyor of juicy prime steaks and succulent outsize lobsters—established in 1926 and still run by its founding family—also has a branch in Atlanta, and it's a beauty. Glossy oak floors, soft lighting, a lofty pressed-tin ceiling, potted palms, and tables spaced for power-lunch privacy create the classic Palm setting—a setting that would not be complete without the restaurant's signature "Wall of Fame," plastered with celebrity caricatures from Frank Sinatra to famous locals Jane Fonda and Ted Turner.

The expense-account crowd is mostly from affluent Buckhead: folks looking for the kind of food served at Chops or Bone's (two premier steakhouses), but in a brasher, more boisterous setting. Preparations are simple here (nothing drizzled or infused); the emphasis is on the freshest seafood and the highest-quality cuts of meat, all served up in satisfying hungry-man portions. The strip steak is huge and divine, done exactly to order. But the most popular entree is the lobster, a hefty critter weighing from 3 to 7 pounds. Other excellent choices are fluffy jumbo-lump crab cakes and linguine with garlicky white-clam sauce. The Palm also serves breakfast, much to the delight of Westin Buckhead hotel guests. Service here is always exceptional.

At the Westin Buckhead Atlanta, 3391 Peachtree Rd. (btw. Lenox and Piedmont roads, just south of Lenox Square). © **404/814-1955.** www.thepalm.com. Reservations recommended. Lunch items $13–$23; dinner main courses $21–$67. Lobster market priced by the pound. AE, DC, MC, V. Mon–Fri 11:30am–10:30pm; Sat noon–11pm; Sun noon–10pm. MARTA: Lenox or Buckhead.

Expensive

Anis Café & Bistro ★ 🍴 FRENCH/MEDITERRANEAN   In the midst of pricey Buckhead, this unpretentious cafe serves great food at the right price. Set in a converted cottage on a side street, it's the perfect spot for a light lunch or dinner with a French accent. The specialties are Provençal versions of healthy Mediterranean cuisine, and the atmosphere is reminiscent of that region, especially if you're lucky enough to snag a table on the tree-shaded brick patio. The key word here is *informal*. The service is sometimes maddeningly casual, and occasionally there are glitches in the kitchen, but if you relax and pretend you've been invited to a friend's house in the south of France, you won't be disappointed.

Starters include pastis-scented escargots with crispy polenta, garlic, and crushed tomatoes. The mussels, which are plump and plentiful, make a full meal when paired with the goat-cheese salad. The saffron linguine and monkfish, with leeks, tomatoes, and white wine butter, is a great entree choice. There are several specialty coffee drinks, including espresso over ice cream. The wine list is quite respectable, and there's a full bar as well.

2974 Grandview Ave. (1 block south of Pharr Rd.). © **404/233-9889.** www.anisbistro.com. Reservations recommended. Lunch $6–$17; dinner entrees $19–$29. AE, DC, MC, V. Daily 11:30am–2:30pm and 6–10pm (until 10:30pm Fri–Sat); Sun 6–9pm. Free valet parking Fri–Sat. MARTA: Lenox.

Atlanta Fish Market ★★ SEAFOOD/SUSHI   It's hard to miss this place, and you really don't want to. It's a great mix of whimsy outside (there's a 65-ft. copper fish standing on its tail out front) and serious seafood inside—some of the best you'll find anywhere. Like the Buckhead Diner (see below), the Atlanta Fish Market is simultaneously glitzy and informal. You'll want to dress up, but not too much. Housed in a brick building inspired by a 1920s Savannah train station, it has a dramatic interior with a soaring ceiling, plush leather booths, and distressed pine tables; there's also

💬 A BUCKHEAD fish TALE

Traveling down Pharr Road in Buckhead, it's pretty hard not to notice the huge fish sculpture outside the Atlanta Fish Market, one of the city's finest seafood restaurants. The fish, which is perched on its swooped tail and appears to be about to leap over the restaurant, caused quite a commotion when it was first proposed. Although the restaurant was enthusiastic about its construction, many folks in the surrounding neighborhoods were not exactly hooked on the idea. Despite protests, the project was approved, and the enormous creature, which resembles a cross between a salmon and a trout, was unveiled in late 1995. Here are some fish facts about a

sculpture that, like it or not, is on its way to becoming an Atlanta landmark:

- The fish is about 65 feet high and weighs 50 tons.
- Measured from head to tail, it's 100 feet long, about the size of a large whale.
- It sports more than 600 copper scales, 3½ feet each, which will age to a patina over the years.
- Made of solid copper and steel, it is supported by a welded-iron infrastructure that is connected to a 35-foot-deep steel-and-concrete casing.
- Cost was in excess of $360,000.

an enclosed porch that feels very beachy. The 15-year-old interior just had a noticeable refresher.

The menu is vast, and the seafood as fresh as it's possible to get. To some folks, seafood in the South means fried, and the fried dishes are okay, but the other preparations are exceptional. There are several daily specials and a list of at least a dozen fresh-catch items that can be ordered charbroiled or Hong Kong–style, spiked with soy sauce, ginger, and scallions. You'll also find steaks and chops, as well as a vast number of appetizers, many almost large enough for a meal.

265 Pharr Rd. (btw. Peachtree Rd. and N. Fulton Dr.). © **404/262-3165.** www.buckheadrestaurants. com. Reservations recommended. Sandwiches $9–$16; lunch and dinner entrees $16–$37; seafood at market prices. AE, DC, DISC, MC, V. Daily 11:30am–1pm (until 11pm Fri–Sat). MARTA: Lenox.

Au Pied de Cochon ★★ FRENCH   Located in the InterContinental Buckhead, Au Pied de Cochon is the Atlanta venture of prominent French restaurant group Les Freres Blanc, which operates a Parisian brasserie, also named Au Pied de Cochon. Known for the fresh seafood and the signature roasted "pig trotter"—or pigs' feet, to be frank—the restaurant is open 24 hours a day, so there is no excuse for not coming here at some point. This spot provides diners with private booths curtained with red velvet as well as traditional seating options. Nearby, the XO bar specializes in old cognacs. Live jazz is played Tuesday through Saturday from 6 to 11pm. If you're not up for the action, plan to come early, as the noise from the bar can get pretty intense.

At the InterContinental Buckhead, 3315 Peachtree Rd. NE. © **404/946-9070.** www.aupiedde cochonatlanta.com. Reservations recommended. Main courses $17–$32; seafood at market prices. AE, DC, DISC, MC, V. Daily 24 hr. MARTA: Buckhead.

Horseradish Grill ★ CONTEMPORARY SOUTHERN   This restaurant had a previous incarnation as the Red Barn Inn, and it still retains some of the rustic atmosphere: wood barn walls, a raftered pine ceiling, and a massive stone fireplace. Big windows overlook the organic garden on one side and Chastain Park on the other; patio seating is under ancient oaks. The view is lovely, whether you're inside or out, but go for the patio if you have a choice. It's also Atlanta's oldest continuously operating restaurant.

Chef Daniel Alterman emphasizes innovative southern recipes, simply prepared. Ingredients are seasonal and regional: no salmon or lobster, no tomatoes in winter, no turnip greens in summer. The excellent specialties include spicy North Carolina barbecue on corncakes, Georgia mountain trout, hickory-grilled double-cut pork chop, and so on. The wine list is predominantly American, but there are international selections, too. Kentucky oatmeal spice cake is the not-to-be-missed dessert. At lunch, there are sandwiches, small plates, and salads. The brunch menu is especially good; try the white omelet with goat cheese, Roma tomatoes, caramelized onions, and spinach.

4320 Powers Ferry Rd. (at Chastain Park). © **404/255-7277.** www.horseradishgrill.com. Reservations recommended. Lunch items $7–$16; dinner main courses $20–$34. AE, DC, DISC, MC, V. Mon-Sat 11:30am–2:30pm; Mon-Thurs 5:30–10:30pm; Fri-Sat 5–10pm; Sun 11am–9pm. MARTA: Lenox.

Kyma ★★ GREEK   Kyma is a contemporary Greek seafood tavern unlike any other. The restaurant is absolutely stunning, with 16-foot solid marble columns weighing 55,000 pounds each, a ceiling lit by twinkling stars, a broken-plate wall mosaic, and a fountain cascading over a marble display of iced fresh whole fish. The predominantly Greek staff adds authenticity to the experience.

Chef Pano I. Karatassos led the menu development for Kyma, showcasing his love of French fundamentals and his clean technique, featuring spices, acidity, and finesse. Kyma will delight you with its cuisine full of true Greek flavors, including *mezedakia* (assorted Greek appetizers), whole fresh fish flown in daily from Mediterranean waters, and spreads. The *mezedes* are typically shared and enjoyed with ice-cold ouzo, a Greek liqueur flavored with anise. Try a combination tasting of appetizers, from traditional Greek red-caviar mousse to roasted red-pepper puree with feta cheese, to get the full range of flavors and textures. Sides serve two people, so you can choose your main dish and accompaniments separately. Vegan and vegetarian menus are also available. You might not be able to pronounce anything on the menu, but the waitstaff is used to the grunt-and-point method.

3085 Piedmont Rd. © **404/262-0702.** www.buckheadrestaurants.com. Reservations required. Entrees $19–$42; fish by the pound. AE, DC, MC, V. Mon–Thurs 5–10pm; Fri–Sat 5–11pm; Sun 4–10pm. Valet parking available. MARTA: Lindbergh.

Nava ★★ SOUTHWESTERN   Nava's tri-level, earth-toned interior is gorgeous—the work of architect Bill Johnson, who is known for creating fabulous settings. There's a bundled spruce ceiling beamed with tree trunks, a *kiva*-style fireplace, a copper-hooded exhibition kitchen, and a rustic and elegant decor rich with southwestern and Native American art.

Don't come here expecting a beans-and-burritos Tex-Mex meal. This is truly inventive southwestern cuisine; you'll find enchiladas, tostadas, and the like, but they're stuffed with such treats as rock shrimp and jalapeño honey mustard, or ancho-chili steak and portobello mushrooms. You can even make a meal from the long list of starters—an easy way to sample the creative menu. The appetizer of mussels dry-roasted in a hot-iron skillet and served in spicy chipotle broth is a favorite among regulars. Save room for the roasted-banana enchilada, served with warm caramel sauce—a great combination. Gluten-free lunch and dinner menus are also available. Nava's extensive wine list was composed to complement the contemporary southwestern dishes. There's also a large selection of tequilas, beers, and margaritas; the prickly pear margarita is a big seller.

3060 Peachtree Rd. (at W. Paces Ferry Rd.). © **404/240-1984.** www.buckheadrestaurants.com. Reservations recommended. Lunch items $10–$15; appetizers $7.50–$13; dinner main courses $18–$30. AE, DC, DISC, MC, V. Mon–Fri 11:30am–2:30pm; Sun–Thurs 5:30–10pm; Fri 5:30–11pm; Sat 5–11pm. Valet parking available. MARTA: Lenox.

Paces 88 NEW AMERICAN   Being located in one of the swankiest hotels in the city, Paces 88 has a lot to live up to when it comes to discerning patrons. Serving three meals a day, the restaurant offers traditional breakfasts, lunches of soups, salads, sandwiches, and pastas, and seafood and grilled meats for the evening meal. The rack of lamb with lyonnaise potatoes, fava beans, white asparagus, and roasted garlic jus is tender and succulent. A Chef's Selection menu changes frequently, and Thai steamed mussels with ginger, lemon grass, cilantro, and coconut curry sauce offers a change of pace. The wine list is especially impressive, featuring some 520 wines, 60 available by the glass.

88 West Paces Ferry Rd. (in the St. Regis Atlanta). © **404/563-7910.** www.paces88.com. Reservations recommended. Breakfast items $12–$24; lunch items $15–$19; dinner main courses $15–$29. AE, MC, V. Daily 6:30–10am (from 7am Sat–Sun); 11:30am–2:30pm; 5:30–10pm (until 11pm Sat–Sun). MARTA: Buckhead.

Prime ★★ SEAFOOD/STEAK/SUSHI Don't be put off by the fact that this restaurant is located in a shopping mall. For one thing, it's in Lenox Square, *the* shopping mall of the Southeast. And what better finish to a shopping spree than a martini and a steak, or sushi? If you're going to indulge, you might as well go all the way, and this is an extremely indulgent place—a suave, hip atmosphere with food to match. It's a steakhouse, but it's bright and contemporary rather than dark and clubby.

Do start with a martini; several specialty martinis are available. The sushi is the freshest you can get and is available at all times, the steaks are sublime and huge, and the seafood is stylish. At lunch, you'll find lighter entrees, sandwiches, and salads. Steak specials nightly before 6pm.

3393 Peachtree Rd. NE (upstairs at the main entrance to Lenox Square shopping mall). © **404/812-0555.** www.h2sr.com. Reservations recommended. Lunch items $6–$39; dinner main courses $16–$39. AE, DC, DISC, MC, V. Mon–Sat 11:30am–10pm (until 11pm Fri–Sat); Sun 4–9pm. MARTA: Buckhead or Lenox.

Restaurant Eugene ★ CONTEMPORARY SOUTHERN Yet another venture in the city's current popularity of farm-to-table establishments, Restaurant Eugene opened to wide acclaim, the effort of Executive Chef Linton Hopkins, who named the eatery for his grandfather. He's also responsible for Atlanta's Holeman and Finch Public House and H&F Bread Co. A recipient of a pair of James Beard Award nominations, Hopkins shines in preparation of Georgia meat and produce, drawing from seasonal bounties and regional offerings. Because of that food philosophy, the menu here changes frequently. Typical fare includes a lamb tasting, confit pork belly, and duck breast with creamed green onion. Veggies are a big deal here, so prime your taste buds for a fresh twist on old favorites such as succotash and crowder peas (similar to black-eye peas). **Note:** Nonsoutherners are often surprised to learn not all peas are green and come in a can. Five- and seven-course tasting menus are also available, $75 and $95 respectively.

2277 Peachtree Rd. © **404/355-0321.** www.restauranteugene.com. Reservations recommended. Dinner entrees $13–$48. AE, MC, V. Daily 5:30–10pm (Sat–Sun until 11pm). MARTA: Buckhead or Arts Center.

Thirsty Dog Tavern ★ ITALIAN Opened a few years as ago as Vita by 30-year restaurant veteran Tony LaRocco, Thirsty Dog Tavern retains the Italian menu of Vita but is now dog friendly (they even have a menu of tasty tidbits for Fido) and offers wall-to-wall televisions for sports lovers. Family-style Italian-American fare is served by women clad in Catholic school uniforms, giving a religious nod to the Hooter waitresses, to the delight of those who have discovered the place. The restaurant's old-world style is comfortable and inviting.

Homemade sausages and meatballs, and a number of paninis, wraps, and po' boys make for a varied menu. Along with a healthy number of chicken and veal dishes, they also serve steaks and chops, and the fresh mussel appetizer is a reason to return. Of course, cannoli ranks high on the dessert menu, so don't fill up too much. Late hours here make it a popular stop for post-theater or clubbing crowds.

2110 Peachtree Rd., Ste. B. © **404/367-8483.** www.thirstydogtavern.com. Reservations for groups of 6 or more. Lunch items $10–$12; dinner entrees (family style) $13–$54. AE, DC, DISC, MC, V. Mon–Fri 5pm–2am; Sat 11am–2am; Sun 11am–midnight. MARTA: Lindbergh.

Woodfire Grill ★★ NEW AMERICAN Many of us wept tears of joy when chef/owner Michael Tuohy announced that he was opening this restaurant, and wept again when he sold it. But incoming owner/chef Kevin Gillespie has a huge following in Atlanta and does not disappoint. A recent finalist on Top Chef, Gillespie takes advantage of seasonal offerings of local farms when crafting his menu. The interior is warmly decorated, with a stunning copper bar inside the entrance. Entering the dining room, you'll find the wood-fired grill and rotisserie in plain view, providing a dinner theater of sorts for diners whose tables are in the vicinity. Just two complaints: It's noisy, and the hardwood seats are uncomfortable (pillows are available).

The local, sustainable, organic menu changes daily, so no matter how often you dine here, you'll always find something different. Woodfire boasts an impressive wine list, with most selections available by the glass. The desserts are quite elaborate, though you might not have room for them.

1782 Cheshire Bridge Rd. ✆ **404/347-9055.** www.woodfiregrill.com. Reservations recommended. Entrees $28–$32; 5-course chef's tasting $65, 7 courses $85. AE, DC, DISC, MC, V. Tues–Thurs 5:30–10pm; Fri–Sat 5:30–11pm. Complimentary valet parking. MARTA: Lindbergh.

Moderate

Buckhead Diner ★★ NEW AMERICAN/TRADITIONAL AMERICAN   As sleek as a Thunderbird convertible, the exterior of this nouvelle diner glitters with neon tubing and chrome, and the posh interior conjures images of the *Orient Express.* It's almost always crowded, so be prepared to wait at peak times (it's usually worth it—the place is full of hustle and bustle and lots of fun). Open since 1987, the diner has a full bar, offering excellent bloody marys.

Main courses are a mix of Mom's cooking and modern cuisine, some quite heavy on the calories (but who's counting?). Longtime favorites include the veal and wild-mushroom meatloaf with celery mashed potatoes, as well as the ahi tuna burger. The sweet and spicy calamari appetizer is a favorite. If you order nothing else, be sure to get the homemade potato chips slathered with melted Maytag blue cheese—big enough for the table to share, and I bet you won't be too embarrassed to lick the plate. Dessert must-haves include a to-die-for chocolate chunk crème brûlée. All the breads are baked fresh daily at the Buckhead Bread Company (see below).

3073 Piedmont Rd. (at E. Paces Ferry Rd.). ✆ **404/262-3336.** www.buckheadrestaurants.com. Reservations not necessary. Snacks, sandwiches, and salads $6–$16; lunch and dinner main courses $10–$24. AE, DC, DISC, MC, V. Mon–Sat 11am–midnight; Sun (including brunch) 10am–10pm. MARTA: Lenox.

Colonnade ★ SOUTHERN/REGIONAL   This Atlanta institution, established in 1927, serves authentic southern specialties without any newfangled twists (thank goodness). The Colonnade is unpretentious and comfortable, with most of the seating at butcher-block tables in a large room. A cozy bar with a working fireplace is a nice place to sit if you have to wait for a table—and you probably will.

The fried chicken is some of the best in town—four huge pieces done the way Mama used to make it. The homemade yeast and whole-wheat rolls will melt in your mouth. In addition to the menu listings, there are economical early bird specials and fancier offerings ranging from salmon croquettes to prime rib. The portions are huge, so it's doubtful you'll have room for dessert. But if you decide to squeeze it in, the butterscotch meringue and banana pudding will satisfy any sweet tooth.

1879 Cheshire Bridge Rd. NE (btw. Wellborne Dr. and Manchester St.). ✆ **404/874-5642.** www.colonnadeatl.com. Reservations not accepted. Entrees $9–$22. No credit cards; personal checks accepted. Mon–Fri 5–9pm (until 10pm Fri); Sat noon–10pm; Sun 11:30am–9pm. MARTA: Midtown.

Fat Matt's Rib Shack BARBECUE   This blues and barbecue shack is a favorite among locals who like their ribs as smoky as their music. Don't expect much in the way of decor. This is truly a shack, where patrons order at the counter, then sit elbow-to-elbow at plastic tables while chowing down on pork ribs, barbecued chicken, and pulled-pork sandwiches. There are sides of coleslaw, baked beans, and Brunswick stew—a southern concoction that's a cross between a thick gravy and a thicker meat stew. Snack on an "appetizer" of peanuts in the shell, along with ice-cold beer, while waiting for your order.

Live music—authentic blues by a variety of local and regional groups—starts every night around 8pm. People pack into the small space, and it's usually standing room only, especially on weekends, so come early if you want to see the show.

1811 Piedmont Rd. (a few blocks south of Cheshire Bridge Rd.). *C* **404/607-1622.** www.fatmatts ribshack.com. Reservations not accepted. Ribs and chicken $3.75–$19; chopped pork sandwiches $3.95. AE, DISC, MC, V. Mon–Thurs 11:30am–11:30pm (until 12:30am Fri–Sat); Sun 1–11:30pm. MARTA: Lindbergh.

Houston's ★ ☺ TRADITIONAL AMERICAN Part of an Atlanta-based group with restaurants throughout the country, Houston's serves lavish portions of fresh, top-quality fare in an exciting yet informal spot. It's always packed with people, and service is as snappy as the food. There's usually a wait, but you won't mind spending time on the front patio, a terrific people-watching spot, or in the bar. (If you're in a rush during lunch, eat at the bar.)

Thick, hickory-grilled burgers are a specialty, as are the tender, meaty ribs, served with a choice of side dishes: skillet beans, fries, coleslaw, or couscous. A lighter main course is the salad of sliced grilled chicken, tossed with chopped greens and juli-enned tortilla strips in a honey-lime vinaigrette, garnished with a light peanut sauce. For dessert, you can indulge in a huge, chewy brownie topped with vanilla ice cream and Kahlúa.

There are three additional locations around town, including one in the Brookwood Square Shopping Center, 2166 Peachtree Rd., at Colonial Homes Drive (*C* **404/351-2442**).

3321 Lenox Rd. (at E. Paces Ferry Rd.). *C* **404/237-7534.** www.hillstone.com. Reservations not accepted. Burgers and salads $9–$17; main courses $15–$25. AE, MC, V. Daily 11am–10pm. MARTA: Lenox.

OK Café ☺ TRADITIONAL AMERICAN The specialties here are down-home classics served in a simple setting of leather booths and old-style Formica tables. A jukebox is stocked with oldies, and waiters wear white diner uniforms. There's a witty sculpture of a money tree in the dining room—perhaps to pay homage to the mon-eyed crowd, which comes here for updated comfort food.

The place is full of memories of Mom: Blue-plate specials such as meatloaf, pot roast, and roast turkey with corn-bread dressing are all served with corn muffins and two side dishes (the best is six-cheese macaroni). Sandwiches, burgers, salads, and thick, old-fashioned shakes are other options. They also have a dessert list to die for, including coconut cake, hot pecan pie, and banana bread pudding. It's a good spot to bring the whole family, especially if you have kids who turn up their noses at anything more complex than mashed potatoes. OK Café is also known for its country-style breakfasts and brunches. Takeout is available.

1284 W. Paces Ferry Rd. NW (at Northside Pkwy., in the West Paces Ferry Shopping Center). *C* **404/233-2888.** www.okcafe.com. Reservations not accepted. Burgers, salads, and sandwiches $7–$13; lunch and dinner $12–$14. AE, DC, DISC, MC, V. Daily 7am–10pm (until 11pm Fri–Sat). Closed major holidays. MARTA: Lenox.

5

WHERE TO DINE | Buckhead

Pasta Vino ☺ 🍴 ITALIAN/PIZZA   This may not be the very best Italian restaurant in town, but the combination of high quality and low prices makes it a favorite neighborhood stop—and a great choice when you want good food but don't want to dress up and go "out." Billy Petrucci runs this little trattoria; his father, Nico, runs chic, upscale Abruzzi in the same shopping center.

The yeasty, chewy pizzas, most of which are available by the slice, are as good as they come. Seafood and veal, served with a side of pasta marinara, are done especially well. And the mussels appetizer is large enough for an entree. The best traditional Italian dish on the menu is the lasagna, made with the most tender noodles, a little ground beef, delicate béchamel and tomato sauces, and lots of mozzarella. It's worth twice the price. The eggplant lasagna is even better. The house salad is made with boring iceberg lettuce, so choose the huge Caesar instead and split it. The wine is limited to the house varieties—one white, one red—but they're not bad. This place is extremely kid friendly and usually filled with families from the local, well-heeled neighborhood. The patio is a great spot in summer.

2391 Peachtree Rd. NE (in the Peachtree Battle Promenade at Peachtree Battle Ave.). ✆ **404/231-4946.** www.pvbuckhead.com. Reservations not accepted. Pizzas $14–$21; pastas $10–$19; main courses $13–$21. MC, V. Mon–Fri 11:30am–2pm; daily 5–9pm (until 10pm Fri–Sat). MARTA: Lenox or Buckhead.

Pricci ★ ITALIAN   Pricci is strikingly glamorous, with part of its drama stemming from an open kitchen where a team of white-toqued chefs engage in a culinary frenzy around an oak-fired pizza oven. The decor is also theatrical—Art Deco chrome and brass dividers, rich decorative woods, cozy banquettes, and a snazzy bar. The downside is the noise; it's hard to escape all the dining clatter.

Pricci's fare is hearty regional Italian cuisine: thin-crusted oak-fired pizzas, pastas such as beef short-rib ravioli, *osso buco* with borlotti beans and gremolata, and so on. The specialty of the house, which serves two, is an excellent whole roasted fish with grilled asparagus. A good value on the lunch menu is the three-pasta tasting. The award-winning wine list highlights every wine-producing region of Italy and features a good selection of grappa (an Italian brandy).

500 Pharr Rd. (at Maple Dr.). ✆ **404/237-2941.** www.buckheadrestaurants.com. Reservations recommended. Lunch $10–$16; dinner entrees $11–$29. AE, DC, DISC, MC, V. Mon–Fri 11:30am–2:30pm; daily 5–11pm (until 10pm Sun). MARTA: Lenox.

R. Thomas Deluxe Grill ★★ ECLECTIC   Conveniently located in Midtown, R. Thomas is open 24 hours a day, 7 days a week, so there's no excuse to go hungry. Its eclectic menu is about as healthy a choice as you can make in today's world of fast food. Now in its 20th year in Atlanta, this Peachtree Street icon will please the meat eater and the vegetarian alike, with delicious fare such as collard greens with millet-corn casserole, mashed potatoes, and shiitake-mushroom gravy. Menu items include gourmet sandwiches, southwestern fare, pasta dishes, and noodle bowls. Breakfast can be enjoyed at any time—day or night. The store sells books and other items for healthy living.

1812 Peachtree St. NW. ✆ **404/872-2942.** www.rthomasdeluxegrill.com. Entrees $8–$19. AE, MC, V. Daily 24 hr. MARTA: Midtown.

Swan Coach House 🏛 CONTINENTAL/TRADITIONAL AMERICAN   If you visit the Atlanta History Center in Buckhead (p. 115), this delightful restaurant is a great lunch option. It's a genteel spot with a "ladies who lunch" ambience, and the menu mirrors the setting, featuring fare such as salmon croquettes with cucumber relish and Dijon dill sauce. There's even a 1950s-style congealed salad on the list. The best choice, which has been on the menu for 30 years, is the Swan's Favorite: chicken salad in pastry timbales served with cheese straws and creamy frozen fruit salad. For dessert, order the French silk swan—a meringue base filled with chocolate mousse and covered with whipped cream and slivered almonds. There's a full bar, and Swan's champagne punch is delightful, especially if you're celebrating a special occasion.

Note: You don't have to visit the Atlanta History Center to dine here; the restaurant has a separate entrance. A gift shop and art gallery adjoin the dining room and are well worth the extra time for browsing.

At the Atlanta History Center, 3130 Slaton Dr. NW. © **404/261-0636.** www.swancoachhouse.com. Reservations accepted for groups of 10 or more. Main courses $12–$15. AE, MC, V. Mon–Sat 11am–2:30pm. Closed New Year's Day, Memorial Day, July 4th, Labor Day, Thanksgiving, and Christmas.

Toulouse ★ 🏢 NEW AMERICAN   The name is French, but the cuisine is New American, with influences from the south of France. Toulouse is tucked away behind a strip of shops along Peachtree Road; it's a bit hard to spot, but you'll be glad you sought it out. The neighborhood crowd, attired in anything from blue jeans to black tie, likes to keep this place a secret, revealing it only to friends and special visitors. It's casual and charming, a spacious loft with a large wooden bar and an open kitchen in full view.

The menu changes seasonally, perhaps more often depending on the whims of the chef, but you're likely to find some of the house specialties always available. A good bet is the plump roast chicken done to perfection in a wood-fired oven. Another favorite is the braised lamb shank with a Kalamata olive/sweet-pepper sauce and roasted vegetables. The excellent wine list has lots of good values and recently landed Toulouse a top ranking from *Wine Spectator*. There's no corkage fee on Sundays.

2293 Peachtree Rd. NE (south of Peachtree Battle Ave.). © **404/351-9533.** www.toulouserestaurant. com. Reservations recommended. Main courses $15–$24. AE, DC, MC, V. Daily 5:30–10pm (until 11pm Fri–Sat). MARTA: Lenox or Buckhead.

Inexpensive

Corner Café/Buckhead Bread Company ★ BAKERY/CAFE   This spot is a combination of an upscale cafe and a gourmet bakery. The cafe portion is more casual and relaxed than the Buckhead Diner, its glitzy cousin across the street, but the food is still upscale. The menu is large and varied, with wonderful soups and hearty sandwiches on bread baked in the neighboring bakery. There are also interesting main-dish salads, including the longtime favorite, a chicken-, egg-, and tuna-salad trio. Weekday breakfasts include fresh-baked pastries, crepes, Belgian waffles, and traditional fare such as poached eggs with cheddar-cheese grits. Weekend brunch is a busy time here, with a fancier menu that features delicious dishes such as two pan-poached eggs with portobello mushrooms and crispy prosciutto topped with a port-wine glaze.

About half the space is given over to a vast bakery, the Buckhead Bread Company, which displays many varieties of fresh-baked bread each day—everything from focaccia flavored with fresh rosemary and basil to honeyed eight-grain loaves studded with roasted sunflower seeds. The gorgeous pastries have a French pedigree that will transport you to the Left Bank. You can get your sweets to go, or enjoy them on the small patio with a cup of specialty coffee.

3070 Piedmont Rd. (at E. Paces Ferry Rd.). © **404/240-1978.** www.buckheadrestaurants.com. Reservations not accepted. Sandwiches and main-dish salads $8–$17; brunch items $6–$17. AE, DC, DISC, MC, V. Mon–Fri 6:30am–3:30pm; Sat–Sun 8am–3:30pm. MARTA: Lenox.

Fellini's Pizza ☺ PIZZA   You won't get chèvre or cilantro on your pizza here, but you will get traditional toppings such as anchovies, Italian sausage, meatballs, pepperoni, fresh mushrooms, and onions. These cheesy New York–style pies have thin, doughy crusts that exude the heavenly aroma of fresh-baked bread. Besides the pizzas, some of which are available by the slice, there are immense, well-stuffed calzones. The beer is always ice-cold.

Fellini's is a classic pizza joint, and a damn good one at that. It's a wacky place, very atypical for Buckhead. Most of the seating is at tables on a large outdoor patio centered on a tiered fountain, with statues of angels and gargoyles. Because it fronts Peachtree Road, it's a great spot to sit and watch the city go by. If you're wilting from the heat, you can always retreat to the funky, spare interior.

There are several additional locations; the most convenient for visitors are at 1991 Howell Mill Rd. (© **404/352-0799**) and 909 Ponce de Leon Ave. (© **404/873-3088**).

2809 Peachtree Rd. (at Rumson Rd.). © **404/266-0082.** www.fellinisatlanta.com. Reservations not necessary. Slice $3–$4; medium pie $12 and up; calzones $5.50 and up. No credit cards. Mon–Sat 11am–2am; Sun noon–midnight. MARTA: Lenox or Buckhead.

La Fonda Latina SPANISH   Funky and festive, La Fonda is a brightly painted hole in the wall consisting of a small interior dining area with an open kitchen, a covered outdoor patio, and an open-air rooftop patio with seating in wooden booths amid lots of plants. Outdoor areas are heated in winter and cooled by large fans in summer.

The food is both fresh and refreshingly authentic. You might simply order a bottle of *vino blanco* and a delicious *ensalada mixta* (tuna, black olives, lettuce, onions, and peppers in a classic vinaigrette that you can soak up with Cuban bread). There are several different kinds of quesadillas, three types of paella (traditional, seafood, and vegetarian), Latin sandwiches served on crusty Cuban bread, and a nicely grilled chicken served with rice and beans. Try the creamy, homemade flan for dessert.

La Fonda has four other locations, including 923 Ponce de Leon Ave. (© **404/607-0665**).

2813 Peachtree Rd. NE (btw. Rumson Rd. and Sheridan Dr.). © **404/816-8311.** www.fellinisatlanta.com. Reservations recommended. Main courses $6–$19. MC, V. Mon–Thurs 11am–11pm; Fri–Sat 11am–midnight; Sun noon–11pm. MARTA: Lenox or Buckhead.

VIRGINIA-HIGHLAND & INMAN PARK

A meal in this charming district can be an occasion to see a nontouristy part of Atlanta. Come a little early so you can browse the area's great little shops and galleries. For dining establishments, see the map on p. 101.

Expensive

TWO Urban Licks ★ NEW AMERICAN   One of Atlanta's hottest dining spots, TWO Urban Licks is among a handful of area restaurants turned gold by creators Bob Amick and Todd Rushing of Concentrics Restaurants. (Others include ONE Midtown Kitchen and Murphy's.) TWO's executive chef, Cameron Thompson, has created a menu of fiery American cooking in a high-energy, urban environment.

Where to Dine in Virginia-Highland

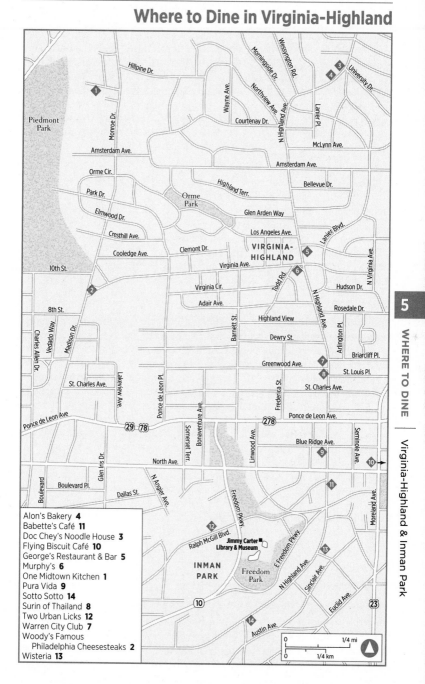

Alon's Bakery **4**
Babette's Café **11**
Doc Chey's Noodle House **3**
Flying Biscuit Café **10**
George's Restaurant & Bar **5**
Murphy's **6**
One Midtown Kitchen **1**
Pura Vida **9**
Sotto Sotto **14**
Surin of Thailand **8**
Two Urban Licks **12**
Warren City Club **7**
Woody's Famous
    Philadelphia Cheesesteaks **2**
Wisteria **13**

Specializing in wood-fired meat selections such as duck, fish, and barbecue, the restaurant cooks dishes "in the round" on a 14-foot rotisserie in a wide-open kitchen, smack-dab in the middle of the bustling eatery. Try the lamb lollipops and smoky corn soup for starters. Just as exciting as the menu here is the innovative domestic wine program, consisting of 42 stainless-steel barrels of wine displayed in a 26-foot glass-and-steel temperature-controlled tower just inside the front door. Enjoy live blues starting at 7:30pm Tuesday through Saturday; on Sundays at 6pm, there's the Low Country boil.

820 Ralph McGill Blvd. © **404/522-4622.** www.twourbanlicks.com. Reservations recommended. Main courses $14–$30. AE, MC, V. Mon–Thurs 5:30pm–midnight; Fri–Sat 5:30pm–1am; Sun 5:30–10pm. Complimentary valet parking. MARTA: Five Points and bus 16.

Wisteria ★ SOUTHERN/REGIONAL   In this former grocery store, chef Jason Hill has given Southern cuisine his own twist, starting with the black-eyed pea hummus with sweet-potato chips and his crawfish and corn fritters. This casual, upscale setting is perfect for special events, and the wine list is brief but interesting. Belly up for supper when you can enjoy such down-home delights as jumbo shrimp and grits or southern fried catfish over a warmed green tomato, okra, and spicy crawfish ragout with rémoulade.

471 N. Highland Ave. © **404/525-3363.** www.wisteria-atlanta.com. Reservations recommended. Main courses $15–$29. AE, DC, DISC, MC, V. Daily 5:30–10pm (until 11pm Fri–Sat). MARTA: North Ave.

Moderate

Babette's Café ★★ EUROPEAN PROVINCIAL   Owner/chef Marla Adams has put together a menu that's decidedly anti–haute cuisine, full of excellent interpretations of comfy, everyday provincial dishes. The crowd is made up of loyal locals, and the French farmhouse ambience matches the fare.

The restaurant has some of the best mussels in town. Start with the mussel appetizer, and don't let the offbeat combination of ingredients scare you off. Bivalves are Adams's specialty, and this unusual dish—steamed mussels with white wine, strawberries, and serrano peppers—is excellent. A longtime favorite entree—grilled lamb loin chops with red-wine reduction and shoestring potatoes—is kept on the menu by popular demand.

Most of the selections from the reasonably priced wine list are available by the glass, part of Adams's strategy to encourage customers to sample different wines. There are special prix-fixe dinners held each season, the most famous of which are at New Year's. It's a re-creation of the food and wine from the book *Babette's Feast*, for which the restaurant is named. Babette's is a great place to stop after a visit to the Carter Center, which is just around the corner.

573 N. Highland Ave. (just north of Freedom Pkwy.). © **404/523-9121.** www.babettescafe.com. Reservations recommended, and required for wine dinners held once a season. Brunch items $7–$26; dinner main courses $16–$26. AE, DC, DISC, MC, V. Tues–Sat 5:30–10pm; Sun 10:30am–2pm and 5–9pm. MARTA: North Ave.

Murphy's ★★★ TRADITIONAL AMERICAN   Murphy's, a wine-and-cheese shop that evolved into a restaurant and bakery, comprises a cozy warren of rooms. It's one of the most popular places in Atlanta for weekend brunch. The interior is charming and innlike, with French doors flung open and ceiling fans spinning in nice weather. Up front is the bakery/wine shop, with glass display cases overflowing with

outdoor DINING

Food always seems to taste better outdoors, and Atlanta's temperate climate makes alfresco dining possible 6 to 8 months out of the year. It's true that there are always some stifling midsummer days, but things usually cool off enough in the evening to make outdoor dining quite pleasant. Many of these places heat their patios during the winter, closing them only on the most frigid days. Here are a few prime spots:

Anis Café & Bistro (p. 92): This tree-shaded spot outside a converted Buckhead bungalow is reminiscent of a terrace in the south of France. You can easily imagine you're in Provence here.

Canoe (p. 106): Lovely gardens surround a covered terrace on the banks of the Chattahoochee River, creating a perfect setting. Wear your best Ralph Lauren outfit.

Fellini's Pizza (p. 100): Have a beer or a slice of pizza, and watch the world sail down Peachtree Road.

French American Brasserie (p. 78): Known to its friends as FAB, this downtown spot offers a great view of the city's skyline from its canopied rooftop seating area and bar.

George's Restaurant and Bar (p. 106): There are only a few tables outside this plain neighborhood tavern, but it's in the heart of trendy Virginia-Highland, prime people-watching territory.

Horseradish Grill (p. 93): If you're looking for a place to propose, this is it. A candlelit patio is set under ancient oaks and overlooks lovely Chastain Park.

Nava (p. 94): Located at the busy intersection of Peachtree and West Paces Ferry roads, but comfortably set back from the street, the lovely brick terrace here is a great perch from which to watch all the Buckhead activity while enjoying $5 Patio Party cocktails and appetizers.

South City Kitchen (p. 80): There's limited seating outside this converted Midtown house, but it's a perfect spot to watch the comings and goings of all the beautiful young people who dine here.

Warren City Club (p. 105) The Warren in popular Virginia-Highland has a delightful third-level garden terrace where guests can enjoy cocktails or a full meal.

pastries, crusty fresh-baked breads, and luscious desserts. At dinner, you'll find a variety of entrees, including North Georgia trout. For lunch, the hefty sandwiches are always winners, especially the crab-cake version with smoky chili mayo; there's a selection of pastas and salads as well. Brunch includes egg dishes, breads, waffles, pancakes, salads, and sandwiches.

Murphy's is a popular destination for locals in the surrounding neighborhood, which is full of young professionals who like casual dining. It's a good stop if you're exploring the Virginia-Highland area; if there's a wait, you can kill some time in the nearby shops. Murphy's is also perfect for dessert and coffee, which is otherwise hard to find around here.

997 Virginia Ave. NE (at N. Highland Ave.). © **404/872-0904.** www.murphysvh.com. Call-ahead seating for dinner only. Lunch, brunch, and breakfast items $5–$15; dinner main courses $11–$25. AE, DC, DISC, MC, V. Mon–Thurs 11am–10pm; Fri 11am–11pm; Sat 8am–11pm; Sun 8am–10pm. Closed Thanksgiving and Christmas. MARTA: North Ave.

ONE Midtown Kitchen ★ NEW AMERICAN   You'll feel like you're in the heart of New York when you dine at this sophisticated restaurant, the creation of renowned restaurateur Bob Amick. It manages to be both delicious and not too pricey (someone finally figured it out). Chef Drew VanLeuvan heads the kitchen here. The wine list is eclectic and affordable, and the atmosphere is high energy—maybe the high spirits are left over from the restaurant's previous life as a swinging club. Located on the edge of Piedmont Park, ONE takes the cake when it comes to creativity in powder rooms (you'll see what I mean). This place is a local favorite, especially with a younger crowd working their way up the ladder to six figures.

559 Dutch Valley Rd. NE. ✆ **404/892-4111.** www.onemidtownkitchen.com. Reservations recommended. Starters $6–$22; entrees $10–$25. AE, MC, V. Sun–Mon 5:30–10pm; Tues–Thurs 5:30–11pm; Fri–Sat 5:30pm–midnight. Free valet parking. MARTA: Midtown.

Pura Vida TAPAS   With cuisine inspired by that of the Latin Caribbean and South America, plus some Spanish influences thrown in for good measure, Pura Vida is the best tapas eatery in the city. Among the tasty $6-to-$10-a-plate tapas designed to share are the *empanada de picadillao de pollo.* Translated, that would be turnovers stuffed with chicken, olives, capers, raisins, and diced eggs served with chili–sugar cane vinegar. Another popular plate is the Ponce de Leon—18-month cured Serrano ham, Spanish chorizo, and olives. Pura Vida also offers an extensive wines-by-the-glass menu, as well as specialty drinks such as "Sex in Santiago," its version of a cosmopolitan cocktail. Folks come here not only to eat but to enjoy the activities including scheduled cooking classes. On the second and fourth Thursdays, the city's dramatic tango community performs the Argentine tango while guests enjoy Argentine wines. Monday nights feature mojitos and dominos. The atmosphere is fun, but if you're not up for noisy crowds, plan to dine early.

656 N. Highland Ave. ✆ **404/870-9797.** www.puravidatapas.com. Reservations recommended. Tapas $6–$10. AE, DC, DISC, MC, V. Mon–Thurs 5:30–10pm; Fri–Sat 5:30–11:30pm; Sun 5–9pm (tapas menu not available on Sun). MARTA: North Ave.

Sotto Sotto ★★ ITALIAN   Sotto Sotto means "hush hush" in Italian. How ironic: The food is divine here, but the noise is incredible. It seems that half of Atlanta has determined this is the place of the moment and now tries to wedge into the tiny restaurant on the same night, at the same time. It's an energetic crowd, and they all appear quite content to shout at one another over their seafood risotto. If you don't mind noise, then by all means go. But if you're looking for a quiet, romantic spot, forget it.

That's the bad news. There's lots of good news: the duck breast with polenta; the meltingly tender homemade pastas and creamy risottos; the inventive appetizers; the attentive service; and the small but tempting selection of desserts. The unbelievably rich chocolate soup (yes, soup) of dark Belgian chocolate with hazelnut whipped cream and sugar croutons will make you swoon. The bartender makes a top-notch martini, and the all-Italian wine list is extensive, with several excellent selections by the glass. You may have to wait to be seated even if you have a reservation, but it's worth it.

313 N. Highland Ave. (at Elizabeth St.). ✆ **404/523-6678.** www.sottosottorestaurant.com. Reservations recommended. Entrees $16–$34. AE, DC, MC, V. Mon–Thurs 5:30–11pm; Fri–Sat 5:30pm–midnight; Sun 5:30–10pm. Free valet parking. MARTA: North Ave.

Surin of Thailand ★ THAI   This charming Thai restaurant is full of neighborhood regulars and suburbanites looking for consistent Asian cooking in an upbeat, contemporary setting—bare oak floors, candlelit tables covered in royal-blue cloths, and cheerful yellow walls. On weekends, arrive early or late to avoid a wait, and try for a table in the window or along the wall. There's more seating in the small back rooms, but the noisy and crowded main dining area is much more fun.

The same menu is offered throughout the day, with specials at both meals. The fresh basil rolls are some of the best around. Another appetizer favorite is chef Surin Techarukpong's exquisite deep-fried edible "baskets" filled with shrimp, chicken, and corn, served with a piquant vinegar-chili-peanut sauce. Entrees range from seafood dishes to traditional noodles and curry. If it's on the specials menu, opt for *neur nam tok*—strips of grilled beef tenderloin seasoned with lime, hot serrano chili peppers, fresh basil, fish sauce, and green onion; it's eaten rolled in cabbage leaves. For a cool finale, try the creamy homemade coconut ice cream or one of the mango, green tea, or ginger versions.

810 N. Highland Ave. (at Greenwood Ave.). ℂ **404/892-7789.** www.surinofthailand.com. Reservations not accepted. Entrees $7-$20. AE, DC, DISC, MC, V. Mon-Fri 11:30am-2:30pm; Sat-Sun noon-2:30pm; daily 5:30-10:30pm (until 11:30pm Fri-Sat). MARTA: North Ave.

Warren City Club ★ NEW AMERICAN   Don't let the name scare you away— you can be a member of this club, but don't have to be in order to enjoy the great food in a comfortable setting, including an outdoor deck. The Warren offers a full bar and comfortable seating areas around five wood-burning fireplaces. Dishes include Captain Crunch–crusted salmon, lobster ravioli, and, of course, the Warren burger, recently voted the best burger in the city.

Friday and Saturday nights the party goes on until 3am, with DJ music and dancing. The $4 mimosa brunches are a can't-miss, with menu items ranging from $8 to $12. Stand-up comedy on Wednesdays is a popular event. You'll find an extensive list of fine wines and special spirits.

818 N. Highland Ave. (at Greenwood Ave.). ℂ **404/475-1991.** www.thewarrencityclub.com. Appetizers $7-$12; entrees $11-$26. AE, MC, V. Wed-Sat 6pm-2am; Sun brunch 11am-3pm. MARTA: North Ave.

Inexpensive

Doc Chey's Noodle House ☺ ASIAN   This may not be the most authentic noodle house in the city, but it's a neighborhood standby that won't let you down if you're looking for a good, inexpensive meal. It's kid friendly, too, and offers two children's meals (Chinese chicken soup or chicken, carrots, and broccoli over rice) that should please finicky little eaters. The rest of us have a lot to choose from: fragrant basil rolls, Chinese scallion pancakes, soup bowls, noodle bowls, rice bowls, and salads, each with a Thai, Chinese, Japanese, or Vietnamese accent. You can ask for most dishes to be prepared vegetarian. The decor is nothing fancy, but the patio is large and pleasant, the Asian beer is cold, and at these prices, there's not much to complain about.

There are a couple of other locations in Atlanta, including Doc Chey's in Emory Village near Emory University, 1556 N. Decatur Rd. (ℂ **404/378-8188**), open for lunch Monday through Saturday and dinner nightly.

1424 N. Highland Ave. (at University Dr.). ℂ **404/888-0777.** www.doccheys.com. Reservations not accepted. Main dishes $7-$9. AE, DISC, MC, V. Daily 11:30am-10pm. MARTA: North Ave.

Flying Biscuit Cafe ★ ▮▮ NEW AMERICAN   This totally unpretentious neighborhood hangout has the best biscuits in town, but that's not all that makes folks willing to wait up to 1½ hours for a table. A cozied-up storefront near the funky Little Five Points area, this place has a round-the-clock breakfast menu that will get you over the worst day-after-the-night-before, plus an assortment of dishes that are best described as comfort food for the granola crowd. Breakfast and lunch are served all day. You can get a cup of coffee while you wait outside for your table, but to avoid the serious crowds, come on a weekday or in the early afternoon. If you have any sullen teenagers in your party, they'll think you're really cool for bringing them here.

The orange-scented French toast with raspberry sauce and honey crème anglaise is hard to beat. But the aptly named Love Cakes, a mix of black beans and cornmeal, sautéed and topped with tomatillo salsa, sour cream, feta, and raw onion spears, will steal your heart away. Though there's a vegetarian slant to the menu, there's also plenty to please carnivores, from the grilled turkey meatloaf to the ever-popular warm chicken salad atop organic field greens. Look for nightly chicken, seafood, and pasta specials, too.

There are a number of locations around the city, including a second one in Midtown at 1001 Piedmont Ave. (© **404/874-8887**).

1655 McLendon Ave. (at Clifton Rd.). © **404/687-8888.** www.flyingbiscuit.com. Reservations not accepted. Breakfast $6–$10; main courses $7–$14. AE, MC, V. Daily 7am–10pm (until 10:30pm Fri–Sat). MARTA: Midtown.

George's Restaurant and Bar 🍴 TRADITIONAL AMERICAN   Smack in the middle of trendy Virginia-Highland, surrounded by chic boutiques and cafes, is a comfy old neighborhood tavern—nearly a juke joint—that's managed so far to buck the gentrification sweep. This place, which has been operated by the Najour family for more than 40 years, is not trendy, so gear up for solid bar fare—burgers, sandwiches, fries, and the like. The refreshingly unpretentious attitude attracts neighborhood regulars and a couple of book-discussion groups, which meet here regularly.

Good bets are the substantial homemade black-bean soup and the crispy onion rings—even better than the Varsity's. When you order a burger, be sure to specify how you want it done. The charbroiled chicken salad, chunks of tender breast atop mixed greens, is nicely prepared. On a sunny day, grab a table on the sidewalk out front; it's a great place for watching the world (and some unusual folks) go by.

1041 N. Highland Ave. NE (near Virginia Ave.). © **404/892-3648.** www.georgesbarandrestaurant.com. Reservations not accepted. Main courses $6–$9. AE, MC, V. Mon 11:30am–10:30pm; Tues–Thurs 11:30am–11pm; Fri–Sat 11:30am–midnight; Sun 12:30–9:30pm. MARTA: North Ave.

Woody's Famous Philadelphia Cheesesteaks ☺ TRADITIONAL AMERICAN   Gourmet it ain't, but if you and the kids are all tuckered out from a romp in nearby Piedmont Park, walk on over to this casual little spot for lunch. It's barely bigger than a glorified hot-dog stand, but since 1975 has served excellent Philly cheese steaks, Italian subs, Polish sausages, and hot dogs. The ordering line (there's no table service) often snakes all the way out the door, so arrive at off-peak hours or be prepared to wait. There are five small booths inside, but the best place to sit on a nice day is the covered deck—perfect for enjoying an orange freeze or one of Woody's extra-thick, old-fashioned milkshakes.

981 Monroe Dr. NE (at 10th St.). © **404/876-1939.** Reservations not accepted. Hot dogs and sandwiches $4–$9. DISC, MC, V. Sun–Thurs 11am–10pm; Fri–Sat 11am–4am. MARTA: North Ave.

VININGS

Expensive

Canoe ★★ NEW AMERICAN   Canoe's cuisine is exceptional, and the setting is divine—a picturesque spot on the Chattahoochee River, surrounded by heavenly gardens. Unfortunately, that proximity to the river left Canoe underwater during flooding in Atlanta last year. Not to worry, all is back to normal now. The interior is ultra-upscale boathouse, with polished wood, classy fabrics, and fun, sophisticated metalwork (wrought-iron kudzu vines trail through the dining room). The canoe motif is everywhere; there's even a canoe-shaped phone booth.

The menu is American with Asian accents. The appetizer of duck-stuffed crispy Georgia quail with local baby collards and star anise boiled peanuts is a great start to dinner. If it's available, try the slow-roasted rabbit with Swiss chard, apple wood bacon ravioli, and candied garlic jus. Any of the fish options are good, but for a regional dish with a twist, try the seared local rainbow trout with lobster succotash. The excellent wine list is encyclopedic, and even includes a few organic options. If the weather is good, ask for a table on the large, canopied patio. Frequent live music riverside is a real treat.

4199 Paces Ferry Rd. NW (at the Chattahoochee River), in Vinings. ⓒ **770/432-2663.** www.canoeatl. com. Reservations essential on weekends. Lunch items $6–$28; brunch items $7–$16; dinner main courses $20–$29. AE, DC, DISC, MC, V. Mon–Fri 11:30am–2:30pm; Mon–Thurs 5:30–10pm; Fri–Sat 5:30–11pm; Sun 10:30am–2:30pm and 5:30–9:30pm.

DECATUR

Expensive

Floataway Café ★★ COUNTRY FRENCH/ITALIAN Tucked away on a secluded industrial street in a renovated warehouse near Emory University, the Floataway Café is not easy to find, but people have been flocking here since the restaurant opened in 1998. This is the second venture by Anne Quatrano and Clifford Harrison of the renowned Bacchanalia in Midtown; the restaurant and menu here are less formal, but the food is of the same high quality. The only drawback to this place is that it can be as loud as a working warehouse. Ask for a table away from the bar, which can be quite boisterous.

The menu changes daily, with an emphasis on fresh and local organic produce and unusual ingredients. You'll find succulent wood-grilled or roasted meats and seafood, homemade pastas, even a couple of pizzas—all inventively prepared. One favorite is a house specialty: wood-grilled steak with pommes frites and red-wine shallot butter. You can make a meal of the starters including the Star Provisions charcuterie. The wine list has an international slant and complements the food.

1123 Zonolite Rd., Ste. 15 (west of the intersection of Johnson and Briarcliff roads), Decatur. ⓒ **404/892-1414.** www.starprovisions.com. Reservations essential. Main courses $15–$24. AE, DC, MC, V. Tues–Sat 6–10pm.

Moderate

Leon's Full Service ★ GASTROPUB This community establishment has a big local following and a waiting line is the norm during prime hours, as no reservations are accepted. A big draw is the unique beers on tap—more than a dozen at any given time. The bar is always lively, and the outdoor seating is hugely popular. Monday nights are Flight Night, featuring micro flights of beer and wine paired with menu items. Pub fries are served with your choice of two of a dozen sauces, masaman curry and bacon and tarragon mayonnaise, for example. A selection of fine meats and cheeses are paired with homemade mustards and are among a long list of starter choices. A handful of sandwiches and another of entrees, including a panko-fried turkey schnitzel, round out the offerings.

cheesecake FIT FOR A PRESIDENT

Sweet potatoes are a staple in many southern homes, and they find their way into recipes that never cease to surprise me. From sweet-potato casserole and sweet-potato pie to the popular sweet-potato biscuits served during brunch at the Horseradish Grill (p. 93), this tasty tuber is very versatile. One Atlanta treat in particular does true justice to this spectacular spud: the sweet-potato cheesecake from **Sweet Auburn Bread Company.** The creation of Atlanta chef Sonya Jones, this sweet treat is known far and wide. In fact, former president Bill Clinton stopped by the market to try it for himself. Let's just say he didn't let any go to waste.

Trained at the Culinary Institute of America (CIA) in Hyde Park, New York, Jones grew up in the restaurant business watching every move her mother made around the kitchen. She fell in love with baking. After graduating from the CIA, she went on to share her culinary talents as a baking and pastry-chef instructor at a local technical college.

Soon she had opened her own bakery and was turning out pound cakes, buttermilk and lemon chess pies, even cakes made from towers of Krispy Kreme doughnuts. But in 1998 her name became synonymous with the famed sweet-potato cheesecake. "I wanted to come up with something really southern and yet gourmet," she said of the smooth sweet pie resting atop a pound-cake crust. The cheesecake has been featured in numerous magazines and newspapers and even on the Food Network. Now her goods are available at Atlanta Whole Foods markets.

Formerly housed in the Sweet Auburn Curb Market, her bakery is now right at home at 234 Auburn Ave. NE, in the same neighborhood where she grew up and learned to love baking as a young girl. Retail hours are Monday through Friday from 7:30am to 5pm and Saturday from 8am to 3pm. Special orders may be placed by calling ⓒ **404/221-1157** or visiting the website at www.sweetauburnbread.com.

131 E. Ponce de Leon Ave., Decatur. ⓒ **404/687-0500.** www.leonsfullservice.com. Entrees $11–$19. AE, MC, V. Mon 5pm–1am; Tues–Thurs and Sun 11:30am–1am; Fri–Sat 11:30am–2am.

Thai Chili ★ ☺ THAI   Owner Robert Khankiew, who was a chef at several other local Thai restaurants, has been packing people in since he and his family opened the doors of this friendly restaurant. The dishes are authentic, the flavors bold, and the dining room casual yet polished (tablecloths, soft lighting).

Start off with traditional basil rolls with plum sauce, or try the *namsod*—minced pork with chili, ginger, onion, and lime juice, which you roll up in a cabbage leaf. The spicy basil lamb (charbroiled chops with mushroom and onions) is succulent and exceptional, and the curries are quite good. When in doubt, stick with the daily specials or the chef's special section of the menu; all are good bets. There is no children's menu, but the restaurant is very child friendly. On weekends, you're likely to wait if you arrive without a reservation.

2169 Briarcliff Rd. NE (at LaVista Rd. in the Briarvista Shopping Center), Decatur. ⓒ **404/315-6750.** www.thaichilicuisine.com. Reservations recommended for dinner. Lunch items $8–$16; dinner main courses $9–$23. AE, DISC, MC, V. Sun–Thurs 11am–10pm; Fri–Sat 11am–11pm.

Watershed ★ SOUTHERN/REGIONAL   Watershed is a hip eatery housed in a former gas station in Decatur. Okay, it's better than it sounds. Owned in part by Emily

Saliers, one of the Indigo Girls (she's often spotted on-site), and bearing the name of one of the folk duo's songs, Watershed works on several levels—hip restaurant, wine bar, and retail store featuring wine, cookbooks, kitchen-related items, and other gifty little things. All of these attractions are found in a bright, airy, retro-style space whose industrial feel is softened by its pastel decor.

There are three or four entrees on the lunch menu, but sandwiches are the thing here—highly inventive and served on a variety of buttered, toasted breads. Two standouts include the version with garlic thyme-roasted pork and fig conserve; and the white-truffle chicken salad with sultanas and pine nuts. Oh, yes, and you can't ignore the tangy but comforting pimento-cheese sandwich made with extra-sharp cheddar. Whichever sandwich you choose to go with, the onion rings are a must. At dinner, more entrees are added to the seasonal list of sandwiches, sides, and soups. You might find grilled plantation quail with black-eyed peas, or cornmeal-crusted sea scallops. While Joe Truex is putting his own signature on the menu, Tuesday remains fried-chicken night, so arrive early to avoid a long wait. The wine list is extensive and well chosen, and the desserts, from the chocolate/pecan-praline parfait to the organic Georgia pecan tart with shortbread crust, are scrumptious.

406 W. Ponce de Leon Ave. (just west of the square), Decatur. © **404/378-4900.** www.watershed restaurant.com. Reservations recommended. Lunch entrees $8–$16; dinner entrees $12–$27. AE, MC, V. Mon–Sat 11am–10pm; Sun brunch 10am–2pm.

Inexpensive

Athens Pizza House 🍴 GREEK/PIZZA Who says pizza has to have an Italian pedigree? The Papadopoulos family has been serving Greek specialties and their interpretation of pizza in Atlanta since 1977. Their restaurant draws a large number of families and Emory University students from the surrounding area. The interior is ultra-casual, with Naugahyde booths and Formica-topped tables, and you'll be welcome in shorts or jeans.

There's quite a variety of Greek dishes, from gyros to pastitsio to rotisserie-cooked lamb. Portions are generous, prices are reasonable, and everything is authentic. It's home-style rather than fancy—exactly what you would get if the Papadopouloses invited you over for dinner. The signature creation is the pizza, and if you've never had it Greek-style, it's worth a try. It has a thick, yeasty crust and comes in several varieties; the best is the vegetarian special, with fresh tomatoes, onions, sweet green peppers, Kalamata olives, and a generous portion of feta cheese. A good ending is the honey-soaked baklava.

Note: There are several Athens Pizza restaurants and Athens Pizza Express takeout stores around town. Check the phone book for other locations.

1341 Clairmont Rd. (at N. Decatur Rd.), Decatur. © **404/636-1100.** www.athenspizzaatlanta.com. Reservations not accepted. Pizzas $7–$23; main courses $7–$12. AE, DC, DISC, MC, V. Sun–Fri 10am–11pm; Sat 11am–11pm.

Brick Store Pub GASTROPUB On the square in Decatur, this pub has old-world charm without being dark and gloomy, and features one of the most eclectic beer menus in Atlanta. Each of the 17 drafts—from Germany, England, and even the Czech Republic—is served in its own special glass. The 79 bottled beers might make it difficult for you to decide, and Brick Store also offers 26 single-malt scotches, nine Irish whiskeys, and eight small-batch bourbons. Many patrons come here for the drinks as much as for the diverse food. Starters include such treats as baked brie or roasted-red-pepper hummus with warm pita points. Pierogies fried in brown butter with caramelized onion and crispy sage is another popular item, as is that classic comfort food, shepherd's pie. Sit around the horseshoe bar for a real pub experience, or opt for one of several tables outdoors.

There are several great shops in the area for some before- or after-dinner shopping; you'll also find a coffee shop and an ice-cream shop.

125 E. Court St. (on the square), Decatur. © **404/687-0990.** www.brickstorepub.com. Reservations not accepted. Salads, sandwiches, and burgers $3.50–$8; dinner entrees $7–$9. AE, MC, V. Mon 11am–1am; Tues–Sat 11am–2am; Sun noon–1am.

Raging Burrito MEXICAN   A Decatur favorite, the Raging Burrito is the place to go when you need a salsa, guacamole, and margarita fix, not to mention the out-of-this-world burritos. From the barbecued-chicken burrito with caramelized onions and cilantro to the Sydney Salad burrito with fresh guacamole (voted best in town year after year) and a salad filling, Raging is sure to satisfy even the biggest hunger pangs. Choose from flour, wheat, spinach, or sun-dried tomato tortillas to build your dream burrito. Chase down the chow with any of 50 tequilas offered, and you might be hanging around at an outside table for a while. Nachos, quesadillas, and vegetarian chili are also popular menu items. Brunch is offered on Sundays. This is also home to Azul Tequila Lounge.

141 Sycamore St. (on the square), Decatur. © **404/377-3311.** www.ragingburrito.com. Reservations not accepted. Burritos $5.35–$9. AE, DC, DISC, MC, V. Daily 11am–10pm (until late Fri–Sat). Free 90-min. validated parking next to the patio.

DORAVILLE
Moderate

Han il Kwan ★ KOREAN   Frequently named best Korean barbecue in the city, Han il Kwan is popular with families and offers an attractive dining room, including a number of tables with charcoal grills. Cook your own thinly sliced beef over the grill in the center of your table and choose from a dozen sides to enjoy with it, including the popular and spicy kimchi. Like many other entrees, the hot pots are sized and priced for two or three people and are always consistent. A variety of Korean soups are warm and soothing options, as are the *bulgogi*, a marinated barbecued beef, and *bibimbap*, rice topped with vegetables, meat, an egg, and chili pepper paste. Always good is the rib-eye that your server will cook for you. A variety of pickles and other spicy snacks are provided for all guests to enjoy. Han il Kwan offers late-night noshing and is just one of many ethnic restaurants along Buford Highway, so pick a different one for each day of your visit.

5458 Buford Hwy, Doraville. © **770/457-3217.** Lunch combos under $10; dinner entrees under $20. MC, V. Daily 10am–2am.

Little Szechuan CHINESE   Little Szechuan is a perennial favorite among the ethnic restaurants that now line Buford Highway in northeast Atlanta. It's nothing fancy, but the price is right. Most of the patrons are Chinese or regulars (or both), who make a point of seeking out good ethnic food. Two Chinese-restaurant clichés are pointedly absent here: egg rolls and fortune cookies. When you're seated, you'll be given a small bowl of spicy sprouts to munch on while you peruse the extensive menu. And when your check arrives at the end of the meal, it will be accompanied by a piece of fresh, seasonal fruit—perhaps a slice of watermelon.

The standout entree is also the most expensive: fresh steamed red snapper with black-bean sauce; it's best when you request it spiced up a little. (Even though the name of the restaurant would suggest otherwise, not everything on the menu is spicy Szechuan-style Chinese.) Skip the limited wine list, and have an ice-cold Tsing-Tao beer instead.

5091-C Buford Hwy. (just north of Shallowford Rd. in Northwoods Plaza), Doraville. © **770/451-0192.** www.littleszechuanchefkongs.com. Lunch combination plates $7–$9; dinner entrees $8–$22. MC, V. Daily 11:30am–3pm and 5–9pm.

WHAT TO SEE & DO IN ATLANTA

People truly began flocking to Atlanta following its unveiling during the 1996 Olympics. Finally, outsiders had a reason to come to the city, and while they were here for those international games, they discovered that Atlanta has a huge offering for visitors and residents alike. Word spread like wildfire. Despite the complaints about traffic—which can still be an issue—tourists pour into the city at an average rate of 36 million people a year to see what this gateway to the New South has to offer. And they're not disappointed.

A lot has happened since Atlanta's humble beginnings as a railroad depot, and the city is rich in historic attractions—Civil War sites, landmarks of the civil rights movement, and monuments to the businesses that have energized the city's development (such as World of Coca-Cola). And all those elements that make Atlanta a great place to live make the city a terrific place to visit, too. You can take a stroll through a world-class botanical garden, visit the world's largest indoor aquarium, picnic in a scenic park, raft down a river, visit a major art museum, splash through the Olympic-rings fountain, take in an enchanting puppet show, and much more.

Consider the CityPass and see eight of Atlanta's top attractions ($74 for adults, $54 kids 3–12; it's a bargain, take my word for it) while avoiding most ticket lines at the same time. For info, call ☎ **770/256-0490,** or visit **www.citypass.com**.

MARTA stops near attractions are listed where applicable. If you need information on bus routes, call ☎ **404/848-4711.**

THE TOP ATTRACTIONS

The APEX (African-American Panoramic Experience) Museum

This museum chronicles the history of Sweet Auburn, once Atlanta's foremost black residential and business district, and serves as a national African-American museum and cultural center. The museum's Trolley Car Theater, a replica of a turn-of-the-20th-century tram that ran on Auburn Avenue, shows a 12-minute multimedia presentation, *Sweet Auburn: Street of Pride*, acquainting visitors with the area's history. Sweet Auburn also comes to life in tableaux such as a replica of an Auburn Avenue barbershop and a re-creation of the 1920s-era Yates & Milton's Drugstore (Atlanta's first black pharmacy), featuring some original furnishings. There are interactive displays for children, too. The APEX recently added a tribute to the late Maynard Holbrook Jackson, Jr., Atlanta's first black mayor. Inquire about special events and workshops taking place during your visit to Atlanta.

Across the street, at 100 Auburn Ave., is **Herndon Plaza,** where you can see a permanent exhibit on the Herndon family (former slave Alonzo F. Herndon founded the Atlanta Life Insurance Company) and changing shows featuring the works of African-American artists.

135 Auburn Ave. (at Courtland St.). © **404/523-2739.** www.apexmuseum.org. Admission $4 adults, $3 seniors and students, free for children 4 and under. Tues–Sat 10am–5pm. Closed Sun–Mon and all major holidays. MARTA: Bus 113 from the Five Points station.

Atlanta Botanical Garden This delightful botanical garden, occupying 30 acres in Piedmont Park, includes the Fuqua Orchid Center, a children's garden, an education center, and the Dorothy Chapman Fuqua Conservatory. In the $4.8-million, 25,000-square-foot Fuqua Orchid Center, a collection of rare high-elevation orchids, which flourish on cool, wet mountains in South America, are being grown in the warm Southeast. Typically, one would have to go to San Francisco or Seattle to see such plants. There is beauty here year-round, but peak orchid-bloom season lasts through March.

The latest and greatest here is the Canopy Walk, offering a view from 40 feet above one of the city's last remaining urban forests. Along with the Edible Garden and Cascades Garden, the Canopy Walk marked the completion of a major expansion that nearly doubled the garden's size. The 600-foot walk is the only tree canopy-level walk of its kind in the country.

Nearby, the 16,000-square-foot, glass-walled Dorothy Chapman Fuqua Conservatory houses rare and endangered tropical and desert plants—and a fascinating exhibit of poison dart frogs (more about them later). With acres of irreplaceable rainforest being bulldozed every minute, the plant species in the conservatory seem all the more special. Approached via an arbored promenade and fronted by a lily pond, the entrance to the conservatory has a revolving globe showing the many regions of the world where plant life is endangered.

The focal point of the conservatory is the misty Tropical Rotunda, housing fern collections, cycads (the most primitive seed-bearing plants known), epiphytes (plants that don't require soil to grow), gorgeous orchids, carnivorous plants, a wide variety of begonias, and towering tropical palms. It's a lush and humid jungle, with brightly hued tropical birds warbling overhead, a splashing waterfall, and winding pathways lined with fragrant hibiscus, ginger, and flowering jasmine vines. Of special interest is a double coconut palm from the Seychelles, growing from the largest and heaviest seed in the plant kingdom. Its first 12-foot leaves have already begun to grow, but it will be 100 years before the tree reaches its full height.

In the midst of all this is an intriguing exhibit of Central and South American poison dart frogs—small, active ground dwellers in unbelievably bright colors (yellow, orange, lime green, cobalt blue) and vivid patterns. About 12 species are exhibited in three large terrariums filled with tropical rainforest plants and designed to simulate the climates in the frogs' native lands. This exhibit is a big hit with visiting children.

Another main section of the garden highlights plants that thrive in North Georgia's extended growing season. Displays in this area include a rock garden, a dwarf conifer garden, an English knot herb garden, a tranquil moon-gated Japanese garden, a rose garden, and annual and perennial displays. The delightful children's garden, with its wonderful climbing structures and whimsical sculptured fountains, has become a hot spot for young families.

Another section of the garden consists of two wooded areas. The 5-acre Upper Woodland features a paved path, a fern glade, camellia and hosta gardens, gurgling streams, beautiful statuary, and a habitat designed to show visitors how to attract wildlife to their own backyards. Still more rustic is Storza Woods, 15 acres of natural woodlands and one of the few remaining hardwood forests in the city. Even though its path is unpaved, it makes for an easy and interesting walk.

The arid Desert House displays Madagascan succulents, such as a unique family of spiny plants called *Didieriaceae*. Here, too, are "living stones" (desert succulents that nature designed to look like pebbles to protect them from predators), tree aloes, caudici-forms (with swollen stems and roots for storing water), and conifers from Africa. The building also houses an orangery of tropical mango, papaya, star-fruit, litchi, coffee, and citrus trees. An "Olympic" olive tree presented by Greece in honor of the 1996 Centennial Olympic Games in Atlanta resides here as well.

There are flower shows throughout the year, along with lectures and other activities. Call to find out what's scheduled during your visit. The Café serves sandwiches, salads, and snacks, and it also has a children's menu. It's open Tuesday through Sunday, with outdoor seating available. A marvelous gift shop is on the premises; your purchases help support the garden.

1345 Piedmont Ave. NE (adjacent to Piedmont Park at Piedmont Ave. and the Prado). (C) **404/876-5859.** www.atlantabotanicalgarden.org. Admission $15 adults, $12 seniors and children ages 3–17, free for children 2 and under. Tues–Sun 9am–5pm, until 7pm during daylight saving time, Thurs May–Oct 9am–10pm. The gardens are closed every Mon except Mon holidays. All areas accessible to visitors with disabilities. Free parking. MARTA: Bus 27 stops at the main entrance on Piedmont Avenue.

Atlanta Cyclorama & Civil War Museum ★★ Though it sounds like something out of Disney World, the Atlanta Cyclorama was created in the 1880s, and the concept—a huge, 360-degree cylindrical painting viewed from a rotating platform—dates from a century earlier. Cycloramas were the rage of 18th- and 19th-century Europe, Russia, Japan, and, later, the United States, depicting subject matter ranging from the splendors of Pompeii to Napoleonic battles. Enhanced by multimedia effects and faux terrain extending 30 feet from the painting into the foreground, they were the forerunners of newsreels, travelogues, and TV war coverage.

The one you'll see here—a 42-foot-high cylindrical oil painting, 358 feet in circumference (on about 16,000 sq. ft. of canvas)—depicts the events of the Battle of Atlanta, on July 22, 1864, in meticulous detail. It took 11 Eastern European artists, working in the United States in the studio of William Wehner, 22 months to complete the project.

For 21st-century tourists, the concept and story of the Cyclorama are as interesting as the action depicted, and the restoration is incredibly impressive. Though painted on fine Belgian linen in the painstaking style of the 19th-century art academies, the work suffered in moves from city to city, and later (when motion-picture epics made cycloramas passé) from neglect. Well-intentioned but incompetent attempts at restoration caused further damage. In the 1970s, a severe storm waterlogged the painting, causing seemingly irreversible damage. But Mayor Maynard Jackson recognized the historical and artistic importance of the Cyclorama; under his auspices, $11 million was raised for its restoration. It took 2½ years for renowned conservator Gustav Berger and his crew to repair the damaged work, a process that included mending more than 700 rips in the canvas. The fascinating story of the Cyclorama's development and restoration is related in a video near the auditorium entrance.

The Cyclorama's central theme is General John B. Hood's desperate attempt to halt General William Tecumseh Sherman's inexorable advance into the city. Comprehensively narrated, and complete with music and sound effects (including galloping horses and cannon fire), it vividly depicts the troop movements and battles on the day that the Confederates lost 8,000 men and the Yankees lost 3,722. A figure highlighted far beyond his historical importance is General John A. Logan of the Federal Army of Tennessee (who commissioned the painting at a cost of $42,000 as a campaign move in his bid for the Union vice presidency). He's shown gloriously galloping into the fray, bravely exposing himself and his men to enemy fire. (The work was originally called *Logan's Great Battle.*) A 14-minute film about the Battle of Atlanta precedes the Cyclorama viewing. The total program lasts about 35 minutes.

The building housing the Cyclorama also contains a museum of related artifacts, the most important being the steam locomotive *Texas* from the 1862 "Great Locomotive Chase." Other exhibits include displays of Civil War arms and artillery, Civil War–themed paintings, portraits of Confederate and Union leaders, "life in camp" artifacts and photographs, and uniforms. You'll need about an hour and a half to see the museum in full if you visit both floors.

Note: No video cameras are allowed inside the Cyclorama auditorium.

800 Cherokee Ave. (in Grant Park). © **404/658-7625.** www.atlantacyclorama.org. Admission $10 adults 13–64, $8 seniors (65 and up), $8 children 4–12, free for children 3 and under. Tues–Sat 9:15am–4:30pm. Guided tours hourly on the half-hour starting at 9:30am. Closed Thanksgiving, Christmas, New Year's Day, and Martin Luther King, Jr., Day. By car, take I-20 E. from downtown to exit 59A. Free parking. MARTA: From Five Points Station take bus 97 to Grant Park.

Atlanta History Center ★★★   The Atlanta History Center chronicles the past of Georgia and the Southeast, as well as the history of Atlanta, with a vast collection of photographs, maps, books, newspaper accounts, furnishings, Civil War artifacts, and decorative arts. It occupies 32 woodland acres, with self-guided walking trails and five gardens. Plan to spend the better part of a day here. And call ahead, or inquire on the premises, about lectures, films, festivals, and other events that take place on a regular basis; activities range from sheep-shearing demonstrations to decorative-arts forums. When you call, also check on house-tour times for the day of your visit (these tours are described below). **Note:** House-tour tickets are limited and can be purchased only on the day of your visit. Arrive early to avoid disappointment.

Begin your visit at the **Atlanta History Museum,** where you can buy tickets and get information about historic house tours and other activities. The museum is the single best place to go for a cultural record of the city and the South. The major permanent exhibit, "Metropolitan Frontiers: Atlanta, 1835–2000," traces Atlanta's history from the Native Americans and rural pioneer settlements to the present day. Displays, enhanced by hands-on discovery areas and informative videos, feature hundreds of photographs, documents, and artifacts. Included is an entire 1890s shotgun house, a fire engine that was used in Atlanta's great fire of 1917 (when 50 city blocks were ravaged by flames), a rare 1920 Hanson Six touring car, and a model of Atlanta's most complex interstate intersection, known locally as "Spaghetti Junction."

A $10-million, 20,000-square-foot addition houses a highly interactive exhibition about the 1996 Centennial Olympic Games in Atlanta. Also on the center's grounds is the beautifully restored **Swan House,** the 1928 estate of Edward Hamilton Inman, scion of an old Atlanta family. The house and gardens were designed by renowned architect Philip Trammell Shutze and are considered his finest residential work, and, ironically, his first. The formal gardens include terraced lawns and water-falls, retaining walls with recessed ivy arches, and fountain statuary. Swan House is fronted by a classical colonnaded *porte-cochere* leading to a circular entrance hall with Ionic columns and a dramatic floating stairway. In the entrance hall, you'll notice that the fanlight over the door features a swan, announcing the theme of the house. There is at least one swan emblem or decoration in each room—see if you can find all 24 of them. The house is interesting not only architecturally, but also for its eclectic contents and furnishings, which comprise a veritable museum of decorative arts. It's a fascinating glimpse into the lifestyle enjoyed by upper-crust Atlantans in the early 20th century. Tours of the house begin every 30 minutes.

Tullie Smith Farm gives a sense of the life of Georgia's mid-19th-century farm-ers. A two-story "plantation-plain" house built in the early 1840s, it was brought to Atlanta along with period outbuildings in 1972. This was no Tara-like colonnaded mansion—just an everyday farmhouse whose occupants lived in rustic simplicity. Costumed docents give tours throughout the day, and there are frequent demonstra-tions of 19th-century farm activities. In a bedroom with a rope bed and a crib (always occupied by the youngest baby), a docent will demonstrate how to use a spinning wheel. The basket of pomander balls in this room was typical—the 19th century's answer to today's air fresheners. You'll find weaving demonstrations in the back room. During cooler months, demonstrations of hearth cookery take place in the white-washed kitchen, where herbs hang from the rafters. Additional outbuildings include a barn, corncrib, root cellar, blacksmith shop, and smokehouse. The gardens and grounds are authentic to the period.

Leave some time to stroll the many gardens, most notably the forested mile-long **Swan Woods Trail.** It includes plants native to Georgia, plus the Garden for Peace, home to a sculpture by noted Soviet artist Georgi Dzhaparidze and Atlanta artist Hans Godo Frabel. If you're visiting during lunchtime, the **Swan Coach House** (p. 98) is a delightful restaurant on the premises, famous for the chicken salad in timbales.

130 W. Paces Ferry Rd. NW (at Slaton Dr.). © **404/814-4000.** www.atlantahistorycenter.com. Admis-sion $17 adults, $13 seniors and students 13 or older, $11 children 4-12, free for children 3 and under. General admission is all-inclusive. Mon-Sat 10am-5:30pm; Sun and some holidays noon-5:30pm. Ticket sales end at 4:30pm. Closed Thanksgiving, Christmas Eve, Christmas, and New Year's Day. MARTA: Rte. 38 offers hourly service Mon-Sat from 5:30am-8:30pm to the History Center via East Andrews Dr., Pharr Rd., and Slaton Dr.

Birth Home of Martin Luther King, Jr. ★★   Martin Luther King, Jr., was born in this two-story Queen Anne–style house on January 15, 1929, the oldest son of a Baptist minister and an elementary-school music teacher. His childhood was a nor-mal one. He preferred baseball to piano lessons, liked to play board games, and got a kick out of tearing the heads off his older sister's dolls (nonviolence came later). To quote his sister, Christine King Farris, "My brother was no saint ordained at birth; instead he was an average and ordinary man, called by . . . God . . . to perform extraordinary deeds."

A Spot of History

Dr. Martin Luther King, Jr., won the Nobel Peace Prize in 1964 at the age of 35, the youngest person ever to do so. He was killed 4 years later.

King lived here through the age of 12, and then moved with his family to a house a few blocks away. A visit provides many insights into the formative influences on one of the greatest leaders of our time. The Rev. A. D. Williams, King's maternal grandfather and pastor of Ebenezer Baptist Church, bought the house in 1909. Reverend Williams was active not only in the church but in the community and in early manifestations of the civil rights movement. He was a charter member of Atlanta's NAACP and led a series of black registration and voting drives as far back as 1917. He was instrumental in getting black officers onto the Atlanta police force. Martin Luther King, Sr., moved in on Thanksgiving Day 1926, when he married Williams's daughter Alberta. When Reverend Williams died in 1931, King became head of the household and took over Williams's pulpit at Ebenezer Church.

The King family retained ownership of the house at 501 Auburn Ave. even after they moved away. King's younger brother, Alfred Daniel, lived here with his family from 1954 to 1963. In 1971, King's mother deeded the home to the King Center. It has since been restored to its appearance during the years of King's boyhood. The furnishings are all originals or period reproductions, and some personal items belonging to the family are on display. Christine was actively involved in the restoration, providing a wealth of detail about the former appearance of the house, as well as anecdotal material about life in the King family.

Tours of the house, conducted by national park rangers, begin in the downstairs parlor, where you'll see family photographs showing Martin Luther as a child. The parlor was used for choir practice, for the dreaded piano lessons, and as a rec room where the family gathered around the radio to listen to shows like *The Shadow*. In the dining room, world events were regularly discussed over meals, and every Sunday before dinner, each child was required to recite a newly learned Bible verse from memory. You'll also see the coal cellar (stoking coal was one of King's childhood chores); the children's play area; the upstairs bedroom of King's parents, in which Christine, Martin Luther, and Alfred Daniel were born; Reverend Williams's den, where the family gathered for nightly Bible study; the bedroom King shared with his brother ("always in disarray," says Christine); and Christine's bedroom.

Note: In summer, especially, tickets often run out early; for your best chance at touring the home, arrive at 9am.

501 Auburn Ave. ℂ **404/331-6922.** www.nps.gov/malu. Free admission. Tickets are available at the National Park Service Visitor Center, 450 Auburn Ave. Accessible only by tour. Tours depart from Fire Station No. 6 (at Boulevard and Auburn Ave.) about every 30 min. in summer, every hour the rest of the year. June 15–Aug 15 daily 9am–6pm; Aug 16–June 14 daily 9am–5pm. Closed Thanksgiving, Christmas, and New Year's Day. From I-75/85 S., exit at Freedom Pkwy./Carter Center (exit 248-C). Turn right at first stoplight onto Boulevard. Follow signs to Martin Luther King, Jr., National Historic Site. MARTA: Take bus 3 east from the Five Points station or take bus 99 from the Midtown and Georgia State stations.

Centennial Olympic Park ★★★ ☺ Centennial Olympic Park, one of the most enduring legacies of the 1996 Olympic Games, is a living monument to the city's memories—both good and bad—of that seminal event. Conceived as a town square, it represents the heart of the Olympic effort, the site where everyone flocked to celebrate the games. And when the games resumed after the bombing in the park that claimed one life, it was where people gathered to try to revive the Olympic spirit. Ongoing upgrades keep the park in tiptop shape for the more than three million visitors who come here each year.

A 21-acre swath of green space and bricks, the park was carved out of a blighted downtown area. It's an oasis of rolling lawns crisscrossed by brick pathways and

Pricey Parkland

If you really, really, really had a good time at Centennial Olympic Park, you can have it all to yourself for a small fee. Though it's a public park, it's also a moneymaker managed by the Georgia World Congress Center Authority, and parts of the park are sometimes rented for various business functions, parties, and other celebrations. There have even been a few weddings. You can rent the entire park for, um, $15,000. If you're short on cash, you can always buy the park for $1 million in Monopoly money, as it's a featured Atlanta location in the Monopoly Here and Now board game. Call © **404/222-7275** for facility rental details.

punctuated by artwork, rock gardens, pools, and fountains. There are usually a few free events each month—festivals, artists' markets, concerts, and other performances, some private, some open to the public. The park is home to a number of concert series, a huge Fourth of July celebration, and the Holiday in Lights, including an ice skating rink. Call for a complete listing of happenings or visit their website.

If you're visiting the park on your own, and not coming for a specific event, your first stop should be the Visitor Center on Andrew Young International Boulevard, in the southwest corner of the park, across from the CNN Center. This is where you'll find information about the park. If you bought a $35 commemorative brick in 1996, someone will help you locate it among more than 500,000 engraved bricks that were used to pave the plaza and walkways. Even if you didn't buy a brick, it's fun to wander around and read the names and messages (some pretty intriguing) engraved on them.

The best part of the park is the Fountain of Rings and its 251 water jets in the shape of the five interlocking Olympic rings. It's the focus of a vast paved plaza bordered by 23 flags honoring the host countries of the summer games from 1996 and earlier. If you're here in summer, you and the kids can frolic in the Fountain of Rings (wear shoes, please, and bring a bathing suit), a good way to cool off in the sizzling southern heat. Don't be shy—just about everybody in Atlanta has done this at one time or another. If getting drenched is not your thing, you can still enjoy one of the "concerts" put on by the fountain—choreographed water-and-light displays, during which the water jets, which normally shoot 12 feet into the air, can reach 35 feet during special effects.

Located along the east border are the Quilt Plazas, five plazas of contrasting bricks that tell the story of the Centennial Olympic Games. The best "quilt" is also the most moving. Titled the *Quilt of Remembrance,* it pays respect to the bombing victims and contains colored marble from five continents. Be sure to read the inscriptions on its borders.

265 Park Ave. W. NW (at Baker St.). © **404/222-PARK** (7275). www.centennialpark.com. Free admission. Daily 7am–11pm. MARTA: Philips Arena/Dome/GWCC or Peachtree Center.

CNN Studio Tour ★★★   This tour of the world's largest newsgathering organization is lots of fun and a uniquely Atlanta experience. The CNN Center is headquarters for CNN, CNN International, and Headline News. During 50-minute guided walking tours, visitors get a behind-the-scenes look at the high-tech world of 24-hour TV network news in action.

You'll find the tour desk in the main lobby near the base of an eight-story escalator. While you're waiting for the tour to begin, you can have a videotape made of yourself reading the day's top stories from behind a CNN anchor desk. The tour starts in an exhibit area where you'll find timelines covering the history of CNN and Turner Broadcasting, interactive kiosks where you can surf the CNN websites or access clips from the top 100 stories that CNN has covered, memorabilia from some of those events, and a journalism ethics display. A theater that re-creates CNN's main control room allows you to experience the behind-the-scenes elements of a news broadcast.

Next, you'll enter a special-effects studio and get a glimpse of the technology that goes into the production of global news. Here you'll discover the magic of a high-tech Blue Chromakey system (it's what's used to broadcast that big map behind the weather folks), see how on-air graphics are made, and learn the secrets of the Tele-PrompTer.

On another level, visitors get a bird's-eye view of the main CNN newsroom from a glass-walled observation station. From here, you'll see the hustle and bustle of writers composing news scripts. If a live broadcast is in progress—and chances are good that one will be—you can see CNN newscasters at work. Tour guides are knowledgeable and can answer virtually any question.

The longer, more extensive VIP tour allows visitors to actually step out onto the main CNN newsroom floor and explore production areas not normally accessible to the public.

After your visit, stop by the Turner Store, which carries network-logo clothing and gift items, along with MGM movie paraphernalia. For sports fans, there's the Braves Clubhouse store, featuring the Atlanta Braves logo on every item you can imagine. There are several restaurants and numerous fast-food outlets in the atrium of the CNN Center, as well as a few shops. Remember that the tour includes quite a bit of walking and a very steep escalator ride, which carries you to great heights to begin your visit. Those afraid of heights might want to consider skipping the tour.

CNN Center, 190 Marietta St. NW (at Techwood Dr.). ℭ **877/4-CNN-TOUR** (266-8687) or 404/827-2300. www.cnn.com/studiotour. Admission $13 adults, $12 seniors, $11 student (13–18 or with valid college ID), $10 children 4–12. A more in-depth, Morning Express tour costs $49 (includes breakfast, souvenirs, and more behind-the-scenes opportunities), Inside CNN VIP Tour $35. **Note:** Reservations highly recommended. Tours are given daily every 10 min. 9am–5pm. Arrive early for the tour you wish to take, as most tours sell out. Closed Easter, Thanksgiving, and Christmas. MARTA: Omni/Dome/GWCC. Many parking lots around the building.

Ebenezer Baptist Church   Founded in 1886, Ebenezer was a spiritual center of the civil rights movement from 1960 to 1968, when Martin Luther King, Jr., served as copastor. King's grandfather, the Rev. A. D. Williams, dedicated the church to "the advancement of black people and every righteous and social movement." His son-in-law and successor, Martin Luther King, Sr., worked for voting rights and other aspects of black civil and social advancement, following Williams's activist example. Later, Martin Luther King, Jr., would join his ancestors in pursuing justice for African Americans.

The congregation has built a new sanctuary directly across the street, but the older building, where Martin Luther King, Jr., preached, continues to be open to the public. Short but informative tours of the sanctuary, conducted by members of the Ebenezer congregation, are given Monday through Friday from 9am to 4pm, Saturday from 9am to 2pm, and Sunday from 2 to 4pm. One of the best things to do is attend a Sunday-morning worship service in the new sanctuary. The public is welcome—and you'll realize just *how* welcome when the members of the congregation leave their seats at the beginning of the service to shake the hands of as many visitors as possible. It's a living testimonial to all that the church's most famous son stood for. Sunday services are at 7:45 and 10:45am. The sanctuary is usually packed, so it's a good idea to arrive well ahead of time. Groups of six or more should call the church office at ℂ **404/688-7263** to make reservations. An ecumenical service also takes place here every year during King Week (Jan 9–15).

407 Auburn Ave. NE. ℂ **404/688-7300.** http://new.historicebenezer.org. Free admission (donations appreciated). Mon–Sat 9am–5pm; Sun 1–5pm. From I-75/85 S., exit at Freedom Pkwy./Carter Center. Turn right at first stoplight onto Boulevard. Follow signs to Martin Luther King, Jr., National Historic Site. MARTA: King Memorial station is about 8 blocks away, or take bus 3 from the Five Points station.

Fernbank Museum of Natural History ★★ ☺ The largest museum of natural sciences in the Southeast, this architecturally stunning facility borders 65 acres of pristine forest. Architect Graham Gund has achieved a marvelous integration of interior/exterior space: The building, which nearly eclipses the attractions inside, centers on a soaring three-story, sky-lit Great Hall—an Italianate brick atrium with spiral staircases, lofty columns, and windows revealing the woodlands beyond. Look closely at the museum floors, where ancient fossil remains from the late Jurassic period are embedded.

When the Great Hall was designed, it was meant to one day be the home of a large-scale permanent dinosaur exhibition, and in 2000, Fernbank became the only place in the world to display a complete mounted skeleton of *Argentinosaurus,* the largest dinosaur ever found. The dramatic permanent exhibit, "Giants of the Mesozoic," features the 90-foot-long plant eater as it defends its nest of eggs against the 45-foot-long *Giganotosaurus,* the largest meat-eater ever classified. Hovering above in the 86-foot-tall hall are two flying *Pterosaurs.* Dinosaurs just don't get any bigger than this, and it's a little hair-raising to walk into the hall and see these beasts towering over the tiny humans below.

There are several other permanent exhibits, including "A Walk Through Time in Georgia," which uses the state as a microcosm to tell the story of the earth's development through time and the chronology of life upon it. Visitors travel back 15 billion years to experience the origins of the universe (the Big Bang) and the formation of galaxies and solar systems, and into the future to consider the fate of our planet. Eighteen galleries re-create landform regions from the rolling pine-forested foothills of the Piedmont Plateau to the mossy Okefenokee Swamp, from the Cumberland Plateau (where you can walk through a typical limestone cavern) to the marshy Coast and Barrier islands. Exhibits are enhanced by creative films and videos, informational audiophones, interactive computers, sound effects, and old-fashioned field guides—not to mention more than 1,500 fabricated plants and mounted specimens of birds and animals.

"Sensing Nature" tantalizes your senses with hands-on exhibits that explore how we experience the natural world. The room swims with computers, colored lights, and mirrors, and you can step into a life-size kaleidoscope, play with perspective, gaze into infinity, see physical evidence of sound waves, and mix colors on a computer.

The Children's Discovery Room, open daily June through August and on a limited basis during the school year, includes Fantasy Forest, a colorful play area designed for preschoolers (ages 3–5), where kids can become bees and pollinate flowers, climb a tree house, walk through a swamp, and play at being farmers. The state-shaped Georgia Adventure is a similar discovery room for ages 6 to 10.

While you're here, be sure to catch a stunning IMAX film (buy tickets as soon as you enter the museum; they sometimes sell out). The immense screen—five stories high and 72 feet wide—puts you right in the middle of all the action.

Other museum attractions include a wetlands exhibit, a dramatically colorful living coral reef aquarium, a unique shell display, a gemstone collection, and the McClatchey Collection of jewelry and textiles from the old Silk Road countries. The museum store is stocked with entertaining and educational gifts and books, and there's a restaurant with arched windows overlooking Fernbank Forest and outdoor patio seating. See p. 192 for a description of the adult-geared Martinis & IMAX Friday nights.

767 Clifton Rd. NE (off Ponce de Leon Ave.). ✆ **404/929-6300** for information, or 929-6400 for tickets. www.fernbankmuseum.org. Admission $15 adults ($23 includes an IMAX theater ticket), $14 seniors and students ($21 includes an IMAX theater ticket), $13 children 3–12 ($19 includes IMAX theater ticket), free for children 2 and under. IMAX theater admission alone $13 adults, $12 seniors and students, $11 children 3–12, free for children 2 and under. Mon–Sat 10am–5pm; Sun noon–5pm. The IMAX theater until 11pm on Fri nights Jan–Nov for Martinis & IMAX. Closed Thanksgiving and Christmas. Free parking. MARTA: Bus 2, ask driver to drop you at Clifton Rd. Walk north and Fernbank is first drive on right.

Fox Theatre ★★   Originally conceived as a Shriners' temple in 1916, this lavish, block-long Moorish-Egyptian fantasyland ended up as a movie theater when the Shriners realized that their grandiose plan had far exceeded their budget. In 1927, they sold the temple to movie magnate William Fox, who created a peerless pleasure palace. French architect Oliver J. Vinour designed the building, using motifs of the Middle East, including replicas of art and furnishings from King Tut's tomb.

Atlanta's new theater opened in 1929 as a masterpiece of Eastern splendor, its Moorish facade, onion domes, and minarets in exotic contrast to the surrounding Victorian boardinghouses. A brass-trimmed marble kiosk imported from Italy served as a ticket booth. The 140-foot entrance arcade led to a lushly carpeted lobby with blue-tiled goldfish pools. The auditorium was an Arabian courtyard under a twinkling starlit sky that, with state-of-the-art technology, could be transformed to a sky at sunrise or sunset. A striped Bedouin canopy sheltered the balcony, and sequin- and rhinestone-studded stage curtains depicted mosques and Moorish horsemen.

As the show began, a gigantic gilded 3,610-pipe Möller organ rose majestically from its vault, its rich chords accompanied by a full orchestra. A medley of popular songs, cartoons, a follow-the-bouncing-ball singalong, a stage-show extravaganza by a bevy of Rockette-like chorines called the Fanchon and Marco Sunkist Beauties, and a newsreel preceded every main feature. At night, there were dances in the Egyptian Ballroom, designed to replicate Rameses' temple. Even the men's lounge was exotically appointed with hieroglyphic adornments, winged scarab-motif friezes, bas-reliefs of royal figures, and throne chairs.

Unfortunately, the Fox's opening coincided with the Great Depression, and it proved impossible to maintain its opulence. In 1932, the company declared bankruptcy and closed its doors. The theater reopened 3 years later for occasional concerts. By the 1940s, it was a successful concern once more, and in 1947, the Metropolitan Opera began performing here for a week each year—an offering that lasted 2 decades. An oversize panoramic screen was installed in the 1950s, along with a 26-speaker stereo system. But like monumental movie palaces nationwide, the Fox inevitably declined in the age of television. In 1975, its doors were padlocked once again.

An organization of concerned citizens called Atlanta Landmarks raised $1.8 million and saved the Fox from the wrecking ball in 1978, foiling Southern Bell's plans to purchase and demolish it to make way for a regional headquarters building. Ever since, it's been a thriving entity, featuring Broadway shows, headliners, dance companies, and comedy stars. Best of all, the theater has been restored to its former glory, its fabulous furnishings and fixtures all refurbished or replaced with replicas.

You cannot explore the building on your own, so call to find out when you can take a tour, or come to see a performance in the theater.

660 Peachtree St. NE (at Ponce de Leon Ave.). © **404/881-2100** for performance tickets, or 688-3353 for tours. www.foxtheatre.org. Tours $10 adults, $5 seniors and students. The Atlanta Preservation Center conducts walking tours of the Fox Theatre and the surrounding area 10am Mon, Wed–Thurs, and 10am, 11am Sat; call to verify times before you go, as tours are occasionally canceled due to production rehearsals. MARTA: North Ave.

Georgia Aquarium ★★★ ☺   Since it opened to continual massive crowds in late 2005, the world's largest aquarium has had Atlanta abuzz about its 8 million gallons of fresh and marine water, home to more than 100,000 animals representing 500 species from around the globe. The aquarium continues to add to its collection, including a 9-foot, 456-pound manta ray named Nandi, which joined the aquarium in 2008. A $110-million dolphin exhibit opening is planned for 2011 and will include a 1.3-million-gallon exhibit, offering dolphin encounters, viewing windows, and dolphin shows.

The aquarium includes five stunning permanent exhibits, including Cold Water Quest, Georgia Explorer, Ocean Voyager, River Scout, and Tropical Diver, each featuring inhabitants of those environments. Visitors are fascinated by the ghostly beluga whales in the Cold Water Quest, along with Australian weedy sea dragons, giant Pacific octopus, and Japanese spider crabs. Georgia Explorer includes an interactive gallery with touch pools of horseshoe crabs, sea stars, stingrays, and shrimp. See a loggerhead sea turtle and right whales, which live just off the Georgia coast. Feel like a scuba diver in a sea of fish as you walk through an acrylic tunnel surrounded by water and creatures in the Ocean Voyager exhibit. Watch out for the gigantic whale sharks that call this tunnel home; they'll swim right over your head. River Scout highlights wildlife of rivers from Georgia to Asia, including a large exhibit of Amazonian fish. See electric fish from Africa and get up close and personal with a toothy piranha. Kids delight at the playful Asian small-clawed otters that spend their days playing and eating. Tropical coral reefs round out the exhibit Tropical Diver, where kids love to look for "Nemo" among the hundreds of sea creatures that pop in and out among the reef. Three jellyfish exhibits are also located here, performing a mesmerizing watery ballet.

A number of behind-the-scenes tours are available, including Journey with Gentle Giants, an opportunity to swim or scuba-dive with whale sharks and tons of other fish in the Ocean Voyager exhibit. Fees are steep: $190 for swimmers and $290 for certified divers, but where else could you have this experience in a metropolitan setting? The swim/dive tour is limited to six people a day and reservations are booked months ahead, so plan early. For another $50 you can purchase a DVD of yourself swimming with the fishes to take home to impress friends and family. Other tours are less expensive and allow guests to visit areas typically off-limits to see how these creatures are cared for by staff.

While numbers have leveled out since the opening year, crowds are still big enough that tickets are issued based on your preferred time to enter the aquarium. Tickets to the 4-D theater are a few bucks extra, or for an additional $50, visitors can experience

WATER, water EVERYWHERE

Folks in Atlanta were pretty sure the Georgia Aquarium would be a big hit, but even the most optimistic about this world-class project underestimated the numbers of people who'd be clamoring to see it. Nine months after its opening in November 2005, the world's largest indoor aquarium was already welcoming its three-millionth visitor.

Aquarium benefactor Bernie Marcus had it pegged pretty well, though—he predicted the facility would welcome three million people within its first year. The aquarium is a gift to the people of Georgia from Marcus, cofounder of Home Depot, and his wife, Billi, through the Marcus Foundation.

The initial crowds were so huge, sales of annual memberships were actually suspended because management feared that hordes of return visitors would overwhelm their ability to welcome first-time guests. Of the first three million visitors, more than 50,000 were Atlanta-area teachers and students, who were among the earliest supporters of the facility. The aquarium has now served as Atlanta's second-largest tourism boost since the Centennial Olympic Games were held here in 1996.

Since the opening, aquarium visitors and staff have found reason to both celebrate and mourn. From an announcement of $14 million in building improvements less than a year after opening to the 2007 death of Gasper, one of two beluga whales housed here, the Georgia Aquarium continues to draw international attention.

a behind-the-scenes tour. Advance booking online is highly recommended. Café Aquaria serves grilled items, pasta, pizza, salads, sandwiches, and more.

If you plan to see the World of Coca-Cola and the Georgia Aquarium, a Pemberton Pass will save you a few bucks. In addition, the two attractions share a huge covered parking garage with a $10 fee. Pemberton Place includes an expansive lawn, perfect for a picnic, as well as a cafe and public restrooms.

225 Baker St. ℂ 404/581-4000. www.georgiaaquarium.org. Admission $26 adults, $22 seniors, $20 children 3–12. Sun–Fri 10am–5pm; Sat 9am–6pm. 365 days, but holiday hours vary slightly. Covered parking (attached) $10. MARTA: Peachtree Center or Dome/GWCC/PhilipsArena/CNN.

High Museum of Art ★★★   The High's $130-million, three-building expansion brought the museum to truly world-class status. The additions include more gallery space for the museum's permanent collection, enlarged special-exhibit space, a coffee bar, and a new retail shop. Not to be overshadowed, the original facility—designed by architect Richard Meier and part of the Woodruff Arts Center complex—is itself a work of art. A dazzling white-porcelain-tiled building with an equally pristine white interior, the museum houses four floors of galleries connected by semicircular pedestrian ramps girding a spacious, sun-filled four-story atrium.

The permanent collection here includes more than 10,000 pieces, among them a significant group of 19th- and 20th-century American paintings. Hudson River School artists such as Thomas Cole and Frederic Church are featured, as are Thomas Sully, John Singer Sargent, and William Harnett. The Virginia Carroll Crawford Collection of American Decorative Arts comprehensively documents trends in decorative arts from 1825 to 1917. The Samuel H. Kress Foundation collection includes Italian paintings and sculpture from the 14th through the 18th centuries. The Uhry Print

SEARCHING FOR Margaret Mitchell

More than 6 decades after Margaret Mitchell published *Gone With the Wind*, the novel continues to attract new fans and fascinate people around the world. And thousands of them come to Atlanta each year looking for some trace of Tara or the woman who wrote about it. Well, Tara doesn't exist, no matter how much the book and movie brought it to life for us. The white-columned mansion we equate with Tara was more the product of Hollywood's fancy than of Mitchell's imagination. She begged filmmakers to represent the house as she envisioned it, as a plain structure without columns, which is far closer to the reality of a working plantation than the image that's been perpetuated.

Until the Margaret Mitchell House & Museum opened in 1997, evidence of Mitchell herself was nearly as elusive as the fictional Tara. An extremely private person, she left a will stipulating that her papers and manuscripts be burned upon her death. Only a portion of the manuscript of *Gone With the Wind* was spared—enough to prove that Mitchell was its author. Several places where Mitchell lived fell victim to development or were destroyed in 1917, when a great fire swept the city.

Still, it's possible to walk the streets of Atlanta and find traces of the famous author, either by viewing exhibits honoring her or by retracing some of her steps:

- The house at **1401 Peachtree St.** is gone, but a plaque commemorates the site of the home where Mitchell spent her adolescence. She ordered that the house be torn down after her death, possibly because she wasn't happy there. Her mother's dream house, it was a white, two-story Colonial Revival with Doric columns. MARTA: Arts Center.

- **Margaret Mitchell House & Museum,** 990 Peachtree St., at 10th Street (📞 **404/249-7015**). In 1925, newlywed Mitchell and her husband, John Marsh, moved into apartment 1 on the bottom floor of this building, living here until 1932. It was in "the dump," as she called it, that Mitchell wrote much of her novel. See p. 128 for details. MARTA: Midtown.

- **Georgian Terrace,** 659 Peachtree St. NE. It was here in 1921 that debutante Mitchell shocked polite society by performing an Apache dance—all the rage in Paris—with her partner at a charity ball. As a result, she was blackballed from the Junior League. Years later, when the Junior League held a costume ball the night before the world première of *Gone With the Wind*, Mitchell declined their invitation to be the guest of honor. It was also here that Mitchell handed over her manuscript to Harold Latham, an editor for Macmillan. MARTA: North Avenue.

- **Margaret Mitchell Square,** intersection of Peachtree and Forsyth streets and Carnegie Way. It's possible to walk right by this spot and not even know that you've just passed one of the few public memorials to Atlanta's most famous author, which is probably just the way Mitchell would have preferred it. (Friends and acquaintances say she would have disliked the idea of a monument to her life.) The understated square contains a fountain, an inscription, and a sculpture symbolizing the columns of Tara. A block away is the famous intersection known as Five Points, which Mitchell referred to in her book. MARTA: Peachtree Center.

○ Across the street from the square is the **Atlanta-Fulton Public Library** (✆ **404/730-1700**), which has a permanent Margaret Mitchell exhibit on its third floor. Among the interesting memorabilia, you'll find numerous photographs, a facsimile copy of one of the pages of the original manuscript, and Mitchell's library card. The library also possesses Mitchell's personal literary collection, including the books she used to research *Gone With the Wind,* her typewriter, and her Pulitzer Prize. If you sign the guest book at the exhibit, look back through the previous pages. You'll be astounded at the number of people from overseas who have visited the display. The current library is the site of an earlier building, the Carnegie Library, where Mitchell did much of her research. Her father was one of the founders of the library, and in the years after his death, Mitchell made many contributions in his name. The Carnegie Library was razed in 1977 to make way for the present building. Open Monday from 9am to 6pm, Tuesday through Thursday from 9am to 8pm, Friday and Saturday from 9am to 6pm, and Sunday from 2 to 6pm. MARTA: Peachtree Center.

○ Across Peachtree Street is the rose-granite **Georgia-Pacific Building,** built on the site of the Loew's Grand Theatre, where *Gone With the Wind* had its première on December 15, 1939. The theater burned in 1979, but there's an inscription to the right of the main entrance to the current building. See if you can find the misspelling. MARTA: Peachtree Center.

○ **Accident scene,** Peachtree and 13th streets. On August 11, 1949, Mitchell and her husband were crossing the street to attend a play. Mitchell accidentally darted into the path of a taxi rounding the curve, was struck, and died 5 days later. MARTA: Peachtree Center.

○ **Gravesite,** 248 Oakland Ave. SE. Mitchell was laid to rest in Oakland Cemetery on August 17, 1949. Only 300 guests were allowed to attend, but fans invaded the cemetery after the service, many taking funeral flowers as souvenirs. The cemetery (✆ **404/688-2107**), which is an interesting place in and of itself, is open daily from dawn to dusk. Admission is free, and a map of famous graves is available for a small fee at the cemetery foundation office Monday through Thursday from 9am to 5pm and Friday from 9am to 4pm. MARTA: King Memorial.

○ **Atlanta History Center,** 130 W. Paces Ferry Rd. NW (✆ **404/814-4000**). For a look at what plantation life was really like, visit the Tullie Smith Farm on the grounds of the history center. The house itself, built in 1845 and moved here in 1972, is a plain, columnless two-story building, typical of an antebellum working plantation in North Georgia. See p. 115 for more details on the Atlanta History Center. MARTA: Arts Center.

For more information on Margaret Mitchell, read *Looking for Tara,* a small but informative guidebook to Mitchell's Atlanta. It's written by Don O'Briant and is available in local bookstores.

Collection contains important works by French Impressionists and post-Impressionists, German expressionists, and 20th-century American artists. Also notable are collections of sub-Saharan African art, a folk-art collection, and works by noted 19th- and 20th-century American and European photographers.

In addition to the permanent collection, which is shown on a rotating basis, the museum hosts a number of major traveling exhibitions each year, complemented by films, lectures, workshops, gallery talks, concerts, and other events, including Friday Jazz, the third Friday of each month. Ask at the desk about special events during your visit. Free guided gallery tours of the High's permanent collection are offered Tuesday through Sunday at 1pm; free guided family tours are given every Saturday and Sunday at 2pm. Special headsets for audio guides are available for special exhibits.

The museum's wonderful gift shop boasts an impressive stock of books, prints, and interesting art-related objects. Since the opening of the contemporary Table 1280, the on-site restaurant, many now visit the High specifically for the food. It serves American-inspired fare as well as a delightful mix of small plates of seasonal ingredients, and the meal can be as memorable as the museum visit. The restaurant is open Tuesday through Saturday from 11am to 2pm for lunch, Sunday from 11am to 2pm for brunch, and Tuesday through Sunday from 5 to 10pm for dinner and tapas. The lounge remains open until midnight Tuesday through Saturday. Don't miss this experience.

1280 Peachtree St. NE (at 16th St.). ☎ **404/733-HIGH** (4444). www.high.org. Admission $18 adults, $15 seniors and students with ID, $11 children 6–17, free for children 5 and under. Fees subject to change for special exhibitions. Tues–Wed and Fri–Sat 10am–5pm; Thurs 10am–8pm; Sun noon–5pm; Fri Jazz 3rd Fri of every month (except Dec.) from 5–10pm. Closed July 4th, Thanksgiving, Christmas, and New Year's Day. MARTA: Arts Center (a covered walkway links the station to the museum). Parking is available in the garage across from the museum.

Jimmy Carter Library & Museum   Set on 30 acres of gardens, lakes, and waterfalls, this impressive presidential library houses some 27 million pages of documents, memoranda, and correspondence from Jimmy Carter's White House years. There are also 1.5 million photographs and hundreds of hours of audio- and videotapes. The library's hilltop site is a historic one; it was from this spot that Sherman watched the Battle of Atlanta.

In the extensive museum, you'll find an exact replica of the Oval Office during Carter's presidency—an exhibit enhanced by a recording of Carter speaking about his experiences in that office. A large display of "gifts of state" runs the gamut from a Dresden figurine of George and Martha Washington (a gift from Ireland) to a carpet from the Shah of Iran. You'll also see the table setting used when the Carters entertained Chinese Vice Premier Deng Xiaoping and his wife in the State Dining Room; a video of artists such as the late pianist Vladimir Horowitz performing in the East Room; campaign memorabilia; and a large display devoted to the activities of Rosalynn Carter. Other exhibits focus on Carter's support of human rights (there's a letter from Soviet dissident Andrei Sakharov and Carter's reply); his boyhood days (you'll see his sixth-grade report card and a photo of the Plains High basketball team); and his pre-presidential life as a peanut farmer, governor, and state senator.

There are informative videos throughout, including an interactive "town meeting" video through which visitors can ask Carter questions on subjects ranging from world affairs to his personal life. Another intriguing participatory video lets you respond to a terrorist crisis and learn the probable consequences of your choice.

Consider having lunch here. There's an excellent cafeteria, run by one of the city's top catering companies, with patio seating overlooking a Japanese garden and pond.

The APEX Museum **10**
Centennial Olympic Park **5**
CNN Center **4**
Georgia Aquarium **7**
Georgia Dome **2**
Georgia State Capitol **12**
Herndon Home **1**
Imagine It! Children's
  Museum of Atlanta **9**
National Museum of
  Patriotism **6**
Philips Arena **3**
Underground Atlanta **11**
World of Coca-Cola **8**

If you're still in a political mood, stop at nearby **Manuel's Tavern,** a local pub at 602 N. Highland Ave. that's popular with journalists and politicians. President Carter himself stops in occasionally.

441 Freedom Pkwy. (exit 248-C off I-75/85). (C)**404/865-7100.** www.jimmycarterlibrary.org. Admission $8 adults, $6 seniors 60 and over, free for children 16 and under. Mon–Sat 9am–4:45pm; Sun noon–4:45pm. Library Mon–Fri 8:30am–4:30pm. Closed New Year's Day, Thanksgiving, and Christmas. Free parking.

The King Center ★ Martin Luther King, Jr.'s, commitment to nonviolent social change lives on at this memorial, museum, and educational center. A nongovernmental member of the United Nations, the center works with government agencies and the private sector to reduce violence within individual communities and among nations.

The tour of the center, which is self-guided, begins in Freedom Hall, where memorabilia of King and the civil rights movement are displayed. Here, you can see King's Bible and clerical robe, a handwritten sermon, a photographic essay about his life and work, and, on a grim note, the suit he was wearing when a deranged woman stabbed him in New York City. Also on display is the key to his room at the Lorraine

Motel in Memphis, Tenn., where he was assassinated. In an alcove off the main exhibit area is a video about King's life and works. Additional exhibits include a room honoring Rosa Parks (whose refusal to give up her seat on a city bus led to the Montgomery bus boycott), and another honoring Mahatma Gandhi, whose emphasis on nonviolence was a major influence on King.

The center's library and archives house the world's largest collection of books and other materials documenting the civil rights movement, including Dr. King's personal papers and a rare 87-volume edition of *The Collected Works of Mahatma Gandhi,* a gift from the government of India. The library is open by appointment only for scholarly research.

In addition to serving as a museum and hub of social-justice activity, the center is Martin Luther King, Jr.'s, final resting place, a living memorial to this inspiring leader that is visited by tens of thousands each year. Dr. King's white-marble crypt rests outside in the Freedom Plaza, surrounded by a beautiful five-tiered Reflecting Pool, a symbol of the life-giving nature of water. The tomb is inscribed with his words: "Free at Last. Free at Last. Thank God Almighty I'm Free at Last." An eternal flame burns in a small circular pavilion directly in front of the crypt, and the late Coretta Scott King is laid to rest here as well. The Freedom Walkway, a vaulted colonnade paralleling the pool, will eventually be painted with murals depicting the civil rights struggle. Located at the end of Freedom Walkway is the Chapel of All Faiths, symbolizing the ecumenical nature of Dr. King's work and the universality of the basic tenets of the world's great religions.

A store on the premises sells King memorabilia and a wide selection of books and audiovisual resources. Ranger talks focusing on the community and the civil rights movement take place frequently on Freedom Plaza.

449 Auburn Ave. NE (btw. Boulevard and Jackson St.). ✆ **404/526-8900.** www.thekingcenter.org. Free admission. Mon–Fri 8:30am–5:30pm. Closed Thanksgiving, Christmas, and New Year's Day. From I-75/85 S., exit at Freedom Pkwy./Carter Center. Turn right at first stoplight onto Boulevard. Follow signs to Martin Luther King, Jr., National Historic Site. MARTA: King Memorial station is about 8 blocks away, or take bus 3 east from the Five Points Station.

Margaret Mitchell House & Museum (Birthplace of *Gone With the Wind*) ★   Eight decades after it was first published, *Gone With the Wind* continues to fascinate people around the world. But until this attraction opened in 1997, after a 10-year effort to preserve the house from demolition, disappointed pilgrims found precious little evidence here of the famous book or its author. Now the house and museum are a must-see for visiting *GWTW* fans.

It's rather surprising that it took so long for restoration efforts to get underway on the dilapidated Tudor Revival apartment house where Margaret Mitchell wrote most of her epic novel and lived with her husband, John Marsh, from 1925 to 1932. The structure was built as a single-family dwelling in 1899, then moved to the back of the lot in 1913 and converted into a 10-unit apartment building 6 years later. It remained an apartment building until 1979, when it was abandoned and eventually boarded up. When the newlyweds moved in, they called it "the dump." It was not an affectionate nickname; according to a friend of Mitchell's, she disliked living here (finances left few alternatives) and would probably be offended by the notion of its restoration. But the house has attracted its share of visitors—from all 50 states and more than 70 countries.

The house and museum tell the complex story of the famous novelist. Guided tours, which last 1 to 1½ hours, begin in the visitor center. Before beginning the tour,

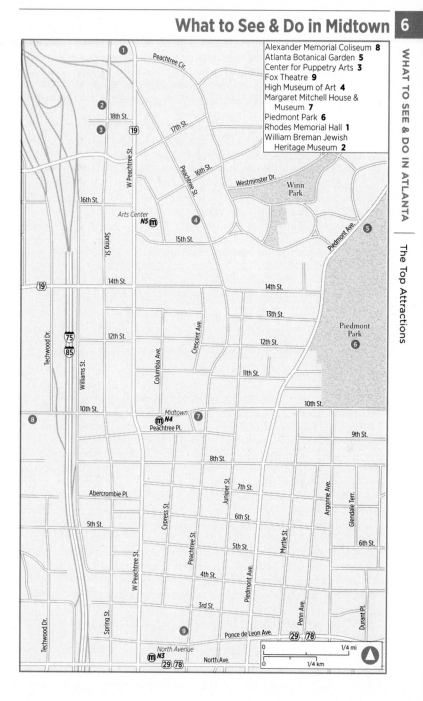

Alexander Memorial Coliseum **8**
Atlanta Botanical Garden **5**
Center for Puppetry Arts **3**
Fox Theatre **9**
High Museum of Art **4**
Margaret Mitchell House &
  Museum **7**
Piedmont Park **6**
Rhodes Memorial Hall **1**
William Breman Jewish
  Heritage Museum **2**

guests enter the theater to see a 17-minute film titled *It May Not Be Tara,* featuring an overview of Mitchell's life, and interviews with some of her friends and family members. Also in the theater is an exhibit of photos taken of Mitchell in her teens and 20s. The tour of the house includes a visit to the Mitchell-Marsh apartment, which is furnished much as it was when the couple lived here. Mitchell wrote much of her novel in the front room, seated at a typewriter and desk below the beveled-glass windows in the small corner alcove. Like most writers, she preferred to keep her literary efforts private and would throw a towel over her typewriter when friends dropped in—which was often.

The museum contains movie memorabilia and chronicles the making of the movie, its première in Atlanta, and the impact that the book and movie had on society. The tour concludes in the museum shop, which features a variety of *GWTW* collectibles. If you finish your tour around mealtime and you're ready for a real change of pace, walk a few blocks south on Peachtree Street to the Vortex (p. 86), a rowdy burger joint and bar that serves some of the best hamburgers in town.

990 Peachtree St. (at 10th St.). © **404/249-7015.** www.gwtw.org. Admission $13 adults, $10 seniors and students, $8.50 children 4–12, free for children 3 and under. Mon–Sat 10am–5:30pm; Sun noon–5:30pm. Closed Thanksgiving, Christmas Eve, Christmas, and New Year's Day. Free parking. MARTA: Midtown.

Martin Luther King, Jr., National Historic Site   Under the auspices of the National Park Service (NPS), this area of about 2 blocks around Auburn Avenue was established to preserve the birthplace and boyhood surroundings of the nation's foremost civil rights leader. Designated a national historic site, these blocks include King's boyhood home and the Ebenezer Baptist Church, where King's father and grandfather were ministers and King served as a copastor. Free tours of King's birth home start at Fire Station No. 6, which was recently restored by the NPS; tickets are available on a first-come, first-served basis at the National Park Service Visitor Center, 450 Auburn Ave., across from the King Center. For more information on King's birth home, see p. 116.

Other Auburn Avenue attractions, not under NPS auspices, include the King Center, where King is buried (see above), and the APEX Museum (p. 112). Several additional surrounding blocks have been designated as a preservation district; this area is known as Sweet Auburn. John Wesley Dobbs, maternal grandfather of former Atlanta mayor Maynard Jackson, is the person who first called it such, after Oliver Goldsmith's *The Deserted Village,* the first line of which reads, "Sweet Auburn! loveliest village of the plains." Mayor Jackson says his grandfather called the area "sweet" because the keys to black liberation existed here in the form of "the three Bs—bucks, ballots, and books." (See chapter 7 for tips on exploring the area.)

The NPS Visitor Center provides a complete orientation to area attractions and includes a theater for audiovisual and interpretive programs, interactive exhibits, and a bookstore. It's fronted by a beautifully landscaped plaza with a reflecting pool, King's crypt (which his wife had returned to the site several years ago), and an outdoor amphitheater for NPS programs.

450 Auburn Ave. NE © **404/331-6922.** www.nps.gov/malu. Free admission and parking. Labor Day to Memorial Day weekend daily 9am–5pm; rest of year daily 9am–6pm. Closed Thanksgiving, Christmas, and New Year's Day. MARTA: Bus 3 from the Five Points station.

Michael C. Carlos Museum of Emory University 🏛   Emory University began its antiquities collection in 1875, and this intriguing museum dates from 1919, when it was founded to display the art and artifacts collected by Emory faculty in Egypt, Cyprus, Greece, Sicily, the Sea of Galilee, and the sites of ancient Babylon and Palestine. Today, the museum also maintains collections of ancient art and archaeology from Rome, Central and South America, the Near East, and Mesoamerica; works of the native cultures of North America; art of Asia and Oceania; and some 1,000 objects from sub-Saharan Africa. Additionally, a sizable collection of works on paper encompasses illuminated manuscript pages, drawings, and prints from the Middle Ages and the Renaissance to the 20th century.

The museum is housed partly in a 1916 Beaux Arts building that is on the National Register of Historic Places; architect Michael Graves redesigned the interior in 1985. The remainder of the collection occupies a 35,000-square-foot exhibition space (also designed by Graves). The first-floor galleries feature exhibits from the extensive permanent collection—objects that were part of the daily life of people from five continents as early as the 7th millennium B.C. They include Bronze and Iron Age clay pots, jugs, loom weights, and oil lamps from Palestine; Egyptian mummies, pottery, cosmetic containers, and headrests; Greek and Cypriot pottery, flasks, and statuary; and Mesopotamian pottery, coins, tools, sculpture, and cuneiform tablets inscribed with ancient writing. Also on this level: the Thibadeau pre-Columbian collection, comprising more than 1,300 objects spanning 2,000 years of creativity—gold jewelry, pottery, and statues, including many ceramic, volcanic stone, greenstone, and gold sculptures from ancient Costa Rica.

The upper floor is used for changing exhibits ranging in subject matter from Pueblo Indian pottery to Impressionist art. Throughout the museum, 210 plaster casts of ancient architectural elements—reliefs, friezes, column capitals, and decorative elements from temples and monuments—adorn hallway and lobby walls.

Allow at least an hour to see the collections. There are many interesting workshops, lectures, films, and gallery tours here; call to find out what's on during your stay. A nice museum shop tempts with a variety of educational books and gifts, as well as jewelry inspired by the collections. Caffè Antico, on the third floor, serves a seasonal menu of salads, sandwiches, and entrees and is open Monday through Saturday 11am to 4pm and Sunday noon to 4pm.

571 S. Kilgo Circle (near the intersection of Oxford and N. Decatur roads on the Main Quadrangle of the Emory campus). ℰ **404/727-4282.** www.carlos.emory.edu. Admission $8. Tues–Sat 10am–4pm; Sun noon–4pm. Closed major holidays. Parking can be difficult on the Emory campus. Paid visitor parking is available in the Fishburne Parking Deck and at the B. Jones Center lot. After 6pm, free parking is available in any space on campus not marked by an orange PARK or handicap sign. MARTA: Bus 6 Emory from Candler Park station or Lindbergh station, or bus 36 N. Decatur from Avondale station or Arts Center station.

Oakland Cemetery ★ 👬 Listed on the National Register of Historic Places, this outstanding 88-acre Victorian cemetery was founded in 1850. It survived the Civil War and remained the only cemetery in Atlanta for 34 years. Among the more than 48,000 people buried here are Confederate and Union soldiers (including five Southern generals), prominent families, paupers, governors and mayors, golfing great Bobby Jones, and *Gone With the Wind* author Margaret Mitchell. There's a Jewish section (consecrated by a temple), a black section (dating from segregation days), and a potters' field (a section for unknown or poor people). Two monuments honor the Confederate war dead. Standing at the marker that commemorates the "Great Locomotive Chase," you can see the trees from which the Yankee raiders were hanged; the Confederate train conductor Captain William Fuller is buried nearby. The cemetery is not only famous for historical reasons, but also because it is a virtual outdoor museum of Gothic and Classical Revival mausoleums, bronze urns, stained glass, and Victorian statuary.

Almost every grave has a story. Real-estate tycoon Jasper Newton Smith had a life-size statue of himself erected on his grave so he could watch the city's goings-on into eternity. (The sculptor originally gave Smith a tie, but Smith, who never wore one, refused to pay for the piece until the tie was chiseled off.) Dr. James Nissen, Oakland's first burial, feared being buried alive; his will directed that his jugular vein be severed prior to interment. And John Morgan Dye was a baby who died during the siege of Atlanta; his mother walked through the raging battle to the cemetery carrying the small corpse. The smallest grave, however, is that of "Tweet," a pet mockingbird buried in its family's lot.

Though you can visit whenever the cemetery is open, try to come when you can take a guided tour. It's a fascinating way to learn about the history of the graveyard and about graveyard symbolism (a lopped-tree-trunk marker indicates a life cut short or goals unachieved, rocks on a grave denote a life built on a solid foundation, a shell means resurrection, and so on). Every October, there's a celebration to commemorate the cemetery's founding, with turn-of-the-20th-century music, food, and storytelling.

Dozens of people jog and walk on the rolling terrain every day, and picnickers are a common sight. However, a tornado swept through in the spring of 2008, damaging several sections. Restoration, which is always a huge task at Oakland, where most of the mausoleums are more than 100 years old, went into overdrive. Trees and debris were cleaned up and the cemetery is once again fully navigable to visitors, though repairs to individual sections continue. Completed repairs and restoration improved many sections of the cemetery from their prestorm condition. Leashed pets are welcome.

248 Oakland Ave. SE (main entrance at Oakland Ave. and Martin Luther King, Jr., Dr.). © **404/688-2107.** www.oaklandcemetery.com. Free admission. Daily dawn–dusk; visitor center Mon–Sat 9am–5pm, Sun 1–5pm. Purchase an informative, self-guided walking-tour map brochure at the visitor center for $1. Guided walking tours available Mar–Nov for $10 adults, $5 seniors and students. Free parking inside the cemetery. MARTA: King Memorial.

Stone Mountain Park ★ ☺   A monolithic gray-granite outcropping (the world's largest) carved with a massive monument to the Confederacy, Stone Mountain is a distinctive landmark on Atlanta's horizon and the focal point of its major recreation area, which includes 3,200 acres of lakes and beautiful wooded parkland. Having celebrated its 50th anniversary in 2008, Stone Mountain is Georgia's number-one tourist attraction, and one of the 10 most-visited paid attractions in the United States.

Stone Mountain itself was formed about 300 million years ago, when intense heat and pressure caused molten material just below the earth's surface to push upward. That material cooled slowly (it took 100 million years) and formed compact, uniform crystals. Initially, a 2-mile-thick overlay of the earth's surface covered the hardened granite, but over the next 200 million years, that layer eroded, exposing the mountain we see today. The dome-shaped rock rises 1,683 feet above sea level and covers 583 acres. Half of Georgia and part of North Carolina rest on the mountain's base.

Make your first stop the **Discovering Stone Mountain Museum** to get some perspective on the mountain's history. Exhibits take you through an intriguing chronological journey from the area's past into its present.

Although the best view of the mountain is from below, the vistas from the top are spectacular. Visitors who are part mountain goat can take the **walking trail** up and

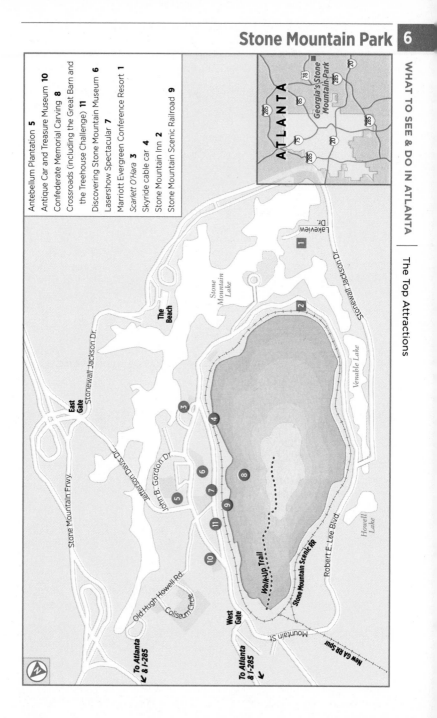

Antebellum Plantation **5**
Antique Car and Treasure Museum **10**
Confederate Memorial Carving **8**
Crossroads (including the Great Barn and the Treehouse Challenge) **11**
Discovering Stone Mountain Museum **6**
Lasershow Spectacular **7**
Marriott Evergreen Conference Resort **1**
Scarlett O'Hara **3**
Skyride cable car **4**
Stone Mountain Inn **2**
Stone Mountain Scenic Railroad **9**

The Face of a Mountain

Over half a century in the making, Stone Mountain's neoclassical carving—90 feet high and 190 feet wide—is the world's largest bas-relief sculpture. Originally conceived by Gutzon Borglum, it depicts Confederate leaders Jefferson Davis, Robert E. Lee, and Stonewall Jackson galloping on horseback throughout eternity. Borglum started work on the mountain sculpture in 1923, but abandoned it after 10 years due to insurmountable technical problems and rifts with its sponsors. (He went on to South Dakota, where he gained fame carving Mount Rushmore.) No sign of his work remains at Stone Mountain, but it was his vision that inspired the project. Augustus Lukeman took over in 1925, but 3 years later, the work still far from complete, the family that owned the mountain lost patience and reclaimed the property. It wasn't until 1963, after the state purchased the mountain and surrounding property for a park, that work resumed under Walter Kirtland Hancock and Roy Faulkner. It was completed in 1970.

down its moss-covered slopes, especially lovely in spring when they're blanketed in wildflowers. The trail is 1.3 miles each way. Or you can ride the **Skyride cable car** to the top, where you'll find an incredible view of Atlanta and the Appalachian Mountains. The best approach is to take the cable car up and then walk back down. A new view can be had from the **Sky Hike** attraction, a quarter-mile family adventure course four stories high.

For a different perspective, check out the park from onboard a World War II amphibious vehicle: The park's **Ride the Ducks Tour** is a 40-minute adventure that moves from land into the waters of Stone Mountain Lake. Tours run from 11am daily; tickets are $9 for ages 3 and up, or $6 when added to the One-Day All-Attractions Pass. Duck Tours are included on the One-Day Pass on "Limited Attraction Days" (Mon–Thurs in the fall) at no additional charge.

A highlight at Stone Mountain is the **Lasershow Spectacular,** an astonishing display of laser lights and fireworks with animation and music. The brilliant laser beams are projected on the mountain's north face, a natural 1-million-square-foot screen. Shows are presented on Saturdays at 8:30pm from March through October, except from Memorial Day weekend through Labor Day, when they take place every night at 9:30pm. They're free with park admission. Bring a picnic supper and arrive early to get a good spot on the lawn at the base of the mountain.

Other major park attractions include the **Stone Mountain Scenic Railroad,** an open-air train that chugs around the 5-mile base of Stone Mountain. The ride takes 40 minutes and includes a live "train robbery" skit. Trains depart from Railroad Depot, an old-fashioned train station, where there's a restaurant with all the fixings for a fried-chicken picnic, just in case you forgot to bring your own.

The **Antique Car and Treasure Museum** is a jumble of old radios, jukeboxes, working nickelodeons, pianos, Lionel trains, carousel horses, and clocks, along with classic cars. The *Scarlett O'Hara,* a paddlewheel riverboat, cruises the 363-acre Stone Mountain Lake.

Visitors can now travel back in time at **Crossroads ★**, where you can explore an 1870s rural southern town, complete with a cast of authentically costumed characters who sing, play instruments, tell stories, and demonstrate crafts such as glass blowing, candle making, and blacksmithing. In addition to the town's quirky and talented characters, other special treats include a gristmill and bakery, a general store with candy and ice-cream production facilities, and a boardinghouse restaurant that serves up tasty Southern cuisine, from chicken and dumplings to fried catfish. If you plan to eat, you might want to stop by and add your name to the list before you explore the town, as there is often a wait.

Another part of the Crossroads attraction is the **Great Barn,** a hit with children and adults. Join in the fun as you help "harvest" fruits and vegetables throughout this multi-level foam factory to rack up points for your team. The **Treehouse Challenge** is a one-of-a-kind outdoor adventure that pits boys against girls to control balls on a large track that links the two tree houses (sort of a life-size pinball game). The town's centerpiece is the **Tall Tales of the South** theater, where visitors use special glasses to view a 3-D film with 4-D (yes, four) special effects. The frog's tongue, which stretches into the movie audience from its perch on a swamp log, is just one of the surprises of the experience. Small children might not enjoy the film, as some of the effects are a bit unnerving.

The 19-building **Antebellum Plantation** offers self-guided tours assisted by hosts in period dress at each structure. Highlights include an authentic 1830s country store; the 1845 Kingston House (which represents a typical overseer's house); the clapboard slave cabins; the 1790s Thornton House, elegant home of a large landowner; the smokehouse and well; the doctor's office; a barn, a coach house, and crop-storage cribs; a privy; a cook house; and the 1850 neoclassical Tara-like Dickey House. The grounds also contain formal gardens and a kitchen garden. It takes at least an hour to tour the entire complex. Often (especially in summer), there are Civil War reenactments, craft and cooking demonstrations, storytellers, and balladeers on the premises. Children will enjoy getting up close and personal with the critters at Grandpa's Farm at the Plantation, featuring domesticated farm animals such as pigs and goats.

Additional activities: golf (on top-rated courses designed by Robert Trent Jones and John LaFoy), miniature golf, 15 tennis courts, a sizable stretch of sandy lakefront beach with four water slides, carillon concerts, rowboats and paddleboats, bicycle rental, fishing, hiking, picnicking, and more.

Stone Mountain is one of the most beautiful parks in the nation and hosts a number of major events throughout the year, so visit its website for dates and details. Consider spending a few days of your trip here; it's a great place for a romantic getaway or a family vacation. See p. 70 for details about on-site accommodations. If you can only spare a day, it's an easy drive (about 30 min.) from downtown.

U.S. Hwy. 78E, Stone Mountain (16 miles east of downtown Atlanta). ☎**800/401-2407** outside metropolitan Atlanta, or 770/498-5690. www.stonemountainpark.com. A ticket for all major attractions is $27 adults, $24 seniors/military, $21 children 3–11. Year-round, gates 6am–midnight. Major attractions fall and winter 10am–5pm; spring and summer 10am–8pm. Parking $10 a day (one-time-only charge if you stay on the grounds) or $35 for 12-month pass. Attractions only are closed Christmas Eve and Christmas; park remains open. MARTA: Take MARTA to the Avondale station, where you can transfer to a bus to Stone Mountain Village. The park is 4 blocks from the village.

World of Coca-Cola ★★ ☺ An exposition showcasing the world's most popular soft drink, World of Coca-Cola sounds like a huge Coke commercial—and it is. But it's also one of the biggest attractions in the city and a must-see for anybody who's ever had a taste of the Real Thing (and who hasn't?). The museum, in a 75,000-square-foot facility downtown near Centennial Park, the CNN Center, and the Georgia

Aquarium, houses a massive collection of Coca-Cola memorabilia, along with numerous interactive displays, high-tech exhibits, an art gallery, and video presentations.

The self-guided tour begins with a preshow in the memorabilia-laden Coca-Cola Loft, which includes the oldest artifact, a 1905 "Drink Coca-Cola" Christmas bell decoration, advertising the fizzy beverage for 5¢. From here, visitors gain entrance to the Happiness Factory Theater, where a short film gives them a glimpse into the magic behind every bottle of Coke. Milestones of Refreshment, a series of 10 galleries, traces the history of Coca-Cola from its 1886 debut at Jacob's Pharmacy in downtown Atlanta to its current worldwide fame. Gathering in the Hub, visitors have an opportunity to meet the Coca-Cola polar bear and have their photo taken with him. Adults and kids alike are mesmerized by the Bottle Works exhibit, a working bottling line that allows visitors to stand in the midst of the process. Watch for the small glass bottles to be filled and then be sure to pick up one as your free souvenir before leaving.

The second level holds much, much more—this experience is a total immersion in Coca-Cola. The upper level includes everyone's favorite exhibit—Taste It!—where visitors can have free samples of more than 60 soft drink products from around the world. (**Warning:** You'll soon figure out that America's idea of refreshing isn't the same as that of other countries.) You'll want to let the kids run wild on the lawn outside once they've loaded up on sugar and caffeine here, but what the heck, drinks are on the house, right? The Pop Culture Gallery showcases Coca-Cola as an icon of popular culture and includes artistic expressions of those inspired by the soft drink, including paintings, furniture, home decor, and advertisements.

The Secret Formula 4-D Theater airs a film featuring an eccentric scientist on a quest to uncover the mysterious secret formula for Coke. And a Perfect Pauses Theater showcases some of the best Coca-Cola television advertising throughout the years, as well as three short films on the product. The tour ends in the massive gift shop (you can't leave without going through here first—smart marketing, huh?), which sells a mind-boggling array of Coca-Cola logo items, everything from T-shirts to Coke polar bears.

Allow about 90 minutes to drink it all in. Weekdays are the prime time to visit if you want to avoid long lines. If you plan to see the World of Coca-Cola and the Georgia Aquarium, a Pemberton Pass will save you a few bucks. In addition, the two attractions share a huge covered parking garage with a $10 fee. Pemberton Place includes an expansive lawn, perfect for a picnic, as well as a cafe and public restrooms.

121 Baker St. NW. © **404/676-5151.** www.woccatlanta.com. Admission $15 adults, $13 seniors 65 and over, $10 children 3-12, free for children 2 and under with adult admission. Sun–Thurs 10am–5:30pm; Fri–Sat 9am–6:30pm. Closed Easter, Thanksgiving, and Christmas; abbreviated hours on Christmas Eve and New Year's Eve. Parking garage costs $10 per vehicle per day on Central Ave. off Martin Luther King, Jr., Dr. MARTA: Peachtree Center or Dome/GWCC/Philips Arena/CNN Center.

MORE ATTRACTIONS IN ATLANTA & BEYOND

Callanwolde Fine Arts Center A magnificent Gothic-Tudor–style mansion built for Coca-Cola heir Charles Howard Candler in 1920, Callanwolde today serves as a fine-arts center for city residents. Ongoing classes are given in pottery, painting, photography, drawing, and more, and there are numerous workshops for both adults and children. The estate occupies 12 acres in the Druid Hills section of Atlanta, an area planned by Frederick Law Olmsted, designer of New York's Central Park. You may be surprised that most of the rooms are bare; only Callanwolde's exquisite walnut paneling, beautifully carved ceilings and moldings, grand staircase, magnificent marble and stone fireplaces, and leaded-glass windows evoke its luxurious past.

Visitors are welcome to peruse shows of local artists in the Petite Hall gallery upstairs; enjoy the lawns and formal gardens, which are maintained by the county; and take in the concerts, storytelling evenings, 1- and 2-day workshops, and dance performances. Check the website to see what's going on when you're in town, as attending an event here is the best way to experience the estate. Especially memorable is Christmas at Callanwolde, when the entire house is decorated for the season, crafts shops are set up in different rooms, and special events and performances are scheduled for children and adults.

980 Briarcliff Rd. NE (north of Ponce de Leon Ave.). 🕽 **404/872-5338.** www.callanwolde.org. Free admission, except for special events. Mon–Fri 9am–10pm; Sat 9am–4pm. Self-guided tours available at all times, except during special events. MARTA: Bus 6 (Emory route) from Edgewood/Candler Park or Lindbergh stations.

Château Elan Winery & Resort   Surrounded by verdant countryside just 40 minutes north of Atlanta, the four-diamond/four-star Château Elan is a hilltop winery that replicates a 16th-century-style French estate. Though its first wines were produced in 1985, the winery has already garnered more than 200 awards.

Guided tours are given Monday through Friday between 11am and 6pm, Saturday and Sunday between noon and 4pm. Self-guided tours are free, or $5 with wine tasting for those 21 and over, except on Saturdays when tours are $10 and include a souvenir glass. On view are the crushing and pressing machines, oak barrels used to age and flavor the wines, the cask room, and the bottling area. The tours conclude with a wine tasting. Grapes ripen in July and August, so if you're here during harvesting in August and September, you'll actually see the winemaking procedure. More than 300 tons of grapes are harvested and processed each year. Saturday cooking demonstrations in the winery's Culinary Studio are popular events, but limited to 20 people at $20 per pop.

The interior of the château, a stage-set version of a Paris street, has a quarry-stone floor, wrought-iron fences, and street lamps. The building houses a gallery with monthly exhibits by regional and national artists, displays of antique European winemaking equipment, and a wine market.

There are also some on-premises restaurants, so plan to eat lunch or dinner here. **Café Elan,** open daily from 11am to 10pm, serves sandwiches, salads, and light entrees. It's a charming setting, with seating under a green awning. **Paddy's Irish Pub,** open Friday through Sunday at noon, the rest of the week at 2pm (closing hours vary), serves traditional Irish fare and spirits. Seating just 28 guests, the fancier **Le Clos,** with pale-pink walls, lace-curtained French doors, and tables covered with crisp white linen, is open for dinner Thursday through Sunday evenings, with seatings from 6 to 9pm. A five-course prix-fixe meal features haute-cuisine entrees; appropriate Château Elan wines are served with each course. Reservations are imperative; men are required to wear a coat and tie.

You might also consider an overnight stay at the 277-room **Inn at Château Elan,** a luxurious resort where facilities include three golf courses (two 18-hole and one par-3, 9-hole) and seven tennis courts (offering pro shops and instruction), an equestrian center, a full-service European-style health spa and salon, an outdoor Olympic-size pool, an indoor heated pool, a fitness center, and a rock-climbing tower. Room

Atlanta Cyclorama & Civil War Museum **9**
Atlanta History Center **5**
Callanwolde Fine Arts Center **11**
Fernbank Museum of Natural History **13**
Fernbank Science Center **14**
Grant Park **9**
Hammonds House Galleries &
　　Resource Center of African-American Art **6**
Jimmy Carter Library & Museum **10**
Kennesaw Mountain/National Battlefield Park **2**
Michael C. Carlos Museum of Emory University **12**
Six Flags Over Georgia **4**
Southern Museum of Civil War &
　　Locomotive History **1**
Stone Mountain Park **15**
Turner Field **8**
White Water **3**
Wren's Nest **7**
Yellow River Game Ranch **16**
Zoo Atlanta **9**

rates begin at $180 double; call for details and to inquire about golf, tennis, spa, and other packages. If the lovely grounds beckon, you can order a gourmet picnic basket from the kitchen at the hotel.

100 Rue Charlemagne Dr., Braselton (30 miles north of Atlanta at exit 126 off I-85). ☎ **800/233-WINE** (9463) or 678/425-0900. www.chateauelan.com. Winery open daily 10am–8pm.

Georgia State Capitol　It wasn't until after the Civil War (1868) that Atlanta became, once and for all, the state capital; its present capitol building, completed July 4, 1889, was hailed as a testament to the city's recovery. Modeled after the nation's Capitol, another neoclassical edifice atop a "crowning hill," its 75-foot dome, covered in gold leaf and topped by a Statue of Freedom, is a major Atlanta landmark. The building is fronted by a massive four-story portico with a pediment supported by six Corinthian columns set on large stone piers. In the rotunda, with its soaring 237-foot ceiling, are busts of famous Georgians, including signers of the Declaration of Independence and the Constitution. The governor's office is off the main hall. The capitol building's public spaces are currently being restored to their 1889 grandeur.

Grand staircases in both wings rise to the third floor, where you'll enter the House of Representatives and, across the hall, the Senate chambers. The legislature meets for 40 days, beginning the second Monday in January (it can also be called into special sessions); all of its sessions are open to the public. The fourth floor houses legislative galleries and the Georgia Capitol Museum, with exhibits on cotton-, peach-, and peanut-growing; cases of mounted birds, fish, deer, insects, and other species native to Georgia; rocks and minerals; American Indian artifacts; and more. Note, too, the museum displays on the first floor.

Tours begin on the main floor; this level also serves as an information center for city and state attractions. The tours take 45 minutes; allow at least another 30 minutes to browse around on your own afterward. Highlights of the grounds are detailed in a brochure available at the tour desk. *Note:* For security reasons, your bag will be searched when you enter.

If you're visiting in December or January, take note of two special treats: A beautifully decorated 40-foot tree adorns the rotunda at Christmas, and on January 15, Dr. Martin Luther King, Jr.'s, birthday, there's a memorial program featuring speeches by local dignitaries, including the governor.

206 Washington St. ☎ **404/656-2844.** www.sos.state.ga.us. Free admission. Mon–Fri 8am–5pm. Tours given year-round at 9:30, 10, 10:30, 11am, with additional times Sept–Apr of 10:30am and 1:30pm. Self-guided tours are possible any time the capitol is open. Closed major holidays, including state holidays. Parking lot behind the capitol building on Capitol Ave. is closed to the public during legislative sessions; other lots are on Martin Luther King, Jr., Dr. at Central Ave. and on Courtland St. btw. Martin Luther King, Jr., Dr. and Central Ave. MARTA: Georgia State.

Hammonds House Galleries & Resource Center of African-American Art　Occupying the 1857 Eastlake Victorian–style former home of Dr. Otis T. Hammonds, a black anesthesiologist and art patron, Hammonds House is a national center for the exhibition, preservation, research, and documentation of African-American art and artists. The permanent collection includes Hammonds's extensive compilation of works by African-American and Haitian artists, as well as his African masks and carvings. These works are complemented by later acquisitions, including pieces by Romare Bearden, William H. Johnson, Robert S. Duncanson, and Elizabeth Catlett. The permanent collection is shown on a rotating basis and is supplemented by exhibitions featuring the work of renowned black artists from all over the world.

The Resource Center, housing documents on African-American art and artists, is open to the public by appointment.

The house is located in the thriving West End neighborhood, which was declared a historic district in 1991. While you're in the area, take a look at the other lovingly restored Victorian bungalows and houses. A short walk away is the Atlanta University Center, the largest historically African-American education complex in the world, home to prestigious Morehouse College. Dr. Martin Luther King, Jr., is Morehouse's most famous alumnus; a chapel was built on the campus to honor his memory.

503 Peeples St. SW (at Lucile St., 2 blocks north of Ralph David Abernathy Blvd.). © **404/612-0500.** www.hammondshouse.org. Admission $4 adults; $2 seniors, children, and students. Tues–Fri 10am–6pm; Sat–Sun 1–5pm. MARTA: Bus 71 from the West End station or bus 67 from West Lake station.

Herndon Home   Alonzo Herndon was born in 1858, during the last decade of slavery. After emancipation, he worked as a field hand and sharecropper, supplementing his meager income by selling peanuts, homemade molasses, and axle grease. He arrived in Atlanta in the early 1880s, taking on work as a barber and eventually owning several barbershops of his own. Herndon used the earnings from these shops to acquire Atlanta real estate, and by 1900, fewer than 40 years out of slavery and with only a year of formal education, he was the richest black man in Atlanta. In 1905, Herndon purchased a church burial association, which, with other small companies, became the nucleus of the Atlanta Life Insurance Company, today the nation's second-largest black-owned insurance company.

In 1910, Herndon built this elegant 15-room house in the Beaux Arts–neoclassical style, complete with a stately colonnaded entrance. Herndon and his wife, Adrienne McNeil, a drama teacher at Atlanta University, were the primary architects of the house, and construction was accomplished almost completely by African-American artisans. Because their son Norris occupied the home until 1977, much of the original furniture remains, and there are family photographs throughout. Adrienne died about a week after the house was completed.

The house tour begins in a receiving room with a 10-minute introductory video called *The Herndon Legacy.* The tour then takes you through the reception hall; the music room, with rococo gilt-trimmed walls and Louis XV–style furnishings; the living room, with a frieze on its walls depicting the accomplishments of Herndon's life; the dining room, furnished in late Renaissance style with family china and Venetian glass displayed in a mahogany cabinet; the butler's pantry; and the sunny breakfast room. Upstairs, you'll see the bedroom used by Herndon's second wife, Jessie, with its Jacobean suite and Louis XV–style furnishings; Herndon's Empire-furnished bedroom, where a book from a Republican National Convention is displayed on a table, letting you know his political bent; the collection room (Norris collected ancient Greek and Roman vases and funerary objects); Norris's bedroom; a sitting room; and a guest bedroom.

587 University Place NW (btw. Vine and Walnut sts.). © **404/581-9813.** www.herndonhome.org. Admission $5 adults, $3 students and children. Tues–Sat 10am–4pm. Guided tours available by appt. only. Closed New Year's Day, July 4th, Thanksgiving, Christmas Eve, and Christmas. MARTA: Vine City.

Kennesaw Mountain/National Battlefield Park   This 2,884-acre park, run by the National Park Service, was established in 1917 on the site of a crucial Civil War battle in the Atlanta campaign of 1864. Some two million visitors come annually to explore the Confederate entrenchments and earthworks, some of them equipped with actual Civil War artillery.

The action began in June 1864. A month earlier, General Ulysses S. Grant had ordered Sherman to attack the Confederate army in Georgia, telling him to "break it up, and go into the interior of the enemy's country as far as you can, inflicting all the damage you can upon their war resources." In response to this order, Sherman's army, 100,000 strong, pushed back Confederate forces composed of General Joseph E. Johnston's 65,000 men. By June 19, Union troops had driven Johnston's men back to a well-prepared defensive position on Kennesaw Mountain. Southern engineers had built a line of entrenchments in its rocky slopes, allowing the Confederates to cover every approach with rifle or cannon. An Ohio officer later commented that if the mountain had been constructed for the sole purpose of repelling an invading army, "it could not have been better made or placed."

On June 27, following a few weeks of skirmishing, Sherman, underestimating the strength and still-feisty morale of the rebels, attempted to break through Confederate lines and annihilate the troops in a grand no-holds-barred assault from two directions. Confederate General Samuel French described the onset of the attack: "As if by magic, there sprang from the earth a host of men, and in one long, waving line of blue the infantry advanced and the battle of Kennesaw Mountain began." Weeks of torrential rain had turned these battlegrounds into muddy mire, adding significantly to the misery on both sides.

Sherman's men were repelled by massive bursts of firepower and huge rocks that the Confederates rolled down the mountain at them. Union casualties far outnumbered Confederate losses in this first attack. Meanwhile, 8,000 Union infantrymen in five brigades attacked from another angle; in this battle, the Union lost 3,000 men, the Confederates 500, resulting in a tremendous Confederate victory on these grounds.

Allow at least 2 hours for exploring. Start your tour at the **visitor center,** where you can pick up a map, watch a 20-minute film about the battle, and view exhibits of Civil War artifacts, medicine, and memorabilia. On weekdays, you can drive or hike up the mountain to see the actual Confederate entrenchments and earthworks. On weekends, it may be too crowded to drive, but you can take a shuttle bus for a nominal fee or you can hike (the steep trail is about 2 miles round-trip, so wear comfortable shoes). You'll find interpretive signs at key spots and, on weekends and holidays from Memorial Day through Labor Day, interpretive programs give further information about the battle. You'll also want to drive to **Cheatham Hill,** site of some of the fiercest fighting. There are 16 miles of hiking trails for those who want a more extensive tour (trail maps are available at the visitor center), and picnicking is permitted in designated areas, some of which boast barbecue grills. The scenery is gorgeous, so even if Civil War battles are not your thing (that is, if you're reluctantly accompanying an enthusiastic spouse or friend), you'll find some beautiful hiking or driving.

900 Kennesaw Mountain Dr., Kennesaw. ☎ **770/427-4686.** www.nps.gov/kemo. Free admission. Park daily 7:30am–8pm; visitor center weekdays 8:30am–5pm, Sat–Sun 8:30am–6pm. Closed 6 major holidays. Take I-75 N. to Barrett Pkwy. and then follow the signs.

Rhodes Memorial Hall   Rhodes Hall is one of a few remaining pre–World War I Peachtree Street mansions—a significant reminder that Peachtree was once a fashionable residential street. The house was designed shortly after the turn of the 20th century by Willis Franklin Denny (at the time Atlanta's leading residential architect) as a home for affluent Atlanta businessman Amos Giles Rhodes and his family.

Its medieval-baronial-cum-High-Victorian-Romanesque style was inspired by Rhineland castles. The Stone Mountain granite exterior is replete with arched Romanesque windows, battlements and buttresses, parapets, towers, and turrets. A large Syrian-arched veranda wraps the east and north facades. The interior is grandiose, with maple- and mahogany-bordered oak parquet floors, mosaics surrounding the fireplaces, and a gracefully winding, hand-carved Honduran mahogany staircase with nine stained-glass stairwell panels depicting "The Rise and Fall of the Confederacy." The house and stables originally occupied 150 acres of land and included servants' quarters, a carriage house, and other outbuildings. When it was built, this site was in suburbia, an afternoon's drive from downtown.

Upon Rhodes's death in 1929, his residence was deeded to the state of Georgia in keeping with his desire to preserve his home. The house was entered on the National Register of Historic Places in 1974. Today, it is the headquarters for the Georgia Trust for Historic Preservation and is in an ongoing process of restoration. To date, the original dining-room suite and some other furnishings are in place, and all the mahogany woodwork and decorated ceilings on the first floor have been restored. The original landscaping—with white and red cedars, dogwoods, banana trees, and a circular flower bed—has been re-created in the front yard.

You can see the house only by guided tour. On weekdays, the 45-minute Historical Tours explain Rhodes Hall's background while guiding visitors through the first floor of the house. The special Behind-the-Scenes Tours, on Sunday at noon, are comprehensive 3-hour experiences that explore the entire house.

1516 Peachtree St. NW (at Peachtree Circle). © **404/885-7800.** www.rhodeshall.org. Behind-the-scenes tour of all 4 floors, $7; 1st floor only tour $5 adults, $4 seniors, students and children 6–12, free for children 5 and under. Tours on the hour every hour. Tues–Fri 11am–3pm; Sat 10am–2pm. Closed major holidays. Free parking in designated lot behind building on Spring St. MARTA: Arts Center.

Southern Museum of Civil War and Locomotive History   Previously the Kennesaw Civil War Museum, this museum is now operated in association with the Smithsonian Institute, which means that Civil War and transportation objects from the Smithsonian will be incorporated into the exhibits here.

It was here that the wild adventure known as the "Great Locomotive Chase" began. The Civil War had been underway for a year on April 12, 1862, when Union spy James J. Andrews and a group of 21 Northern soldiers disguised as civilians boarded a locomotive called the *General* in Marietta, buying tickets for diverse destinations to avert suspicion. When the train made a breakfast stop at the Lacy Hotel in Big Shanty, they seized the locomotive and several boxcars and fled northward to Chattanooga. The goal of these daring raiders was to destroy tracks, telegraph wires, and bridges behind them, thus cutting off the Confederate supply route between Virginia and Mississippi.

Conductor William A. Fuller, his breakfast interrupted by the sound of the *General* chugging out of the station, gave chase on foot, then grabbed a platform car and poled along the tracks. With him were a railroad superintendent and the *General*'s engineer. At the Etowah River, Fuller and crew commandeered a small locomotive called the *Yonah* and made better progress. Meanwhile, the raiders tore up track behind them, and when the pursuers got close, the raiders slowed them down by throwing ties and firewood onto the tracks. Andrews, a very smooth talker, managed to convince station attendants en route that he was on an emergency mission running ammunition to Confederate General Beauregard in Mississippi.

Fuller's chances of catching the *General* improved when he seized the southbound *Texas* and began running it backward toward the raiders, picking up reinforcements along the way and eventually managing to get a telegraph message through to General Danville Leadbetter, commander at Chattanooga. The chase went on, with Andrews sending uncoupled boxcars careening back toward Fuller as obstructions. Fuller, who was running in reverse, merely attached the rolling boxcars to his engine and kept on. At the covered Oostanaula Bridge, the raiders detached a boxcar and set it on fire in hopes of finally creating an impassable obstacle—a burning bridge behind them. But the *Texas* was able to push the flaming car off the bridge. It soon burned out, and Fuller tossed it off the track and continued.

By this time the *General* was running low on fuel and water, the *Texas* was hot on its heels, and the raiders realized that all was lost. Andrews gave his final command: "Jump off and scatter! Every man for himself!" All were captured and imprisoned within a few days. Some escaped, others were exchanged for Confederate prisoners of war, and the rest were hanged in Atlanta, most of them at a site near Oakland Cemetery. Though the mission failed, the raiders, some of them posthumously, received the newly created Medal of Honor for their valor.

The museum, occupying a building that was once the Frey cotton gin, houses the *General* (still in running condition, but don't get any ideas); a walk-through caboose; exhibits of Civil War artifacts, memorabilia, and photographs (including those relating to the chase and its participants); and exhibits on railroads. You can view a 20-minute narrated video about the chase, but if you really want the full story, rent the Disney movie *The Great Locomotive Chase*, starring Fess Parker as the dashing Andrews. (You can also buy a copy in the museum gift shop.)

The museum is 3 miles from Kennesaw Mountain/National Battlefield Park (p. 141), so consider visiting both of these Civil War–related sights on the same day.

2829 Cherokee St., Kennesaw. © **770/427-2117.** www.southernmuseum.org. Admission $7.50 adults, $6.50 seniors 60 and over, $5.50 children 4–12, free for children 3 and under. Guided tours given hourly at the half-hour. Mon–Sat 9:30am–5pm. Closed major holidays. Free parking. Take exit 273 off I-75 N. and follow the signs.

Underground Atlanta 👃 In 1969, a group of Atlanta businesspeople decided to create an underground entertainment complex of restaurants, shops, and bars in the historic hub of the city, centered on the Zero Milepost that marked the terminus of the Western & Atlantic Railroad in the 1800s. The area had flourished until the early 1900s, until it became so congested that permanent concrete viaducts were constructed over it, elevating the street system and routing traffic over a maze of railroad tracks. Merchants moved their operations up to the new level, using the lower level for storage space. For most of the 20th century, it remained a deserted catacomb.

The 1969 entertainment development idea was great, but unfortunately the complex declined and closed after a little more than a decade. In 1989—after a public-private infusion of $142 million—a larger, livelier Underground reopened to much fanfare, becoming once again an entertainment mecca and urban marketplace. Local civic leaders pinned their hopes for downtown revival on the complex, and for some time it looked as if the concept would work. But, beset by lease disputes, financial problems, and changes of management, Underground has failed to sustain its early promise, and its most recent management company struggles to overcome the complex's seedy reputation.

Occupying 12 acres in the center of downtown, Underground Atlanta sports oscillating searchlights emanating from a 138-foot light tower, an outdoor staging area used for performances and concerts, and the cascading waters of Peachtree Fountain Plaza. Underground comprises about 75 retail operations and restaurants, many of them national chains. Markers throughout the complex indicate historic sites. Their origins are fascinating, so be sure to pick up an information sheet at the visitor booth and take your own self-guided tour. Humbug Square—where street vendors and con artists flourished in the early 1900s—has a colorful market with turn-of-the-20th-century pushcarts and wagons displaying offbeat wares. The complex is still worth a look if you're in the downtown area, but keep in mind that it's mostly a tourist attraction at this point. It's still struggling to find its place in the urban mix, perhaps because locals prefer the shopping and entertainment areas in Buckhead and Virginia-Highland.

The **Atlanta Convention & Visitors Bureau (© 404/222-6688)** operates its most comprehensive center in Underground Atlanta, at 65 Upper Alabama St. Open Monday through Saturday from 10am to 6pm, Sunday from noon to 6pm, it includes displays and interactive exhibits depicting the city's rich history. There's also **Atlan-TIX!,** a ticket booth where visitors can purchase day-of-show, half-price tickets to theater, dance, and other live performances throughout the metro area.

50 Upper Alabama St. (bounded by Wall St., Central Ave., Martin Luther King, Jr., Dr., and Peachtree St.). © **877/859-4891** or 404/523-2311. www.underground-atlanta.com. Free admission. Mon–Sat 10am–9pm; Sun 11am–7pm. Some restaurants and clubs until midnight (or later) nightly. Paid parking in the garages off Martin Luther King, Jr., Dr. MARTA: Five Points station has a short pedestrian tunnel that connects directly with Underground Atlanta.

William Breman Jewish Heritage Museum This museum, the largest of its kind in the Southeast, offers a unique glimpse into Atlanta's history, exploring Jewish heritage with a special emphasis on the Atlanta Jewish experience. Two main galleries juxtapose the destruction of the Holocaust with the reemergence of Jewish communities in Atlanta and throughout the world. The stories are told through photographs, documents, and memorabilia uncovered in the attics and basements of local families and individuals. Especially moving are the stories and possessions generously shared by Holocaust survivors living in Atlanta.

In addition to the two main galleries, there's a Discovery Center with hands-on activities related to the exhibitions, a community archive, a genealogy center, a library, and a gift shop.

1440 Spring St. NW (in the Selig Center at 18th St.). ☎**678/222-3700.** www.thebreman.org. Admission $12 adults, $8 seniors (62 and older), $6 students, $4 children 3–6, free for children 2 and under. Mon-Thurs 10am–5pm; Fri 10am–3pm; Sun 1–5pm. Archives by appt. only. Closed Sat, major Jewish holidays, and some secular holidays. Limited free parking. MARTA: Arts Center.

ESPECIALLY FOR KIDS

Though the following attractions are great choices if you're traveling with kids, don't pass them up even if you're not. Especially worthwhile are the Center for Puppetry Arts, Imagine It! Children's Museum of Atlanta, Wren's Nest, and Zoo Atlanta (visit in conjunction with Atlanta Cyclorama and Oakland Cemetery). In addition, be sure to take the kids to the Fernbank Museum of Natural History (p. 120), the Birth Home of Martin Luther King, Jr. (p. 116), and the King Center (p. 127), all described earlier in this chapter.

Center for Puppetry Arts ★ ☺ Dedicated to expanding public awareness of puppetry as a fine art and to presenting all of its international and historical forms, the center opened in 1978, with Kermit the Frog cutting the official ribbon (he had a little help from the late Jim Henson). Staff and loyal visitors are all aglow with the latest acquisition: more than 500 of the late Henson's Muppets, as well as props, videos, and memorabilia from such classics as *The Muppet Show* and *Sesame Street.* The collection will be housed in a Jim Henson Wing when the new center is unveiled soon. Until then, a number of Henson puppets are on display at the current location.

It encompasses a 300-seat theater, a smaller theater, gallery space, and a permanent museum. The puppet shows are marvelous—sophisticated, riveting, full-stage productions with elaborate scenery. Some are family oriented; others, with nighttime showings, are geared to adults. Call ahead to find out what's on (reservations are essential). You can also call a week or so in advance to enroll yourself or your kids in a puppet-making workshop.

The center's permanent exhibit, "Puppets, The Power of Wonder," is stunning, featuring one of the largest and finest puppet collections in North America. It includes such treasures as ritualistic African figures, Punch and Judy, Henson's Pigs in Space, turn-of-the-20th-century Thai shadow puppets, Indonesian *wayang golek* puppets used to tell classic stories (a centuries-old tradition), Chinese hand puppets, rod-operated marionettes from all over Europe, original Muppets, pre-Columbian clay puppets that were used in religious ceremonies (ca. A.D. 1200), and Turkish shadow figures made of dried animal skins. Visitors get the opportunity to use joysticks to manipulate more than 350 of these puppets. A video hosted by Jim Henson provides an overview of puppetry and takes visitors around the world to meet masters of the art. Another gallery features visiting exhibits from other countries. Reservations are required for guided 1-hour tours of the permanent exhibit.

The gift shop is like no other, with oodles of marionettes, one-of-a-kind handmade puppets, masks, videos, and other related items.

1404 Spring St. NW (at 18th St.). ☎**404/873-3391.** www.puppet.org. Museum admission $8 adults, children, or free if you see a show or take a workshop. Family show performance tickets $16 (workshop and museum admission included in single show ticket), teen/adult performances $20–$24 (includes museum admission). Workshop prices vary. Tues–Fri 9am–3pm; Sat 9am–5pm; Sun 11am–5pm. Closed New Year's Day, Memorial Day, July 4th, Labor Day, Thanksgiving, and Christmas. Limited free parking. MARTA: Arts Center.

Fernbank Science Center ☺   Owned and funded by the DeKalb County School System, this museum/planetarium/observatory, located adjacent to the 65-acre Fernbank Forest, is an educational partner of the Fernbank Museum of Natural History (p. 120). Plan to visit the entire complex on the same day. There's a 1.5-mile forest trail here, with trees, shrubs, ferns, wildflowers, mosses, and other plants marked for identification. An extensive rose garden is next-door to the museum.

The indoor facility houses exhibits such as a video display on geological phenomena (volcanoes, earthquakes, mountain formation, and so on); a gem collection; an exhibit tracing the development of life in Georgia from 500 million to 1 million years ago; a complete weather station; fossilized trees; the original *Apollo 6* space capsule and space suit (on loan from the Smithsonian); computer games; a replica of the Okefenokee Swamp, complete with sound effects; and models of dinosaurs that roamed Atlanta in prehistoric times. At the Observatory, which contains the largest telescope in the world dedicated to public education, an astronomer gives talks and helps visitors to spot celestial objects. Planetarium shows are held daily.

156 Heaton Park Dr. NE (at Artwood Rd. off Ponce de Leon Ave.). ℂ **678/874-7102.** www.fernbank. edu. Free admission to exhibit hall Mon–Wed noon–5pm; Thurs–Fri noon–9pm; Sat 10am–5pm. Planetarium shows $4 adults, $3 students and seniors. Planetarium shows vary (see website for latest info). Observatory Thurs–Fri 9 (or whenever it gets dark) to 10:30pm, weather permitting. Forest trails Mon–Fri 2–5pm; Sat 10am–5pm. From downtown, go east on North Ave. to Piedmont Ave. and turn left. Turn right on Ponce de Leon Ave., drive 4½ miles, and turn left at the light onto Atwood Rd. Turn right on Heaton Park Dr. Fernbank is on the left across from Fernbank Elementary School.

Imagine It! Children's Museum of Atlanta ☺   Imagine It! is a 30,000-square-foot children's museum conveniently located across the street from Centennial Olympic Park, in an area undergoing some exciting urban renaissance. Based on Howard Gardiner's theory of multiple intelligences, Imagine It! features colorful hands-on exhibits and activities that allow children the opportunity to look, listen, touch, and explore in order to discover firsthand how things work. Fun is the priority in this high-energy environment (the learning just sneaks up). There are four major learning zones: Fundamentally Food, Let Your Creativity Flow, Tools for Solutions, and Leaping into Learning, the specialty zone for toddlers. The Morph Gallery has changing exhibits, such as Bob the Builder, the Amazing Castle, and Curious George's Let's Get Curious.

The museum is recommended for children 2 to 8, but all are welcome. However, all grown-ups must be accompanied by a kid, and all kids must be accompanied by a grown-up. Snacks and drinks are available in the Eats and Treats area, and Chick-fil-A offers a limited menu during lunch hours. Due to high visitor volume, Imagine It! encourages visitors to purchase advance tickets online to ensure entrance to the museum upon arrival. Make a day of it and visit Centennial Park, the new World of Coca-Cola, or the Georgia Aquarium across the street either before or after your museum visit.

275 Centennial Olympic Park Dr. NW. ℂ **404/659-KIDS** (5437). www.imagineit-cma.org. Admission $13 (plus tax) for adults and children 2 and above, free for children 1 and under. Advance ticket reservations encouraged. Mon–Fri 10am–4pm; Sat–Sun 10am–5pm. Closed Thanksgiving and Christmas. Parking available throughout the area. MARTA: Peachtree Center.

Six Flags Over Georgia ☺   One of the state's major family attractions, Six Flags provides a great day's entertainment. Arrive early (at least 30 min. before opening), note where you've parked in the vast lot, and take 10 minutes or so to plan out your show and ride schedule.

The park's various areas have themes centered around different regions, from southern (Cotton States, Confederate, Georgia, Lickskillet, and Promenade) and European (France, Britain, Spain) to American (U.S.A.) and Gotham City (featuring Batman The Ride). Costumed Looney Tune characters (Sylvester, Daffy Duck, and others) roam the park greeting kids (check out the gazebo in the Promenade section to meet that wascally wabbit Bugs Bunny). Summertime is busy in the park's water-themed venue, Skull Island, a Caribbean pirate adventure, with six slides and a spewing volcano among other watery playground treats.

Thrill rides include several additional watery options, such as Splashwater Falls (a plummet down a soaring 50-ft. waterfall), a log flume, and Thunder River (a simulated white-water rafting adventure). White-knuckle coasters include the Georgia Scorcher (one of the Southeast's tallest and fastest stand-up roller coasters), Ninja (the "black belt" of roller coasters, turning riders upside down five times and offering thrilling loops, dives, and corkscrew turns), the Georgia Cyclone (a classic wooden coaster with 11 dramatic drops, patterned after Coney Island's famous thrill ride), the Great American Scream Machine (another classic wooden coaster), and Mind Bender (a triple-looper). Other highlights are Batman The Ride (a twisting roller coaster with ski-lift-like seats), Great Gasp (a 20-story parachute jump), Riverview Carousel (a merry-go-round from the early 1900s), and Free Fall (ever wonder what it would be like to fall off a 10-story building?). A less dizzying adventure is Monster Mansion, a Disney-esque boat ride through an antebellum mansion haunted by more than 100 animated monsters. And there's much, much more.

Shows vary from year to year, but they usually include a major musical revue, a country-music show, a golden-oldies show, thrill cinema adventures on a 180-degree screen, and an animated character show. In addition, headliners such as SheDaisy and John Michael Montgomery play the 8,072-seat (with lawn seating for 4,000) Southern Star Amphitheatre.

There are restaurants and snack bars throughout the park, though you might consider bringing a picnic.

275 Riverside Pkwy. SW (at the Six Flags exit off I-20 W.), Austell. ✆ **770/948-9290.** www.sixflags. com/overgeorgia. Admission at the park $50 (plus tax) adults, $35 children 48 in. and under, free for kids 2 and under; online special, everyone $35. A nominal fee is charged for amphitheater concerts. Sat–Sun only Mar to mid-May and Sept–Oct; daily Memorial Day to Labor Day. Gates 10am; closing hours vary. Parking $15.

White Water ☺ A Six Flags park encompassing 40 acres of wet, splashy fun, White Water is the largest water park in the South, with more than 30 slides. Its star attraction is the $1-million Tree House Island, a four-story fantasy treehouse with more than 100 different activities—curvy slides, net bridges, water cannons, chutes, and more. A 1,000-gallon bucket of water empties over the whole attraction every few minutes. Other park highlights include Cliffhanger, a 990-foot free fall (one of the tallest such attractions in the world); the 735-foot Run-A-Way River, an enclosed tunnel raft ride; the "Atlanta Ocean," a 750,000-gallon wave pool; and a host of different slide and splash experiences. There's much more, including a special section for children 48 inches and under called Little Squirt's Island, with 25 tot-size water attractions. Adjacent Captain Kid's Cove has dozens of additional activities for kids 12 and under. Restaurants and snack bars are on the premises, as are rental lockers ($13–$19) and shower facilities. Swimsuits are essential and no outside food, beverages, or coolers are allowed.

Next to White Water is **American Adventures** (✆ **770/428-5217;** www.american adventuresfunpark.com), a year-round indoor/outdoor family amusement park with children's rides in the Fun Forest (bumper cars, a small roller coaster, a tilt-a-whirl, and others); a classic carousel; a go-cart track; a penny arcade with more than 130 games; Professor Plinker's Laboratory (a large children's play area with ball crawls and nets to climb); 18-hole miniature golf; and the Foam Factory, a huge, multilevel interactive play area with scads of foam-ball activities. It's all geared to children 12 and under. A family-style restaurant is on the grounds. Admission to American Adventures is $20 for a full-day pass or $16 for 3 hours. Or pay just for those attractions you want to use. Some attractions are free for adults accompanying children, and most attractions offer discounted pricing for adults. American Adventures is connected to the water park, so you can go back and forth if you want, though you'll pay entrance fees to both. Hours vary with the season, so call first.

250 N. Cobb Pkwy. NE (exit 265 off I-75), Marietta.✆ **770/424-9283.** www.sixflags.com/whitewater. Admission $37 adults, $27 children under 48 in. tall. Parking $10. Sat–Sun only starting in mid-May 10am–6pm; daily Memorial Day to late summer and Labor Day weekend 10am to late evening (closing hours vary). Closed early Sept to Apr.

Wren's Nest ☺   Named for a family of wrens that once nested in the mailbox, Wren's Nest is the former home of Joel Chandler Harris, who chronicled the wily deeds of fictional African characters Br'er Rabbit and Br'er Fox. It's been open to the public since 1913, when Harris's widow sold it to the Uncle Remus Memorial Association.

Harris's literary career began at the age of 13, when he apprenticed on the *Country-man,* a quarterly plantation newspaper. During the 4 years that he spent learning at the *Countryman,* young Harris spent many an evening hanging about the slave quarters, drinking in African folk tales and fables spun by George Terrell, a plantation patriarch who became the prototype for Uncle Remus. When the *Countryman* went out of business, Harris went on to other newspapers, working his way up to editorial writer at the *Atlanta Constitution* by his early 30s. There, filling in for a sick colleague, he remembered the plantation stories of his youth and evoked Uncle Remus to fill his column. Enthralled readers clamored for more, and the rest is history.

The house itself is an 1870s farmhouse with a Queen Anne–style Victorian facade added in 1884. Harris lived here from 1881 until his death in 1908, doing most of his writing in a rocking chair on the wraparound front porch. On the 30-minute tour, you'll see a good deal of memorabilia: the stuffed great horned owl over the study door

---

Impressions

I seem to see before me the smiling faces of thousands of children—some young and fresh—and some wearing the friendly marks of age, but all children at heart, and not an unfriendly face among them. And while I am trying hard to speak the right word, I seem to hear a voice lifted above the rest saying, "You have made some of us happy." And so I feel my heart fluttering and my lips trembling and I have to bow silently and turn away and hurry into the obscurity that fits me best.

—Joel Chandler Harris, former owner of Wren's Nest, who died on July 3, 1908. He wrote these words, which later appeared on his gravestone.

(a gift from Theodore Roosevelt, whose White House Harris visited); the original wren's-nest mailbox on the study mantel; and all of Harris's books, along with signed first editions from major authors of his day (an unverified Mark Twain among others) displayed in a bookcase. Guided tours are held every half-hour on Tuesday, Thursday, and Saturday.

The house itself is certainly more than worthy of a visit here, but a favorite attraction is the **storytelling** every Saturday at 1pm, when the resident storyteller shares stories culled from African and African-American folklore; it's a real treat.

1050 Ralph David Abernathy Blvd. SW (2 blocks from Ashby St.). © **404/753-7735.** www.wrens nestonline.com. Admission $8 adults, $7 seniors and students, $5 children 3–12, free for children 2 and under. Tues–Sat 10am–2:30pm. Closed major holidays. Take I-20 W. to Lowery Blvd., turn left on Ashby St., then right on Ralph David Abernathy Blvd.; Wren's Nest is 2 long blocks down on the left. MARTA: Bus 71 from West End station.

Yellow River Game Ranch ☺   Bordering the Yellow River, this 24-acre animal preserve allows for close encounters of the four-legged kind—a chance to view, pet, feed, and generally mingle with some 600 animals (always including quite a few babies) who live in open enclosures or right out in the open along a 1-mile oak- and hickory-shaded forest trail. The ranch is home to one of the largest buffalo herds east of the Mississippi. Owner Art Rilling knows every animal on the ranch by name and can give you chapter and verse on each one's personality, preferences, and, in some cases, romantic history. The animals know they're among friends here and are highly socialized, so you'll have a unique chance to study them up close. Keep in mind that all these animals smell like, well, animals. If a barnyard atmosphere bothers you, don't visit.

Inhabitants include donkeys named Rhett and Scarlett, Georgia black bears that stand up and beg for marshmallows, goats, dozens of rabbits in Bunny Burrows (kids can pet the bunnies), an assortment of interesting-looking chickens, a herd of buffalo, sheep, burros, goats, ponies, and a groundhog named General Beauregard Lee (we are in Georgia, after all) who lives in a white colonnaded southern mansion complete with miniature satellite dish.

Consider packing a picnic lunch. There are tables throughout the property, and one especially nice picnic area overlooks the river.

4525 Hwy. 78, Lilburn. © **770/972-6643.** www.yellowrivergameranch.com. Admission $8 adults, $7 children 2–11, free for children 1 and under with adult admission. Winter hours weekdays 10am–5pm, Sat–Sun 10am–6pm; summer hours 10am–6pm; ticket sales end at 4pm during winter weekdays and 5pm all other times. Closed major holidays. Take I-85 N. to I-285 E. Exit at State Hwy. 78 and follow it east for 10 miles.

Zoo Atlanta ★★ ☺   This delightful 40-acre zoo dates from 1889, when George W. Hall (aka "Popcorn George") brought his traveling circus to town. Employee claims for back wages forced Hall to relinquish his menagerie, and the animal entourage was purchased by a prominent Atlanta businessman who donated the collection to the city as the basis for a zoological garden in Grant Park. It grew considerably over the years and was a popular local attraction, but had fallen into disrepair by the mid-1980s. Director Terry Maple was brought in to rescue the zoo and oversee a multi-million-dollar renovation.

The turnaround has been dramatic. Today, Zoo Atlanta is one of the finest zoos in the country, with animals housed in large open enclosures that simulate their natural habitats. The zoo participates in breeding programs, many of them focusing on endangered species, and is home to endangered animals that include black rhinos,

Fond Farewell

When Willie B., the beloved Zoo Atlanta gorilla, died a number of years ago, so many people came to his memorial service to pay their last respects that many had to be turned away. In all, close to 8,000 mourners attended.

Sumatran orangutans, 19 western lowland gorillas, two African elephants, two Komodo monitors, and big-mouthed African dwarf crocodiles. The Australian-themed Outback Station in the Orkin Children's Zoo introduced two new species—red kangaroos and kookaburras. The Living Treehouse, a revitalized home for drill baboons, Mona monkeys, and red ruffed lemurs, also houses an open-air aviary for 15 species of African birds. Turner Broadcasting made a $5-million donation in 2004, the single largest gift in Zoo Atlanta history. The money allowed the zoo to enhance the public offerings and educational programs in its Conservation Action Resource Center.

Currently, the exhibit creating the biggest stir is the Asian Forest, home to Lun Lun and Yang Yang, two giant pandas and their first offspring, Mei Lan, born in 2006 after a couple years of pressure on the two to procreate. The happy couple welcomed their second baby in 2008, much to the delight of the public and fans who kept up with the cub's progress via webcam on the zoo's website. The cub, named Xi Lan ("Atlanta's Joy" in Chinese), through a public vote—by tradition remained unnamed until he was 100 days old—was the only giant panda born in the U.S. that year. A third offspring was expected as this guide went into production. The two Chinese natives and their adorable offspring are a huge hit with adults and children alike. Although the pandas' rowdiest period is in the afternoon, they put on quite a show most of the day: munching bamboo, tussling with each other, playing on their log swing, or climbing on the swinging ladder. When Lun Lun has had enough of Yang Yang's roughhousing, she heads for the water. In the summer, the two can be especially entertaining; if it's really sweltering, zoo officials give each of them a huge block of ice to help them cool off. Yang Yang likes to hug his until it melts.

Your first stop at the zoo will probably be Flamingo Plaza. Farther on, Mzima Springs and Masai Mara house elephants, rhinos, lions, zebras, giraffes, gazelles, and other African animals and birds. The landscape in this section resembles the plains of East Africa, with honey locust trees and yuccas, and the lion enclosure replicates an East African *kopje* (rocky outcropping). Frequent animal demonstrations, African storytelling, and educational programs take place under the Elder's Tree in Masai Mara. Here you'll find the young waterbuck, daughter of Kokopelli (who was aptly named for the ancient fertility god).

The lushly landscaped Ford African Rain Forest—one of the most popular sections—centers on four vast gorilla habitats separated by moats. Studies on gorilla behavior take place here, and there are usually quite a few adorable babies (they're hard to spot sometimes, so be sure to ask if there are any to be seen). The zoo's long-time mascot, Willie B. (named for former Atlanta mayor William B. Hartsfield), died in 2000, but his daughters Kudzoo and Olympia live in the forest and usually put on a pretty good show. The best time to visit is around 2pm, when the gorillas are fed. Also in this section are a walk-through aviary of West African birds, an exhibit of small

African primates, and the Gorillas of Cameroon Museum. Landscaping includes burned-out areas of forest and deadfall trees—gorillas do not live in manicured gardens. In addition, the rainforest is home to the zoo's African lions, including three cubs new to the property in 2008: Christos, Mikalos, and Athanaisi.

In the Ketambe section, several families of high-climbing orangutans show off their skills among the trees and bamboo clusters of an Indonesian tropical rainforest. If you're lucky enough to be here at feeding time—around 2:30pm—you might see them swinging on ropes from tree to tree. In the Sumatran Tiger Forest, rare Sumatran tigers prowl a lush forest, sometimes dipping into a stream or waterfall. Nearby is a superb Reptile House—the zoo is home to one of the finest reptile collections in the country—and a special exhibit area, often used to house visiting animals.

A zoo train travels through the Children's Zoo area. Here, you'll find a playground and petting zoo where kids can get friendly with llamas, sheep, pot-bellied pigs, goats, and more. There are aviaries here, too. Kids (and adults) will love the entertaining and informative free animal shows at the zoo; these shows are held in the Wildlife Theater during summer, and African elephant demonstrations are given daily year-round. The zoo's "Wild Like Me" indoor play experience highlights similarities between people and animals.

There are snack bars (including a McDonald's) throughout the zoo. You can also picnic in tree-shaded areas in Grant Park just outside the zoo. The Zoo Atlanta Trading Company sells zoo memorabilia and gifts.

800 Cherokee Ave. SE (in Grant Park). © **404/624-WILD** (9453). www.zooatlanta.org. Admission $20 adults, $16 seniors, $15 children 3–11, free for children 2 and under. Strollers can be rented. Weekdays 9:30am–5:30pm, Sat–Sun 9:30am–6:30pm; ticket booths close at 4:30pm weekdays and 5:30pm Sat–Sun. Closed Thanksgiving and Christmas. Free but limited parking. Take I-75 S. to I-20 E. Get off at the Boulevard exit (59A) and follow signs to Grant Park. MARTA: Bus 97 from the Five Points station or bus 397 from the King Memorial station.

SPECIAL-INTEREST TOURS

The **Atlanta Preservation Center,** a private nonprofit organization headquartered at 327 St. Paul Ave. SE (© **404/688-3353**), offers a variety of 1- to 2-hour guided walking tours of the city. Cost of each tour is $10 for adults and $5 for seniors, students, and children. Tours of the Fox Theatre are given year-round; the remaining options are noted below. Call or visit www.preserveatlanta.com for days, hours, and departure points.

On the **Fox Theatre Tour,** you'll explore this restored 1920s Moorish movie palace in depth. The theater's auditorium resembles the courtyard of a Cairo mosque, and the architecture and interior were influenced by the discoveries at King Tut's tomb (p. 121 for a full description of the theater). This tour is subject to change due to special events or matinee performances.

Grant Park, the centerpiece of a revitalized neighborhood, became a favorite spot thanks to its beautiful lake, numerous springs, and amusement area. It's now home to the Atlanta Cyclorama and Zoo Atlanta. The **Grant Park Tour** (Sun in Mar–Nov) uses the park as the setting for a walk through Atlanta's history, from antebellum times (you'll see the Grant Mansion and Confederate fortifications) through the Victorian era to the present day.

The **Historic Downtown Tour** (Fri–Sat in Mar–Nov) is an architectural survey of Atlanta's downtown, from Victorian buildings to modern high-rises. You'll learn

RUN THE peachtree

The Peachtree Road Race is more than just the world's largest 10K road race. It's a social event in Atlanta, as thousands of spectators line Peachtree Street, Atlanta's main drag, to cheer the runners.

If you're lucky enough to be in town on July 4th, you can do the same. Pack a breakfast and station yourself just about anywhere along Peachtree from Lenox Square to 14th Street. Or go straight to the finish in Piedmont Park and take part in the chaos of the finale. Be sure to arrive early. The wheelchair division of the race begins at 7am, and the official footrace begins at 7:30am. Peachtree is closed to traffic that morning, and you'll have difficulty crossing the street—even on foot—after 7am.

The race is quite a sight to behold, as 55,000 runners surge down Peachtree, a far cry from the 110 runners who gathered to run the first race in 1970. (The only spectators then were a few surprised pedestrians walking their dogs.) The race is so popular now that it takes 500 volunteers to coordinate the start and 50 minutes for the final group to pass the starting line. By then, the winner has already covered the 6.2-mile distance and rested for at least a quarter of an hour.

Don't even think about entering the race at the last minute. Many more applicants than can be accommodated vie for the available spots, and the event always closes out in a few days. You can, however, run the course on other days of the year. There are sidewalks all the way down Peachtree, so it's a fairly safe course. Here's the route you should follow:

Start at the corner of Peachtree and Lenox roads, right across from Lenox Square. Proceed down Peachtree through Buckhead. Along the way, you'll pass by some of Atlanta's most elegant neighborhoods. Just after West Wesley Road, you'll have a magnificent view of the downtown skyline. Don't let the easy, downward trend of the first few miles fool you. This is a tough run, and just about halfway through the course, there's a fairly steep incline—appropriately dubbed Heartbreak or Heart Attack Hill. (Fortunately, the top of the hill is right in front of Piedmont Hospital.) In Midtown, proceed on Peachtree to 10th Street, turn left, and continue to the end of the course, which is at the Charles Allen Drive entrance to Piedmont Park. To return to Lenox Square, backtrack to the Midtown station on 10th Street a block off Peachtree, and take MARTA to the Buckhead or Lenox station.

For more information, call the Atlanta Track Club at ☎ **404/231-9064.**

about the architects, the businesspeople, and the prominent families who created the city's early commercial center. The tour includes peeks at historic interiors.

The **Inman Park Tour** (2pm Sun in Mar–Nov, Twilight Tours Apr–Oct) visits Atlanta's first trolley suburb, where you'll see preserved and restored Victorian mansions (exterior views only). Highlights include the homes of Coca-Cola magnates Asa Candler and Ernest Woodruff.

The **Sweet Auburn/Martin Luther King, Jr., Historic District Tour,** offered only as a special prearranged group tour, focuses on the area that 20th-century African-American entrepreneurs developed into a prosperous commercial hub. You'll also visit the church where Martin Luther King, Jr., preached, and discover landmarks of the civil rights movement.

Frederick Law Olmsted's Druid Hills Tour (Mar–Nov, Twilight Tours Apr–Oct) explores the neighborhood that was the setting for the play and film *Driving Miss Daisy.* The gracious parklike area was laid out by noted landscape designer Frederick Law Olmsted and contains many architecturally important homes.

Margaret Mitchell's Ansley Park Tour (Twilight Tours Apr–Oct) explores one of Atlanta's first garden suburbs (today a charming Midtown neighborhood), partly designed by Frederick Law Olmsted. Its broad lawns, majestic trees, parks, and beautiful houses make for a lovely tour. It's easy to get lost in Ansley Park, so if you want to explore the area, this walking tour is a good idea.

The **Historic Midtown Tour** (Mar–Oct) explores the many faces of the booming Midtown area, from its bungalows and skyscrapers to its restaurants and churches.

PARKS & OUTDOOR PURSUITS

Parks

GRANT PARK

Named for Confederate Capt. Lemuel P. Grant, who helped build Atlanta's defense line, Grant Park (bordered by Sydney St., Atlanta Ave., Boulevard, and Cherokee Ave.) still contains vestiges of his fortifications. Near the intersection of Boulevard and Atlanta Avenue, you can see the remaining earthwork slopes of Fort Walker, a commanding artillery bastion with its original gun emplacements. Its cannons and caissons can be seen in the museum area of the Atlanta Cyclorama (p. 114), one of Grant Park's two major attractions. The other is Zoo Atlanta (p. 150). The park is open daily from 6am to 11pm; it's best to visit during daylight hours.

PIEDMONT PARK ★

Piedmont Park, the city's most popular and centrally located recreation area (with its main entrance on Piedmont Ave. at 14th St.), was once a farm and a Civil War encampment. Its first public usage was by the elite Gentlemen's Driving Club, which bought the property as a site for horseback riding and racing. It soon became a venue for state fairs, including the spectacular Cotton States and International Exposition of 1895. In 1904, the property's 180-plus acres of woodsy meadow and farm were transformed into a city park with a varied terrain of rolling hillsides, verdant lawns, and lush forest around Lake Clara Meer.

Today, Piedmont Park is the setting for many popular regional events such as concerts and music festivals, and recently opened a 53-acre expansion. It contains softball fields, soccer fields, public tennis courts, a public swimming pool, and paths for jogging, skating, and cycling. The expansion added a public skate park and an interactive fountain. The park hosts a Green Market from 9am to 1pm every Saturday from May through mid-December, selling locally grown produce, artisan cheeses, fresh-cut flowers, and other merchandise. The park gets a lot of use, and in some spots can be downright scruffy-looking, but the Piedmont Park Conservancy and the city of Atlanta continue to upgrade the landscaping. A visitor center, where you can find information on the park and the surrounding area, is located at the Piedmont Avenue and 12th Street entrance. The park is a great place for children, with plenty of open, car-free spaces. Don't let the kids miss PlayScape at the 12th Street entrance; created by well-known sculptor Isamu Noguchi, it's a climbable series of brightly colored geometric shapes complete with ladders and slides. The people-watching in the park is superb, and the Midtown skyline beyond is magnificent. The Atlanta Botanical Garden (p. 113) is next-door.

Parking was also expanded recently, but it can still be difficult during special events, and authorities are quick to tow cars parked illegally. It's easiest to take MARTA to the Arts Center station and walk the few blocks down 14th Street. During special events, it's usually possible to take a shuttle to and from the station.

A great way to see the park and soak up some of its history is on a **walking tour** sponsored by the Piedmont Park Conservancy. These free tours depart from the visitor center at 11am on the first and third Saturdays in May through early December. During the 1½-hour tour, guides will point out many historic areas, including remnants of the 1895 Piedmont Exposition, the Walker Farm, and the 1895 Cotton States and International Exposition. Call ✆ **404/876-4024** for information.

STONE MOUNTAIN PARK

See p. 132 for a full description of Stone Mountain Park, one of the best places in the region for all kinds of outdoor activities: picnicking, boating (rowboating, canoeing, and sailing), biking (rentals are available), fishing, hiking, golfing, playing tennis, and swimming. The entrance fee (which includes parking) is $8 per car per day; an annual pass is $35.

Outdoor Pursuits

BIKING

See "In-Line Skating & Biking," below.

FISHING

There's good trout fishing on the Chattahoochee River, in the North Georgia Mountains, about 1½ hours from downtown. Many lakes in the area are good for bass and striper; these include **Lake Lanier** (www.lakelanier.com), a 38,000-acre reservoir about 45 minutes away. Fishing licenses, which can be bought at most sporting-goods stores, Walmarts, Kmarts, and online at www.gadnr.org, are $3.50 for 3 days and $9 for the season (for Georgia residents; nonresidents pay $20 for 3 days, $45 for season). A trout-fishing stamp is $8 (in season) or $13 for non-Georgia residents.

The **Fish Hawk,** 3095 Peachtree Rd. (✆ **404/237-3473;** www.thefishhawk. com), has been selling quality tackle for more than 25 years. Specializing in fly-fishing, the store carries all kinds of fishing gear and outdoor clothing and can also supply the requisite license. The staff is extremely knowledgeable and can tell you where to find the fish you seek and anything you need to know about applicable state regulations. They also offer a fishing guide service. Hours are Monday through Friday from 9:30am to 6pm, Saturday from 9am to 5pm.

For additional information, serious anglers can contact the **Georgia Department of Natural Resources,** License and Boat Registration Unit (✆ **800/366-2661;** www.gadnr.org).

GOLF

The **Stone Mountain Golf Club** (✆ **770/465-3278;** www.stonemountaingolf. com) is a beautiful nationally ranked public facility, boasting some areas that are adjacent to the park's lake. Robert Trent Jones, Sr., designed 18 of the 36 holes. A pro shop is on the premises, and lessons are available. For weekends and holidays, reserve the Tuesday before the day you want to play; at other times, reserve a week in advance. A restaurant/clubhouse has a large deck overlooking the lake. Greens fees, including cart and taxes, are $39 Monday through Thursday from 7:30 to 10:50am; $55 Friday to Sunday and holidays from 7:30 to 10:50am; prices may be lower in the off season. There is a parking fee of $10 per car to enter the park. The course is open daily from 7:30am to an hour before dark.

IN-LINE SKATING & BIKING

Piedmont Park is the place to skate, and the nearby **Skate Escape,** 1086 Piedmont Ave. NE, at 12th Street (© **404/892-1292;** www.skateescape.com), is the place to rent equipment. This establishment has all kinds of bicycles and skates for rent or sale, plus helmets, bike locks, and accessories. You can also buy skateboards here. Conventional and in-line skates can be rented for $6 per hour, $15 per day; three-speed or children's bikes are $6 per hour, $25 per day. If you have an out-of-state driver's license, a major credit card is required as ID; alternately, you can leave a deposit of $150 for skates, $250 for bikes. Skate Escape is open daily in the spring and summer from 11am to 7pm, and the folks here will give you good advice about routes through the park. MARTA: Midtown.

Also see the information on the PATH Foundation under "Nature Walks & Scenic Strolls," below.

NATURE WALKS & SCENIC STROLLS

Atlanta offers many wonderful places for quiet nature walks and easy day hikes. Below are just a few of the options.

The **Atlanta History Center,** 130 W. Paces Ferry Rd. (© **404/814-4000**), described fully on p. 115, stands on 32 woodland acres and has self-guided walking trails and five gardens. You'll discover many plants native to the region along the forested mile-long Swan Woods Trail.

The **Chattahoochee River National Recreation Area** is a series of parklands that punctuate the 48 miles along the Chattahoochee River—from Buford Dam at Lake Lanier, north of the city, to Paces Mill at Vinings, just outside Atlanta's northwestern limits. Along the way, trails range from flat, easy walks to more strenuous ridge and valley hikes. Lace up your sneakers to enjoy some of the unspoiled parts of the scenic Chattahoochee River. Admission is free, but there is a $3 parking fee. For maps and more information, contact the National Park Service (© **678/538-1200;** www.nps.gov/chat).

Stone Mountain Park, 16 miles east of downtown on U.S. 78, is also covered in more detail in this chapter (p. 132). It has thousands of acres of beautiful wooded parkland and lakes. There's a walking trail that goes up and down the moss-covered slopes of the mountain; you'll be delighted by the wildflowers that bloom here each spring. Twenty acres of wildlife trails crisscross the park, passing through natural animal habitats and a petting zoo. Hard-core hikers will enjoy the challenging hiking trails.

Sixteen miles of extensive hiking trails meander through the beautiful scenery at **Kennesaw Mountain/National Battlefield Park,** Old Hwy. 41 and Stilesboro Road, Kennesaw (© **770/427-4686**). Trail maps are available at the visitor center. See p. 141 for more information.

Piedmont Park, centrally located with its main entrance on Piedmont Avenue at 14th Street, provides a glorious setting for strolls, jogs, and bike rides. The wonderful **Atlanta Botanical Garden** is next door. See p. 154 for a full description of the park, and p. 113 for coverage of the botanical garden.

Château Elan, 30 miles north of Atlanta at exit 126 off I-85 in Braselton (© 678/ 425-0900), has nature trails along St. Emilion Creek (forested with tulip, poplar, oak, hickory, and beech trees) and by Romanée–Conti Pond. There are picnic areas on the lovely grounds, and custom picnic boxes can be purchased at Café Elan. See p. 137 for a complete description of the château's offerings.

The **Fernbank Science Center,** 156 Heaton Park Dr. NE (© 678/874-7102), has 1.5 miles of paved trails with trees, wildflowers, and plants labeled for identification. This unspoiled natural environment is home to many animals and birds; in addition, a small pond teems with aquatic life. See p. 147 for a complete description of the science center.

The nonprofit **PATH Foundation** (© 404/875-PATH [7284]; www.path foundation.org) is dedicated to creating and maintaining a network of walking and biking trails in metropolitan Atlanta. So far, the organization has completed more than 100 miles of greenway trails. The most accessible is around **Chastain Park** in the northern part of the city; it's an easy, paved 2.6-mile trail looping around the rolling hills of the park and golf course. The **Atlanta–Stone Mountain Trail,** which goes from the Carter Center to Stone Mountain Park, is another popular trek. Maps are available at most biking and sporting-goods stores. Call the above phone number for more information and advice about where to begin your journey.

RIVER RAFTING/CANOEING/KAYAKING

The **Nantahala Outdoor Center** (© 888/905-7238; www.noc.com) leads white-water rafting adventures on the scenic Chattooga River in North Georgia (it's the one you saw in the movie *Deliverance*) and the Ocoee River in Tennessee (which was an Olympic venue). Put-in points for both rivers are about a 2-hour drive from Atlanta. Trips vary in length (from a few hours to a few days) and difficulty.

The Chattooga has Class II and III rapids in Section III, and Class III, IV, and V in Section IV. The roller coaster Ocoee has Class III and IV rapids only. Kids must be at least 10 years old for easy trips, 12 or older for more difficult rapids. The company also offers canoeing and kayaking trips, plus excursions of varying difficulty on other rivers. All of the expeditions are immensely popular, so make reservations as far in advance as possible.

Prices vary depending on the length and difficulty of the trip, and weekends are more expensive than weekdays, summer trips more expensive than spring and fall. Half-day trips begin at about $35, full-day trips at about $85; both rates include equipment, a guide, and transportation from the outpost to the river. Rafting season is April 1 to October 31, with occasional trips in March and November.

The **Chattahoochee River National Recreation Area** (see "Nature Walks & Scenic Strolls," above) has several spots where canoers, kayakers, and rafters have access to the cold, slow-moving Chattahoochee River. Call the National Park Service (© 678/538-1200) for more information. Watercraft can be rented year-round from the **Chattahoochee Outdoor Center** (© 770/395-6851) at the Johnson Ferry and Powers Island units in the recreation area.

SWIMMING

Almost every Atlanta hotel has a swimming pool. In addition, there is a sandy lake-front beach (complete with water slides) in Stone Mountain Park (p. 132).

If you're *really* serious about getting wet, there's also **White Water,** exit 265 off I-75 on North Cobb Parkway in Marietta (© 770/424-9283), a water theme park described in detail on p. 148.

TENNIS

The City of Atlanta Parks and Recreation Department operates 12 outdoor hard courts at the Sharon Lester Tennis Center at **Piedmont Park** (© **404/853-3461**), all of them lit for night play. No reservations are taken; it's first-come, first-served. There's free parking at the courts, and showers and lockers are available on the premises. Hours are Monday through Thursday from 10am to 10pm, Friday 10am to 9pm, and weekends 9am to 6pm. Fees are $3 per person per hour during the day, $5 per person per hour when courts are lit.

The city also has 13 outdoor clay courts and 10 outdoor hard courts (16 are lit) at the **Bitsy Grant Tennis Center,** 2125 Northside Dr., between I-75 N. and Peachtree Battle Avenue (© **404/609-7193**). Courts are available on a first-come, first-served basis; no reservations are taken. There are showers and lockers available. The courts are open Monday to Thursday 9am to 10pm, Friday 9am to 7pm, and weekends 9am to 6pm. Hours from Labor Day to April are abbreviated; call ahead for details. Court fees are around $6 per person per hour on a soft court and $3 per person per hour on a hard court, depending on the hour of play. There's a lot of team tennis played here, so call ahead to check court availability. For information about other city courts, call the **Office of Recreation** (© **404/817-6766**).

SPECTATOR SPORTS

Atlanta has five professional major league teams: the Braves, the Hawks, the Falcons, the Thrashers, and the Dream. Good tickets can be extremely hard to come by during a winning season, so plan in advance. Tickets can be obtained from the individual teams or through **Ticketmaster** (© **800/326-4000** or 404/249-6400; www.ticket master.com). Note that a service charge will be added to each ticket purchased through Ticketmaster.

Auto Racing

From beginning to end, **Atlanta Motor Speedway** has race fans covered. Hosting two NASCAR Sprint Cup races a year—one in early March and one on Labor Day weekend—as well as NASCAR Nationwide Series and NASCAR Camping World Truck Series events, this track in Hampton, 30 miles south of Atlanta, is where folks come to see the big boys run. The smart fans are those who come in a day early and camp or RV—they get to avoid the traffic. The others aren't so lucky. Unreserved campsites are $60 during race week. Reserved camping for self-contained RVs is $100 to $150; hookups are available. If you don't want to wait for a free parking space for your car, $75 reserved vehicle parking is in the Champions Reserve Lot. Race tickets are usually available right up until the start of the race, and some are quite reasonably priced. Tours of the speedway are available through the gift shop. Call © **770/946-4211** or visit www.atlantamotorspeedway.com for more information.

Situated on 700 scenic wooded acres about 45 minutes north of downtown Atlanta, **Road Atlanta** is one of the Southeast's premier road-racing motor-sports facilities. Its 2.5-mile Grand Prix racecourse has a challenging combination of turns, elevation changes, and high-speed straightaways. A year-round season includes sports-car, motorcycle, truck, and vintage/historic racing, among other events. Call © **800/849-RACE** (7223) or 770/967-6143, or go to www.roadatlanta.com, for information and a schedule of events. Tickets usually run $20 to $75, with higher prices for the Petit Le Mans, a 1,000-mile race. Infield parking is $5. Road Atlanta is

Kudzu, a fast-growing vine that smoth-
ers anything and everything in its path,
once stopped an Atlanta Braves baseball game. On August 29, 2000, in the
ninth inning of a game between the
Braves and the Cincinnati Reds, the
lights abruptly went out at Turner Field.
It seems that a kudzu vine had snaked
around a critical terminal area, causing
the 12-minute blackout. It was the first-
ever kudzu delay in Major League Baseball. The Braves lost 4 to 2.

located in Braselton on Georgia Hwy. 53 between I-85 and I-985 (take I-85 N. to exit 129, make a left, and follow the signs).

Baseball

Although they've won the World Series only once in recent memory, in 1995, the **Atlanta Braves** consistently post a terrific record. The team plays in Turner Field, a stadium that was modified to function as a world-class ballpark after hosting the Centennial Olympic Games (see "Stadiums," below, for details). The regular season runs from the first week of April until the first week of October; post-season play is over by the end of October.

Advance-purchase seats run from $6 (in the Upper Pavilion) to $56 (on the Dugout Level), and ticket availability is proportional to the team's success. Call customer service (✆ **404/522-7630**) for more information, or visit the website at www.atlanta braves.com. You can charge tickets online or by phone through **Ticketmaster** (✆ **800/326-4000** or 404/249-6400; www.ticketmaster.com), or buy directly from the stadium box office, which is located at the northwest corner of the ballpark. It's open Monday through Friday from 8:30am to 6pm, Saturday from 9am to 5pm, and Sunday from 1 to 5pm. Even if you can't get tickets in advance, it's sometimes possible to get $1 Skyline tickets (bleacher seats) and $5 standing-room-only tickets. Skyline tickets are available only on game day and go on sale 3 hours before game time. Fans are limited to one ticket per customer, and immediate entry to the ballpark is required. Standing-room-only tickets are sold only on game day and are available 1 hour before the first pitch, but only when all other tickets for the game have been sold. Check the designated ticket window in the main ticket area.

Basketball

The **Atlanta Hawks** are the local NBA franchise, and their season runs from November to April. The Hawks play in Philips Arena, which was built downtown on the site of the old Omni Coliseum, adjacent to CNN Center (see "Stadiums," below, for details). Tickets range from $10 for a nosebleed seat to $90 for something up close and personal. Call **Ticketmaster** (✆ **800/326-4000** or 404/249-6400; www.ticket master.com) or ✆ **404/827-3865** for information.

New to Atlanta and to the WNBA since 2008, the fledgling **Atlanta Dream** is the local women's professional basketball franchise, with a season that runs from May to September. The Dream plays in Philips Arena, adjacent to CNN Center (see "Stadiums," below, for details). Tickets range from $10 to $45 for regular seating areas and $53 to $212 courtside. Call ✆ **404/604-2626** for information.

On the college front, the **Georgia Tech Yellow Jackets** play in the highly competitive Atlantic Coast Conference (ACC). Their season runs from mid-November to early March, and home games are played in Alexander Memorial Coliseum, on the campus at 10th and Fowler streets (see "Stadiums," below, for details). Tickets range from $13 to $31, but they are often difficult to come by. Available tickets go on sale at the Coliseum on the day of the game. Call ✆ **888/832-4849** or 404/894-5447 for information.

Football

The **Atlanta Falcons** are the city's NFL franchise, playing eight games (plus exhibition games) each season in the Georgia Dome (see "Stadiums," below, for details). Watching a game in the Dome is an interesting, noisy experience. The regular season begins in September and runs through December, with post-season games played in January. Pre-season games begin in August. Ticket prices are $62 to more than $189, depending on how close to the action you want to sit. For information, call ✆ **404/ 249-6400,** or visit www.atlantafalcons.com.

As for college football, the "Ramblin' Wrecks from **Georgia Tech**" have played their home games at 43,000-seat Bobby Dodd Stadium/Grant Field, on campus at North Avenue and Techwood Drive, since 1913. The season runs from September to November. Call ✆ **888/832-4849** or 404/894-5447 for information. Tickets are $25 and $40 and are usually available, except for home games against the University of Georgia, which are always sold out. Games are played on Thursday nights and Saturday afternoons. Parking is limited; taking MARTA to the North Avenue station is the best option. Go early and stop at the Varsity for a hamburger or a hot dog; it's on North Avenue between the MARTA station and the stadium.

Hockey

The **Atlanta Thrashers,** an NHL team named after Georgia's state bird, take to the ice in Philips Arena, which was built downtown on the site of the old Omni Coliseum (see "Stadiums," below). The season runs from October through April, and tickets run from $14 to $263. Call ✆ **404/878-3000,** or visit www.atlantathrashers.com for information. Take MARTA to Omni/Dome/GWCC.

Stadiums

Alexander Memorial Coliseum This 10,000-seat stadium—renovated for the Olympics—is home to Georgia Tech's Yellow Jackets college basketball team. Parking is limited around the stadium; it's easiest to take MARTA.
Georgia Institute of Technology, 10th and Fowler sts. ✆ **404/894-5400** for information. MARTA: North Ave.

Georgia Dome Atlanta's $214-million, 71,500-seat domed mega-stadium, home of the Atlanta Falcons, hosted Super Bowl XXVIII in 1994, several Olympic events in 1996, and Super Bowl XXXIV in 2000. In addition, it is the site of the annual Chick-fil-A Bowl (formerly Peach Bowl) each January, and it hosted the NCAA Men's Basketball Final Four in 2002 and 2007. The Dome also holds tennis matches, tractor pulls, college basketball games, track and field events, and Supercross events. Behind-the-scenes tours of the Georgia Dome are available Monday, Wednesday, and Friday on the hour from 10am to 2pm for $6 per person. The stadium's oval shape provides a good view of the action from every seat. Check the papers or call the number below to find out what's on during your stay. Parking is extremely limited and expensive; take MARTA and walk to the Dome instead.

A Grand Golfer

Robert Tyre "Bobby" Jones, who won golf's Grand Slam at the age of 28, never became a professional golfer. Jones, who rarely played in tournaments after 1930, went on to practice law in Atlanta. One of the city's public golf courses is named for him.

1 Georgia Dome Dr. (at International Blvd. and Northside Dr.). © **404/223-4636.** www.gadome.com. MARTA: Omni/Dome/GWCC.

Philips Arena   This spectacular $213-million arena, home to the NHL Atlanta Thrashers, NBA Atlanta Hawks, and WNBA Atlanta Dream, was built on the site of the old Omni Coliseum. Tours of the arena are available daily every half-hour from 9am to 6pm on non-event days, and 9am to 5pm on event days. The 1-hour tours take in the Hawks' and Thrashers' locker rooms, the press box, and the luxury suites. Tickets are $7 for adults, $5 for seniors, $4.50 for children 4 to 12, and free for kids 3 and under. The Philips Experience is an interactive station with five hands-on activities to test your skills in basketball, hockey, and other fun challenges.

The Hawk Walk, which connects the CNN Center with Philips Arena, is worth a look if you're a sports fan. It's an indoor street that sells food, beverages, and Atlanta Hawks, Thrashers, and Dream merchandise. Huge video screens display live action at the arena or shows from one of the Turner networks, while giant billboards flash ticker information from the CNN channels.

1 Philips Dr. (at Marietta St.). © **404/878-3000.** www.philipsarena.com. MARTA: Omni/Dome/GWCC.

Turner Field ★★   This spectacular 50,000-seat ballpark started life as an 80,000-seat stadium built to host the Centennial Olympic Games in 1996. After housing the opening and closing ceremonies and numerous track and field events during the Olympics, the north end of the stadium (with approximately 35,000 seats) was demolished, and the rest of the structure was modified to accommodate baseball.

Turner Field is built in the style of old-time ballparks, but also includes a number of attractions besides the baseball game itself. The folks who run the stadium like to call it a baseball theme park, and it's not a bad idea to come to the game early and take in the various attractions, especially if you have children along. The **Braves Museum and Hall of Fame** features memorabilia commemorating legendary stars and key moments in Braves history (take a gander at the bat Hank Aaron used to hit his 715th home run). The museum is open to ticket holders on game days 3 hours before game time and 1 hour after the completion of the game. **Scouts Alley** is designed to teach fans about the fine art of scouting. Fans can test their hitting and throwing skills, call up scouting reports on former and current Braves, play a trivia game, call a play-by-play inning of a game, learn about Hank Aaron's "hot" spot, and much more. At the **Cartoon Network's Tooner Field,** kids can hang out with Cartoon Network characters or play interactive games in the Digital Dugout. At the **East Pavilion,** fans can have their images inserted into either a baseball card or a photo of a great moment in Braves history. The **Braves Clubhouse Store** is full of Braves-themed merchandise, some of which is available only at the stadium.

Finally, it's possible—and fun—to tour Turner Field. Tours depart every half-hour Monday through Saturday from 9:30am to 4pm and Sunday from 1 to 4pm on nongame days, and Monday through Saturday from 9:30am to noon on game days. Cost is $10 for adults, $5 for military and children 3 to 12, and free for children 2 and under. Tours include the museum, the dugout, the press box and broadcast booth, the clubhouse, Scouts Alley, and more. On nongame days, there's ample free parking in the north lot. Call © **404/614-2311** for more information.

If all this activity makes you hungry, head to the **West Pavilion**—where you can snack on famous food items from other ballparks—or to the **Braves Chop House,** a casual restaurant that overlooks the Braves' bullpen.

Museum-only tickets are $5 on nongame days, $2 on game days; the museum hours vary according to the game schedule.

755 Hank Aaron Dr. SE. © **404/522-7630.** http://mlb.mlb.com/atl/ballpark/index.jsp. Parking $8–$12. Parking for visitors with disabilities in the south lot, east of I-75/85, on a first-come, first-served basis. MARTA: Free parking at MARTA rail stations; ride the train ($2) and then take the free shuttle from the Five Points station to the stadium. Shuttle service begins 1 hr. before game time and continues for 1 hr. after the game ends. Or take MARTA to the Georgia State University station and walk several blocks to the stadium. **Note:** The shuttle fans used to take from Underground Atlanta no longer runs on game days so make other plans. Call MARTA (© **404/848-4711**) for more information.

A WALKING TOUR OF SWEET AUBURN

Y ou never really understand a city until you walk
around it a bit, and Atlanta's climate allows for walking tours almost year-round.

In addition to the tour below, consider taking one of the
guided walking tours beginning on p. 152. Also, note that certain attractions detailed in chapter 6 are walking tours in and of themselves: for
example, Stone Mountain Park, Kennesaw Mountain/National Battlefield
Park, Oakland Cemetery, and the Atlanta History Center in Buckhead.

Sweet Auburn, the focus of the following walking tour, includes the Martin Luther King, Jr., National Historic Site, which comprises about 2
blocks along Auburn Avenue, plus the surrounding preservation district
(about 10 more blocks). A neighborhood that nurtured scores of 20th-
century black businesspeople and professionals, it contains the birthplace, church, and gravesite of Martin Luther King, Jr. The area was a
vibrant commercial and entertainment district for black Atlantans from
the late 1800s until the 1930s, when it went into a steep decline. In the
1980s, the area where Martin Luther King, Jr., was born and raised was
declared a national historic site, and now, under the auspices of the
National Park Service, portions of Auburn Avenue are in an ongoing process of restoration. Although parts of the area are still in sad disrepair, new
landscaping has beautified some of the street, and several homes on the
"Birth Home" block have been restored to their 1920s appearance. For
more information about the national historic site, contact the **National
Park Service** at © **404/331-6922,** or visit the website at www.nps.gov.

This walking tour provides insight into black history, the civil rights
movement, and black urban culture in the South. If you're traveling with
children, it's a wonderful opportunity to teach them about a great American. The major points of interest are covered in detail in chapter 6.

WALKING TOUR: **SWEET AUBURN**

START:	**The corner of Howell and Irwin streets. To get here, take I-75/85 S and exit at Freedom Parkway/Carter Center. Turn right at the first light onto International Boulevard. Follow signs to the Martin Luther King, Jr., National Historic Site. You can park in a lot on the north side of Irwin Street between Boulevard and Jackson Street. By MARTA: King Memorial station is about 8 blocks away, or you can take bus 3 east from the Five Points station.**
FINISH:	**Auburn Avenue and Courtland Street.**
TIME:	**Allow a half-day to explore this area thoroughly. If you want to include a tour of Martin Luther King, Jr.'s, Birth Home (stop no. 3)—and a visit to this area would not be complete without it—start out early in the day and obtain your tickets at the National Park Service Visitor Center at 450 Auburn Ave. Only a limited number of tickets are available each day.**

Begin your stroll at:

1 Howell and Irwin Streets

Walk south along Howell Street, where renovated historic homes and housing (designed to harmonize with the architecture of the neighborhood) provide testimony to the area's continuing renaissance. Note 102 Howell St., built between 1890 and 1895, which was the home of Alexander Hamilton, Jr., Atlanta's leading turn-of-the-20th-century black contractor. Its architectural details include Corinthian columns and a Palladian window.

Turn right on Auburn Ave. As you proceed, look for interpretive markers indicating historic homes (mostly Victorian and Queen Anne) and other points of interest en route to 499 Auburn Ave., home of:

2 The King Center

The organization here (© **404/526-8900;** www.thekingcenter.com) continues the work to which King was dedicated—reducing violence within individual communities and among nations. Freedom Plaza, on the premises, is King's final resting place. Stop in to take a self-guided tour of exhibits on King's life and the civil rights movement. Admission is free; the center is open every day from 9am to 5pm. See p. 127 for more details.

Now double back a few blocks east to 501 Auburn Ave., the:

3 Birth Home of Martin Luther King, Jr.

Free half-hour guided tours are given on a continual basis, daily from 9am to 5pm, at King's birthplace. On weekends, especially, arrive early—demand for tickets often exceeds supply. Tickets are obtained at the National Park Service Visitor Center, at 450 Auburn Ave. See p. 116 for more details on the Birth Home.

Walk back toward stop no. 2, noting the turn-of-the-20th-century homes in the area, such as the:

4 Double "Shotgun" Row Houses

Standing at 472–488 Auburn Ave., these two-family dwellings with separate hip roofs were built in 1905 to house workers for the Empire Textile Company. They were called "shotgun" because rooms were lined up in a row, and one could (theoretically) fire a shotgun straight through the whole house.

Continue west on Auburn Ave. At the corner of Auburn Ave. and Boulevard is:

5 Fire Station No. 6

This is one of Atlanta's eight original firehouses, completed in 1894. The two-story Romanesque Revival building was situated to protect the eastern section of the city. The station houses a museum, open daily from 9am to 5pm, where exhibits include restored fire engines and vintage fire-fighting paraphernalia. Note the Italianate arched windows on the second story. Admission is free.

Continuing west on Auburn Ave., a notable stop on your tour is at 407 Auburn Ave., where you'll find the:

6 Ebenezer Baptist Church

This church (✆ **404/688-7263**), founded in 1886, is where Martin Luther King, Jr., served as copastor from 1960 to 1968. Short but informative tours are given Monday through Friday from 9am to 4pm, Saturday from 9am to 2pm, and Sunday from 2 to 4pm. The church has built a new sanctuary across the street, but the original building remains as a historic site under the auspices of the State Department of Parks and Recreation. The church is open Monday through Saturday from 9am to 5pm. See p. 119 for more details.

One block west, at 365 Auburn Ave., is the:

7 Wheat Street Baptist Church

This church has served a congregation since the late 1800s. Auburn Avenue was originally called Wheat Street in honor of Augustus W. Wheat, one of Atlanta's early merchants. The name was changed in 1893.

Farther west, on Auburn Ave. btw. Hilliard and Fort sts., is the:

8 Prince Hall Masonic Building

This was an influential black lodge led for several decades by John Wesley Dobbs. Today, it houses the national headquarters of the Southern Christian Leadership Conference.

On the other side of the expressway, at 228–250 Auburn Ave., note the:

9 Odd Fellows Building and Auditorium

This was another black fraternal lodge, which originated in Atlanta in 1870. Completed in 1914, the building later became headquarters for an insurance company.

Across the street, at 234 Auburn Ave., is the:

10 Sweet Auburn Bread Company ☕

Auburn Avenue native Sonya Jones is known for her delectable sweets, from her signature sweet-potato cheesecake to red velvet cupcakes. Drop in for a cup of coffee, a one-serving-size cheesecake, and some delightful conversation at this Atlanta gem. For more on Sweet Auburn, see p. 108.

Walking Tour: Sweet Auburn

— Preservation District Boundary
━━ National Historic Site Boundary

Ellis St.

Courtland St.

Piedmont Ave.

Butler St.

Irwin St.

Fort St.

Hilliard St.

Houston Street

Atlanta Life Insurance Co. Bldg.

PRESERVATION DISTRICT BOUNDARY

finish here

Herndon Plaza

Brooks Alley

17

18   16

Auburn Ave.

15   14   9 10

75
85

Old Wheat St.

PRESERVATION

8

11

Bell St.

Atlanta Expressway

PRESERVATION DISTRICT BOUNDARY

Edgewood Ave.

Auditorium Place

Piedmont Ave.

Coca-Cola Pl.

Butler St.

Boaz St.

Atlanta Municipal Market

12
13

Hilliard St.

Tanner St.

1 Howell and Irwin streets
2 The King Center
3 Birth Home of Martin Luther King, Jr.
4 Double "Shotgun" Row Houses
5 Fire Station No. 6

6 Ebenezer Baptist Church
7 Wheat Street Baptist Church
8 Prince Hall Masonic Building
9 Odd Fellows Building and Auditorium
10 Sweet Auburn Bread Co. ☕

Make a left on Butler St., and you'll see the:

11 Butler Street YMCA

Built in the early 1900s, this was a popular meeting place for civil rights leaders. Today, the building is augmented by a modern YMCA across the street.

Continue south along Butler St. to the:

12 Sweet Auburn Curb Market

The market is located just below Edgewood Avenue. Formerly called the Municipal Market, this historic market dates from 1924, when Atlanta was still a segregated city. Whites shopped within, while blacks were only permitted to patronize stalls lining the curb. The market's current name reflects that era. Today, it sells groceries and fresh produce—including many regional and ethnic items, such as ham hocks and chitlins ("We sell every part of the pig here but the oink," says the owner). Fully cooked ethnic meals are available as well, and there is seating so you can dig in right away. Open Monday through Thursday from 8am to 6pm, Friday and Saturday from 8am to 7pm.

11 Butler Street YMCA

12 Sweet Auburn Curb Market

13 Sweet Auburn Curb Market 🍽

14 Big Bethel African Methodist Episcopal Church

15 Royal Peacock Club

16 The APEX (African-American Panoramic Experience) Museum

17 Herndon Plaza

18 Auburn Avenue Research Library on African-American Culture and History

13 Sweet Auburn Curb Market 🍽

This is a delightful mix of scents and sights. Seating is scattered throughout in case you just can't wait to get home to eat your purchases. Variety abounds, with fresh fish, meats, veggies, salads, and flowers to take home, plus fully cooked foods from every corner of the earth—everything from specialty cheesecakes to chitlins. Open Monday through Saturday from 8am to 6pm. 209 Edgewood Ave. ✆ 404/659-1665.

Walk back to Auburn Ave. on Butler St. and turn left. To your right, at 220 Auburn Ave., is the:

14 Big Bethel African Methodist Episcopal Church

This church was originally built in the 1890s, destroyed by fire, and then rebuilt in 1924. In the 1920s, John Wesley Dobbs called the Bethel "a towering edifice to black freedom."

Farther along, at 186 Auburn Ave., is the:

15 Royal Peacock Club

This music club's walls were painted from floor to ceiling with peacocks. It has been closed for years, but in its heyday it presented top black entertainers such as Ray Charles, Aretha Franklin, and Dizzy Gillespie.

At 135 Auburn Ave., the corner of Auburn Ave. and Courtland St., is:

16 The APEX (African-American Panoramic Experience) Museum

This museum features exhibits on the history of Sweet Auburn and the African-American experience, including a children's gallery with interactive displays. You can call ☎ **404/521-2739** to see if there's anything special happening at the museum while you're in town. See p. 112 for further details.

Cross the street to:

17 Herndon Plaza

Here, you can see exhibits on the high-powered Herndon family, including patriarch Alonzo Herndon, a former slave who started the Atlanta Life Insurance Company.

If you'd like to do further research on the history of Auburn Ave.—or on any aspect of African-American history and culture—continue on to 101 Auburn Ave., the:

18 Auburn Avenue Research Library on African-American Culture and History

This is the place to go for answers about African-American history. Operated by the Atlanta-Fulton County Library System, the library's collection includes literature, documents, rare records, and more. A Heritage Center on the premises features special exhibits, workshops, seminars, lectures, and other events. Open Monday through Thursday from 10am to 8pm, and Friday through Sunday from noon to 6pm.

SHOPPING

Atlanta is the shopping mecca of the Southeast—period. Visitors might say they come to Atlanta to steep themselves in southern history, take in a play or two, or contemplate the masterpieces in a museum, but what they really want to do is trot on over to Buckhead for a little retail therapy.

It's not just that there's a lot of shopping here, but the fact that it's so varied. There are chic boutiques that can hold their own with the best of Los Angeles or New York, flea markets bursting at the seams with antiques and collectibles, giant department stores, and interesting little browsable areas such as Virginia-Highland. And even if you don't want to buy anything, it's great fun to wander around the shopping areas, checking out the locals and taking the pulse of the city.

GREAT SHOPPING AREAS

Atlantic Station

Open and growing since 2006, **Atlantic Station** (© **404/876-2616;** www.atlanticstation.com) is a mixed-use development, much of which includes shops with everything from books and boots to furniture and furs. Covering 138 acres, it's as ambitious a development as any this country has seen, and includes 1 million square feet of open-air retail and entertainment venues, including a two-story movie theater. You can easily spend a full day browsing the stores, which include American Eagle Outfitters, Ann Taylor and Ann Taylor LOFT, City Sports, Dillard's, DSW Shoes, Express, Gap, Nine West, Old Navy, West Elm, and Z Gallerie. It's also the location of the city's first IKEA, a shopping experience in itself. This is not only the first branch in the Southeast, but also the first in the world to serve grits and sweet tea in its restaurant. Once you shop 'til you drop, stop in at the Grape, a casual wine bar with outstanding small-plate gourmet fare and a great variety of wines from around the world. Find a new one you really like? Pick up a bottle from its wine shop right next door. There are several locations around the city, so visit www.yourgrape.com for more information and scheduled wine tastings.

Atlantic Station is located on 17th Street, just west of I-75. To get here, take MARTA to the Arts Center station, then hop a free shuttle to Atlantic Station. Shuttles stop at various points throughout Atlantic Station and make the rounds every 20 to 30 minutes.

Buckhead

The stamping ground of well-to-do Atlantans, Buckhead is the ultimate shopping area, with two major malls and lots of little boutiques, antiques shops, and galleries. If you're serious about shopping, this is the place to start. Even though the area has an upscale reputation, don't let that stop you. There's lots of variety, and the competition can mean excellent bargains.

The hot spot for the best of Buckhead is at the corner of Peachtree and Lenox roads, where two major malls—**Phipps Plaza** and **Lenox Square**—face off against each other (p. 177). If your time is limited, pick one of these malls and spend the morning or afternoon there. For about $7, you can park in the "up front" lot, right outside the main entrance.

If you have more time and are interested in art, antiques, or decorative accessories, head straight to **Bennett Street,** where you'll find a healthy concentration of stores in a 2-block strip. There are also many options in **Buckhead West Village,** near the intersection of Peachtree and West Paces Ferry roads. Shops also line the rest of Peachtree Road as well as smaller side streets. Serious interior decorators will want to make the trip to **Miami Circle.**

BENNETT STREET

Located just off Peachtree Road on the south edge of Buckhead is a quaint little street that's become one of the most interesting shopping destinations in the city. Once a supply path linking Atlanta to the surrounding countryside during the Civil War, Bennett Street evolved into a thriving warehouse district around the turn of the 20th century. Those warehouses have been transformed into a handy concentration of shops and galleries specializing in art, decorative accessories, and antiques.

Exploring the street makes for a pleasant afternoon ramble, but if you don't have time to wander the whole strip, check out the Stalls and the Interiors Market, both of which house many dealers in one location. Most shops are open Monday through Saturday from 10am or 11am to 5pm, and a few are open Sunday from 1 to 5pm. Bennett Street—little more than a dead-end alley—is only a couple of blocks long, but it's built on a hill, so wear comfortable shoes. It's just off Peachtree Road between Collier Road and Peachtree Battle Avenue. To get here from downtown, take bus no. 23 from the Arts Center MARTA station to the 2100 block of Peachtree Road.

Here's some of what you'll find along Bennett Street.

Bennett Street Gallery This gallery features contemporary glass, ceramics, jewelry, and fine art, including paintings in oil, acrylic, casein (a plastic substance), and watercolors. 22 Bennett St. NW. ✆ **404/352-8775.** www.bennettstgallery.com.

Interiors Market This is a large consortium of antiques and art dealers all under one roof. Locals looking for just the right home accessory know to start here or at the Stalls (see below) rather than schlepping around to all the different shops in town. There's an ever-changing variety of objects here, with myriad booths featuring everything from fine antiques to old books. 55 Bennett St. NW. ✆ **404/352-0055.** www.interiors market.com.

Nottingham Antiques Direct importers of European antique pine furniture, this shop also sells custom furniture. 45 Bennett St. NW. ✆ **404/352-1890.** www.nottingham antiques.com.

The Stalls Just like the Interiors Market, this is a large assortment of dealers under one roof, which increases the odds that you'll find that special piece you've been searching for. The quality of the antiques and accessories is excellent, attracting designers from around the country. For lunch, you can stop at the Stalls Café, which serves an excellent grilled sandwich—pimento cheese with bacon and tomato. 116 Bennett St. NW. ✆ **404/352-4430.** www.thestalls.com.

MIAMI CIRCLE

Most design centers are open to the trade only, and this street of showrooms and warehouses started out that way. But now, most of the nearly 100 merchants on Miami Circle in Buckhead are open to the public. It's a virtual smorgasbord of furnishings and accessories—from fine European and American antiques to country and primitive pieces. There's antique and reproduction pine, painted furniture, antique statuary, heirloom wicker, fine artwork, majolica, custom and antique rugs, antique books and bookcases, clocks, antique chandeliers, and at least one warehouse of designer fabrics.

This is not a quaint street suitable for a pleasant stroll, but it is a great place to browse for serious merchandise. Most establishments are open Monday through Saturday from 10am to 5pm, and some are open on Sunday as well. If you need something shipped home, it's not a problem. Miami Circle is off Piedmont Road, just a half-mile south of Peachtree Road and about ⅓ mile north of the Lindbergh MARTA station.

WEST VILLAGE OF BUCKHEAD

The intersection of Peachtree and West Paces Ferry roads is the heart of the original Buckhead community. On the east side of Peachtree Road is the center of Buckhead nightlife; the retail shops are on the west side of Peachtree Road, where you'll find everything from art and antiques to women's apparel. The West Village, as the area surrounding the intersection is called, is bounded by West Paces Ferry Road, Roswell Road, and East Andrews Drive. If you're navigating the city via public transportation, use the Buckhead MARTA station to access shopping in this area.

There are a couple of places to stop for a snack or lunch as you wander through the neighborhood. You can stop in at **Fadó**, 3035 Peachtree Rd. (✆ **404/841-0066**), an "authentic" Irish pub that serves commendable Gaelic fare; especially good is the *boxty* (filled Irish potato pancake) and the corned beef and cabbage.

Here's some of what you'll discover in the West Village.

Boxwoods   It's hard to see everything in this delightful shop in one visit. There are intriguing gifts and serious gardening accessories, as well as numerous antiques, lamps, fresh flowers, and greenery. Open Monday through Saturday from 10am to 6pm. 100 E. Andrews Dr. NW. ✆ **404/233-3400.** www.boxwoodsonline.com.

Lagerquist Gallery   The contemporary fine art in this, Atlanta's oldest fine-arts gallery, includes sculpture, paintings, watercolors, and works on paper by regional, national, and international artists. Open Tuesday through Friday from 10am to 5pm and 11am to 5pm Saturday. 3235 Paces Ferry Place NW. ✆ **404/261-8273.** www.lagerquist gallery.net.

Patagonia   There's a lot here for outdoor enthusiasts, no matter what sport you enjoy—canoeing, paddling, skiing, cycling, climbing, surfing, and on and on. You'll find plenty of equipment, as well as boots, outerwear, and organic cotton clothing for men, women, and children. Open Monday through Friday from 10am to 7pm, Saturday from 10am to 6pm, and Sunday from noon to 6pm. 34 E. Andrews Dr. NW. ✆ **404/266-8182.**

Peoples The women's clothing in this friendly shop—suits, tops, skirts, dresses, jackets, and swimwear—is contemporary, with clean, classic lines. It's a sleek, well-chosen collection you won't find in department stores. Open Tuesday through Saturday from 10am to 5pm. 3236 Roswell Rd. NW. ✆ **404/816-7292.**

Razzle Dazzle Razzle Dazzle has been on the Buckhead scene since 1975. Sportswear is the main staple here (great pants, sweaters, jackets, and so on), but there are also stunning little dresses, some evening wear, hats, and a wonderful assortment of jewelry, some of it handmade. You'll find lines by Ella Moss, Splendid, Free People, and more. Open Monday through Saturday from 10:30am to 5pm. 49 Irby Ave. NW. ✆ **404/233-6940.** www.razzledazzleatlanta.com.

Signature Shop & Gallery Everything here is one of a kind, handcrafted by contemporary American artists: dinnerware, turned wood bowls, decorative and functional ceramics, pewter vessels, sterling jewelry and utensils, quilts, furniture, and more. Open Tuesday through Saturday from 10am to 5:30pm. 3267 Roswell Rd. NW. ✆ **404/237-4426.** www.thesignatureshop.com.

White Dove White Dove is full of feminine, sexy, upscale clothing for day and evening. Many of the fabrics are delicate and antiquey—silky rayons, linens, chiffons, and gauzy cottons—and the hats are festooned with silk flowers. Open Tuesday through Saturday from 11am to 6pm. 18 E. Andrews Dr. NW. ✆ **404/814-1994.**

Chamblee's Antique Row

Antique Row (www.antiquerow.com), on New Peachtree Road at Broad Street and North Peachtree Road, is a quaint collection of shops located in historic buildings, some dating from the 1800s. Nearby, there are a few antiques malls, which conveniently house many dealers under one roof. The largest is the **Broad Street Antiques Mall,** 3550 Broad St. (✆ **770/458-6316**), which has around 100 dealers.

In the assorted shops and malls, you'll find antique American and European furniture, glassware, pottery, Victoriana, Orientalia, wicker, collector toys, quilts, Coke memorabilia, jewelry, architectural antiques, Olympics collectibles, and crafts items. Hours vary with each store. Most are open Monday through Saturday from 10am to 5:30pm, Sunday from 1 to 5:30pm. It's a little tough to get here if you don't have a car, but you can take a MARTA train to the Chamblee station, which is about ¾ mile from the shops. On weekdays, take the no. 132 Tilly Mill bus from there; on weekends, walk or take a taxi.

Decatur

Decatur is finally getting some respect as a destination for dining, entertainment, events, and even shopping. With dozens of small boutiques and galleries, Decatur can hold its own when it comes to shoppers looking for one-of-a-kind buys, fine art, and great bargains. From clothing and shoes to books and jewelry, the area has a little of everything and plenty of fun places for a quick bite or full afternoon of wine and noshing.

Boogaloos   If you're looking for the latest in fashion for women for a special night on the town or a date with a new guy (or even an old one), this cute shop carries all the lines today's young women love. Look for clothing lines such as Seven for All Mankind, BCBG Generation, Citizens of Humanity, Envi, and more. The fourth Friday of every month is Fab Friday, with 20% off all full-price merchandise—and wine and hors d'oeuvres! 246 W. Ponce De Leon Ave. ✆ **404/373-3237.** www.boogaloosboutique.com.

Heliotrope   This shop is packed with fun stuff, from holiday decor, candles, and practical-joke ammo to greeting cards, jewelry, and tableware. If you need a gift, you can find it here, regardless of whom you are shopping for. 248 W. Ponce de Leon Ave. ✆ **404/371-0100.** www.heliotropehome.com.

Squash Blossom Boutique   Opened in 1999 by mother and daughter Ettie Wurtzel and Talia Wurtzel Blanchard, Squash Blossom recently doubled its space—and its inventory. Located on the square in Decatur, this shop features hip women's clothing by Echo, Nick & Mo, Hanky Panky, and Bobi, and accessories, including bags, hats, scarves, and jewelry. 113 E. Court Sq. ✆ **404/373-1864.** www.squashblossom boutique.com.

Wiggle   Even if you don't have kids of your own, this is a fun place to ooh and aah over cute clothes for tykes. The shop has apparel for babies, boys, and girls from infant size through size eight. Toys, art, and shoes round out the offerings. Wiggles does monogramming, too, whether on a piece you buy from them or something you bring in. They also do free gift wrapping. 305 E. College Ave. ✆ **404/373-2522.** www. wiggleatlanta.com.

Little Five Points

An area similar to Virginia-Highland (p. 174), though a lot funkier and much rougher around the edges, Little Five Points is a happening and offbeat shopping district. There are still authentic hippies here—and enough young people with wildly colored hair and pierced body parts to give you a '60s flashback. Little Five Points is close to Virginia-Highland, so head over that way if you crave additional browsing; you can cover both areas in a few hours. In addition to the shops, there are a number of taverns and cafes in the area. Plan to have lunch at the Flying Biscuit Cafe (p. 105), which is about a mile up McLendon Avenue.

Begin your stroll on Moreland Avenue just north of Euclid Avenue, and then proceed southwest along Euclid Avenue. Most shops are open Monday through Saturday from 11am to 7 or 8pm, and Sunday from noon to 6pm. But note this is a very laid-back shopping district, so hours can change on a whim. Paid parking is available on weekends in the expanded parking lot around Junkman's Daughter on Moreland Avenue. Take MARTA to the Five Points station to access this area.

Below are some of the shopping highlights of Little Five Points.

Abbadabbas's If you're searching for comfortable shoes and want something a tad offbeat, step into this wild little shoe store that's been a fixture for years. You'll find Birkenstocks, Doc Martens, and Converse, to name a few, as well as a great assortment of socks. There are four other locations around town. 421-B Moreland Ave. NE (btw. Euclid and North aves.). ☏ **404/588-9577.**

A Cappella Books You'll discover new, used, and out-of-print books here, many on topics including the counterculture, literature, history, and the arts. There are signed editions, too. 484 Moreland Ave. ☏ **404/681-5128.**

The Clothing Warehouse Vintage Levi's are the main attraction here, but there's also a selection of other casual used clothing for both men and women. 420 Moreland Ave. NE (btw. Euclid and North aves.). ☏ **404/524-5070.**

Junkman's Daughter This funky 10,000-square-foot megastore looks like a transplant from New York's East Village. The merchandise includes inexpensive club clothing for men and women (often bizarre and totally tasteless), including T-shirts and shoes. The staircase leading to the mezzanine is in the shape of a 20-foot-tall red high-heeled shoe. 464 Moreland Ave. NE (btw. Euclid and North aves.). ☏ **404/577-3188.**

René René *Atlanta* magazine named René René the city's best women's clothing shop in the "funky club scene" category. It's true, but some of owner René Sanning's designs are also sophisticated—possibly even wearable for work. Among the offerings is a glamorous, Old Hollywood–style evening line that has attracted such customers as Faye Dunaway and Halle Berry. Don't miss the interesting accessories. 1142 Euclid Ave. (btw. Moreland and Colquitt aves.). ☏ **404/522-RENE (7363).**

Sevananda This natural foods co-op market is a health junkie's dream. Sevananda, Sanskrit for "the joy of service," offers fresh, local, and organic produce, natural foods, vitamins and supplements, and the largest selection of bulk herbs and spices in the city. Even if you aren't in the market for fresh wheatgrass, you won't be able to pass up the freshly prepared foods, from baked goods and soups to sandwiches and entrees. Also look for earth-friendly household and pet products. 467 Euclid Ave. ☏ **404/681-2831.**

Stefan's Vintage Clothing Most of Stefan's merchandise is vintage clothing for men and women from the early 1900s through the early 1960s, plus accessories such as cigarette cases, cuff links, evening bags, hats, and period costume jewelry. There are cashmere overcoats, lingerie items, cocktail and evening gowns, tuxedos, wedding gowns, Hawaiian shirts, bowling shirts, and suits. Prices are low, and the merchandise is usually in flawless condition. It's definitely the best shop in Little Five Points. 1160 Euclid Ave. NE (btw. Moreland and Colquitt aves.). ☏ **404/688-4929.**

Wax n Facts Looking for that ancient Bob Dylan album that your college girl-friend got custody of when you broke up? It's probably here, along with tons of other old vinyl. 431 Moreland Ave. NE (btw. Euclid and North aves.). ☏ **404/525-2275.**

Virginia-Highland

This charming area of town, centered on North Highland Avenue between University Drive and Ponce de Leon Avenue, boasts antiques shops, boutiques, and art galleries. There are three major areas for shopping: North Highland just south of University Drive; the intersection of North Highland and Virginia avenues; and just north of Ponce de Leon Avenue around St. Charles Place. It's about 1½ miles from one end of Virginia-Highland to the other, but it's a nice walk, and there are cafes where you can stop and take a break. For lunch, try Murphy's (p. 102). If you have limited time

I Scream for Ice Cream

If you happen to be in the Virginia-Highland shopping district in the afternoon or evening, stop in for an authentic Italian gelato at the funky **Paolo's Gelato Italiano,** 1025 Virginia Ave. NE. The place is open during Monday through Thursday 1 to 10pm, Friday from noon to 11pm, Saturday noon to 11:30pm, Sunday noon to 10pm. Its winter hours (Nov–Mar) are the same, but Monday to Wednesday they're open 4 to 10pm. Also in the area, **Cold Stone Creamery,** 231 18th St. NW (and 13 other metro Atlanta locations), limits its flavors only by your imagination, as you get to choose your ice-cream flavor as well as dozens of delicacies that are mixed in on a cold marble slab (hence the name). If you're not feeling creative, choose from the shop's own combinations, including Chocolate Devotion, Birthday Cake Remix, and Cookie Minster. Open daily from 11am to 11pm. Shoppers can enjoy another favorite, **Jake's Ice Cream,** located in the Irwin Street Market at 660 Irwin St. Belly up to the ice cream bar for fun flavors such as Brown Shugah Vanilla and Mexican Hot Chocolate. Jake's is open Tuesday through Saturday from 11am to 9pm.

to browse, go straight to the intersection of North Highland and Virginia avenues and take in the stores there. This area is accessible by MARTA through the Five Points station.

Here's some of what you'll find in the Virginia-Highland area.

Mitzi & Romano   Mitzi Ugolini carries cool and contemporary women's clothing, plus great jewelry and accessories, including fantastic handbags. Most of the selection is affordable. Don't miss the sale section at the back of the store. Open Sunday and Monday from 11am to 7pm, Tuesday through Thursday from 10am to 9pm, and Friday and Saturday from 10am to 10pm. 1038 N. Highland Ave. (btw. Virginia and Los Angeles aves.). *© **404/876-7228.***

Mooncake   The ever-changing inventory of whimsical wearables for women here might include cloche and straw hats, flowing dresses, unusual silk separates, and handcrafted jewelry. The retro-style clothing looks vintage, but everything is new. You'll also find body and bath items, hair accessories, diaries, and greeting cards. Open Monday through Saturday from 11am to 7pm and Sunday 12:30 to 5pm. 1019 Virginia Ave. NE (just off N. Highland Ave.). *© **404/892-8043.***

Natural Body International   This appealing shop invites you to pamper yourself with all manner of skin treatments, oils, soaps, lotions, and cosmetics, as well as an extensive line of aromatherapy products. All offerings are natural and animal and environment friendly. An on-site day spa features a full line of beauty treatments. Open Monday 10am to 6pm, Tuesday through Friday from 10am to 8pm, Saturday from 10am to 7pm, and Sunday from noon to 6pm. There are several other Atlanta locations, including one in Buckhead at 2385 Peachtree Rd., Ste. 3A (© **404/869-7722**); the hours vary. 754 Peachtree St. NE. © **404/876-2131.** www.naturalbody.com.

Ten Thousand Villages   Even though Ten Thousand Villages is not unique to Virginia-Highland, every item sold here is unique in itself. A fair trade retailer of handmade jewelry, home decor, and gifts, Ten Thousand Villages helps support and improve the lives of thousands of artisans in Asia, Africa, Latin America, and the

Middle East. Open Monday to Saturday from 11am to 6pm, Sunday from 1 to 5pm. 1056 St. Charles Ave. NE. ② **404/892-5307.** http://atlanta.tenthousandvillages.com.

The West Side

If you want to end your shopping day with dinner at Bacchanalia (p. 79), be sure to call well in advance for reservations. You can, however, grab a quick lunch at Taqueria del Sol (p. 86).

To reach the West Side, take I-75/85 from downtown, exit at 14th Street, take 14th Street west to Howell Mill Road, turn right, and go to the intersection of Howell Mill and Huff roads. Don't miss the additional stores on Foster Street, about a block down Huff Road, but note that the artists' studios at the end of the street are not open to the public. (And please don't feed the goats and chickens grazing in front of the studios.) Take MARTA to the Arts Center station to reach this area.

Below are some of the shopping highlights in this area.

Bungalow Classic   Simple, comfortable, elegant furniture is what you'll find here, along with linens, books, lamps, and other home accessories. Open Tuesday through Saturday from 10am to 6pm. 1197 Howell Mill Rd. NW, Ste. 110. ② **404/367-8522.** www.bungalow classic.com.

The Garden Path   This is a full-service nursery and landscape company with a selection of gardening paraphernalia and teak furniture. Open Tuesday through Saturday from 10am to 6pm. 1198-B Howell Mill Rd. NW. ② **404/355-0788.**

Provenance Antiques   This store started out small a few years ago, but recently expanded into a larger space that offers more room for the large and interesting collection of antiques, chandeliers, bed linens, rugs, tableware, and accessories. Open Monday through Friday from 10am to 6pm. 1190 Huff Rd. ② **404/351-1217.**

Star Provisions   Owned by Bacchanalia restaurant, Star Provisions is a cooks' marketplace unlike any other in Atlanta. There's a small offering of locally grown organic produce, a cheese shop, a comprehensive wine shop, a bakery, and a specialty fish and meat market featuring Niman Ranch's fantastic meats. There's also a large selection of unique tableware, cookbooks, and other gourmet-quality provisions such as olives, tea, coffee, olive oil, vinegar, and pasta. This place is nirvana if you're a serious foodie, but even if you're not, it's fun to look around and get a sample or two of cheese. And just try to sneak by the bakery, with its fabulous array of goodies, including Bacchanalia's legendary Valrhona chocolate cakes—divine confections with gooey chocolate middles. Open Monday through Saturday from 10am to 10pm. 1198 Howell Mill Rd. NW. ② **404/365-0410.** www.starprovisions.com.

Stone Mountain Village

Stone Mountain Village, just outside the West Gate of Stone Mountain Park (bounded by Second and Main sts. north and south, Lucille St. and Memorial Dr. east and west; ✆ **770/879-4971;** www.stonemountainvillage.com), is worth a visit. This has been a shopping area since the 1800s, and many of the shops are housed in historic buildings. Antiques, crafts, and collectibles are among the most popular merchandise here, so this is the place to stock up on country furniture, imported toys, dolls, baskets, homemade jams, handmade patchwork quilts and quilting fabrics, handcrafted dulcimers, Civil War memorabilia, and out-of-print books. Hours for most shops are Monday through Saturday from 10am to 6pm; many are also open Sunday from 1 to 5pm. Parking is free at several lots in town.

It's great fun to wander around this quaint village, and there's usually some festive event going on—an arts-and-crafts fair, live entertainment, and so on. During the Christmas season, the streets are candlelit and the village becomes a magical place populated by St. Nick, elves, carolers, and harpists. Be sure to stop by the **Village Visitor Center,** housed in a restored 1915 caboose at the corner of Main and Poole streets, to find out about special sales and events. It's open Monday through Saturday from 10am to 4pm, Sunday from 1 to 4pm.

Stop for a meal at the nearby **Village Corner Bakery, Tavern, and German Restaurant,** 6655 Memorial Dr., at Main Street (✆ **770/498-0329**). For breakfast, there are croissants, German apple pancakes, and ham-and-egg platters with homemade biscuits. At lunch, you can chow down on sandwiches, salads, quiche, soups, and home-baked desserts. And the dinner menu features German specialties such as Wiener schnitzel and sauerbraten. Wash it all down with one of the restaurant's German-style beers. The restaurant is open Tuesday through Thursday from 9am to 11pm, Friday 9am to midnight, Saturday 8am to 10pm, and Sunday from 10am to 9pm.

DEPARTMENT STORES & MALLS

Discover Mills   This is Atlanta's newest collection of specialty shops and outlets—200 in all, some offering up to 70% off on designer fashions and brand names. Just 30 minutes northeast of downtown, Discover Mills features a Bass Pro Shops Outdoor World, Burlington Coat Factory, Children's Place Outlet, Eddie Bauer Outlet, Kenneth Cole Outlet, Justice, Mikasa Factory Store, Neiman Marcus Last Call, Off Broadway Shoe Warehouse, Off 5th (Saks Fifth Avenue outlet), OshKosh B'gosh Outlet, Samsonite Company Store, and Sun & Ski Sports. Open Monday through Saturday from 10am to 9pm, Sunday from noon to 6pm. 5900 Sugarloaf Pkwy., Lawrenceville. ✆ **678/847-5000.** www.discovermills.com.

Lenox Square   Vast, upscale Lenox Square, which started out as a humble shopping center in 1959, has grown into one of the most popular shopping destinations in the Southeast. Its interesting mix of stores, many of them exclusive to the region, takes it beyond the usual cookie-cutter mall, and the formula attracts locals and visitors alike. You can buy just about anything here, from hiking boots to an engagement ring—and even if you're not in the mood to buy, there's great people-watching.

Anchors include Neiman Marcus, Macy's, and Bloomingdale's department stores. There are 250 shops, restaurants, kiosks, and services in the mall, including six movie theaters and several fine-dining restaurants. One of the best restaurants is Prime (p. 95). Among the best-known stores are Ann Taylor, Anthropologie, BCBG, Betsey

Johnson, Brooks Brothers, Burberry, Cartier, Club Monaco, Coach, Hermès, J. Crew, Kate Spade, Kenneth Cole, Louis Vuitton, Nicole Miller, Polo/Ralph Lauren, Sephora, St. John, Stuart Weitzman, Urban Outfitters, and Williams-Sonoma. Pottery Barn, Restoration Hardware, and Crate & Barrel all carry a selection of home furnishings and accessories, including many items that are usually available only by catalog.

Open Monday through Saturday from 10am to 9pm, Sunday from noon to 6pm, with extended hours during the Christmas season. A few stores close early on Saturday night. There's valet parking ($6) and a free shuttle to Phipps Plaza at the main entrance on Peachtree Road. 3393 Peachtree Rd. NE (at Lenox Rd.). *℃* **404/233-6767.** www. simon.com. MARTA: Lenox.

Mall at Peachtree Center   Part of the vast Portman-designed Peachtree Center complex, this downtown mall has around 70 shops, restaurants, and services on three levels. It's not exactly a shopping destination, but its location near major downtown hotels makes it convenient if you're in need of certain goods or services. There are a few apparel shops, including Brooks Brothers, and other stores with gifts, jewelry, books, cards, and candy. Services include florists, hairstylists, FedEx, UPS, a dry cleaner, and an optician. A food court dishes up everything from gyros to chocolate-chip cookies, and full-service restaurants include some decent choices: Benihana and Azio. Most stores are open Monday through Saturday from 10am to 6pm, with restaurants opening at 7am. Peachtree St. at International Blvd. *℃* **404/654-1296.** www.peachtree center.com/mall. MARTA: Peachtree Center.

Mall of Georgia   Atlanta's newest megamall, Mall of Georgia is about a half-hour drive from downtown and worth every mile. Anchoring this vast shopping haven are Dillard's, Nordstrom (and Nordstrom Rack), and Macy's. They're joined by 225 of the biggest names in retail, including Ann Taylor, A/X Armani Exchange, Coach, J. Crew, Old Navy, Pottery Barn, Restoration Hardware, Talbots, and Williams-Sonoma. Dining and entertainment options abound here, with Max Lager's American Grill, outdoor cafes, and a 500-seat amphitheater. Mall hours are Monday through Saturday from 10am to 9pm and Sunday from noon until 6pm. 3333 Buford Dr., Buford, GA 30519. *℃* **678/482-8788.** www.simon.com.

Phipps Plaza   Just across the street from Lenox Square is Phipps Plaza, Atlanta's most exclusive shopping venue and one of its prettiest as well, with spacious promenades and grand interior courts. Nordstrom, Parisian (a Birmingham, Alabama–based department store with a fantastic women's shoe department), and Saks Fifth Avenue anchor the mall's 100-plus shops and restaurants. The exclusive Ritz-Carlton Buckhead hotel is just a few steps away.

Phipps Plaza's posh emporia (many of them area exclusives) include A/X Armani Exchange, Barneys New York CO-OP, Cole Haan, Elie Tahari, Gianni Versace, Giorgio Armani, Gucci, Intermix, Jeffrey Atlanta, Juicy Couture, Max Mara, Niketown, Origins, Ross-Simons (for jewelry, china, and silver), Talbots, Theory, Tiffany & Co., and Tory Burch. You'll also find chic boutiques selling ladies' and men's apparel, luggage, jewelry, home furnishings, and specialty gifts.

Services include valet parking ($7) and a free shuttle to Lenox Square at the Lenox Road entrance. There are several restaurants, including the Tavern at Phipps, which has a pleasant, clubby atmosphere. Also on the premises: a food court and a 14-screen movie theater. Stores are open Monday through Saturday from 10am to 9pm, Sunday from noon to 5:30pm. 3500 Peachtree Rd. NE (at Lenox Rd.). *℃***800/810-7700** or 404/262-0992. www.simon.com. MARTA: Lenox.

Underground Atlanta   This 12-acre stretch of shops and restaurants is not as vibrant as it was several years ago, but it can still be fun to browse if you're staying downtown. There are dozens of shops, plus vendors in Humbug Square selling merchandise off antique pushcarts. Shopping options include clothing stores for men, women, and children, running the gamut from lingerie to sportswear. There are also cart vendors and novelty stores such as Atlanta Dollar, a bargain mecca.

Of course, there's a food court with a number of dining options. For lunch, you might try Johnny Rockets, an entertaining 1950s-style burger joint that the whole family will enjoy. If you're driving, there's parking in two garages off Martin Luther King, Jr., Drive. Open Monday through Saturday from 10am to 9pm, Sunday from 11am to 7pm. Alabama St. (btw. Peachtree St. and Central Ave.). © **404/523-2311.** www. underground-atlanta.com. MARTA: Five Points.

MORE SHOPPING AROUND TOWN

Antiques/Flea Markets

Atlanta is home to several permanent flea markets selling everything from custom furniture to antique toys, but the most exciting markets are those that set up shop once a month. The lineup of dealers—from all parts of the country—is ever-changing, so no matter how often you go, you'll always see something new and fresh.

If you're in search of real finds, shop on the first day as soon as the market opens—that's when local dealers swoop in to snatch up the best merchandise. Serious bargaining often takes place in the closing hours of the last day, when many dealers are anxious to avoid lugging their wares home with them. Be sure to keep your admission ticket; it's good for the whole weekend.

Kudzu Antique Market   You can spend half a day browsing this 25,000-square-foot antiques market, featuring one of the best collections of folk art in Atlanta as well as more than 100 dealers selling antiques, furniture, vintage clothing, '50s and '60s retro, garden art, lighting, and more. Open daily from 11am to 7pm. 2928 E. Ponce de Leon Ave. © **404/373-6498.** www.kudzuantiques.com.

Pride of Dixie Antiques Show   Formerly the Pride of Dixie Antiques Market, this is more of a true antiques market than a flea market, featuring 700 dealers who have searched the countryside for fabulous finds. You'll see fine antique furniture as well as interesting primitive painted pieces, heirloom jewelry and silver, antique books, baskets, rugs, linens, roll-top desks, and much more. The market is held inside an air-conditioned building, so weather is not a factor. Open the fourth weekend of each month, Friday and Saturday from 9am to 6pm, Sunday from 11am to 5pm. Admission is $4 for the weekend. Parking is free. At the North Atlanta Trade Center, north of Atlanta. 1700 Jeurgens Ct., Norcross. Take I-85 N. to the Indian Trail exit (about 25 min. from downtown), and then follow the signs. © **770/279-9899.**

Paris on Ponce   This 50,000-square-foot bohemian warehouse in the heart of Midtown features everything from 18th-century antiques to new designer furniture. This is one of the neatest retail spaces for seeing things you never would have dreamed existed, yesterday or today. Open Thursday through Saturday from 10am to 6pm and Sunday from noon to 6pm. 716 Ponce de Leon Place NE. © **404/249-9965.** www. parisonponce.com.

Scott Antique Markets Scott is an immense and immensely popular market that has been so successful that it's had to open another location across the highway from its original spot. It's now garnered much of the market here, following the closing in late 2006 of the popular Lakewood Antiques Market. There are spaces for 2,400 booths, all indoors, and the antiques and collectibles are some of the finest you'll see anywhere. This market is similar in atmosphere to the North Atlanta Antique Show, but much bigger, with loads of heirloom furniture, jewelry, silver, and so on, as well as a huge assortment of collectibles.

There's a free shuttle between the two Scott markets, so it's easy to visit both locations. The markets are held on the second weekend of every month. Open Friday and Saturday from 9am to 6pm, Sunday from 10am to 4pm. Admission is $5. Free parking is available. At the Atlanta Exposition Center, south of the city. Take I-75 S. to I-285. Go east on I-285 to exit 55 (Jonesboro Rd.) and follow the signs. © **404/366-0833.** www.scottantiquemarket.com.

Bookstores

In addition to the independent bookstores in Atlanta, the nationwide chains of Barnes & Noble, Borders, and Doubleday are all represented locally. The main **Barnes & Noble,** 2900 Peachtree Rd. (© **404/261-7747;** MARTA: Lenox), can be found in Buckhead, just a few minutes south of Lenox Square. The main **Borders,** 3637 Peachtree Rd. (© **404/237-0707;** MARTA: Lenox), is also in Buckhead, 3 blocks north of Lenox Square.

Charis Books & More Marketed as an "independent feminist bookstore," Charis is located in the funky Little Five Points district and specializes in diverse and unique children's books, feminist and cultural studies books, and lesbian/gay/bi/trans fiction and nonfiction. Open Monday through Saturday from 11am to 7pm and Sunday from noon to 6pm. 1189 Euclid Ave. © **404/524-0304.** www.charisbooksandmore.com.

Engineer's Bookstore The largest technical bookstore in Atlanta, Engineer's has been in business since 1954 and has an incredible selection of computer and engineering titles as well as the graduate and undergraduate texts for Georgia Tech. Open Monday through Friday from 9am to 5:30pm, Saturday from 10am to 2pm. 748 Marietta St. NW (at Means St., just off Tech Pkwy. and approx. 1 mile from Georgia World Congress Center). © **800/635-5919** or 404/221-1669. www.engrbookstore.com. MARTA: North Ave.

Outwrite Bookstore & Coffeehouse Selling books, magazines, and CDs, this casual Midtown spot caters to the gay and lesbian community and is a sort of clearinghouse for information on local issues and activities. The coffee and pastries are good, and the atmosphere is comfortable. Open daily from 10am to 11pm. 991 Piedmont Ave. (at 10th St.). © **404/607-0082.** www.outwritebooks.com. MARTA: Midtown.

Tall Tales Book Shop, Inc. This general bookstore in the Emory University area has a large selection of mainstream titles with an emphasis on literature. All large publishers, as well as university and small presses, are represented. The staff is knowledgeable and will be happy to process special orders. Open Monday through Thursday from 9am to 10pm, Friday and Saturday from 9am to 11pm. 2105 LaVista Rd., No. 108. © **404/636-2498.** MARTA: Lindbergh.

Factory & Discount Outlets

North Georgia Premium Outlets This 140-store center is a cut above most outlet complexes, with designers and manufacturers such as BCBG, Bose, Brooks

Brothers, Calvin Klein, Coach, Cole Haan, Gap, Kenneth Cole, Nike, Nine West, Saks Fifth Avenue Off 5th, Pottery Barn, Puma, Timberland, and Williams-Sonoma. It's definitely worth the trip. Open Monday through Saturday from 10am to 9pm, Sunday from 11am to 7pm. 800 Hwy. 400 S. (35 min. north of Atlanta), Dawsonville. © **706/216-3609.** www.premiumoutlets.com.

Farmers' Markets

Atlanta State Farmers' Market   The State Farmers' Market is a vast 146-acre outdoor facility where stall after stall is piled high with produce. There are also vendors of home-canned pickles, jams, and relishes; plants and flowers; and seasonal items such as pumpkins in October and holly and Christmas trees in December. It's a colorful spectacle. You can have a good meal at a restaurant on the premises. Open 24 hours daily except Christmas. 16 Forest Pkwy., Forest Park, GA. © **404/675-1782.** www.pickyourown.org. Take I-75 S. to exit 23; the market is on your left.

DeKalb Farmers' Market   Even if you have no intention of purchasing, this incredible market, started in 1977 by Robert Blazer, merits a visit. A mind-boggling array of international food items are temptingly displayed in a 140,000-square-foot building. Tables are laden with mountains of produce from broccoli to bok choy, not to mention winter melons and water chestnuts, lily root, curry leaves, breadfruit, Jamaican jerk marinade, Korean daikon radish, a multiplicity of mushrooms, chickpea miso, a vast beer and wine section, dried fruits, plants and flowers, seafood, meat, poultry, every imaginable fresh herb and hot pepper, fresh-baked breads and pastries, stalks of sugar cane, many varieties of cheese, frogs' legs, conch meat, quail, and on and on. As you shop, you can nibble whatever is offered at sample tables throughout the facility. There's also a small cafeteria on the premises. The market is about a 20-minute drive from downtown. Open daily from 9am to 9pm except Thanksgiving and Christmas. 3000 E. Ponce de Leon Ave., Decatur. © **404/377-6400.** MARTA: Avondale.

Harry's Whole Foods   Like the DeKalb Farmers' Market, this megamarket must be seen to be believed. An Atlanta icon since 1987, Harry's features mountains of fresh produce, incredible selections of cheese, seafood, meats, gourmet items, wines, and beers, plus more exotica than you can imagine. While DeKalb attracts a more international clientele (although the selection of goods is not necessarily more international in scope), Harry's is a bit more upscale and polished, and attracts many suburbanites, probably because of its locations. DeKalb has a wider variety of organic foods and produce, while Harry's does better at baked goods, prepared foods, and

---

Fresh Market Fare

If your idea of fun is watching other people cook for you, stop in at the Morningside Farmers' Market on a Saturday morning. Each week at 9:30am, one of the city's top chefs gives a free cooking demonstration, and the lucky audience gets to sample the results. Afterward, browse the market, a small but beautiful array of organic, locally grown vegetables, fruits, herbs, and flowers. There are also handmade soaps, beeswax candles, primitive furniture, beaded jewelry, and other assorted artisanal items. The market, at 1393 N. Highland Ave., is open on Saturdays in late April through December from 8 to 11:30am. Call © **404/313-5784** for details.

cheeses. Saturday and Sunday are crowded at all markets, but the bustle seems to add to the fun if you don't have to do any serious shopping.

Open Monday through Saturday from 8am to 9pm, Sunday from 8am to 8pm. There is another Harry's located at 70 Powers Ferry Rd., Marietta (✆ **770/578-4400**). 1180 Upper Hembree Rd., Alpharetta. ✆ **770/664-6300.** From I-85 N., take Hwy. 400 north toward Roswell. Turn right onto Alpharetta Hwy./Hwy. 120 and left onto Upper Hembree Rd.

Fashions

See earlier sections of this chapter for more store listings.

The Bilthouse   Set in an old cottage in Buckhead, this is the place to go if you're looking for something casual that's a little out of the ordinary. Most of the clothing is designed for comfort—which is not to say that it doesn't also look great—and much of it is made of natural fabrics. There are linen shifts and separates, cotton sweaters, tights, flowing skirts, lots of one-of-a-kind dresses, and more for women of all ages. There's also unique furniture, jewelry, children's clothing, artwork by local artists, and little goodies for body and bath. Open daily from 10am to 6pm. 511 E. Paces Ferry Rd. NE (5 blocks west of Peachtree Rd., on the corner of Maple Ave.). ✆ **404/816-7702.** MARTA: Buckhead.

K&G Men's Center   K&G is tucked away in an industrial area with a number of other discount stores, but it's definitely worth seeking out. This huge warehouse is crammed with a large selection of top-quality men's clothing, men's shoes, and furnishings. You'll find truly excellent suits, including tuxedos. There are other K&G stores, all in the suburbs, but this is the original. To reach Ellsworth Industrial Drive, take I-75 N., exit at Howell Mill Road, go west to Chattahoochee Avenue, turn right, and then take the next right. Open Monday through Saturday from 10am to 9pm, and Sunday from 11am to 7pm. 1750 Ellsworth Industrial Dr. NW (at Chattahoochee Ave.). ✆ **404/352-3471.**

Luna   A good variety of strictly up-to-the-minute women's clothing and accessories are found here: sportswear, ultrafeminine evening wear, suits, jewelry, handbags, and cool shoes. Open Monday through Saturday from 10am to 7pm, and Sunday from noon to 5pm. 3167 Peachtree Rd. (south of Piedmont Rd.). ✆ **404/233-5344.** MARTA: Lenox.

A Pea in the Pod   This cleverly named boutique chain features maternity clothes, but we're not talking T-shirts with an arrow pointing to your stomach. These are gorgeous clothes, from really chic sportswear to elegant business garb to evening wear. Open Monday through Saturday from 10am to 8pm, Sunday from noon to 5:30pm. In the Phipps Plaza mall, 3500 Peachtree Rd. (at Lenox Rd.). ✆ **404/816-9747.** MARTA: Lenox.

Potpourri   If you're in search of upscale traditional women's apparel, Potpourri will fit the bill. There are lots of lovely sportswear separates, as well as dresses, belts, costume jewelry, and other accessories. Open Monday through Friday from 10am to 5:30pm and Saturday from 10am to 5pm. 3718 Roswell Rd. NW (just north of Piedmont Rd.). ✆ **404/365-0880.** MARTA: Buckhead.

Gifts, Art & Collectibles

Also see the stores listed in the hot shopping neighborhoods under "Great Shopping Areas," earlier in this chapter.

Erika Reade Ltd.   The emphasis here is on interesting home-related accessories and furnishings—paintings, antique and primitive furniture, mirrors, exquisite bed linens, and tabletop items. You'll find French soaps and candles, hand-blown glass, jewelry, wonderful gifts for adults and children, and much more. It's all absolutely up to date and extremely tasteful. Open Monday through Thursday from 10am to 6pm, Friday and Saturday from 10am to 5pm. 3732 Roswell Rd. (just north of Piedmont Rd.). *ⓒ* **404/233-3857.** MARTA: Lindbergh.

Hardware/Woodworking

Highland Hardware   This isn't a hardware store; it's an institution. Woodworkers come from all over the country to browse Highland's huge selection of woodworking supplies and tools, and still more order from its voluminous catalog. But even if you don't know a router from a band saw, it's fun to roam through the large, high-ceilinged store, which has an old-fashioned, neighborly feel. Highland also stocks regular hardware, gardening merchandise, annuals, and perennials. Call in advance if you're interested in attending one of the many woodworking programs or workshops. Open Monday through Friday 9am to 6pm, Saturday from 8:30am to 6pm, and Sunday from noon to 5pm. 1045 N. Highland Ave. NE (at Los Angeles Ave.).*ⓒ* **404/872-4466.** www.tools-for-woodworking.com. MARTA: Five Points.

Kitchenware

The Cook's Warehouse   There's everything you need here—except the kitchen sink—for setting up a gourmet kitchen: top-of-the-line cookware, dinnerware, quality knives, small appliances, cookbooks, chef's clothing, oodles of gadgets, a selection of olive oils and vinegars, and much more. There's a full schedule of cooking classes and demonstrations, too, so check the website for details. Open Monday through Saturday from 10am to 8pm, and Sunday from 11am to 4pm. 180 W. Ponce de Leon Ave., Decatur. *ⓒ* **404/377-4005.** www.cookswarehouse.com. MARTA: Decatur.

Sporting Goods

REI (Recreational Equipment Inc.)   This Seattle-based company sells everything imaginable for the outdoor enthusiast: clothing, shoes, outerwear, and accessories for biking, hiking, camping, rock climbing, canoeing, kayaking, and so on. The staff is extremely knowledgeable, and the sales are frequent and fabulous.

Open Monday through Saturday from 10am to 9pm, Sunday from 11am to 6pm. There's another REI just north of the city at 1165 Perimeter Center W. NE (*ⓒ* **770/901-9200**). 1800 Northeast Expwy. (on the I-85 access road; take the Clairmont Rd. exit and go south). *ⓒ* **404/633-6508.** www.rei.com. MARTA: Brookhaven.

ATLANTA AFTER DARK

This is a city that sizzles after dark, with numerous music clubs featuring jazz, rock, country, and blues, plus a comprehensive cultural scene that includes symphony, ballet, opera, and theater productions. If that's not enough, major artists headline regularly at Atlanta's many large-scale performance venues.

Nightlife turns up all over Atlanta, but the biggest concentration of clubs and bars is in Buckhead (near the intersection of Peachtree and E. Paces Ferry roads); in Virginia-Highland (at the intersection of Virginia and N. Highland aves., and on N. Highland just north of Ponce de Leon Ave.); in Little Five Points (near the intersection of Moreland and Euclid aves.); and downtown near Peachtree Center.

The **Buckhead** scene is often like a huge, unruly fraternity party, with lots of people and cars cruising the streets. It gets rowdier as the night goes on, and has been marked by violence on several occasions. Scores of complaints from area residents led the Atlanta Police Department to close a couple of roads in the Buckhead area every Friday and Saturday night to discourage some of the cruising. Traffic jams and things have been improving ever since. **Virginia-Highland** is full of upper-20- and 30-somethings and professionals. **Little Five Points** is an eclectic mix of wildly, weirdly dressed folks and neighborhood regulars. **Downtown** hosts many out-of-town visitors and conventiongoers.

To find out what's going on during your stay, consult *The Atlanta Journal-Constitution.* Its "Access Atlanta" section, published every Thursday, highlights movies, plays, festivals, gallery openings, and other happenings for the upcoming weekend. There's also an extensive listing of live music. A calendar of events is published other days of the week, but it's not as complete. The newspaper's website at www.ajc.com allows you to access a week's worth of newspaper features, including the events calendar and "Access Atlanta."

A free newspaper called *Creative Loafing,* available at hundreds of locations around town (hotels, restaurants, shops, MARTA stations, sidewalk stands, and so on), lists numerous events and has special sections for "Gay and Lesbian Activities" and "Singles." Visit its website at www. creativeloafing.com, or call © **800/950-5623** to get a copy of the paper before you visit.

It's often possible to purchase tickets directly from the box office where the event is taking place. In addition, tickets to many performances are sold by **Ticketmaster**—call ☎ **404/249-6400** (for large performances) or ☎ **404/817-8700** (for smaller cultural events) to charge by phone. Online, you can reserve tickets at www.ticketmaster.com. Ticketmaster has more than 100 locations throughout Georgia, including all Publix Supermarkets, where customers can purchase tickets in person, though they must be paid for in cash. If you're staying in a large hotel, your concierge service will usually be able to obtain tickets to even the most popular events.

Day-of-show half-price tickets are available at the **AtlanTIX!** ticket booth at the Atlanta Convention & Visitors Bureau in Underground Atlanta (p. 145) and at Lenox Square (p. 177). Customers can see which plays and other live performances have tickets available that day, purchase a voucher for the show, and pick up the ticket at the show's box office before curtain time. Vouchers must be paid for in person; phone sales are not available. Call ☎ **404/588-9890,** or visit www.atlantaperforms.com for more information.

A quick point before you head out: *Forbes* magazine has listed Atlanta as the number-one city for singles, noting the city's "hopping nightlife" as one of the highlights, so get out there and groove.

A word of warning, however: Atlanta's nightclubs are frequently gone with the wind with no prior notice whatsoever, so call ahead to make sure your planned destination is still in business.

THE PERFORMING ARTS

Ballet

Atlanta Ballet   The oldest continuously operating ballet company in the United States, the Atlanta Ballet usually presents six productions each fall-through-spring season. Performances range from classics to new works and include *The Nutcracker* every December. Tickets are available through **Ticketmaster** (☎ **404/817-8700**) or on the day of the performance at the Fox Theatre box office or the Cobb Energy Performing Arts Centre box office, depending on show location. Performances held at the Fox Theatre, 660 Peachtree St. NE (at Ponce de Leon Ave.). ☎ **404/873-5811.** Also at the Cobb Energy Performing Arts Center, 2800 Cobb Galleria Pkwy. ☎ 770/916-2800. www.atlantaballet.com. Tickets $10–$50. MARTA: North Ave. (to Fox Theatre).

Classical Music

Atlanta Symphony Orchestra   The Atlanta Symphony Orchestra performs under music director Robert Spano and principal guest conductor Donald Runnicles. Complementing the orchestra is the 200-voice Atlanta Symphony Orchestra Chorus, enabling performances of large-scale symphonic/choral works. The season runs from September to May in the Woodruff Arts Center, and there are summer concerts at Verizon Wireless Amphitheatre at Encore Park as well as in Chastain Park Amphitheatre. The box office is open Monday from 10am to 6pm, Tuesday through Friday from 10am to 8pm, Saturday noon to 8pm, and Sunday noon to 5pm. Thursday, Friday, and Saturday performances begin at 8pm and Sundays are at 3pm.

The ASO's annual schedule is extensive. The main offering is the **Master Season Series.** Master Season concerts, held on selected Thursday, Friday, and Saturday evenings in the plush 1,762-seat Atlanta Symphony Hall, feature renowned guest artists such as soprano Twyla Robinson, mezzo-soprano Monica Groop, tenor John

Mac Master, and bass Burak Bilgili. Other events during the season are Sunday-afternoon **Family Concerts** geared toward children, **Casual Classics** on selected Saturday afternoons, holiday concerts during the Christmas season, and a tribute to Martin Luther King, Jr., in mid-January.

The ASO's **Classic Chastain Series** concerts are held in the 7,000-seat Chastain Park Amphitheatre from June to August, featuring headliners such as Tony Bennett and Natalie Cole performing with the ASO. All tickets except lawn seating are reserved. It's customary to bring elaborate picnics and wine to these events. In addition to the Chastain series, the ASO gives free evening concerts in parks throughout the Atlanta area during the summer; these run the gamut from full symphony performances to light classical concerts.

The Verizon Wireless Amphitheatre at Encore Park in Alpharetta is the summer home of the Atlanta Symphony Orchestra. The venue boasts 7,000 fixed seats under a roof and 5,000 lawn seats.

Note: Plans for the future construction of a $300-million Atlanta Symphony Center in Midtown have been in place for nearly a decade. However, the project is currently stalled due to lack of funds and the down economy. Performances held at the Woodruff Arts Center, 1280 Peachtree St. NE (at 15th St.). (C) **404/733-5000** (box office) for information and tickets. www.atlantasymphony.org. Most tickets $19–$55. Parking available in the Arts Center Garage on Lombardy Way btw. 15th and 16th sts. MARTA: Arts Center.

Opera

Atlanta Opera   Under the direction of Dennis Hanthorn, the Atlanta Opera has three fully staged productions during the spring and fall at the Cobb Energy Performing Arts Centre. Principal performers are drawn from top opera companies across the United States and Europe. Recent productions included *La Bohème* and *The Magic Flute*. Only four performances are given of each opera, and tickets can be difficult to obtain, so charge them in advance if possible. Performances held at the Cobb Energy Performing Arts Centre, 2800 Cobb Galleria Pkwy., Alpharetta. (C) **800/35-OPERA (6-7372)** or 404/881-8801 for information. www.atlantaopera.org. Tickets $17–$126. Single tickets available through the Cobb Energy Centre box office (in person only) and Ticketmaster ((C) 404/817-8700).

Theater

The **Alliance Theatre Company** is the major theater company in Atlanta, but there are many other excellent companies with performances ranging from experimental to classic. Most are located near downtown and Midtown, but there are a number in the suburbs. Some of the notables include **Actor's Express** ((C) 404/607-7469; www.actors-express.com), **Ansley Park Playhouse** ((C) 404/875-1193; www.ansleyparkplayhouse.com), **Dad's Garage Theatre Company** ((C) 404/523-3141;

www.dadsgarage.com), **Horizon Theatre Company** (© 404/584-7450; www.horizontheatre.com), **Theatre Decatur** (© 404/373-5311), **7 Stages Theatre** (© 404/523-7647; www.7stages.org), the **New American Shakespeare Tavern** (© 404/874-5299; www.shakespearetavern.com), **Theatre Gael** (© 404/876-1138), **Theatre in the Square** (© 770/422-8369; www.theatreinthesquare.com), and **Theatrical Outfit** (© 678/528-1500; www.theatricaloutfit.org). Check the *Atlanta Journal-Constitution* on Thursday to see what's on during your visit. There are also performances by the **Georgia Shakespeare Festival** (© 404/264-0020; www.gashakespeare.org) each summer and fall.

Alliance Theatre Company   The Alliance Theatre Company, under the direction of Susan V. Booth, is the largest regional theater in the Southeast. The company produces about 10 plays a year on three different stages, and the season runs from September through June, with occasional productions during the summer as well. Many well-known actors have played these stages, among them Jane Alexander, Richard Dreyfuss, Esther Rolle, and Morgan Freeman. Recent seasons have included Dickens's *A Christmas Carol* (performed annually); *Lookingglass Alice*; and the world première of Elton John and Tim Rice's musical *Aida*. The **Alliance Children's Theatre** presents plays geared to youngsters from January to May. Tickets for children's productions are $20 for adults and $15 for children. The box office is open Monday from 10am to 6pm, Tuesday through Friday from 10am to 8pm, Saturday from noon to 8pm, and Sunday from noon to 5pm. Most performances begin at 8pm, and children's performances are either 1 or 3:30pm on the weekends. Performances held at the Woodruff Arts Center, 1280 Peachtree St. NE (at 15th St.). © **404/733-5000** (box office) for information and tickets. www.alliancetheatre.org. Tickets $25–$45. "Rush tickets" often available for $15 on the day of a performance; they must be purchased in person at the box office after 5pm. Parking available in the Arts Center Garage on Lombardy Way btw. 15th and 16th sts. MARTA: Arts Center.

Major Entertainment Venues

In addition to the venues listed below, many stadiums host major concerts from time to time. These include the Alexander Memorial Coliseum and Bobby Dodd Stadium at Grant Field at Georgia Tech, Road Atlanta, Philips Arena, and the Georgia Dome. See "Spectator Sports" in chapter 6 (p. 158) for details on some of these stadiums.

Atlanta Civic Center   The Civic Center offers a wealth of entertainment options in its 4,600-seat auditorium, hosting headliners, touring Broadway shows, traveling symphony and opera companies, and fashion shows. 395 Piedmont Ave. NE (btw. Ralph McGill Blvd. and Pine St.). © **404/523-6275** for general information. www.atlantaciviccenter.com. MARTA: Civic Center (about 5 blocks away); buses go to the door.

Chastain Park Amphitheatre ★★ 📷   This delightful 7,000-seat outdoor facility presents concerts under the stars from May to October, featuring big-name performers. Everyone brings food—a picnic on the grass, at your amphitheater seat, or at a table for up to six is a tradition. Some people even bring gourmet feasts, flowers, and candelabra for an extraspecial experience. If you don't feel like piecing together a picnic, you can preorder your meal from on-site caterers **Proof-of-the-Pudding** and **Glorious Events.** Meals are wonderful and come with enough food for four or more. For a fee, the company will dress your table and have everything ready when you arrive; all you'll have to do is open the wine and light the candles. It can be difficult to get tickets at times, so order as far in advance as possible (months ahead if you can). The Atlanta Symphony Orchestra (p. 185) accompanies some performers here. 449 Stella Dr. NW (in Chastain Park at Powers Ferry Rd.). ✆ **404/733-5000,** or 817-8700 for Ticketmaster. www.classicchastain.com. MARTA: Lenox.

Cobb Energy Performing Arts Centre   The first major performing arts facility built in metro Atlanta in 4 decades, Cobb Energy Centre hosts Broadway shows, ballet, concerts, educational shows, family performances, operas, and other events. The venue includes a 2,750-seat theater, a 10,000-square-foot ballroom, and 1,000 on-site parking spaces. Home to the Atlanta Opera and many performances of Atlanta Ballet, the Cobb Energy Centre is located in northwest Atlanta. 2800 Cobb Galleria Pkwy. ✆ **770/916-2800** for information, or 404/817-8700 for Ticketmaster. Tickets available at the on-site ticket booth in person only. www.cobbenergycentre.com.

Fox Theatre ★★   Opened in 1929, when movie theaters were conceived along lavish lines, the Fox is a Moorish-Egyptian extravaganza complete with arabesque arches, onion domes, and minarets. Its exotic interior reflects the Egyptomania of the 1920s—a phenomenon resulting from archaeologist Henry Carter's discovery of the treasure-laden tomb of King Tut. Throne chairs, scarab motifs, and hieroglyphics are seen throughout the theater, and the auditorium evokes a Middle Eastern courtyard under an azure sky. The Fox is home to some performances of the **Atlanta Ballet** (discussed above). In addition, a wide spectrum of headliners play the Fox, along with diverse entertainment ranging from Broadway musicals to rock 'n' roll. See p. 121 for details on the Fox's history and architecture, as well as information on tours. 660 Peachtree St. NE (at Ponce de Leon Ave.). ✆ **404/881-2100** for information, or 800/745-3000 for tickets through Ticketmaster. www.foxtheatre.org. Many paid parking lots nearby. MARTA: North Ave.

Aaron's Amphitheatre at Lakewood   The outdoor Aaron's Amphitheatre—formerly Coca-Cola Lakewood—accommodates 19,000 people with 7,000 reserved seats, plus a sloping lawn that holds an additional 12,000. Needless to say, this is a vast facility used for major shows. Eric Clapton, Elton John, Pearl Jam, and Aerosmith have all performed here. There are picnic tables with umbrellas on the grounds, and though you can't bring in food or drink, a wide variety of refreshments are available, including beer, champagne, fruit, cheese, sandwiches, and pizza. 2002 Lakewood Way (at the Lakewood exit off I-75/85, 3½ miles south of downtown). ✆ **404/443-5000.** Take I-75 or I-85 S. to Lakewood Fwy. exit and follow signs. MARTA: Lakewood/Fort McPherson (shuttle buses take patrons to and from the station).

Rialto Center for the Performing Arts   Located close to the center of downtown on the campus of Georgia State University, this wonderful 833-seat facility hosts a variety of performances, from theater to dance to all types of music. It opened as a theater in 1916, and then became the Rialto movie house before being converted into a multipurpose venue in the late 1990s. 80 Forsyth St. ✆ **404/413-9849.** www.rialtocenter.org. Paid parking in nearby lots. MARTA: Peachtree Center.

Variety Playhouse   Built in the 1930s as a neighborhood movie theater for Little Five Points, the Variety is now an intimate concert hall offering an eclectic array of performances, from folk rock to jazz, that are definitely worth checking out. There are frequent album-release parties here. 1099 Euclid Ave. (near Washita St.). ✆ **404/524-7354** for information. www.variety-playhouse.com. Paid parking lot on Euclid Ave. near Colquitt Ave. MARTA: Inman Park or bus 3 (Auburn Ave.).

THE CLUB & MUSIC SCENE

Nightclubs come and go, so it's always a good idea to call ahead. Most clubs are open until 2, 3, or even 4am.

Blues Clubs

Blind Willie's   This well-known club features live blues from around the country, but local bands are part of the scene as well. The bar opens Monday through Saturday at 7pm, and there's a limited bar menu, but the big attraction is the music, which starts around 10pm. This place gets too packed to move in when there is a big show. 828 N. Highland Ave. (just north of Ponce de Leon Ave.). ☎ **404/873-2583.** www.blindwilliesblues.com. Cover varies. MARTA: Five Points.

Fat Matt's Rib Shack   This barbecue joint packs 'em in every evening for a taste of smoky ribs, beer, and local blues. The food is as good as the sultry music, which starts every night at 8pm. See p. 96 for more information. 1811 Piedmont Ave. (a few blocks south of Cheshire Bridge Rd.). ☎ **404/607-1622.** www.fatmattsribshack.com. MARTA: Lindbergh and a short cab ride.

Northside Tavern   Home of the locally and internationally acclaimed Mudcat blues band, this hole in the wall was obviously a gas station in a previous life. Though the digs aren't anything to write home about and the location might look a bit shady, the music here is fantastic. Mudcat plays every Wednesday night and one weekend a month—when they aren't performing in Europe. Don't worry if you miss the Mudcats, though; this place offers excellent live blues every day of the week. Cold beer, a full bar, and a couple of pool tables round out the offerings. 1058 Howell Mill Rd. NW. ☎ **404/874-8745.** www.northsidetavern.com. Cover varies. MARTA: Arts Center.

A Comedy Club

The Punchline   This popular suburban comedy club, about a 40-minute drive from downtown, features pros on the national comedy-club circuit—the comedians you see on Leno and Letterman. Jeff Foxworthy got his start here. Doors open an hour before showtime. Reasonably priced food is served, and there's a full bar. All shows are smoke-free. Though you can buy tickets at the club, they often sell out, so it's best to reserve by phone. You must be 21 or older and have a valid ID to get in. It's open Wednesday through Sunday, with showtimes usually beginning around 8pm. 280 Hilderbrand Dr. NE (off Roswell Rd. in the Balconies Shopping Center), Sandy Springs. ☎ **404/252-5233.** www.punchline.com. Cover $15–$20, depending on day of the week. MARTA: Sandy Springs.

Dance Clubs

HALO Lounge   HALO is one of the most beautiful bars in Atlanta, featuring a backlit onyx bar. Some of the coolest DJs in town spin here, making HALO a favorite among Atlantans. Hours are Monday to Saturday from 9pm to 3am. *Note:* Don't miss the black-stone entrance on Sixth Street between Peachtree and West Peachtree streets. 817 W. Peachtree St. NW. ☎ **404/962-7333.** www.halolounge.com. Occasional cover varies. $5 covered parking on Cypress St. MARTA: Midtown.

Johnny's Hideaway   "Atlanta's Only Nightclub for Big Kids" has been one of city's top nightspots for the over-40 crowd for 30 years. Ebullient host Johnny Esposito is a well-known Atlanta character, though his age now keeps him from being on hand nightly to greet guests. Locals jokingly refer to the nightspot as "God's waiting room," a dig at the "old folks" who still come here to party (including the couple in their 80s you might spot tearing up the dance floor if you arrive early). The music sweeps through the decades at this Buckhead treasure, from the big-band era to the '80s, attracting a crowd of all ages. The music gets "younger" as the night wears on, and the patrons do, too. This is a place for serious dancing, and though it's unpretentious, there are celebrities (such as George Clooney and Robert Duvall) who drop by when in town. The majority of the bartenders here have been on staff for more than 25 years and can make a night of sitting at the bar a lot of fun, if you get there early enough to claim a stool. They'll even keep your purse safe behind the bar so you can dance the night away. Check out the Frank Sinatra Room, filled with more than 100 pieces of memorabilia. A reasonably priced menu lists items ranging from deli sandwiches to filet mignon main courses. Attire is casual dressy. Open late daily. 3771 Roswell Rd. (2 blocks north of Piedmont Rd.). ✆ **404/233-8026.** www.johnnyshideaway.com. $5 cover on Sun for live music. MARTA: Buckhead.

The Masquerade Popular with the college-age crowd, Masquerade is housed in a century-old, stone-walled, Romanesque former factory. Its interior is divided into three main areas—Heaven, Hell, and Purgatory—all appropriately decorated. Up in Heaven is a concert hall featuring live local and national acts. Hell is a DJ dance party, and Purgatory is the game room, with pool tables and other non-music diversions. Open daily with hours varying on the show. 695 North Ave. NE (just east of Boulevard). ✆ **404/577-8178.** www.masq.com. Cover $5–$8 in Hell and Purgatory, $5–$20 (depending on the performer) in Heaven. Parking $3–$5. MARTA: North Ave.

Opera Nightclub Formerly Eleven50, this elegant Miami-type club draws a mixed crowd. The atmosphere is very laid-back, and well-known DJs visit on weekends. Opera has three dance areas featuring a different style of music in each, ranging from Top-40/mainstream and house to Latin and hip-hop. Cover is typically $20 and up, depending on the DJ's status and what night of the week you visit. It's also a popular venue for private parties and celebrity sightings. Open from 10pm to 3am Wednesday to Saturday. 1150-B Peachtree Rd. ✆ **404/874-0428.** www.operaatlanta.com. MARTA: Lenox.

Sutra Voted one of the top 100 nightclubs in the country, Sutra is sexy and chic, where all the pretty people meet to drink and dance. In the heart of Midtown, Sutra features the talents of one of the most popular DJs in the city, and it draws big crowds. Guests are asked to "dress to impress;" no ball caps, jerseys, or athletic wear allowed. Cover varies depending on event. 1136 Crescent Ave. NE ✆ **404/607-1160.** www. sutraloungeatl.com. MARTA: Art Center.

Folk, Acoustic & Bluegrass Clubs

Eddie's Attic Eddie's Attic is a popular venue for acoustic singer/songwriters. In fact, the Indigo Girls, Billy Pilgrim, and Shawn Mullins all started their careers here. The place is divided into three sections: The main bar is perfect for music lovers, with its small stage, intimate seating arrangement, and excellent acoustics. Rowdier folks will like the poolroom and the covered patio, where there's a full bar and TV monitors playing the live performance from the main stage. The entire family is welcome for the 7pm shows on Friday and Saturday. There is a full menu, offering mostly typical bar fare. 515-B N. McDonough St., Decatur (next to the old courthouse on the square). ✆ **404/377-4976.** www.eddiesattic.com. Cover $5–$25, depending on the performer and whether you want to secure a good seat or take your chances with general admission. Parking available on the square or at the lot on Church St., directly behind Eddie's. MARTA: Decatur.

Red Light Cafe   This classic San Francisco–style coffeehouse, a funky high-ceilinged space decked out with tables and comfy sofas, offers a mix of art, music, conversation, and food and beverages. The big attraction is the music—local bluegrass, folk, rock, and jazz. Locals jam at 7pm and Wednesdays are open mic. You can order salads, fresh pastas, and sandwiches, and there's a good selection of bottled and draft beers, including some locally brewed choices. Closed on Mondays. 553 W. Amsterdam Ave. (west of Monroe Dr.). © **404/874-7828.** www.redlightcafe.com. Cover varies. MARTA: Arts Center.

Jazz Clubs

Dante's Down the Hatch 🏮   For more than 40 years, Dante Stephensen has manned the decks of this jazz supper club, part of an entertainment complex built around the illusion of a well-rigged 18th-century schooner tied to the wharf of a mythical Mediterranean village. The interior is a mix of antiques and nautical kitsch. There are many intimate seating areas, but the most romantic spot is a semienclosed private "cabin" on the lower deck, where a trio plays traditional jazz 6 days a week. Earlier in the evening, classical folk guitarists perform on the "wharf," and on weekend nights, a solo pianist plays on the ship before the show. Dante's has an expansive wine list, with about 90 bottles at $36 and less. If you wish to have dinner during the show, the specialty is fondue, available by reservation only. Amazingly, the menu is available in 55 languages. 3380 Peachtree Rd. NE (across the street from the Lenox Square mall). © **404/266-1600.** www.dantesdownthehatch.com. Cover $7–$9 for seating on the jazz ship; free on the wharf. MARTA: Buckhead.

Sambuca   Part restaurant, part jazz club, Sambuca is the third in a new chain of six national jazz cafes (the first two were in Texas). The big attraction here is the large, chic bar, where a jazz combo plays on the bandstand each night and a crowd fills the dance floor. Upscale couples and singles are often four-deep at the bar, and everyone is dressed in business casual attire. Weeknight shows start at 7pm, and Friday and Saturday shows begin at 8pm; the cover depends on who's performing on Sunday. There's no cover Monday through Thursday, but dining tables require a dinner or entree purchase. If your main interest is the music, come early for a table near the bandstand. There's almost always a wait to get in, especially as the evening wears on. 3102 Piedmont Road NE (btw. Peachtree and E. Paces Ferry roads). © **404/237-5299.** www.sambuca restaurant.com. 2-drink minimum. MARTA: Lindbergh.

THE BAR SCENE

In addition to the neighborhood establishments listed below, there are some excellent bars in the major hotels, many of them mellow enough for conversation. Two of the best are the **Lobby Lounge** at the Ritz-Carlton Buckhead, 3434 Peachtree Rd. (© **404/237-2700;** MARTA: Peachtree Center), and **Park 75 Lounge** at the Four Seasons Hotel, 75 14th St., in Midtown (© **404/253-3840;** MARTA: Arts Center). The **Sun Dial Restaurant, Bar & View,** high atop the Westin Peachtree Plaza, 210 Peachtree St. (© **404/589-7506;** MARTA: Peachtree Center), and **A Point of View at Nikolai's Roof,** at the Hilton Atlanta, 255 Courtland St. (© **404/221-6362;** MARTA: Peachtree Center), have spectacular views of the city skyline. None of the places has a cover charge unless otherwise stated.

Atkins Park   This place hosts a mix of casually dressed regulars from the Virginia-Highland neighborhood and young crowds from other parts of town. The atmosphere is friendly and the ambience mellow and comfortable. Atkins Park began as a deli in

1922 (it holds the oldest existing tavern license in the city) and now includes a full-scale restaurant that stays open until 11pm (until midnight Fri–Sat). After that, better-than-average bar food is available until 2:30am. Atkins Park is known as *the* place to go for Jägermeister—it sells more than almost any other bar in Atlanta. Things get lively when the restaurant closes and the music (rock, blues, and jazz) is turned up. 794 N. Highland Ave. NE (at St. Charles Place, 1 block north of Ponce de Leon Ave.). 📞 **404/876-7249.** www.atkinspark.com. Some free parking in lot off St. Charles; paid parking in nearby lots. MARTA: Five Points.

Dark Horse Tavern This multiple-deck tavern is primarily a neighborhood hangout during the week, but it attracts a mix of young professionals and college students on the weekends. There's live entertainment in the performance area, called 10 High—mostly local bands, but occasionally a nationally known group. Trivia nights are held Wednesdays at 8pm. Upstairs, there's a dining area serving American fare, where you can eat, drink, and socialize into the wee hours. For major sporting events, there's a big-screen TV. 816 N. Highland Ave. NE (2 blocks north of Ponce de Leon Ave.). 📞 **404/873-3607.** www.darkhorseatlanta.com. Cover $5-$7 for entertainment in High 10. Limited free parking in lot around back; paid lot across the street. MARTA: Five Points.

Fadó If you haven't had a good glass of Guinness since your last trip to Dublin, Fadó (Gaelic for "long ago") is the place to pause for a pint or two. The interior is divided into five pub areas, each one distinct from the next: a cottage pub with a peat-burning fireplace, a Victorian pub with dark wood and stained glass, and so on. As the night goes on and serious revelers invade, the pleasant, unhurried atmosphere of the early evening gives way to loud and crowded boisterousness. There's traditional Irish or Celtic music several days a week, and the Irish fare is good, especially the *boxty* (the Irish version of a potato pancake) and the fish and chips in Guinness batter. 3035 Peachtree Rd. NE (at the corner of Buckhead Ave., just south of E. Paces Ferry Rd.). 📞 **404/841-0066.** www.fadoirishpub.com. Limited parking on neighboring streets; paid valet parking out back. MARTA: Buckhead.

Manuel's Tavern 🍴 Not far from the yuppiness of Virginia-Highland and the funkiness of Little Five Points is an authentic neighborhood bar that's been a gathering spot since 1956. Now operated by Brian Maloof, the tavern was opened by his father, the late Manuel Maloof, former DeKalb County chief executive officer (his ashes rest in an urn on a shelf behind the bar). It's the quintessential watering hole for journalists, politicos, cops, students, and writers. Former President Jimmy Carter often drops by with the Secret Service in tow. The main bar, with its dark wood and large booths, is the best spot in the building, but there are two larger rooms with tables to accommodate the considerable crowds. It's lots of fun to watch the Braves here if you can't get tickets to the game. There's a full bar with 26 beers on tap, plus dozens of beer blends and craft beers. Manuel's menu includes his famous meatloaf and lasagna entrees along with other stick-to-your-ribs home-cooked fare such as turkey and dressing, pork chops, and pecan trout. 602 N. Highland Ave. NE (at North Ave.). © **404/525-3447.** www.manuelstavern.com. MARTA: Five Points.

Park Tavern Brewery This restaurant/bar on the edge of Piedmont Park has great views of the park and all its goings-on. There are two cozy, rustic bars inside, but the large patio is the best spot for sipping one of the brewery's handcrafted beers. 500 10th St. (at Monroe Dr.). © **404/249-0001.** www.parktavern.com. Limited parking. MARTA: Midtown.

Star Community Bar Housed in a former bank, this funky and cavernous club features the "Grace Vault"—a small shrine filled with Elvis posters, an all-Elvis juke-box, Elvis clocks, and other memorabilia. Primarily a Little Five Points neighborhood hangout, it's very low-key and offbeat. Live music Wednesday through Saturday nights runs the gamut from rockabilly to R&B. Most of the performers are local and regional, but occasionally bigger names play here as well. It's closed on Sunday. 437 Moreland Ave. NE (btw. Euclid and Mansfield aves.). © **404/681-9018.** www.starbar.net. Cover $3–$10. MARTA: Five Points.

Sports Bars

High Velocity Formerly Champions, this popular spot underwent major renovation as well as a name change. Twenty-one plasma TVs air nonstop sporting events and are located everywhere you look, so catching your sporting event is easy here. Or grab a leather recliner in the Media Room and watch the featured game on a 40-foot matrix theatrical projection screen. Sports celebrities tend to stop by when they're in town. Visitors will find 48 imported and domestic beers, including 24 beers on tap, and a long list of appetizers and munchies. At the Marriott Marquis, 265 Peachtree Center Ave. (btw. Baker and Harris sts.). © **404/586-6017.** www.highvelocityatlanta.com. MARTA: Peachtree Center.

Jocks & Jills This is the only branch of Jocks & Jills still left in the city, and it does attract some sports celebrities. If nobody famous shows up, you can still watch sporting events on one of the many televisions scattered around, or check out the sports memorabilia. 1 Galleria Pkwy. © **770/952-8401.** www.jocksandjills.com.

Gay & Lesbian Bars & Clubs

Also see **Outwrite Bookstore & Coffeehouse** (p. 180).

Blake's on the Park Not too far from Piedmont Park in Midtown, you'll find this landmark: a friendly, mostly gay bar that's popular with locals. A few doors away on Monroe Drive is Outwrite Bookstore & Coffeehouse, another pleasant gay and lesbian hangout. 227 10th St. (at Piedmont Ave.). © **404/892-5786.** Limited parking. MARTA: Midtown.

Burkhart's Located in Midtown's Ansley Square Shopping Center, this two-level gay men's hot spot offers three bars, pool tables, and outdoor seating. Many come for the weekly drag shows officially held Friday through Sunday, but recent visits have proved that a show might happen at any time. Karaoke is also a favorite here, if you can squeeze in a tune before the queens hit the stage or wait until the show is over. 1482 Piedmont Ave. NE. © **404/872-9060.** MARTA: Midtown.

COFFEEHOUSES, CAFES & LATE-NIGHT BITES

Also see the box "I Scream for Ice Cream," on p. 175.

Apres Diem   This popular coffeehouse has an atmosphere that is laid-back and casual, and you can linger undisturbed over an espresso or glass of wine on the comfy couches inside or outdoors on the patio. This spot reinvents itself when the sun goes down—there's a full bar and live music several nights of the week. Apres Diem serves good desserts, a variety of French-style coffee drinks and teas, and an expanded menu if you want something more substantial. 931 Monroe Dr. (south of 10th St.). ℂ **404/872-3333.** www.apresdiem.com. MARTA: Arts Center.

Café Intermezzo   Café Intermezzo, in South Buckhead, is a great place to stop after dinner or the theater, or if you just don't want the evening to end. In the tradition of a Vienna-style cafe, there's excellent coffee to go with the decadent desserts and pastries. Speaking of desserts, there are so many that each patron receives a private "tour" of the sweets cases to choose his or her poison. There's also free Wi-Fi here. 1845 Peachtree Rd. (just south of Collier Rd.). ℂ **404/355-0411.** www.cafeintermezzo.com. MARTA: Lenox.

Majestic Food Shop   Known simply as "the Majestic" to locals, this all-night restaurant has been serving diner food and a slice of life daily since 1929. You'll find obnoxious drunks, middle-class regulars, working girls, cops, street people, couples on dates, you name it. Sooner or later, just about everybody comes to the Majestic for a late-night breakfast, a cup of coffee, or just to take in the scene. The late Nick Bitzis, a longtime owner who used to keep an aluminum baseball bat behind the register, once chased a group of customers with a butcher knife for smoking pot in one of the booths. Since the Majestic is open 24 hours, things invariably get more interesting as the night goes on. 1031 Ponce de Leon Ave. NE (west of N. Highland Ave.). ℂ **404/875-0276.** MARTA: Inman Park.

Outwrite Bookstore & Coffeehouse   This casual Midtown spot caters to the gay and lesbian community and is a sort of clearinghouse for information on local issues and activities. The coffee and pastries are good, and the atmosphere is comfortable. Open Sunday to Thursday from 9am to 10pm, and Friday and Saturday 9am to 11pm. 991 Piedmont Ave. (at 10th St.). ℂ **404/607-0082.** www.outwritebooks.com. MARTA: Midtown.

R. Thomas Deluxe Grill ★★   You won't find this menu available at any other round-the-clock restaurant in Atlanta. The grill serves healthy, eclectic food with a large number of vegetarian dishes among the offerings. Open 24 hours a day, 7 days a week. 1812 Peachtree St. NW. ℂ **404/872-2942.** www.rthomasdeluxegrill.com. MARTA: Midtown.

San Francisco Coffee   It's hard to find a coffeehouse that's strictly local and not part of a national chain, but this is the real McCoy. A neighborhood spot that roasts its own coffee and bakes most of its own pastries, it has a lot of atmosphere and is a great place for just hanging out. 1192 N. Highland Ave. (at Amsterdam Ave.). ℂ **404/876-8816.** MARTA: Five Points or Arts Station.

SIDE TRIPS FROM ATLANTA

I f you looked for antebellum Georgia around Atlanta, you were in the right church but the wrong pew. The state's pre–Civil War moonlight-and-magnolias romance lives on, and you'll find it some 60 to 100 miles east of Atlanta in charming old towns with patriotic names such as Madison and Milledgeville, two classic antebellum towns that Sherman didn't burn. And although the cities of central Georgia that lie along the Antebellum Trail are cut off from the mountains or the seashore, they are at the doorstep of some of the state's most mammoth lakes.

This area also encompasses two of the most famous cities of Georgia, Athens and Augusta. Athens, called "the Classic City," is home of the University of Georgia, and lies in a setting beside the Oconee River. Many of its restored and still-occupied antebellum houses make it a worthwhile stopover. Augusta, founded in 1736, is today famed as the headquarters of the Masters Golf Tournament the first full week in April.

ATHENS ★

58 miles E of Atlanta; 85 miles NW of Augusta

Just below the foothills of the Blue Ridge Mountains, near the confluence of the North and Middle Oconee rivers, lies the city of Athens amid the rolling red-clay hills of North Georgia.

Athens's fame grew because of the University of Georgia (UGA; www.uga.edu), which covers 605 acres and includes 313 buildings in the center. The university was incorporated in 1785, making it America's first state-chartered college. Abraham Baldwin, one of Georgia's four signers of the U.S. Constitution, was named president. Today the University of Georgia is ranked among the nation's top research institutions, and boasts America's 19th-largest library and many nationally recognized programs of study, including pharmacy, business, and journalism. More than 30,000 students attend the university.

In the last 2 decades, Athens has gained national attention for its music scene as well. This is where R.E.M., the Indigo Girls, and the B-52s got their start. These groups occasionally return to Athens to play local clubs, but their presence is felt philanthropically through donations to local homeless shelters and AIDS organizations. The town continues to have a booming music scene; for the latest music news and concert information, see "Athens After Dark," p. 200.

Essentials

GETTING THERE From Atlanta, take I-85 northwest to Hwy. 316, which leads the rest of the way to Athens. From Augusta, take I-20 W. to Atlanta, cutting northwest on Hwy. 78 into Athens via Washington.

US Airways (✆ **800/428-4322;** www.usairways.com) offers flights only between Athens and Charlotte, North Carolina. Planes land at **Athens–Ben Epps Airport** (✆ **706/613-3420;** www.athensairport.net).

Greyhound (✆ **800/231-2222;** www.greyhound.com) and **Southeastern Stages** (✆ **404/591-2750;** www.southeasternstages.com) run service to the **Athens bus station,** 220 W. Broad St. (✆ **706/549-2255**).

VISITOR INFORMATION **Athens Welcome Center,** 280 E. Dougherty St. (✆ **706/353-1820;** www.athenswelcomecenter.com), is open 10am to 6pm Monday to Saturday and 2 to 5pm on Sunday.

SPECIAL EVENTS The best time to visit is during the **Historic Homes Tour,** the last weekend in April. Sponsored by the Athens-Clarke Heritage Foundation, this is one of the most attended events in East Georgia. For information, call ✆ **706/353-1801** or visit www.achfonline.org.

Seeing the Sights

Athens begins Georgia's antebellum trail and showcases several buildings of note, many centered around the University of Georgia.

Taylor-Grady House, 634 Prince Ave. (✆ **706/549-8688;** www.taylorgradyhouse.com), a Greek Revival home constructed in the 1840s by Gen. Robert Taylor, planter and cotton merchant, is open year-round. Filled with period furniture, it has 13 columns said to symbolize the original 13 states. Henry W. Grady, a native of Athens, lived here from 1865 to 1868. As managing editor of the *Atlanta Constitution,* he became a spokesperson for the New South. Admission is $3. Hours are Monday to Friday from 9am to 5pm; closed 1 to 2pm. *Warning:* Call ahead, as the house is sometimes booked for private events.

Athens's **Double Barreled Cannon** is the only one of its kind in the world and is among the most unusual relics preserved from the Civil War. It was designed by John Gilleland and built at a local foundry in 1863. The concept was to load the cannon with two balls connected by a chain several feet in length. When fired, the balls and chain would whirl out, bola style, and cut down the unfortunate enemy soldiers caught in the path of this murderous missile. It stands on the City Hall lawn at College and Hancock avenues.

Tree That Owns Itself, at Dearing and Finley streets, is another Athens landmark. William H. Jackson, a professor at the University of Georgia, owned the land on which a large oak stood. He took such delight in the shade of the tree that he willed the tree 8 feet of land surrounding its trunk. The original tree blew down in a windstorm in 1942. The local garden club planted a sapling on the land in 1946, grown from one of the acorns from the original tree. Locals refer to the tree as "the world's most unusual heir and property owner."

The main campus of the **University of Georgia** ★ extends 2 miles south from "the arch" at College Avenue and Broad Street. For information, call ✆ **706/542-3000** or visit www.uga.edu/visit. The current campus was established in 1801. John Milledge, late governor of the state, purchased and gave the board of trustees the chosen tract of 633 acres on the banks of the Oconee River. The view from the hill

ATTRACTIONS ●
Double Barreled Cannon **3**
Founders Memorial Garden
and Houses **9**
Georgia Museum of Art **10**
State Botanical Garden
of Georgia **12**
Taylor-Grady House **2**
Tree That Owns Itself **8**

ACCOMMODATIONS ■
Holiday Inn Athens **7**
Microtel Inn **1**

DINING ◆
East West Bistro **6**
Farm 225 **4**
Five & Ten **11**
Last Resort Grill **5**

on which the 1832 Chapel now stands reminded Milledge of the Acropolis in Athens, and the hill was named after its Greek forebear, the classical center of learning. The school produced its first graduating class in 1804. Later funds were raised for the first permanent structure on campus, Old College (1806), which still stands today.

The **State Botanical Garden of Georgia** ★, 2450 S. Milledge Ave. (© **706/542-1244;** www.uga.edu/botgarden), encompassing 313 acres, is a "living laboratory" in teaching and research that is open to the public. Its three-story conservatory features a display of tropical and semitropical plants. Along the garden's 5 miles of nature trails are diverse ecosystems, with many plants labeled. There are nearly a dozen specialty gardens. The garden lies a mile from U.S. 441, about 3 miles from the university campus. Admission is free. A visitor center and the conservatory are open Tuesday to

Saturday 9am to 4:30pm and on Sunday 11:30am to 4:30pm. Grounds open daily April to September 8am to 8pm and October to March 8am to 6pm.

The **Georgia Museum of Art,** 90 Carlton St. (© **706/542-4662;** www.uga.edu/gamuseum), is the official state art museum, offering an extensive collection of American paintings, prints, and drawings in a new 52,000-square-foot facility. It reopened in January following the addition of a wing and renovation of the original space. New additions include an outdoor sculpture garden and new galleries to display the permanent collection. Call or check the website for the calendar of events.

Founders Memorial Garden and Houses, 325 S. Lumpkin St. on the University of Georgia campus (© **706/542-4776;** www.uga.edu/gardenclub/foundersgarden.html), became the first garden club in the United States, founded in 1891 by 12 Athens women. Set on 2½ acres, it offers varying landscapes and the seasonal foliage of a southern garden. Plantings range from the native to the exotic, and the gardens are a particular delight in spring when the azaleas burst into bloom. The boxwood garden evokes the formality of bygone ages, and the camellia walk is notable. Admission is free, and the garden is open during daylight hours.

Outdoor Pursuits

Sandy Creek Nature Center, half a mile north of the Athens bypass, off U.S. 441, offers some 200 acres of woodland and marshland, with a live animal exhibit. It has many nature trails for hikers, and on-site is a cabin nearly 2 centuries old. Trails are open daily, sunset to sunrise. For more information, call © **706/613-3615** or visit www.sandycreeknaturecenter.com.

Visitors can enjoy **Sandy Creek Park** (© **706/613-3631;** www.sandycreekpark.com), north on U.S. 441 (signposted). It offers a beach, fishing, playgrounds, softball, volleyball, and shelters for picnics. Paddleboats and canoes can be rented. April to September, hours are Tuesday to Sunday 7am to 9pm. Off-season hours are Tuesday to Sunday 8am to 6pm. Admission is $2.

Where to Stay

In addition to the listings below, there's a **Holiday Inn Athens** at 197 E. Broad St. (© **800/HOLIDAY** [465-4329] or 706/549-4433; www.hi-athens.com).

The Colonels on Angel Oaks Farm ★★ 🛏️ The most atmospheric place to stay in the area is here at this beautifully restored mansion that dates from the year the Civil War was declared. Less than a 15-minute drive from the center of historic Athens, the farm stands on a 30-acre pastoral estate. Many motorists touring the antebellum trail stop off here, especially equestrian enthusiasts. Many of the furnishings came from a Belgium château dating from 1794. Bedrooms are period pieces that still contain their original doors, woodwork, and heart-pine floors. A special feature is a sunken garden with beautiful flowers and brickwork. Your hosts are Beth and Marc, both retired lieutenant colonels. *Note:* Prices are higher on UGA football weekends.

3890 Barnett Shoals Rd., Athens, GA 30605. © **706/559-9595.** www.thecolonels.net. 10 units. $115–$195 double; $200–$380 suite. Additional person $20. MC, V. **Amenities:** 2 breakfast rooms. *In room:* TV, Wi-Fi (free).

Microtel Inn This small-scale chain hotel is one of the most comfortable and best run in town. It also offers superb value. Bedrooms are well maintained, functional in styling, and the free continental breakfast will fortify you until lunch. Because the inn rises only two floors you probably won't mind the lack of an elevator. The location is convenient, at the Junction U.S. 78 business route (Broad St.) and the SR 10 Loop.

105 Ultimate Dr., Athens, GA 30605. © **800/771-7171** or 706/548-5676. Fax 706/613-5153. www. microtelinn.com. 60 units. $40–$57 double. Rates include breakfast. AE, DISC, MC, V. **Amenities:** Breakfast room; snack shop. *In room:* TV, fridge, hair dryer, Wi-Fi (free).

Rivendell Bed & Breakfast ★★

Although it was built in 1989, this inn contains many architectural features that make you think it's much older. Set on the Oconee River on 11 acres of forested private land, it's the finest inn in the area. It contains lofty beamed ceilings, two fireplaces crafted from large stones, antiques collected from around the world, and big windows opening onto views of the surrounding countryside. There are walking paths for woodland strolls, with many nice places to stop for picnicking. Complimentary tea and sherry are provided in the afternoon. *Note:* Rates are slightly higher on UGA football weekends.

3581 S. Barnett Shoals Rd. (10 miles southeast of Athens), Watkinsville, GA 30677. © **706/769-4522.** Fax 706/769-4393. www.negia.net/-rivendel. 4 units. $85–$100 double. Rates include full breakfast. MC, V. Drive 8 miles south on U.S. 441, then 5 miles west on Barnett Shoals Rd. No children 10 and under. **Amenities:** Breakfast room; lounge. *In room:* Wi-Fi (free).

Where to Dine

East West Bistro FUSION

This place, which opened in 1995 on the main street in Athens, is all the rage. Upstairs, dining is more formal, in a classically styled room where the fare of northern Italy is sometimes prepared with zest and flavor, though the other dishes are uneven, at best. Depending on the night, many dishes merit a rave, whereas others, such as shrimp and mussels tossed with spaghetti in a mild red-curry cream sauce, don't make it. Try fresh-grilled yellowfin tuna with a parsley caper butter or chicken breast breaded with shaved ginger and orange. Downstairs is the largest selection of tapas in Athens, including Carpaccio and a Thai ratatouille crepe. Main dishes range from jerk chicken to salmon in rice paper.

351 E. Broad St. © **706/546-9378.** www.eastwestbistro.com. Reservations recommended. Sandwiches and pastas $8–$12; main courses $10–$14. AE, DISC, MC, V. Sun–Thurs 11am–10pm; Fri–Sat 11am–11pm.

Farm 225 ★★ 🍴 SOUTHERN/MEDITERRANEAN

Its food is farm fresh, and its chefs sail the Mediterranean for their culinary influence but definitely have a southern drawl in the kitchen. The menu changes daily and manages to be both elegant and simple at the same time. Most of the ingredients come from their own Full Moon Farms nearby. Many of their recipes have emerged from grandmother's attic. They bake their own pastries, cure meats, and even can their own preserves and pickles. In addition, the restaurant also uses meat and poultry from their livestock operation, Moonshine Meats. Begin perhaps with fried green tomatoes with pimento cheese or the famous Swiss dish *raclette,* made with potatoes. Main courses likely to tempt are shrimp and grits, or a North Carolina Wahoo with leeks and local squash. Always on the menu is their famous burger made from staff-raised beef.

255 W. Washington St. © **706/549-4660.** www.farm255.com. Reservations recommended. Main courses $12–$21. AE, MC, V. Tues–Thurs 5:30–10pm; Fri–Sat 5:30–10:30pm; Sun 11am–2pm.

Five & Ten ★★ SOUTHERN/CONTINENTAL

For the most imaginative food offered by any restaurant reviewed in this chapter, partake of the viands featured at Hugh Acheson's place. He calls his own food "contemporary American with inspirations from Italy and France." The self-trained Acheson has risen to the top of the list among the chefs of Athens. The bright, contemporary restaurant in Five Points,

1 mile south of the University of Georgia, has an enclosed patio for alfresco dining, plus a long metallic bar with wooden accents. We take delight in his specialty, Frogmore stew, a modern version of a Low Country "boil" with shrimp, sausage, potatoes, corn, and other vegetables. Almost any dish you order at Five & Ten (so-called because the building used to be a five-and-dime store) is likely to be good. We've enjoyed the pork tenderloin with roasted pepper, asparagus, and potatoes, and especially the red grouper served with a scallion broth, braised endive, and leek-flecked mashed potatoes. The desserts are the best in town and include a delightful blueberry cinnamon tart with cinnamon ice cream and warm maple syrup.

1653 S. Lumpkin St. © **706/546-7300.** www.fiveandten.com. Reservations required. Main courses $17–$32. AE, DISC, MC, V. Sun–Thurs 5:30–10pm; Fri–Sat 5:30–11pm; Sun 10:30am–2:30pm (brunch).

Last Resort Grill MODERN SOUTHERN   This is the most artsy haunt in town, attracting a mostly college crowd. Although its days as a center for avant-garde music are over, it's still a place to find out what's happening in town. We prefer the booths in the bar area, although other patrons like the courtyard, with its open end protected by ornate grillwork. In chilly weather, a gas heater blasts away. The chefs really try hard, and many of their dishes are among the best in town, but it's a hit-or-miss affair. Check out the blackboard specialties, or try your luck and sample grilled salmon with Charlestonian grits, chicken stuffed with cheese and covered with a honey-praline sauce, or chipotle pork chops grilled and marinated.

174–184 W. Clayton St. © **706/549-0810.** www.lastresortgrill.com. Reservations not accepted. Main courses $14–$18. AE, DISC, MC, V. Mon–Thurs 11am–3pm and 5–10pm; Fri–Sat 11am–3pm and 5–11pm; Sun 10am–3pm and 5–10pm.

Athens After Dark

To find out who's playing and what's on, pick up *Flagpole,* Athens's arts, entertainment, and events weekly, free at many shops, restaurants, bars, and clubs; or go online to **www.athensmusic.net** for the latest band information. Another good barometer of what's happening is the UGA student newspaper, the *Red and Black.* Remember that this is a college town, so the nightlife scene is much hotter during the school year. Most of the music clubs and bars present nightly live bands September through June only, shrinking their offerings to just the weekends in the summer.

Make a pilgrimage to the famous **40 Watt Club,** 285 W. Washington St. (© **706/ 549-7871;** www.40watt.com), the little joint that launched the B-52s and R.E.M. Although you can still hear up-and-coming local bands, these days the 40 Watt is more geared toward national bands, such as Luscious Jackson or the Lemonheads. They also run a late-night disco several times a week, as does the **Georgia Theatre,** 215 Lumpkin St., at the corner of Clayton Street (© **706/549-9918;** www.georgia theatre.com). A former movie theater, it gives local college-rock bands (along with a smattering of blues and southern rock) the chance to jam long into the night. The facility just reopened after being rebuilt, though its historic appeal was well preserved in the new digs. Oh, and that skinny guy in the corner may just be Michael Stipe.

Our favorite bar in town by far, however, is the **Globe,** 199 N. Lumpkin St. at Clayton Street (© **706/353-4721;** www.globeathens.com). In the mix are students, an occasional filmmaker, and a cross-cultural selection of anyone from hip latter-day rebels to necktie-wearing salesmen. It's like an English pub, with the largest selection of exotic beers in Athens—more than 150 brands. It also has a collection of 50 kinds of single-malt whiskeys. There's also wine, port, and sherry, served by the glass, and nine boutique bourbons.

MADISON ★

Madison, off I-20, an hour's drive east from Atlanta, was once populated by wealthy merchants and cotton planters who erected houses that were fine examples of Federal and Greek Revival architecture. Antebellum travelers called it "the wealthiest and most aristocratic village between Charleston and New Orleans." Late in 1864, with Atlanta in flames, Gen. William T. Sherman's Union juggernaut reached Madison's outskirts. Happily for us, they were met by former U.S. senator Joshua Hill, a secession opponent who'd known Sherman in Washington, and the town was spared.

Today thousands of visitors come to see the oak-lined streets, historic homes, parks, gardens, churches, galleries, and antiques shops. The Historic District was recognized by the Department of the Interior as one of the finest such districts in the South.

Essentials

The **Madison Chamber of Commerce,** PO Box 826, 115 E. Jefferson St. (✆ **800/709-7406** or 706/342-4454; www.madisonga.org), has information about the area. It's open Monday to Friday 8:30am to 5pm, Saturday 10am to 5pm, and Sunday 1 to 4pm.

Seeing the Sights

Stop first at the **Madison-Morgan Cultural Center,** 434 S. Main St., U.S. 441 (✆ **706/342-4743;** www.mmcc-arts.org). The red-brick schoolhouse (ca. 1895) features a history museum on the Piedmont region of Georgia, an 1895 classroom museum, art galleries with changing exhibits, and an auditorium for presentations. Programs range from Shakespeare to chamber orchestras to gospel singing. Hours are Tuesday to Saturday 10am to 5pm and Sunday 2 to 5pm. Admission is $3 for adults, $2 for students, $2.50 for seniors, and free for children 5 and under.

Pick up a self-guided walking-tour map and other information at the center, and stroll past the majestic Greek Revival, Federal, Georgian, neoclassical, and Victorian homes lining Main Street, Academy Street, Old Post Road, and the courthouse square. You'll find plenty of places to buy antiques and handicrafts.

You can relax outdoors at **Hard Labor Creek State Park** (✆ **706/557-3001** or 557-3006 golf course; www.gastateparks.org/info/hardlabor), near Madison. Leave town via I-20 W. and take exit 49 into Rutledge, then drive 2 miles on Fairplay Road to the park. *Golf* magazine rates the park's 18-hole course as one of the finest public courses in America. You can also swim at a sand beach, fish for bass and catfish, and hike the 5,000 wooded acres. The park has 49 campsites with electricity, water, restrooms, and showers for $28 to $53 a night. There are also 20 fully furnished two-bedroom cottages available for $115 to $125 per night. A Michael J. Fox movie, *Poison Ivy,* was filmed here in the mid-1980s.

Where to Stay

The Brady Inn ★ 🏠 The restored Victorian cottages of the Brady Inn lie in the center of the Historic District (they were once two private homes linked by a walkway). Rooms are tastefully furnished, often with antiques, and the breakfast is most generous. All rooms also have well-kept bathrooms with tub/shower combinations. You get old-fashioned hospitality here, along with a good night's sleep.

250 N. Second St., Madison, GA 30650. © **866/770-0773** or 706/342-4400. www.bradyinn.com. 7 units. $125–$175 double; $200–$350 suite. Rates include full breakfast. AE, MC, V. **Amenities:** Breakfast room; lounge. *In room:* TV, fridge (in some), Wi-Fi (free).

Madison Oaks Inn & Gardens ★ 🏠 In a beautifully restored Greek Revival mansion, this elegant B&B lies only half a mile from the historic town square. If you want a relaxing weekend away from the bustle of Atlanta, this place is for you. Owners Dianne and Roger Simmons rent out four exquisitely furnished rooms, all with an antique aura but with modern amenities. A communal gourmet breakfast is one of the highlights of a stay here, as all the food is homemade and individually prepared. The pool, hammock, and lovely gardens await you. The inn does not accept children.

766 East Ave., Madison, GA 30650. © **706/343-9990.** www.madisonoaksinn.com. 4 units. $185–$250 double. Rates include full breakfast. MC, V. No children. **Amenities:** Breakfast room; outdoor pool. *In room:* TV, hair dryer.

Where to Dine

Old Colonial Restaurant 🍴 SOUTHERN This is the busiest restaurant in Madison. The site it occupies, close to the town's main square, comprises an early-18th-century tavern that later functioned as a bank and a storefront. The staff manages to be friendly, helpful, and restrained all at the same time. Don't expect grand cuisine: Lunches and dinners are copious portions served summer camp–cafeteria style. If you like candied yams, pork chops, and collard greens, come on in. Cornbread is served with everything.

108 E. Washington St. © **706/342-2211.** Breakfast $5–$9; lunch and dinner main courses $6.50–$11. AE, DISC, MC, V. Mon–Sat 5:30am–8:30pm.

EATONTON

21 miles S of Madison; 22 miles N of Milledgeville; 47 miles NE of Macon; 75 miles SE of Atlanta

Home of Br'er Rabbit and the Uncle Remus Tales, this town, filled with antebellum architecture, is a sleepy old place of tree-lined streets and historic homes. Eatonton is not only the original home of Joel Chandler Harris, who created the Uncle Remus Tales, but also of Alice Walker, author and Pulitzer Prize winner for *The Color Purple*.

Essentials

To get here from Madison, take Hwy. 441 S. The **Eatonton-Putnam Chamber of Commerce,** 105 S. Washington St. (© **706/485-7701;** www.eatonton.com), dispenses information Monday to Friday 8:30am to 5pm.

Seeing the Sights

Uncle Remus Museum, Hwy. 441 S. (© **706/485-6856;** www.uncleremus.com), lies in Turner Park, 3 blocks south of the courthouse. It has a kid-pleasing collection of memorabilia about Br'er Rabbit, Br'er Fox, and Harris's other storybook critters. The museum is open Monday to Saturday 10am to 5pm (closed 1 hr. for lunch) and Sunday 2 to 5pm. Admission is $2 for adults and $1 for children 7 and younger. Call ahead on Tuesdays from November to March as the museum is sometimes closed then.

    Bronson House, 114 N. Madison Ave. (© **706/485-6442**), is the home of the Eatonton/Putnam Historical Society. Constructed in 1822 by Thomas T. Napier, it was purchased in 1852 by Andrew Reid, who was the first patron of Joel Chandler Harris. The author lived with his mother in a tiny cottage in back of the mansion. Several rooms of the Greek Revival mansion have been restored, displaying local memorabilia. The house can be visited on Saturday and Sunday from 1 to 5pm, but call for an appointment. Admission is $2.50.

Where to Stay

The Lodge on Lake Oconee ★   Nestled on the shore of Lake Oconee, this is one of the best bets for lodging in the area, its well-furnished bedrooms opening onto waterfront views. The resort is also convenient to golfing, boating, and fishing, and you can dock your boat right behind the lodge after putting in about a half mile up the road. It's also a short drive to the Oconee National Forest and the Hard Labor Creek State Park. Bedrooms are configured with either queen-size beds, one king-size bed, or suites with two queen-size beds and a living room. This is a favorite with families since children's suites are also offered for parents who want a respite from their brood.

930 Lake Oconee Pkwy., Eatonton, GA 31024. ✆ **877/OCONEE-1** (626633) or 706/485-7785. Fax 706/485-3996. www.thelodgeonlakeoconee.com. 81 units. $119–$159 double; $169–$189 suite. Rates include breakfast. MC, V. **Amenities:** Breakfast room; boat rentals. *In room:* TV, fridge, hair dryer, Wi-Fi (free).

Where to Dine

Bone Island Grill at Crooked Creek Marina SOUTHERN/CARIBBEAN   In a scenic location at the marina, this is a favorite among boaters and visitors, and it also does a good business serving local diners. The menu is market fresh and well prepared. The chef lodged time in Key West, and many of the dishes show the influence of the Florida Keys, such as the mahi-mahi sandwich with spicy mayonnaise served at lunch. Fresh appetizers are offered at noon along with poultry, vegetable, and shrimp salads. A good selection of sandwiches is also featured, as well as a fried green tomato BLT on Cuban bread. Dinner is far more substantial, beginning with such appetizers as fried oysters. Two of the best main courses are the seafood gumbo with rice or cornbread, or else the pan-sautéed fresh red snapper with a lemon butter sauce. Hush puppies are always on the menu.

Crooked Creek Marina, 208 Crooked Creek Dr. ✆ **706/485-9693.** No reservations taken. Main courses $22–$50. MC, V. Fri–Sat 11am–4pm; Wed–Thurs 5–10pm; Fri–Sat 4pm–12:30am.

MILLEDGEVILLE

20 miles S of Eatonton; 30 miles NE of Macon; 90 miles SE of Atlanta

This town ranks along with Madison and Washington in historic sights. Carved from Native American territories in 1803, Milledgeville was the capital of Georgia until 1868, when the seat was moved to Atlanta. Milledgeville was miraculously spared by General Sherman and today remains a treasure-trove of antebellum architecture.

Essentials

From Eatonton, follow U.S. 441 S. into Milledgeville. The Welcome Center of the **Milledgeville-Baldwin County Convention & Visitors Bureau** is at 200 W. Hancock St. (✆ **800/653-1804** or 478/452-4687; www.milledgevillecvb.com). It's open Monday to Friday 8:30am to 5pm and Saturday 10am to 4pm.

Seeing the Sights

Old Governors Mansion, 120 S. Clark St. (*(C)* **478/445-4545;** www.gcsu.edu/
mansion), a pink marble Palladian beauty, has been exquisitely restored and refurbished as the home of the president of Georgia College. You may tour the antiques-
rich public rooms. The mansion was the home of Georgia's governors from 1839 to
1868. This National Historic Landmark house is an excellent example of Greek
Revival architecture. Guided tours begin on the hour from Tuesday to Saturday 10am
to 4pm and on Sunday 2 to 4pm. Admission is $10 for adults, $7 for seniors, $2 for
students, and free for children 5 and under.

The mansion is on the campus of **Georgia College & State University,** 231 W.
Hancock St. (*(C)* **478/445-5004;** www.gcsu.edu), a former women's college that
dates from 1889 and today is home to some 5,500 students. The college occupies
four 20-acre plots. You may want to stroll about the campus.

At the college's **Ina Dillard Russell Library,** on Clark Street (*(C)* **478/445-
0988**), you can visit the Flannery O'Connor Room, but check its status before coming here. As this guide went to press, it was closed for renovations. O'Connor,
distinguished author of *The Violent Bear It Away* and *A Good Man Is Hard to Find,*
lived in Milledgeville. You can also visit **Memory Hill Cemetery** (www.friendsof
cems.org/memoryhill), the oldest burial ground in the city, where the author is buried.

O'Connor fans should also visit **Andalusia—Flannery O'Connor's Farm ★**,
2628 N. Columbia St./Hwy. 441 (*(C)* **478/454-4029;** www.andalusiafarm.org), outside of town. It's free and open to the public Monday, Tuesday, and Saturday 10am
to 4pm. The author lived at her family's farm from 1951 until her death from lupus
in 1964. The memorabilia-filled farmhouse is 4 miles northwest of Milledgeville on
the west side of U.S. Hwy. 441. Visitors can see the 544-acre estate, complete with
the main house, main barn, even smaller barns, three tenants' houses, and water
tower, plus a man-made pond. The white two-story, plantation-style main house (ca.
1850) is listed on the National Register of Historic Places.

The easiest way to see the town is to take a **Historic Guided Trolley Tour.** The
2-hour tour explores the major sights in the town, including the old governor's mansion and the former state capitol building (ca. 1807). Tours depart from the Welcome
Center (see "Essentials," above) Monday to Friday at 10am and Saturday at 2pm.
Cost of the tour is $10 for adults, $5 for children 6 to 16, and free for children 5 and
under.

Nearby, you can visit **Lake Sinclair,** north on U.S. 441, a 15,330-acre lake with
417 miles of shoreline. It was created when the Oconee River was impounded and
today it is a venue for fishing and boating. There's a marina, and camping is possible.
Call *(C)* **478/452-1605** for more information.

Where to Stay

Antebellum Inn ★ Innkeeper Jane Lorenz welcomes you to her well-restored
1890 Greek Revival home in the heart of the Antebellum Trail in the center of
Milledgeville, just a block from the Georgia College & State University campus. The
Old Governor's Mansion is just down the street. The inn has two old-fashioned parlors and five spacious guest rooms. Individually furnished guest rooms have beds
covered with tasteful linens and down comforters. Several of the well-kept bathrooms
have antique claw-foot tubs. The town's best B&B breakfast is served in an elegant
dining room. If you'd like to recapture the feel of Georgia's former capital, find a

rocking chair on the wraparound porch. The grounds are beautifully landscaped, and a pool cottage suite is now available.

200 N. Columbia St., Milledgeville, GA 31061. ✆ **478/453-3993.** www.antebelluminn.com. 5 units. $109–$169 double. AE, DISC, MC, V. **Amenities:** Breakfast room; outdoor pool. *In room:* Hair dryer, Wi-Fi (free).

Milledgeville Days Inn 🐾   This modest motel is preferred over its major competitor, the 169-room Holiday Inn out on U.S. 441 N. Days Inn is a two-story inn filled with southern comfort. Its guest rooms are strictly functional, but they're well maintained, with good beds and spacious bathtubs with tub/shower combinations.

2551 N. Columbia St., Milledgeville, GA 31061. ✆ **800/329-7466** or 478/453-8471. Fax 478/453-8482. www.daysinn.com. 95 units. $51–$65 double. Rates include continental breakfast. Children 11 and under stay free in parent's room. AE, DC, DISC, MC, V. Pet $10. **Amenities:** Breakfast room; lounge; exercise room; Jacuzzi; outdoor pool; room service; 2 tennis courts (lit). *In room:* TV, fridge, hair dryer, Wi-Fi (free).

Where to Dine

Bo Jo's Boardwalk Café SOUTHERN/STEAK/SEAFOOD   A local eatery, this regional cafe is known for its helpful staff and large portions. Residents come here for steak and fresh seafood—often fried—and plenty of good-tasting southern favorites such as fried chicken. Dress is informal, and there is also a full bar on-site. The cafe is at the junction of U.S. Business Rte. 44 and U.S. 441 Bypass.

3021 N. Columbia St. ✆ **478/453-3234.** Reservations not needed. Main courses $6–$24. MC, V. Mon-Sat 4–10pm.

AUGUSTA ★

139 miles E of Atlanta; 122 miles N of Savannah

Home to one of the world's most prestigious men's professional golf tournaments, the Masters, Augusta is a southern city of charm and grace. Lying along the banks of the Savannah River, it stands about halfway between Savannah and Atlanta.

Augusta is the state's second-oldest city, dating from 1736, when it was marked off for settlement by Gen. James E. Oglethorpe, founder of Georgia. It was a major winter resort, attracting the Yankee wealthy, such as John D. Rockefeller. Except at the time of the Masters Tournament, Augusta doesn't attract vacationers as it did in its heyday, but that's beginning to change.

Essentials

GETTING THERE   Augusta lies off I-20, the main route from Atlanta, on the west bank of the Savannah River.

   Bush Field Airport (✆ 706/798-3236; http://ags.skyharbors.com) lies just a 15-minute drive from the center of Augusta. Fifty commercial flights wing their way into the airport daily. Connections are possible via **Delta** (✆ 800/221-1212; www.delta.com) or **US Airways** (✆ 800/428-4322; www.usair.com) from both Atlanta and Charlotte.

   Buses run by **Greyhound** (✆ 800/231-2222; www.greyhound.com) and **Southeastern Stages** (✆ 404/591-2750; www.southeasternstages.com) arrive downtown at the **Southeastern Stage bus terminal,** 1128 Greene St. (✆ 706-722-6411).

VISITOR INFORMATION The **Augusta Metropolitan Convention & Visitors Bureau,** 1450 Greene St. (© **800/726-0243** or 706/823-6600; www.augustaga.org), is open Monday to Friday 8:30am to 5pm.

SPECIAL EVENTS It seems that half the world—at least, the golfing half—focuses on Augusta the first full week in April for the nationally televised **Masters Golf Tournament ★★★**, a tradition since 1934 and now the most prestigious golf tournament in the world. Hotel space is at a premium then, and prices for rooms soar to whatever the market will bear. Call © **706/667-6000** or go to www.masters.org for more information.

Seeing the Sights

The major attraction is **Riverwalk ★**, the tree-lined paths at the edge of the Savannah River, between 5th and 10th streets, which are resplendent with greenery and seasonal flowers. Riverwalk includes 5 blocks of unique development, including a full-service, 67-slip marina. It boasts a 1,700-seat amphitheater that plays host to various performances throughout the year. It's perfect for a moonlit stroll or an afternoon spent picnicking, shopping, and enjoying one of the city's many festivals. You can see the river from both bi-level and tri-level platforms, with historical markers along the way.

Although it's not a grand attraction, you can visit the **Boyhood Home of Woodrow Wilson,** 419 7th St. (© **706/722-9828;** www.wilsonboyhoodhome.org), which has been restored and opened to the public. The future president lived here from 1860 to 1870 during the years his father served as pastor of the First Presbyterian Church. Admission is $5 for adults, $4 for seniors, and $3 for students and children, and hours are Tuesday to Saturday 10am to 5pm. (Last tour departs at 4pm.)

Confederate Powderworks, along the Augusta Canal on Goodrich Street, is a 168-foot-tall chimney, all that remains of the second-largest powder factory in the world, which operated between 1862 and 1865. It is the only permanent structure begun and completed by the Confederate government, and it once consisted of 26 buildings.

The best way to introduce yourself to Augusta is to contact **Historic Augusta Tours** (© **706/724-4067;** www.augustaga.org), which conducts tours every Saturday from 1:30 to 3:30pm. The tour leaves from the Museum of History Building at 5 Reynolds St. Reservations are required by noon the Friday before. Cost is $10 for adults and $5 for children.

Ezekiel Harris House Constructed by Ezekiel Harris, a leading Augusta tobacco merchant, this 1797 house re-creates the heyday of the late 18th century, when locals grew rich trading in tobacco. The planter's house is filled with period furnishings.

1822 Broad St. © **706/737-2820.** Admission $2 adults, $1 children 6–17, free for children 5 and under. Sat 10am–5pm; Tues–Fri by appointment.

Gertrude Herbert Institute of Art This Federal-style house was built in 1818 for Augusta mayor Nicholas Ware at the cost of $40,000—a tidy sum back then. It now serves as an art institute, a center not only for art classes, but for changing exhibitions open to the public.

506 Telfair St. © **706/722-5495.** www.ghia.org. Free admission; donations accepted. Tues–Fri 10am–5pm.

Meadow Garden This Sand Hill cottage (ca. 1791) was the home of George Walton, youngest original signer of the Declaration of Independence and twice Georgia

Augusta

ACCOMMODATIONS ■
Marriott Hotel & Suites **8**
The Partridge Inn **3**

DINING ◆
Calvert's **1**
French Market Grille **2**
La Maison Restaurant &
Veritas Wine & Tapas **13**
Veranda Grill in the Partridge Inn **3**

ATTRACTIONS ●
Boyhood Home of Woodrow Wilson **11**
Confederate Powderworks **5**
Ezekiel Harris House **4**
Gertrude Herbert Institute of Art **12**
Meadow Garden **6**
Morris Museum of Art **7**
National Science Center's Fort Discovery **9**
St. Paul's Episcopal Church **10**

governor. It is the oldest documented house in Augusta and the first historic preservation project in the state.

1320 Independence Dr. (near the intersection of 13th St. and Walton Way). ℂ **706/724-4174.** www. historicmeadowgarden.org. Admission $4 adults, $3.50 seniors, $1 children. Mon–Fri 10am–4pm. Last tour leaves at 3:30pm.

Morris Museum of Art   This museum features period galleries that display more than 2,000 works spanning 1790 to the present. The museum, which hosts changing exhibitions quarterly, also has a museum shop and a visitor-orientation gallery. Admission is free on Sunday.

Riverwalk and 1 Tenth St. ℂ **706/724-7501.** www.themorris.org. Admission $5 adults; $3 seniors, students, and military; free for children 6 and under and for all on Sun. Tues–Sat 10am–5pm; Sun noon–5pm.

National Science Center's Fort Discovery ★ ☺   This is a hands-on science, technology, and communications center that attracts families and student groups from all over Georgia. There are some 250 interactive exhibits, and traveling exhibitions, such as "Inventions of Leonardo da Vinci," are presented throughout the year. On-site is a science store selling replications of the most popular custom exhibits.

7th Street. ℂ **800/325-5445** or 706/821-0600. www.nscdiscovery.org. Admission $8 adults, $6 seniors and children 4–7, free for children 3 and under. Thurs–Sat 10am–5pm.

St. Paul's Episcopal Church   The fourth structure to be built on this site, the St. Paul's you see today was built after a fire destroyed much of the downtown area in 1915. The first St. Paul's was constructed in 1750 as part of Fort Augusta, constructed by the British in 1739. The Celtic Cross, used to designate the site, still stands. The cemetery next to the church was used during colonial days through 1819, and many notable Georgians are buried here.

605 Reynolds St. ℂ **706/724-2485.** www.saintpauls.org. Free admission. Guided tours by appointment only. Mon–Thurs 9am–4:30pm; Fri–Sat 9am–noon. Sun service 7:45am, 9am, and 11am.

Golf & Other Outdoor Pursuits

Golf is king in Augusta, but unfortunately, the famous tournament course at Augusta National isn't open to the public. We recommend **Goshen Plantation,** 1601 Goshen House Club Dr. (ℂ **706/793-1035;** www.goshenplantation.com), one of the most beautiful and challenging courses in the Central Savannah River Area (CSRA). It has well-bunkered greens and demanding par 3s, 4s, and 5s, and requires you to use every club in your bag. It also has a fully stocked pro shop and the restaurant On the Green. Greens fees are $32 to $37, and hours are daily 7:30am to dusk.

Augusta Canal (ℂ **888/659-8926** or 706/823-0440; www.augustacanal.com), stretching across two counties from the center of Augusta to Evans-to-Locks Road in Columbia County, is the setting for an array of activities, including bicycling, fishing, canoeing, hiking, running, walking, and picnicking. Visit **Savannah Rapids Park** (ℂ **706/868-3349;** www.savannahrapids.com) for easy access to the canal. For canoe rentals, call ℂ **706/738-8500.**

Thurmond Lake, north on Washington Road (about 20 miles from the center of Augusta), offers 1,200 miles of shoreline bordering Georgia and South Carolina. One of the largest inland bodies of water in the South, it has some of the best outdoor sports around, including swimming, sailing, water-skiing, fishing, hunting, and just plain sunbathing. The lake is surrounded by a 70,000-acre park. A Visitor and Information Center (www.georgialakeinfo.com/thurmond) is located at the South Carolina end of the dam off Hwy. 221.

Where to Stay

If you can't get a room in town for the Masters, try for lodgings in Aiken, South Carolina.

Doubletree Hotel Augusta ★★   The renovated hotel, with its airy atrium lobby, is ideal for the business traveler or the vacationer seeking first-class accommodations in a conventional hotel. Rising six floors, it's about 2 miles from the Augusta Mall and some 10 miles from downtown attractions. The hotel facilities are the best in the area, with a heated indoor pool. Guest rooms are spacious and elegantly decorated, from the granite countertops to the cherrywood vanities. The most desirable rooms come with "jetted" bathtubs, microwaves, and refrigerators.

2651 Perimeter Pkwy., Augusta, GA 30909. ✆ **706/855-8100.** Fax 706/860-1720. www.augusta. doubletree.com. 179 units. $116–$134 double; $138–$349 suite. AE, DC, MC, V. **Amenities:** 2 restaurants; bar; exercise room; 2 pools (1 indoor); room service. *In room:* TV, hair dryer, Wi-Fi (free).

Marriott Hotel & Suites ★   This chain hotel enjoys the best location in town; its well-furnished but standard rooms open onto the Savannah River and historic River-walk. Frommer's readers Michael Barnas and Phyllis Feingold-Barnas likened the spacious second-floor concourse of the hotel to a trip back to the "Castle of Versailles, with its sweeping marbled floor length, chandelier after chandelier ceiling, and profusion of flower-filled oversize vases." Augustino's serves only fair Italian dishes, and an adjoining lounge offers big-screen sports. The staff will direct guests to 19 premium golf courses in the area, challenges to both novices and pros alike.

2 Tenth St., Augusta, GA 30901. ✆ **800/868-5354** or 706/722-8900. Fax 706/823-6513. www.marriott. com. 372 units. $149–$199 double; $259 suite. AE, DC, DISC, MC, V. **Amenities:** Restaurant; bar; exercise room; Jacuzzi; 2 pools (1 indoor); room service. *In room:* TV, hair dryer, kitchenette (in some), Wi-Fi (free).

The Partridge Inn ★   During Augusta's heyday as a winter resort—roughly from 1889 to 1930—the Partridge Inn was known as the city's grand dame. The resort's fame faded when Henry Flagler extended the railroad to Florida and the Great Depression hit. By the early 1980s, the hotel was slated for demolition. Fortunately, it was saved, and in 1988, after a major restoration, it reopened. Today's accommodations come in an almost dizzying array of combinations, from standard double to queen- and king-size beds, and some rooms offer views or kitchenettes. Dining at the Inn's **Veranda Grill** (p. 210) is an Augusta tradition.

2110 Walton Way, Augusta, GA 30904. ✆ **800/476-6888** or 706/737-8888. Fax 706/731-0826. www. partridgeinn.com. 144 units. $139–$179 double. AE, DC, DISC, MC, V. **Amenities:** Restaurant; bar; exercise room; outdoor pool; room service. *In room:* TV, hair dryer, kitchenette (in some), Wi-Fi (free).

Where to Dine

Calvert's ★★ AMERICAN   Since it opened in 1977, Calvert's has emerged as the best restaurant in Augusta. In the Surrey Center, the elegant restaurant lures with its dark paneling and candlelit tables. Traditional cuisine is based, whenever possible, on fine local ingredients. The crab cakes are made with Virginia fried ham, a zesty concoction, as is the velvety blend of shrimp, clams, and spinach into a seafood bisque perked up with a touch of Pernod. The main courses are impressive in their wise simplicity and superb cooking technique. Especially notable is the leek-wrapped salmon with a grilled shrimp skewer and a lemon white butter, or pan-seared duck breasts with a black-cherry port sauce. Desserts are made fresh daily.

475 Highland Ave. ✆ **706/738-4514.** www.calvertsrestaurant.com. Reservations recommended. Main courses $20–$35. AE, DISC, MC, V. Tues–Sat 5–9pm.

French Market Grille ★ LOUISIANA In a faux French-market atmosphere located in a shopping center, this restaurant is often hailed as the best in Augusta. It's good, but we give our vote to Calvert's (see above). Po'boys are featured at lunch and might be stuffed with everything from spicy chicken to soft-shell crab. Recommended is the chef's crab chop à la Charles (crabmeat bound by white sauce, with the added flavors of green onions and other seasonings). The étouffée (choice of either shrimp or crawfish) was suitably spicy, Cajun style. The desserts, including pecan praline pie and New Orleans bread pudding, have been voted "best desserts in Augusta" by *Augusta Magazine* several years in a row.

425 Highland Ave. ✆ **706/737-4865.** www.frenchmarketaugusta.com. Reservations not accepted. Main courses $18–$32. AE, DISC, MC, V. Mon–Thurs 11:30am–10pm; Fri–Sat 11:30am–11pm.

La Maison Restaurant & Veritas Wine & Tapas ★ FRENCH/AMERICAN In a Southern Revival home, this elegant choice for dining is perhaps the finest in Augusta in terms of cuisine, ambience, and service. Its special feature is a wine bar and tapas lounge, recognized by *Wine Spectator* for its excellence. This is the finest choice in Augusta for a romantic dinner. Appetizers are often typical, though excellent: French appetizers such as snails in garlic butter, and delightful surprises such as smoked ostrich carpaccio with arugula and vine-ripened tomatoes misted with truffle oil. Chef Heinz's signature dishes (and we endorse them with enthusiasm) include rack of lamb with fresh herbs and an apricot teriyaki glaze, and Dover sole sautéed in butter with grapes and almonds. The five-course light dinner is the best value in the city.

404 Telfair St. ✆ **706/722-4805.** www.lamaisontelfair.com. Reservations recommended. Main courses $17–$43. AE, DC, DISC, MC, V. Mon–Sat 6–9:30pm.

Old McDonald Fish Camp, Inc. ★ 🍴 SEAFOOD When locals from Augusta hanker for catfish and hush puppies and all those good things, they head right to this old fish camp. It's known for serving the best catfish in the area, although you can also order ocean perch, fried shrimp, scallops, crabs, oysters, and even fried gator. One feature is a Low Country boil, with shrimp, sausage, potatoes, corn, and coleslaw. The Thursday-night special is an all-you-can-eat fry of catfish, fish filet, and perch filet—a real bargain. It's a family favorite, even if the fish is often overcooked—hey, that's the way the locals like it.

355 Currytown Rd., N. Augusta. ✆ **803/279-3305.** www.oldmcdonaldfishcamp.com. Main courses $14–$20. MC, V. Thurs 5–9pm; Fri 5–9:30pm; Sat 4–9:30pm. Take I-20 E. to exit 1 in South Carolina, turn left, and go 5 miles.

Veranda Grill in the Partridge Inn ★ 🍴 STEAKHOUSE/SEAFOOD/SOUTHERN Dining at the legendary Partridge Inn has long been an Augusta tradition. The chef, Dominic Simpson, brings a fresh innovative approach to certified Angus beef, fresh seafood from the coast, and old-time Georgia favorites. A breakfast buffet is offered every morning with freshly prepared dishes or else a la carte choices such as blackened shrimp with roasted peppers and Tasso (gravy with smoked pork and spices) over creamy grits. The lunch buffet is the best in Augusta, or you can order menu favorites such as she-crab bisque followed by grilled pesto chicken breast. At night the chef really shines with his beef dishes, including grilled hangar steak and seared venison medallions on a butter bean and country ham ragout.

In the Partridge Inn, 2110 Walton Way. ✆ **706/737-8888.** www.partridgeinn.com/dining. Reservations recommended. Breakfast $12 buffet, $7.95–$11 main courses; lunch $12 buffet, $12–$14 main courses; dinner main courses $18–$27; Sun brunch $22. AE, DC, DISC, MC, V. Sun–Thurs 6am–10pm; Fri–Sat 6am–11pm.

CALLAWAY GARDENS ★★★

70 miles S of Atlanta

One of the most beautiful spots in the South, Callaway Gardens embraces 14,000 acres of gardens, woodlands, and lakes, with wildlife and outdoor activities. Some 750,000 visitors are attracted to this site annually, especially in spring, when its Azalea Trail displays some 700 colorful varieties. But every season brings something new into bloom, from rhododendron and holly trails to wildflowers.

Callaway Gardens at Pine Mountain was begun back in the 1930s. Cason Callaway, head of one of Georgia's most prosperous textile mills, set about rebuilding the soil, nurturing and importing plant life, building the largest man-made inland beach in the world, and providing inn and cottage accommodations—and opened it all to citizens of modest means.

Essentials

GETTING THERE   From Atlanta, take I-85 S. to I-185, continue on I-185 S. to exit 14, and then turn left on U.S. 27 and drive 11 miles to Callaway Gardens. Driving north on either I-185 or I-85, exit east on Ga. 18 to Pine Mountain, and then turn right on U.S. 27 and enter Callaway Gardens.

Seeing the Gardens

Callaway Gardens, at Pine Mountain (© **800/225-5292** or 706/663-2281; www. callawaygardens.com), include floral and hiking trails and acres of picnic grounds. Special events abound, particularly the Spring Celebration. In May, Callaway plays host to the Masters Waterski Tournament. July 4th is the occasion of the sunrise-to-sunset Surf and Sand Spectacular, giving way to the Sky High Balloon Festival over Labor Day weekend. The Fall Festival celebrates the beauty of the chrysanthemums, and Fantasy in Lights at Christmas is a brilliant ride through the gardens with a display of lights and music.

The park has many attractions. The **Cecil B. Day Butterfly Center ★**, a $5.3-million center, ranks with the world's foremost conservatories in London, Melbourne, and Tokyo. The octagonal conservatory houses more than 1,000 free-flying butterflies and numerous birds. The conservatory includes a 12-foot waterfall and lush tropical foliage.

The **John A. Sibley Horticultural Center,** one of the most advanced garden and greenhouse complexes in the world, encompasses 5 acres with 20,200 square feet of indoor floral displays, plus 30,675 square feet of greenhouse space. Floral displays integrate indoor and outdoor settings.

Mr. Cason's Vegetable Garden, started in 1960, was the last major project initiated by Mr. Callaway. On 7½ acres, gardeners demonstrate scientific, educational, and practical applications of fruit and vegetable cultures. A trio of large terraces in a semicircular design, the vegetable garden produces more than 400 varieties of crops that range from traditional southern fruits and vegetables to wildflower test plots. The PBS show *Victory Garden* films its southern segments from here.

The **Ida Cason Callaway Memorial Chapel,** in the English Gothic style, was built to honor Mr. Callaway's mother, Ida Cason. It was dedicated in 1962 by Dr. Norman Vincent Peale. It's patterned much like a rural wayside chapel of the 16th and 17th centuries.

The park is open daily from 9am to 6pm, with extended summer hours. Admission is $18 for adults, $9 for children 6 to 12, and free for children 5 and under.

Outdoor Pursuits

BEACH RESORT   **Robin Lake Beach,** on a 65-acre lake, is the largest inland man-made white-sand beach anywhere in the world. It offers a center for children with a large outdoor playground, as well as miniature golf, badminton, and rides on a riverboat. In summer, a show is presented by Florida State University's Flying High Circus. A trail stretches nearly a mile around the lake with 20 fitness stations. Robin Lake Beach is a virtual miniresort, with sand, surf, and dozens of activities. Admission is $18 for adults, $9 for children 6 to 12, and free for children 5 and under. The beach is open daily from 9am to 6pm in summer. It is closed from Labor Day until the first of June.

BIKING   Callaway Gardens has 7½ paved miles for bikers who'd like to see the gardens up close instead of from a car. The Discovery Bicycle Trail is a family favorite. It begins at Bike Barn near the beach parking lot at Robin Lake, where you can rent bikes and helmets (some bikes are equipped with child safety seats). A ferry is available near the end of the trail at the boat dock to transport riders across Mountain Creek Lake back to their starting point. The Bike Barn rents bikes daily from 8am to 6pm, charging $14 for 2 hours and $20 for a half-day.

FISHING   Fishing is available on Mountain Creek Lake, where two persons can rent a boat for $45 per half-day or $60 per full day.

GOLF   Callaway's well-groomed courses, hailed by *Golf Digest* and *Golf* magazine, are set in the midst of clear lakes, lush landscaping, and wooded shores. **Mountain View,** designed by Dick Wilson, is viewed as the best by many golfers. Tight, tree-lined fairways are characteristic of this championship course. At hole no. 15 (par 5), the threat of water looms over both tee and approach shots. This hole is ranked as one of the most difficult par 5s by *USA Today.* The first course built here, **Lake View** was designed only in part by Dick Wilson. Mr. Callaway himself provided the inspiration for this course, whose challenge lies in its 9 water holes. The par-70 course is known for its no. 5 with its island tee and serpentine bridge over Mountain Creek Lake to the green in front of the Gardens Restaurant. Mountain View is the most expensive course to play, at a cost of $100, while Lake View goes for $80. Call ℂ **800/225-5292** to make reservations for either course.

TENNIS   *Tennis* magazine awarded Callaway a "Top 50" national rating. Nine courts are hard surfaced, and eight have Rubico surfaces. Two glass-walled racquetball courts and a pro shop are also located in Callaway's sports complex.

Where to Stay

Callaway Gardens Resort ★★   In 1951, as the success of Callaway Gardens attracted visitors from around the country, Cason Callaway engaged Holiday Inn to build a motel on gently sloping terrain across the highway from the gardens. Eventually, Callaway acquired the property and enlarged it. It now encompasses the **Mountain Creek Inn,** the **Cottages at Callaway Gardens,** the **Villas at Callaway Gardens,** and the **Lodge and Spa at Callaway Gardens.**

Adjacent to the resort's freshwater beach, rustic two-bedroom cottages contain fireplaces, kitchens, and lots of modern luxuries. Popular with families, they're what you'd expect at an outdoor camping retreat: They have endured their share of wear and tear. More stylish are the villas; all have kitchens, relatively formal furnishings, fireplaces, screened-in verandas, and a greater emphasis on style and comfort.

The Lodge and Spa offers deluxe guest rooms and suites, with private balconies opening onto the forest. This first-class lodge is furnished with an eclectic mix of furnishings, some in the style of an elegant southern estate. In the beautiful landscaping is a swimming pool with a cabana-style bar. The spa features 13 treatment rooms, with "nature-based massages" and nourishing facials. The fitness center features the latest equipment and also has a yoga studio.

17800 U.S. 27 S., Pine Mountain, GA 31822. © **800/CALLAWAY** (225-5292) or 706/663-2281. Fax 706/663-5090. www.callawaygardens.com. 900 units. $79–$167 double; $189–$900 suite; $252–$617 2- to 4-bedroom villa. Honeymoon, sports, and monthly packages available. AE, DC, DISC, MC, V. **Amenities:** 7 restaurants; 2 bar lounges; babysitting; concierge; 2 18-hole golf courses; exercise room; 3 pools (1 indoor); room service; 10 tennis courts (lit). *In room:* A/C, TV, hair dryer, Wi-Fi (free).

Magnolia Hall Bed & Breakfast ★ ▥   Open year-round, this B&B lies 5 miles from the entrance to Callaway Gardens. An 1890s Victorian home, it's surrounded by an acre of land with azaleas, tea olives, camellias, and the namesake magnolias. Potted ferns and cushioned wicker evoke the Deep South. Antiques-filled rooms, a grand piano in the sitting room, and high ceilings add grace notes. Guest rooms are spacious and contain well-kept bathrooms. This is not necessarily a place for kids.

127 Barnes Mill Rd. (P.O. Box 326), Hamilton, GA 31811. © **877/813-4394** or 706/628-4566. Fax 706/628-5802. www.magnoliahallbb.com. 5 units. $115–$135 double. Additional person $30 extra. Rates include breakfast. AE, MC, V. **Amenities:** Breakfast room; 2 lounges. *In room:* A/C, TV, hair dryer, no phone, Wi-Fi (free).

Valley Inn Resort ☺   There's nothing special here, but as motels go, it's one of the best of the lot. Families, especially in summer, like this small resort set on 52 acres near a lake. Guest rooms are comfortably furnished. Some contain kitchens, and all contain well-kept bathrooms. You can park your RV in the Travel Trailer Park or rent a two-bedroom mobile home unit that sleeps up to six. All rooms are nonsmoking.

14420 Hwy. 27, Hamilton, GA 31811. © **800/944-9393** or 706/628-4454. 20 units. $59 double; $105 1-bedroom cottage; $125 2-bedroom cottage. AE, DC, DISC, MC, V. **Amenities:** Cafe; lounge; outdoor pool. *In room:* A/C, TV, kitchenette (in some).

White Columns Motel   One mile from Callaway Gardens, this small family-owned and -operated white-columned motel is a favorite budget choice in the area. There's a large swing on an old magnolia tree on the front lawn, a great place to spend a lazy summer afternoon. Rooms are basic but clean and comfortable, and have been recently "fixed up." Within walking distance of the motel are two good and moderately priced restaurants.

Hwy. 27 S. (P.O. Box 531), Pine Mountain, GA 31822. © **800/722-5083** or 706/663-2312. Fax 706/663-2311. www.whitecolumnsmotel.com. 14 units. $60–$79 double. Rates include continental breakfast. MC, V. *In room:* A/C, TV, fridge, hair dryer, kitchenette (in some), Wi-Fi (free).

Where to Dine

The Country Kitchen SOUTHERN   First things first: Don't come here looking for health food. Despite that, its premises (a stone-built roadside country store about a mile south of the Callaway Gardens entrance, near the top of Pine Mountain) are usually mobbed with families looking for a taste of wholesome country nostalgia. The setting is rustic and woodsy. Menu items include chicken or country ham with biscuits and gravy, an array of vegetables, burgers, and club sandwiches. Dessert might be a portion of muscadine ice cream. If you need grits to get your day started right, have them along with "Mama's pancakes" or a country omelet.

Hwy. 27, near Callaway Gardens. © **706/663-2281.** Breakfast platters $6.25–$9.50; main courses $8–$13. AE, DISC, MC, V. Daily 8am–8pm.

The Gardens ITALIAN/INTERNATIONAL   The Gardens occupies a sprawling and immensely atmospheric building whose stout timbers and rambling verandas resemble a grange in eastern France or Germany. Our favorite tables are perched on a balcony overlooking a landscape of golf fairways and a pond that has a serpentine bridge zigzagging across its waters. The menu emphasizes grilled steaks, seafood, and chops, and the kitchen prepares this fare exceedingly well.

Hwy. 27, at Callaway Gardens. © **706/663-2281.** Reservations recommended. Main courses $12–$19. AE, DC, DISC, MC, V. Tues–Sat 5–9pm.

The Plantation Room 🍴 SOUTHERN   The buffets here celebrate culinary traditions of the Old South. Vegetables are the freshest in summer, when they come to your table just hours after being picked from Mr. Cason's vegetable garden. If you've never eaten corn just pulled from the stalk, you'll find how different it is from store-bought corn pulled days or weeks before. It can get very crowded here, especially on Friday nights when the theme is seafood.

At Callaway Gardens. © **706/663-2281.** Buffet $11 breakfast, $13 lunch, $17–$25 dinner. AE, DISC, MC, V. Daily 6:30–10:30am, 11:30am–2pm, and 5:30–9pm.

PLANNING YOUR TRIP TO ATLANTA

GETTING THERE

By Plane

Hartsfield-Jackson Atlanta International Airport (✆ **404/530-7300;** www.atlanta-airport.com; airport code: ATL), 10 miles south of downtown, is the world's largest and busiest passenger airport and transfer hub, accommodating 78 million passengers a year. It provides 186 U.S. cities with nonstop service.

Delta Air Lines (✆ **800/221-1212;** www.delta.com), which is based at Hartsfield-Jackson, is the major carrier to Atlanta, connecting the city to the rest of the U.S. as well as 62 countries internationally. It carries 80% of the air passengers who come into Atlanta and serves more than 350 international cities.

Other major carriers include **AirTran** (✆ 800/247-8726; www.airtran.com), **American Airlines** (✆ 800/433-7300; www.aa.com), **British Airways** (✆ 800/247-9297; www.british-airways.com), **Continental** (✆ 800/525-0280; www.continental.com), **Japan Airlines** (✆ 800/525-3663; www.jal.com), **Lufthansa** (✆ 800/645-3880; www.lufthansa-usa.com), **Northwest/KLM** (✆ 800/225-2525; www.nwa.com), **United Airlines** (✆ 800/241-6522; www.united.com), and **US Airways** (✆ 800/428-4322; www.usairways.com).

GETTING INTO TOWN FROM THE AIRPORT

Those flying into Atlanta have several options for getting from the airport to the downtown area. Most large hotels offer their guests shuttle service, accessible through a courtesy phone located near baggage claim at Hartsfield-Jackson Atlanta International Airport. Other options include taxi, MARTA rapid-rail or bus service, and rental cars.

By Bus

Bus travel is often the most economical form of public transit for short hops between U.S. cities, but it's certainly not an option for everyone (particularly when Amtrak, which is far more luxurious, offers similar rates). **Greyhound** (✆ **800/231-2222;** www.greyhound.com) is the sole nationwide bus line and connects the entire country with Atlanta via bus.

The bus terminal is located at 232 Forsyth St., at the Garnett Street MARTA station, one stop south of Five Points (the main MARTA station downtown). Taxis are available, but it's both convenient and inexpensive to take MARTA into the central city.

The fare structure on buses is complex and not always based on distance traveled. The good news is that when you call Greyhound, you'll always get the lowest-fare options. Advance-purchase fares booked 3 to 21 days before travel can garner big savings.

International visitors can obtain information about the **Greyhound North American Discovery Pass.** The pass can be obtained from foreign travel agents or through www.discoverypass.com for unlimited travel and stopovers in the U.S. and Canada.

By Car

Navigating Atlanta by car can be freeing or terrifying, depending on your approach to major traffic. While city and state officials continue to stumble around improvements to traffic flow, there is much to be said for having your own ride in this sprawling metropolis. Of course, the use of Global Positioning System (GPS) makes navigation much easier, though frequent and ongoing road construction can result in it leading you to a dead-end or blocked road. Three major interstate highways (**I-20, I-75,** and **I-85**) converge near the center of downtown Atlanta.

Below is a list of approximate mileage from other major cities in the region:

      Birmingham, Ala.: 148
      Charleston, S.C.: 320
      Charlotte, N.C.: 240
      Jacksonville, Fla.: 346
      Louisville, Ky.: 417
      Nashville, Tenn.: 244
      New Orleans, La.: 473
      Norfolk, Va.: 555
      Orlando, Fla.: 441
      Savannah, Ga.: 252
      Tampa, Fla.: 458

For information on car rentals and gasoline (petrol) in Atlanta, see "Getting Around: By Car," below.

By Train

Amtrak operates the *Crescent* daily between Atlanta and New York, with stops in Washington, D.C., Philadelphia, and other intermediate points. Travel time between New York and Atlanta is approximately 18½ hours. The *Crescent* also goes beyond Atlanta to many points south each day, terminating in New Orleans. Other Amtrak trains connect with most of the country. To find out if your city connects via rail with Atlanta, call ✆ **800/USA-RAIL** (872-7245), or check www.amtrak.com.

Like the airlines, Amtrak offers discount fares, and though not all are based on advance purchase, reserving early may pay off.

Contact **Amtrak Vacations** (✆ **800/321-8684;** www.amtrak.com) to inquire about money-saving packages that include hotel accommodations and attraction tickets with your train fare.

Trains arrive in Atlanta at 1688 Peachtree St., just off I-85. From this central location, you can take a taxi to your hotel or to the nearest MARTA station (Arts Center). For information, call ✆ **800/USA-RAIL** (872-7245) or 404/881-3060.

International visitors can buy a **USA Rail Pass,** good for 15 or 30 days of unlimited travel on **Amtrak** (✆ **800/USA-RAIL** [872-7245]; www.amtrak.com). The pass is available online or through many overseas travel agents. See Amtrak's website for the cost of travel within the western, eastern, or northwestern United States. Reservations are generally required and should be made as early as possible. Regional rail passes are also available.

GETTING AROUND

Note to visitors to the U.S. from abroad: Some major airlines offer transatlantic or transpacific passengers special discount tickets under the name **Visit USA,** which allows mostly one-way travel from one U.S. destination to another at very low prices. Unavailable in the U.S., these discount tickets must be purchased abroad in conjunction with your international fare. This system is the easiest, fastest, cheapest way to see the country. Inquire with your air carrier.

By Car

Traffic can be a nightmare in Atlanta, and the region's leaders are working hard to figure out what to do about it. Rush hours—roughly 6:30 to 9am and 3:30 to 6:30 or 7pm—can be vicious, especially when traveling into town in the morning or out of town in the afternoon on any of the interstates. The Downtown Connector (where I-75 and I-85 become one) is almost always congested, even during nonrush times, mostly because travelers on their way to points north, south, east, and west join the locals trying to make their way through the city. The area looks a lot like a pig trying to pass through a python. Atlanta drivers are generally courteous, but they tend to travel at breakneck speeds well above the posted limit, so it's wise to stay off the interstates during peak hours. I-285, which circles the city and supports a lot of truck traffic, should be avoided if at all possible. It's possible to reach most major Atlanta sights via the transit system (MARTA); public transportation is usually the best bet during sporting and entertainment events and conventions.

Even if you're here for just a few days, you'll get a pretty good feel for the layout of the city. Just remember that the main drag is **Peachtree Street** (becoming Peachtree Rd. to the north), and use it to get your bearings. Just don't fall prey to the confusion created by dozens of streets with "Peachtree" in their name.

Georgia law requires the driver and front-seat passengers to wear seat belts while the car is in motion. Children 4 and under must be buckled into safety seats in the rear; those 5 to 12 must sit in the rear seat if the car is equipped with air bags.

Gas stations and public parking lots are plentiful and toll roads are nearly nonexistent. That being said, while parking isn't a problem in Atlanta's outlying areas, it's getting to be a headache downtown and in some commercial areas of Midtown and Buckhead. It can be especially scarce and expensive downtown during conventions and other major events. If you can't find a spot close to your destination, there's often parking available a block or two away, and it's likely to be cheaper.

If you're visiting from abroad and plan to rent a car in the United States, keep in mind that foreign driver's licenses are usually recognized in the U.S., but you should get an international one if your home license is not in English.

Check out **Breezenet.com,** which offers domestic car-rental discounts with some of the most competitive rates around. Also worth visiting are Orbitz, Hotwire, Travelocity, and Priceline, all of which offer competitive online car-rental rates.

International visitors should note that insurance and taxes are almost never included in quoted rental-car rates in the U.S. Be sure to ask your rental agency about additional fees for these. They can add a significant cost to your car rental.

At press time, the cost of gasoline (also known as gas, but never petrol) in the U.S. averaged $2.65 a gallon for unleaded at most Atlanta stations. Taxes are already included in the printed price. One U.S. gallon equals 3.8 liters or .85 imperial gallons. Fill-up locations are known as gas or service stations.

RENTING A CAR

Renting a car in Atlanta is not a problem. All of the major rental agencies maintain branch offices in the city. In addition, **Atlanta Rent-A-Car (© 800/542-8278;** www.atlantarac.com), a local independently owned company, has been serving the area for more than 25 years and its rates are often lower than most. It has 20 metro locations, including one close to the airport, and provides free courtesy pickup anywhere in metro Atlanta.

If you pick up your rental car at Hartsfield-Jackson Atlanta International Airport, expect to pay a 10% government tax (which includes a 7% local sales tax) and a 10% airport tax. Elsewhere in the metro area, car rentals incur only the local sales tax, which can range from 5% to 7%.

SAVING MONEY   Car-rental rates vary even more than airline fares. The price you pay will depend on the size of the car, where and when you pick it up and drop it off, the length of the rental period, where and how far you drive it, whether you purchase insurance, and a host of other factors. A few key questions could save you hundreds of dollars. Here are some things to ask:

- Are weekend rates lower than weekday rates? Ask if the rate is the same for pickup Friday morning, for instance, as it is for Thursday night.
- Is a weekly rate cheaper than the daily rate? Even if you need the car for only 4 days, it may be cheaper to keep it for 5.
- Does the agency assess a drop-off charge if you don't return the car to the same location where you picked it up? Is it cheaper to pick up the car at the airport compared to a downtown location?
- Are special promotional rates available? If you see an advertised price in your local newspaper, be sure to ask for that specific rate; otherwise, you may be charged the standard cost. Terms change constantly.
- Are discounts available for members of AARP, AAA, frequent-flier programs, or trade unions? If you belong to any of these organizations, you may be entitled to discounts of up to 30%.
- How much tax will be added to the rental bill? Local tax? State-use tax?
- What is the cost of adding an additional driver's name to the contract?
- How many free miles are included in the price? Free mileage is often negotiable, depending on the length of your rental.

○ How much does the rental company charge to refill your gas tank if you return with the tank less than full? Though most agencies claim these prices are "competitive," fuel is almost always cheaper in town. Try to allow enough time to refuel the car yourself before returning it. Some companies offer "refueling packages," in which you pay for an entire tank of gas upfront. The price is usually fairly competitive with local gas prices, but you don't get credit for any gas remaining in the tank. If a stop at a gas station on the way to the airport will make you miss your plane, then by all means take advantage of the fuel purchase option. Otherwise, skip it.

ONLINE RENTALS   Internet resources make comparison shopping easier. **Expedia** (www.expedia.com) and **Travelocity** (www.travelocity.com) can help you compare prices and locate car-rental bargains from various companies nationwide. They will even make the reservation for you once you've found the best deal.

PACKAGE DEALS   Many packages are available that include airfare, accommodations, and a rental car with unlimited mileage. Compare the price of the package with the cost of booking airline tickets and renting a car separately to see if the offer is a good deal.

DEMYSTIFYING RENTERS' INSURANCE   Before you drive off in a rental car, be sure you're insured. Hasty assumptions about your personal auto insurance or a rental agency's additional coverage could end up costing you tens of thousands of dollars—even if you are involved in an accident that was clearly the fault of another driver.

If you already hold a **private auto insurance** policy, you are most likely covered in the United States for loss of or damage to a rental car, and liability in case of injury to any other party involved in an accident. Be sure to find out whether you are covered in the area you are visiting, whether your policy extends to all persons who will be driving the rental car, how much liability is covered in case an outside party is injured in an accident, and whether the type of vehicle you are renting is included under your contract. (Rental trucks, SUVs, and luxury vehicles such as Jaguars may not be covered.)

Most **major credit cards** provide some degree of coverage as well—provided they were used to pay for the rental. Terms vary widely, however, so be sure to call your credit card company directly before you rent. Most American Express Optima cards, for instance, do not provide any insurance. In addition, American Express does not cover vehicles valued at more than $50,000 when new, or luxury vehicles such as Porsches, or vehicles built on a truck chassis. MasterCard does not provide coverage for loss, theft, or fire damage, and only covers collision if the rental period does not exceed 15 days. Call ahead of time for details; you may also be able to purchase additional coverage from your credit card company.

If you are **uninsured,** your credit card may provide primary coverage as long as you decline the rental agency's insurance. This means that the credit card will cover damage or theft of a rental car for the full cost of the vehicle. If you already have insurance, your credit card will provide secondary coverage—which basically covers your deductible. **Credit cards will not cover liability,** or the cost of injury to an outside party and/or damage to an outside party's vehicle. If you do not hold an insurance policy, you may seriously want to consider purchasing additional liability insurance from your rental company. Be sure to check the terms: Some rental agencies cover liability only if the renter is not at fault, and even then, the rental company's obligation varies from state to state.

The basic insurance coverage offered by most car-rental agencies, known as the **Loss/Damage Waiver (LDW)** or **Collision Damage Waiver (CDW),** can cost as much as $20 per day. It usually covers the full value of the vehicle with no deductible if an outside party causes an accident or other damage to the rental car. In all states but California, you will probably be covered in case of theft as well. Liability coverage varies according to company policy and state law, but the minimum is usually at least $15,000. If you are at fault in an accident, however, you will be covered for the full replacement value of the car but not for liability. Some states allow you to buy additional liability coverage in case of such accidents. Most rental companies will require a police report in order to process any claims you file, but your private insurer will not be notified of the accident.

Question your rental agency about personal safety and ask for a traveler-safety brochure when you pick up your car. Obtain written directions—or a map with the route clearly marked—from the agency showing how to get to your destination. (Many agencies now offer the option of renting a cellphone for the duration of your car rental; check with the rental agent when you pick up the car.)

Recently, more and more crime has involved cars and drivers. If you drive off a highway into a doubtful neighborhood, leave the area as quickly as possible. If you have an accident, even on the highway, stay in your car with the doors locked until you assess the situation or until the police arrive. If you're bumped from behind on the street or are involved in a minor accident with no injuries and the situation appears to be suspicious, motion to the other driver to follow you. Never get out of your car in such situations. Go directly to the nearest police precinct, well-lit service station, or 24-hour store.

Always try to park in well-lit and well-traveled areas if possible. Never leave any packages or valuables in sight. If someone attempts to rob you or steal your car, don't try to resist the thief/carjacker, but immediately report the incident to the police department by calling ✆ **911.**

By Taxi

Atlanta is not New York. It's not possible to step outside and hail a cab at all times, though there are always cabs waiting outside the airport, major hotels, Underground Atlanta, and most MARTA stations, except those found downtown. If a cab is not waiting at your MARTA rail stop, use the white assistance phone in the station and MARTA will call one for you.

Taxi fares are a bit complicated in Atlanta. Within the Downtown Zone, you pay a flat rate of $5 for one passenger, $1 for each additional rider. That's fine if you're going from one end of this extensive zone to the other; unfortunately, though, you pay the same rate even if you go just a block. Rates and rules are the same in Buckhead.

There's also a flat rate for rides between downtown and the airport: $30 for one passenger, plus $2 for each additional passenger. Between the airport and Midtown, the rate is $32 for one passenger, $2 for each additional. Between the airport and Buckhead, the rate is $38 for one, $2 for each additional.

Outside these specified zones, Atlanta cabs charge a minimum $1.50 for the meter drop and first ⅙ mile, 20¢ for each additional ⅙ mile for the first passenger, and a flat rate of $1 for each additional passenger, adult or child. Waiting time is $15 per hour.

There are many taxi companies in town. If you need to call a taxi, try **Atlanta Lenox Taxi** (✆ 404/872-2600), **Yellow Cabs** (✆ 404/521-0200), **Checker Cabs** (✆ 404/351-1111), or **Buckhead Safety Cab** (✆ 404/875-3777). If your destination lies outside of the zone system (which applies flat rates to trips within each zone), the meter won't start running until you get into the cab. Some of these companies accept credit cards.

If you have a complaint about taxi service, call the **Taxi Bureau** (✆ **404/658-7600**).

By Public Transportation

The **Metropolitan Atlanta Rapid Transit Authority (MARTA)** operates a rail (subway) and bus network, making it possible, though not always convenient, to reach just about any part of town by public transportation. While the system is fairly extensive within the city limits, outside the city (except for areas in DeKalb, Fulton, and Clayton counties) the service is quite limited. Even in some areas served by bus and rail lines, it's often necessary to walk a bit to a station or stop.

Cobb County, a suburban county that includes the city of Marietta, operates a bus system separate from MARTA. **Cobb Community Transit (CCT)** has five local routes and express routes that operate between Cobb and the Arts Center, Dunwoody, and H. E. Holmes MARTA stations. Transfers are free between CCT and MARTA. Call ✆ **770/427-4444** for information.

The **Buckhead Area Transportation Management Association (BATMA)** operates "the buc," free shuttle buses that run every 8 to 15 minutes between the two MARTA rail stations in the area—Lenox and Buckhead—and the hotels, malls, and other businesses along Piedmont and Peachtree roads. The buses operate Monday through Friday from 7am to 7pm, Saturday from 10am to 9pm. For more information, inquire at your hotel, or go to www.bucride.com.

MARTA RAPID RAIL

MARTA's rapid-rail (subway) system has been running since 1979. The stations are clean and modern, and the service is reliable. Although MARTA has a good safety record, there is the perception here—as in many big cities—that subway travel is unsafe. MARTA moves more than half a million people every day, and regular riders seem to have more confidence in the security of the trains and stations than infrequent riders do. Visitors should find the subway most pleasant during the day and during early-evening hours, when usage is heavy.

The major problem with MARTA is that not enough parts of the city are served by rail (which is much faster overall than the bus). MARTA will eventually have 45 stations, but the system currently includes only 40 stations. There are two lines: south-north trains (**orange lines** on the MARTA maps) that travel between the airport and Doraville and North Springs; and east-west trains (**blue lines** on the maps) that travel between Indian Creek (east of Decatur) and Hamilton E. Holmes. They intersect at **Five Points Station** in downtown Atlanta, where you can transfer to another train for free. The system's two newest station additions—Sandy Springs and North Springs—were added in late 2000 to the north line that parallels Georgia Hwy. 400.

The fare is $2 for any ride, and passengers must purchase the new Breeze Card from the station vending machines to ride. Multitrip passes, as well as 7- and 30-day passes, are also available.

MARTA trains generally arrive and depart every 8 to 10 minutes, 7 days a week, from 5am to 1am. Free transfers between bus and rail are available when you board a bus or enter a rail station. Parking is free but limited at about half the rail stations. If you wish to park overnight, you must use the long-term secured parking available at the stations of Doraville, Dunwoody, Medical Center, Lenox, Brookhaven, Lindbergh, North Springs, Sandy Springs, and College Park. Cost is $3 per day.

For MARTA schedule and route information, go to www.itsmarta.com, or call ✆ 404/848-4711 Monday through Friday from 6am to midnight, Saturday and Sunday from 8am to 10pm. Printed schedules are available from racks at Five Points and several other stations; instructions are printed in English, French, Japanese, German, and Spanish. All stations and rail cars are fully accessible to passengers with disabilities.

MARTA BUSES

It's possible, but not always efficient, to get anywhere within the city limits by bus. The routes will deliver you to most major attractions and sightseeing stops, but travel can be slow, with long wait times between buses. MARTA buses operate on a 1,550-mile network of 150 routes, and the fare system is the same as described above for rail service. To find out what bus to take, call ✆ 404/848-4711 for route information (same hours as listed above for rail information). You must have exact change ($1.75) or a Breeze Card. Special shuttle buses operate from downtown in conjunction with major stadium sports events and conventions; call the above number for details.

[FastFACTS] ATLANTA

African-American Travelers Agencies and organizations that provide resources for black travelers in particular include **Rodgers Travel** (✆ **800/825-1775;** www.rodgerstravel.com) and the **African American Association of Innkeepers International** (✆ **877/422-5777;** www.africanamericaninns.com).

Black Travel Online (www.blacktravelonline.com) posts news on upcoming events and includes links to articles and travel-booking sites. **Soul of America** (www.soulofamerica.com) is a comprehensive website with travel tips, event information, family-reunion postings, and sections on

historically black beach resorts and active vacations.

For more information, check out the following collections and guides: *Go Girl: The Black Woman's Guide to Travel & Adventure* (Eighth Mountain Press), a compilation of travel essays by writers including Jill Nelson and Audre Lorde; *The African American Travel Guide,* by Wayne Robinson (Hunter Publishing; www.hunterpublishing.com); *Steppin' Out,* by Carla Labat (Avalon); and *Pathfinders Magazine* (✆ **877/977-PATH** [7284]; www.pathfinderstravel.com), which includes articles on everything from

Rio de Janeiro to Ghana as well as information on upcoming ski, diving, golf, and tennis trips.

Area Codes In metro Atlanta, you must dial the area code (404, 770, or 678) and the seven-digit telephone number, even if you are calling a number within the same area code. It is not necessary to dial "1" before the area code when calling between communities within the Atlanta local calling area, even if they have different area codes.

Business Hours Most stores are open until at least 6pm, with extended hours at larger shopping centers and malls. Banks are typically open 9am to 5pm, with some open a half-day on Saturday.

Car Rental See "Getting Around: By Car," earlier in this chapter.

Cellphones See "Mobile Phones," later in this section.

Crime See "Safety," later in this section.

Disabled Travelers
Most disabilities shouldn't stop anyone from traveling in the U.S. Thanks to provisions in the Americans with Disabilities Act, most public places are required to comply with disability-friendly regulations. Almost all public establishments (including hotels, restaurants, museums, and so on, but not including certain National Historic Landmarks), and at least some modes of public transportation, provide accessible entrances and other facilities for those with disabilities.

Before planning a trip to Atlanta, travelers with disabilities should request *A Guide to Atlanta for People with Disabilities,* available from the Shepherd Center, a nationally renowned Atlanta hospital specializing in the treatment of spinal-cord injuries and diseases. The guide rates the accessibility of local museums, parks, restaurants, hotels, theaters, sports venues, and other popular tourist stops. Accessibility is assessed in several categories, including restrooms, parking, main entrances, and

telephones. The booklet also lists services and other information of interest to travelers with disabilities. For a free copy, contact the **Noble Learning Resource Center, Shepherd Center,** 2020 Peachtree Rd. NW, Atlanta, GA 30309 (ⓒ **404/350-7473**). The guide is also available at www.shepherd.org.

Many travel agencies offer customized tours and itineraries for travelers with disabilities. **Flying Wheels Travel** (ⓒ **507/451-5005;** www.flyingwheelstravel. com) provides escorted tours and cruises that emphasize sports, as well as private tours in minivans with lifts. **Access-Able Travel Source** (ⓒ **303/232-2979;** www.access-able. com) offers extensive access information and advice for traveling around the world with disabilities. **Accessible Journeys** (ⓒ **800/846-4537** or 610/521-0339; www.disability travel.com) caters specifically to slow walkers and wheelchair travelers and their families and friends.

Avis Rent a Car has an "Avis Access" program that offers such services as a dedicated 24-hour toll-free number (ⓒ **888/879-4273**) for customers with special travel needs; special car features such as swivel seats, spinner knobs, and hand controls; and accessible bus service.

Organizations that provide assistance to travelers with disabilities include

MossRehab (www.moss resourcenet.org), which provides a library of accessible-travel resources online; **SATH** (Society for Accessible Travel & Hospitality; ⓒ **212/447-7284;** www.sath.org; annual membership fees: $45 adults, $30 seniors and students), which offers a wealth of travel resources for all types of disabilities and informed recommendations on destinations, access guides, travel agents, tour operators, vehicle rentals, and companion services; and the **American Foundation for the Blind (AFB)** (ⓒ **800/232-5463;** www. afb.org), a referral resource for the blind and visually impaired, which includes information on traveling with Seeing Eye dogs.

For more information specifically targeted to travelers with disabilities, check out the magazines *Emerging Horizons* ($15 per year, $20 outside the U.S.; www.emerginghorizons. com) and *Open World* ($13 per year, $21 outside the U.S.; published by SATH, described above).

For more on organizations that offer resources to travelers with disabilities, go to www.frommers. com/planning.

Doctors See "Hospitals," below.

Drinking Laws The legal age for the purchase and consumption of alcoholic beverages is 21; proof of age is required and often requested at bars, nightclubs, and restaurants, so it's always a good idea to bring ID when you go out. Do not carry open containers of alcohol in your car or any public area that isn't zoned for alcohol consumption. The police can fine you on the spot. Don't even think about driving while intoxicated.

Beer and wine are sold in most grocery stores and all liquor stores. Some areas of the Atlanta region do not allow liquor sales on Sundays, but it can often be purchased by the drink after noon on Sundays in restaurants that serve alcohol. Closing times for bars and clubs in Atlanta vary and can be as late as 2, 3 or even 4am.

Electricity   Like Canada, the United States uses 110–120 volts AC (60 cycles), compared to 220–240 volts AC (50 cycles) in most of Europe, Australia, and New Zealand. Downward converters that change 220–240 volts to 110–120 volts are difficult to find in the United States, so bring one with you.

Wherever you go, bring a **connection kit** of the right power and phone adapters, a spare phone cord, and a spare Ethernet network cable—or find out whether your hotel supplies them to guests.

Embassies & Consulates   All embassies are in the nation's capital, Washington, D.C. Some consulates are in major U.S. cities, and most nations have a

mission to the United Nations in New York City. If your country isn't listed below, call for directory information in Washington, D.C. (☎ **202/555-1212**) or check **www.embassy.org/embassies**.

The embassy of **Australia** is at 1601 Massachusetts Ave. NW, Washington, DC 20036 (☎ **202/797-3000;** www.usa.embassy.gov.au). Consulates are in New York, Honolulu, Houston, Los Angeles, and San Francisco.

The embassy of **Canada** is at 501 Pennsylvania Ave. NW, Washington, DC 20001 (☎ **202/682-1740;** www.canadainternational.gc.ca/washington). Other Canadian consulates are in Buffalo (New York), Detroit, Los Angeles, New York, and Seattle.

The embassy of **Ireland** is at 2234 Massachusetts Ave. NW, Washington, DC 20008 (☎ **202/462-3939;** www.embassyofireland.org). Irish consulates are in Boston, Chicago, New York, San Francisco, and other cities. See website for complete listing.

The embassy of **New Zealand** is at 37 Observatory Circle NW, Washington, DC 20008 (☎ **202/328-4800;** www.nzembassy.com). New Zealand consulates are in Los Angeles, Salt Lake City, San Francisco, and Seattle.

The embassy of the **United Kingdom** is at 3100 Massachusetts Ave. NW, Washington, DC 20008 (☎ **202/588-6500;** http://ukinusa.fco.gov.uk). Other

British consulates are in Atlanta, Boston, Chicago, Cleveland, Houston, Los Angeles, New York, San Francisco, and Seattle.

Emergencies   Call ☎ **911** in an emergency.

Family Travel   To locate accommodations, restaurants, and attractions that are particularly kid friendly, look for the "Kids" icon throughout this guide. If you have enough trouble just getting your children out of the house in the morning, it may seem like an insurmountable challenge to drag them hundreds of miles away. But as any veteran family vacationer will assure you, a trip with the kids can be among the most pleasurable and rewarding times of your life. See p. 146 for some of Atlanta's best attractions for families. See a list of kid-friendly hotels on p. 54 and a list of restaurants that kids will love on p. 78.

Familyhostel (☎ **800/733-9753**) takes the whole family, including kids 8 to 15, on moderately priced domestic and international learning vacations. Lectures, field trips, and sightseeing are guided by a team of academics.

Recommended family-travel websites include **Family Travel Forum** (www.familytravelforum.com), a comprehensive resource that offers customized trip planning; **Family Travel Network** (www.familytravelnetwork.com), an award-winning site that offers travel features, deals, and tips; and **Family Travel Files** (www.thefamilytravelfiles.com), which offers an online magazine and a directory of off-the-beaten-path tours and tour operators for families.

Frommer's Unofficial Guide to the Southeast with Kids (Wiley Publishing, Inc.) also includes information on kid-friendly attractions in and around Atlanta.

For a list of more family-friendly travel resources, visit www.frommers.com/planning.

Gasoline   Please see "Getting Around: By Car" on p. 217.

Hospitals   **Piedmont Hospital,** 1968 Peachtree Rd., just above Collier Road (© **404/605-3297**), provides 24-hour full emergency-room service, as does **Grady Health Systems,** 35 Butler St., downtown (© **404/616-6200**). For life-threatening medical emergencies, dial © **911.**

Insurance   For information on traveler's insurance, trip cancellation insurance, and medical insurance while traveling, please visit www.frommers.com/planning.

Internet & Wi-Fi   More and more hotels, cafes, and retailers are signing on as Wi-Fi (wireless fidelity) "hotspots." **T-Mobile Hotspot** (www.t-mobile.com/hotspot) offers wireless connections at more than 1,000 Starbucks coffee

shops nationwide. **Boingo** (www.boingo.com) and **Wayport** (www.wayport.com) have set up networks in airports and high-class hotel lobbies. To find public Wi-Fi hotspots around Atlanta, go to **www.jiwire.com**; its Hotspot Finder holds the world's largest directory of public wireless hotspots. iPass providers (see below) also give you access to a few hundred wireless hotel-lobby setups. To locate other hotspots that provide free wireless networks in cities around the world, go to **www.personaltelco.net/index.cgi/WirelessCommunities**.

Most business-class hotels in the U.S. offer dataports for laptop dial-up modems, and many hotels now offer free high-speed Internet access using an Ethernet network cable. You can bring your own cables, but most hotels rent them for around $10. Call your hotel in advance to see what your options are.

In addition, major ISPs have **local access numbers** around the world, allowing you to go online by placing a local call. Check your ISP's website or call its toll-free number and ask how you can use your current account away from home and how much it will cost.

The **iPass** network also has dial-up numbers around the world. You'll have to sign up with an iPass provider, who will then tell you how to set up your computer for your destination. For a list of iPass providers,

go to www.ipass.com and click on "Individuals Buy Now." One solid provider is **i2roam** (www.i2roam.com; © **866/811-6209** or 920/235-0475).

Wherever you go, bring a **connection kit** of the right power and phone adapters, a spare phone cord, and a spare Ethernet network cable—or find out whether your hotel supplies them to guests.

For information on electrical currency conversions, see "Electricity," above.

Most major airports have **Internet kiosks** that provide basic Web access for a per-minute fee that's usually higher than cyber-cafe prices. Check out copy shops such as **FedEx Office,** which offers computer stations with fully loaded software (as well as Wi-Fi).

Legal Aid   While driving, if you are pulled over for a minor infraction (such as speeding), never attempt to pay the fine directly to a police officer; this could be construed as attempted bribery, a much more serious crime. Pay fines by mail, or directly into the hands of the clerk of the court. If accused of a more serious offense, say and do nothing before consulting a lawyer. In the U.S., the burden is on the state to prove a person's guilt beyond a reasonable doubt, and everyone has the right to remain silent, whether he or she is suspected of a crime or actually arrested. Once arrested, a person can make one telephone call to a party of his or her choice. The international visitor should call his or her embassy or consulate.

LGBT Travelers

Atlanta has a large gay community. You'll want to check out *Southern Voice,* a newspaper that covers gay issues across the Southeast. Call (☎ **404/876-1819** for information, or go to www.southernvoice.com for a comprehensive online edition, including information on distribution points near your hotel.

Once you arrive, you might want to visit **Outwrite Bookstore & Coffeehouse,** 991 Piedmont Ave., at 10th Street (☎ **404/607-0082;** www.outwritebooks.com). It's a popular Midtown gathering spot for gay men and lesbians, and a sort of unofficial clearinghouse for information on local gay and lesbian resources, events, and issues.

Gay.com Travel (☎ **800/929-2268** or 415/644-8044; www.gay.com/travel or www.outandabout.com) is an excellent online successor to the popular *Out & About* print magazine. It provides regularly updated information about gay-owned, gay-oriented, and gay-friendly lodging, dining, sightseeing, nightlife, and shopping establishments in every important destination worldwide. It also offers trip-planning information

for gay and lesbian travelers for more than 50 destinations, along various themes, ranging from Sex & Travel to Vacations for Couples.

The **International Gay and Lesbian Travel Association (IGLTA)** (☎ **800/448-8550** or 954/776-2626; www.iglta.org), the trade association for the gay and lesbian travel industry, offers an online directory of gay- and lesbian-friendly travel businesses; go to its website and click on "Members."

The following guides are available at most travel bookstores and gay and lesbian bookstores, or you can order them online or from **Giovanni's Room,** 1145 Pine St., Philadelphia, PA 19107 (☎ **215/923-2960;** www.giovannisroom.com): *Out and About* (☎ **800/929-2268;** www.outandabout.com), which offers guidebooks and a newsletter ($20 per year; 10 issues) packed with solid information on the global gay and lesbian scene; *Spartacus International Gay Guide* (Bruno Gmünder Verlag; www.spartacusworld.com/gayguide) and *Odysseus: The International Gay Travel Planner* (Odysseus Enterprises Ltd.), both good, annual English-language guidebooks focused on gay men; the *Damron* guides (www.damron.com), with separate, annual books for gay men and lesbians; and *Gay Travel A to Z: The World of Gay & Lesbian Travel Options at Your*

Fingertips, by Marianne Ferrari (Ferrari International; Box 35575, Phoenix, AZ 85069), a very good gay and lesbian guidebook series.

For more gay and lesbian travel resources, visit www.frommers.com/planning.

Mail Open 24 hours a day, Atlanta's main post office is located not in the downtown area, but close to Hartsfield-Jackson Atlanta International Airport at 3900 Crown Rd. (☎ **800/ASK-USPS** [275-8777]). At press time, domestic postage rates were 28¢ for a postcard and 44¢ for a letter. For international mail, a first-class letter of up to 1 ounce costs 98¢ (75¢ to Canada and 79¢ to Mexico); a first-class postcard costs the same as a letter. For more information, go to **www.usps.com**.

If you aren't sure what your address will be in the United States, mail can be sent to you, in your name, c/o General Delivery at the main post office of the city or region where you expect to be. (Call ☎ **800/275-8777** for information on the nearest post office.) The addressee must pick up mail in person and must produce proof of identity (driver's license, passport, and so on). Most post offices will hold mail for up to 1 month, and are open Monday to Friday from 8am to 6pm, and Saturday from 9am to 3pm.

Always include zip codes when mailing items in the U.S. If you don't know your zip code, visit www.usps.com/zip4.

Medical Requirements Unless you're arriving from an area known to be suffering from an epidemic (particularly cholera or yellow fever), inoculations or vaccinations are not required for entry into the United States. If you have a medical condition that requires **syringe-administered medications,** carry a valid signed prescription from your physician; syringes in carry-on baggage will be inspected. Insulin in any form should have the proper pharmaceutical documentation. If you have a disease that requires treatment with **narcotics,** you should also carry documented proof with you—smuggling narcotics aboard a plane carries severe penalties in the U.S.

For **HIV-positive visitors,** requirements for entering the United States are somewhat vague and change frequently. For up-to-the-minute information, contact **AIDSinfo** (© **800/ 448-0440,** or 301/519- 6616 from outside the U.S.; www.aidsinfo.nih.gov) or the **Gay Men's Health Crisis** (© **212/367-1000;** www.gmhc.org).

Mobile Phones Just because your cellphone works at home doesn't mean it'll work everywhere in the U.S. (thanks to our nation's fragmented cell-phone system). It's a good bet that your phone will work in major cities, including Atlanta, but take a look at your wireless company's coverage map on its web-site before heading out; T-Mobile, Sprint, and Nextel are particularly weak in rural areas, but service is available in metro Atlanta from those companies, as well as Verizon, Tracfone, Virgin Mobile, and AT&T. If you need to stay in touch at a destination where you know your phone won't work, rent a phone that does from **InTouch USA** (© **800/872-7626;** www. intouchglobal.com) or a rental-car location, but be aware that you'll pay $1 a minute or more for airtime. InTouch USA delivers to hotels, and **Rent-A-Cellular** kiosks are located throughout the Hartsfield-Jackson Atlanta International Airport.

If you're not from the U.S., you'll be appalled at the poor reach of the **GSM** (Global System for Mobile Communications) **wireless network,** which is used by much of the rest of the world. While your phone will work in Atlanta, it

definitely won't work in many rural areas. To see where GSM phones work in the U.S., check out www. t-mobile.com/coverage. And you may or may not be able to send SMS (text messaging) home. Assume nothing—call your wireless provider and get the full scoop.

If you have Web access while traveling, consider a broadband-based telephone service (in technical terms, **Voice-over Internet Protocol,** or **VoIP**) such as Skype (www.skype.com) or Vonage (www.vonage.com), which allow you to make free international calls from your laptop or in a cyber-cafe. Neither service requires the people you're calling to also have that service (though there are fees if they do not). Check the websites for details.

Money & Costs Atlanta is a reasonably priced city, whether you live there or just visit. While there are plenty of high-dollar hotels and restaurants for those who don't mind spending money, there are an equal number of options for the more money-conscious spenders. On average, a standard hotel room will run about $120 a night, though rates vary depending on the day of the week and any special events in town. Taxis

THE VALUE OF THE U.S. DOLLAR VS. OTHER POPULAR CURRENCIES

US$	Aus$	Can$	Euro (€)	NZ$	UK£
1	A$1.01	C$1.12	0.73€	NZ$1.29	£0.62

	US$
Taxi from the airport to downtown Atlanta	18.00
Double room, moderate	90.00
Double room, inexpensive	70.00
Three-course dinner for one without wine, moderate	15.00–25.00
Bottle of beer	3.00–4.50
Cup of coffee	1.00–3.50
1 gallon/1 liter of premium gas	2.65/1.57
Admission to most museums	8.00–15.00
Admission to most national parks	10.00

and public transportation costs are in line with other metro areas and when it comes to shopping, well, the sky's the limit.

The most widely used form of payment in the United States is credit cards: **Visa** (Barclaycard in Britain), **MasterCard** (Euro-Card in Europe, Access in Britain, Chargex in Canada), **American Express, Diners Club,** and **Discover.** Nearly every store, hotel, and restaurant in the city will accept all major credit cards and bank debit cards. It's highly recommended that you travel with at least one major credit card. You must have one to rent a car, and hotels and airlines usually require a credit card imprint as a deposit against expenses. Credit cards also provide a convenient record of all your expenses, and they generally offer relatively good exchange rates. You can withdraw cash advances from your credit cards at banks or ATMs, provided you know your PIN. Visitors from outside

the U.S. should inquire whether their bank assesses a 1% to 3% fee on charges incurred abroad.

Nationwide, the easiest and best way to get cash away from home is from an ATM (automated teller machine), sometimes referred to as a "cash machine" or "cashpoint." The **Cirrus** (© 800/424-7787; www.mastercard. com) and **PLUS** (© 800/843-7587; www.visa.com) networks span the country; you can find them even in remote regions. Look at the back of your bank card to see which network you're in; then call or check online for ATM locations at your destination. Be sure you know your personal identification number (PIN) and daily withdrawal limit before you depart. *Note:* Remember that many banks impose a fee every time you use a card at another bank's ATM, and that fee can be higher for international transactions (up to $5 or more) than for

domestic ones (where they're rarely more than $2). In addition, the bank from which you withdraw cash may charge its own fee. To compare banks' ATM fees within the U.S., use **www.bankrate.com**. For international withdrawal fees, ask your bank.

ATM cards with major credit card backing, known as **debit cards,** are now a commonly accepted form of payment in most stores and restaurants. Debit cards draw money directly from your checking account. Some stores enable you to receive "cash back" on your debit card purchases as well. The same is true at most U.S. post offices.

Beware of hidden credit card fees while traveling. Check with your credit or debit card issuer to see what fees, if any, will be charged for overseas transactions. Recent reform legislation in the U.S., for example, has curbed some exploitative lending practices. But many banks have responded by increasing fees in other areas, including fees for customers who use credit and debit cards while out of the country—even if those charges were made in U.S. dollars. Fees can amount to 3% or more of the purchase price. Check with your bank before departing to avoid any surprise charges on your statement.

Traveler's checks are something of an anachronism from the days before the ATM made cash accessible at any time. Traveler's checks used to be the only sound alternative to traveling with dangerously large amounts of cash. They were as reliable as currency, but, unlike cash, could be replaced if lost or stolen.

These days, traveler's checks are less necessary because most cities have 24-hour ATMs that allow you to withdraw small amounts of cash as needed. However, keep in mind that you will likely be charged an ATM withdrawal fee if the bank is not your own, so if you're withdrawing money every day, you might be better off with traveler's checks—provided that you don't mind showing identification every time you want to cash one.

You can get traveler's checks at almost any bank. **American Express** offers denominations of $20, $50, $100, $500, and (for cardholders only) $1,000. You'll pay a service charge ranging from 1% to 4%. You can

also get American Express traveler's checks over the phone by calling ✆ **800/221-7282;** AmEx gold and platinum cardholders who use this number are exempt from the 1% fee.

Visa offers traveler's checks at Citibank locations nationwide, as well as at several other banks. The service charge ranges between 1.5% and 2%; checks come in denominations of $20, $50, $100, $500, and $1,000. Call ✆ **800/732-1322** for information. AAA members can obtain Visa checks without a fee at most AAA offices or by calling ✆ **866/339-3378.**

MasterCard also offers traveler's checks. Call ✆ **800/223-9920** for a location near you.

If you choose to carry traveler's checks, be sure to keep a record of their serial numbers separate from your checks in the event that they are stolen or lost. You'll get a refund faster if you know the numbers.

For visitors from outside the U.S. who choose to use cash, the American money system is fairly simple to grasp. The most common bills are the $1 (a "buck"), $5, $10, and $20 denominations. There are also $2 bills (seldom encountered), $50 bills, and $100 bills (the last two are usually not welcome as payment for small purchases).

Coins come in seven denominations: 1¢ (1 cent, or a penny); 5¢ (5 cents, or

a nickel); 10¢ (10 cents, or a dime); 25¢ (25 cents, or a quarter); 50¢ (50 cents, or a half dollar); the gold-colored Sacagawea coin, worth $1; and the rare silver dollar.

For help with currency conversions, tip calculations, and more, download Frommer's convenient Travel Tools app for your mobile device. Go to www.frommers.com/go/mobile and click on the Travel Tools icon.

Newspapers & Magazines The major newspaper in town is the *Atlanta Journal-Constitution* (www.ajc.com). Its "Access Atlanta" section, published every Thursday, highlights plays, festivals, live music, gallery openings, and other happenings for the weekend and the week ahead. It includes restaurant and movie reviews as well. You'll also find it helpful to pick up a current issue of *Atlanta* magazine when you're in town. And keep an eye out for *Creative Loafing* (www.cln.com), an offbeat free publication available in shops, restaurants, and on the street; it has lots of interesting information, including excellent restaurant reviews.

Packing For helpful information on packing for your trip, download our convenient Travel Tools app for your mobile device. Go to www.frommers.com/go/mobile

and click on the Travel Tools icon.

Passports Virtually every air traveler entering the U.S. is required to show a passport. All persons, including U.S. citizens, traveling by air between the United States and Canada, Mexico, Central and South America, the Caribbean, and Bermuda are required to present a valid passport. **Note:** U.S. and Canadian citizens entering the U. S. at land and sea ports of entry from within the Western Hemisphere must now also present a passport or other documents compliant with the Western Hemisphere Travel Initiative (WHTI; see www.get youhome.gov for details). Children 15 and under may continue entering with only a U.S. birth certificate, or other proof of U.S. citizenship.

o **Australia:** Australian Passport Information Service (✆ 131-232, or visit www. passports.gov.au).

o **Canada:** Passport Office, Department of Foreign Affairs and International Trade, Ottawa, ON K1A 0G3 (✆ 800/ 567-6868; www.ppt. gc.ca).

o **Ireland:** Passport Office, Setanta Centre, Molesworth Street, Dublin 2 (✆ 01/671-1633; www.foreignaffairs. gov.ie).

o **New Zealand:** Passports Office, Department of Internal Affairs, 47 Boulcott St., Wellington, 6011 (✆ 0800/225-050 in New Zealand, or 04/474-8100; www. passports.govt.nz).

o **United Kingdom:** Visit your nearest passport office, major post office, or travel agency or contact the Identity and Passport Service (IPS), 89 Eccleston Sq., London, SW1V 1PN (✆ 0300/222-0000; www.ips.gov. uk).

o **United States:** To find your regional passport office, check the U.S. State Department website (travel. state.gov/passport) or call the National Passport Information Center (✆ 877/487-2778) for automated information.

Petrol Please see "Getting Around: By Car" on p. 217.

Police Call ✆ **911** in an emergency. Otherwise, call ✆ **404/853-3434.**

Safety Atlanta's neighborhoods are relatively safe, but it's wise to exercise caution at night near Underground Atlanta, as well as around the major venues for sporting events. Most of the central city is primarily a business district that closes up after dark, so it's a good idea to stay within the downtown

hotel-and-entertainment district, which is likely to be much busier.

Buckhead, a major restaurant and bar scene, is safe as long as the crowds are out. Recently, however, a few square blocks of Buckhead's entertainment district—where most of the bars are located—have been plagued by overly rowdy behavior and incidents of violent crime. Much of the undesirable activity takes place after midnight or in the wee hours as the bars are winding down, so be alert.

Avoid carrying valuables with you on the street, and don't display expensive cameras or electronic equipment. If you are using a map, consult it inconspicuously—or better yet, try to study it before you leave your hotel. Hold onto your pocketbook, and place your billfold in an inside pocket. In theaters, restaurants, and other public places, keep your possessions in sight.

Remember also that hotels are open to the public, and in a large hotel, security may not be able to screen everyone entering. Always lock your room door—don't assume that once inside your hotel you are automatically safe and no longer need to be aware of your surroundings.

Senior Travel Mention the fact that you're a senior when you make your travel reservations. Although all of the major U.S. airlines except America West have canceled their senior discount programs, many hotels still offer discounts for seniors. In most cities, those age 60 and over qualify for reduced admission to theaters, museums, and other attractions, as well as discounted fares on public transportation.

Members of **AARP** (formerly known as the American Association of Retired Persons), 601 E St. NW, Washington, DC, 20049 (✆ **888/687-2277;** www.aarp.org), get discounts on hotels, airfares, and car rentals. AARP offers members a wide range of benefits, including *AARP The Magazine* and a monthly newsletter. Anyone over 50 can join.

Many reliable agencies and organizations target the 50-plus market. **Road Scholar** (✆ **877/426-8056;** www.roadscholar.org) arranges study programs for those 55 and over (and a spouse or companion of any age) in the U.S. and in more than 80 countries around the world. Most courses last 5 to 7 days in the U.S. (2–4 weeks abroad), and many include airfare, accommodations in university dormitories or modest inns, meals, and tuition. Elderhostel has a number of Atlanta programs, including those that focus on the city's history, culture, fine arts, and homes and gardens. Atlanta trips range from 3 to 8 nights.

Recommended publications offering travel resources and discounts for seniors include the quarterly magazine *Travel 50 & Beyond* (www.travel50 andbeyond.com); *Travel Unlimited: Uncommon Adventures for the Mature Traveler* (Avalon); *101 Tips for Mature Travelers,* available from Grand Circle Travel (✆ **800/221-2610** or 617/350-7500; www.gct. com); and *Unbelievably Good Deals and Great Adventures That You Absolutely Can't Get Unless You're Over 50* (McGraw-Hill).

For more information and resources on travel for seniors, see www.frommers. com/planning.

Smoking While the city of Atlanta has yet to impose a smoking ban on the city, statewide "no smoking" efforts have drastically reduced the number of places that remain smoker friendly. Smoking is still allowed in bars and some restaurants, and efforts to pass a more stringent code that would ban smoking in all bars, restaurants, and other public places have been unsuccessful to date. Designated smoking areas can be found in some public places, such as the airport and some sports/entertainment venues.

Taxes Sales tax in Atlanta is 8%. A total of 15% is paid by hotel and motel guests within the city of Atlanta and Fulton County. Of that tax, 8% is sales tax and 7% is room tax. Car rentals at Hartsfield-Jackson Atlantic International Airport are assessed 20% in taxes, but rentals in the metro area incur only the local sales tax. The United States has no value-added tax (VAT) or other indirect tax at the national level. Every state, county, and city may levy its own local tax on all purchases, including hotel and restaurant checks and airline tickets. These taxes will not appear on price tags.

Telephones Generally, hotel surcharges on long-distance and local calls are astronomical, so you're better off using your **cellphone** or a **public pay telephone.** Many convenience groceries and packaging services sell **prepaid calling cards** in denominations up to $50; for international visitors, these can be the least expensive way to call home. Many public phones at airports now accept American Express, MasterCard, and Visa. **Local calls** made from public pay phones in most locales cost either 25¢ or 35¢. Pay phones do not accept pennies, and few will take anything larger than a quarter.

Most long-distance and international calls can be dialed directly from any phone. **For calls within the United States and to Canada,** dial 1 followed by the area code and the 7-digit number. **For other**

international calls, dial 011 followed by the country code, city code, and the number you are calling.

Calls to area codes **800, 888, 877,** and **866** are toll-free. However, calls to area codes **700** and **900** (chat lines, bulletin boards, "dating" services, and so on) can be very expensive—usually a charge of 95¢ to $3 or more per minute, and they sometimes have minimum charges that can run as high as $15 or more.

For reversed-charge or collect calls, and for person-to-person calls, dial the number 0, then the area code and number; an operator will come on the line, and you should specify whether you are calling collect, person-to-person, or both. If your operator-assisted call is international, ask for the overseas operator.

For local directory assistance ("information"), dial 🕐 **411;** for long-distance information, dial 1, then the appropriate area code and 555-1212.

Time Atlanta is in the Eastern Standard Time Zone. The United States is divided into **four time zones:** Eastern Standard Time (EST), Central Standard Time (CST), Mountain Standard Time (MST), and Pacific Standard Time (PST). Alaska and Hawaii have their own zones. For example, when it's 9am in Los Angeles (PST), it's 7am in Honolulu (HST),10am in Denver (MST), 11am in Chicago (CST), noon in New

York City (EST), 5pm in London (GMT), and 2am the next day in Sydney.

Daylight saving time (summer time) is in effect from 1am on the second Sunday in March to 1am on the first Sunday in November, except in Arizona, Hawaii, the U.S. Virgin Islands, and Puerto Rico. Daylight saving time moves the clock 1 hour ahead of standard time.

For help with time translations, and more, download our convenient Travel Tools app for your mobile device. Go to www.frommers.com/go/mobile and click on the Travel Tools icon.

Tipping In hotels, tip **bellhops** at least $1 per bag ($2–$3 if you have a lot of luggage) and tip the **chamber staff** $1 to $2 per day (more if you've left a big mess for him or her to clean up). Tip the **doorman** or **concierge** only if he or she has provided you with some specific service (for example, calling a cab for you or obtaining difficult-to-get theater tickets). Tip the **valet-parking attendant** $1 every time you get your car.

In restaurants, bars, and nightclubs, tip **service staff** and **bartenders** 15% to 20% of the check, tip **checkroom attendants** $1 per garment, and tip **valet-parking attendants** $1 per vehicle.

As for other service personnel, tip **cabdrivers** 15% of the fare; tip **skycaps** at

airports at least $1 per bag ($2–$3 if you have a lot of luggage); and tip **hairdressers** and **barbers** 15% to 20%.

For help with tip calculations, currency conversions, and more, download our convenient Travel Tools app for your mobile device. Go to www.frommers.com/go/mobile and click on the Travel Tools icon.

Toilets You won't find public toilets or "restrooms" on the streets in most U.S. cities but they can be found in hotel lobbies, bars, restaurants, museums, department stores, railway and bus stations, and service stations. Large hotels and fast-food restaurants are often the best bet for clean facilities. Restaurants and bars in resorts or heavily visited areas may reserve their restrooms for patrons.

VAT See "Taxes," above.

Visas · The U.S. State Department has a **Visa Waiver Program (VWP)** allowing citizens of the following countries to enter the United States without a visa for stays of up to 90 days: Andorra, Australia, Austria, Belgium, Brunei, Czech Republic, Denmark, Estonia, Finland, France, Germany, Greece, Hungary, Iceland, Ireland, Italy, Japan, Latvia, Liechtenstein, Lithuania, Luxembourg, Malta, Monaco, the Netherlands, New Zealand, Norway, Portugal, San Marino,

Singapore, Slovakia, Slovenia, South Korea, Spain, Sweden, Switzerland, and the United Kingdom. (**Note:** This list was accurate at press time; for the most up-to-date list of countries in the VWP, consult http://travel.state.gov/visa.) Even though a visa isn't necessary, in an effort to help U.S. officials check travelers against terror watch lists before they arrive at U.S. borders, visitors from VWP countries must register online through the Electronic System for Travel Authorization (ESTA) before boarding a plane or a boat to the U.S. Travelers must complete an electronic application providing basic personal and travel eligibility information. The Department of Homeland Security recommends filling out the form at least 3 days before traveling. Authorizations will be valid for up to 2 years or until the traveler's passport expires, whichever comes first. Currently, there is a $14 fee for the online application. Existing ESTA registrations remain valid through their expiration dates. **Note:** Any passport issued on or after October 26, 2006, by a VWP country must be an **e-Passport** for VWP travelers to be eligible to enter the U.S. without a visa. Citizens of these nations also need to present a round-trip air or cruise ticket upon arrival. E-Passports contain computer chips capable of storing biometric information, such as the required

digital photograph of the holder. If your passport doesn't have this feature, you can still travel without a visa if the valid passport was issued before October 26, 2005, and includes a machine-readable zone; or if the valid passport was issued between October 26, 2005, and October 25, 2006, and includes a digital photograph. For more information, go to **http://travel.state.gov/visa**. Canadian citizens may enter the United States without visas, but will need to show passports and proof of residence.

Citizens of all other countries must have (1) a valid passport that expires at least 6 months later than the scheduled end of their visit to the U.S.; and (2) a tourist visa. For information about U.S. Visas go to **http://travel.state.gov** and click on "Visas." Or go to one of the following websites:

Australian citizens can obtain up-to-date visa information from the **U.S. Embassy Canberra,** Moonah Place, Yarralumla, ACT 2600 (© **02/6214-5600**) or by checking the U.S. Diplomatic Mission's website at **http://canberra.usembassy. gov/visas.html**.

British subjects can obtain up-to-date visa information by calling the **U.S. Embassy Visa Information Line** (© **09042-450-100** from within the U.K. at £1.20 per minute, or 866/382-3589 from within the U.S. at a flat rate of $16

and is payable by credit card only) or by visiting the "Visas to the U.S." section of the American Embassy London's website at **http://london.usembassy.gov/visas.html**.

Irish citizens can obtain up-to-date visa information through the **U.S. Embassy Dublin,** 42 Elgin Rd., Ballsbridge, Dublin 4 (© 1580-47-VISA [8472] from within the Republic of Ireland at €2.40 per minute; **http://dublin.usembassy.gov**).

Citizens of **New Zealand** can obtain up-to-date visa information by contacting the **U.S. Embassy New Zealand,** 29 Fitzherbert Terrace, Thorndon, Wellington (© **644/462-6000;** http://newzealand.usembassy.gov).

Visitor Information As soon as you know you're going to Atlanta, write or call the **Atlanta Convention & Visitors Bureau (ACVB),** 233 Peachtree St. NE, Ste. 2000, Atlanta, GA 30303 (© **800/ATLANTA** [285-2682] or 404/222-6688). They'll send you a copy of *Atlanta Heritage Guide,* a visitors' guide, a book of discount coupons, a *Metro Atlanta Map and Attractions Guide,* and a 2-month calendar of events; they can also advise you on anything from Atlanta's hotel and restaurant scene to the best tour packages available. Visit the ACVB website at **www.atlanta.net** for lots of information.

You can also learn a lot about the city and its latest happenings by visiting

www.accessatlanta.com, a website whose partners include the *Atlanta Journal-Constitution* and WSB-TV and radio. There, you'll find current local news, a 5-day weather forecast, street maps, and up-to-date information about special events, the arts, entertainment, sports, recreation, restaurants, shopping, and more. There's even a link to the Atlanta Yellow Pages.

Another site worth checking out is **www.atlanta.citysearch.com**. Although it's not as complete as www.accessatlanta.com, it still has lots of useful information about the arts, entertainment, attractions, restaurants, shopping, and hotels. Finally, **Creative Loafing** (**www.cln.com**) features loads of entertainment information and great restaurant reviews.

Wi-Fi See "Internet & Wi-Fi," earlier in this chapter.

Index

Accommodations

Restaurants

NOTES